RELIGION IN GREEK LITERATURE

'Urania speaks with darkened brow'

Σύγγνωθ', Οὐρανία, θύγατερ Διός, εἴ σε προσαυδῶν
ἠλιτόμην, καινῆς ὀψιμαθὴς σοφίας.

RELIGION

IN

GREEK LITERATURE

A SKETCH IN OUTLINE

BY

LEWIS CAMPBELL

κρείσσον' ἢ μορφὴ καλή
SOPH. Œd. Col.

 BOOKS FOR LIBRARIES PRESS
FREEPORT, NEW YORK

First Published 1898
Reprinted 1971

INTERNATIONAL STANDARD BOOK NUMBER:
0-8369-5645-1

LIBRARY OF CONGRESS CATALOG CARD NUMBER:
79-148874

PRINTED IN THE UNITED STATES OF AMERICA

PREFACE

After my retirement from the Greek chair at St. Andrews I was appointed by my former colleagues to the Gifford Lectureship in that University for the years 1894, 1895. I chose for my subject the Religion of the Ancient Greeks, and delivered two courses of twelve lectures each, besides several intermediate lectures. In venturing to bring before the public some part of what was then put forth, I have limited myself to the portion of the subject which was most familiar to me, and which at present perhaps receives less attention than it deserves. Recent researches into the culture of prehistoric times have tended rather to obscure the abiding interest of the age of classical literature in Greece. While endeavouring to carry out the intention of the Gifford bequest, I have sought to emphasise the element of religious feeling and reflection which pervades that literature and is a possession which forms part of the inalienable heritage of mankind.

Of late years much has been written on the subject of Greek religion, and in revising my work I have availed myself, as far as I could find opportunity, of the books which have recently appeared. I would mention specially Theodor Gomperz's 'Griechische Denker,' vol. i.; Foucart on the

'Eleusinian Mysteries,' the writings of Wide, Immerwahr, and Bérard, Farnell's 'Cults of the Greek States,' and Frazer's 'Pausanias.'

In quoting from Plato and Thucydides, I have availed myself of Professor Jowett's translations. And I am specially indebted to the kindness of two other friends— Mr. Peter Giles, of Emmanuel College, Cambridge, who read the work in MS., and Professor Menzies, of St. Andrews, whose criticism and encouragement have been of great assistance to me in revising the proofs.

LEWIS CAMPBELL.

LONDON: *October* 5, 1898.

CONTENTS

―――・◇・―――

CHAPTER I

INTRODUCTORY

CHAPTER II

ANTECEDENTS AND SURVIVALS

CHAPTER III

RELIGION IN THE ILIAD

CHAPTER IV

RELIGION IN THE ODYSSEY

a

CHAPTER X

ATHENIAN WORSHIPS

CHAPTER XI

THE MYSTERIES

CHAPTER XII

ATTIC RELIGION IN THE EARLIER FIFTH CENTURY

CHAPTER XIII

PHILOSOPHY AND SCEPTICISM

CHAPTER XIV

SOCRATES AND THE SOCRATICS

CHAPTER XV

PLATO AND PLATONISM

CHAPTER XVI

RELIGION IN ARISTOTLE—SUBSEQUENT DEVELOPMENTS—CONCLUSION

RELIGION IN GREEK LITERATURE

CHAPTER I

INTRODUCTORY

General remarks—Limitation of subject—Previous factors—Archaeology
—'The Greek spirit'—Religion and statecraft—Worship and mythology
—Superstition—Divination—Stages of culture—Morality.

In answer to one who remarked, 'my chief desire is to leave
the world a little better than I found it,' the late Lord
Tennyson replied, 'my chief desire is to have a new vision
of God.' That was the aspiration of a poet, who had something also of prophetic fire. Another thinker of our time
once said, 'the deepest want of our age is to have a new
definition of God.' Such indeed is the ever-recurring want
of humanity in passing from one stage of enlightenment to
another, and this is a cause of the perplexity which inevitably
haunts the mind in approaching a subject such as that which
is here proposed—the religious element in Greek literature.
The acceptance of each new form of belief implies that our
predecessors were mistaken, and if we look back far enough
their leading thoughts assume an air of grotesque or even
repulsive absurdity. However firmly we may rely upon our
convictions, there is something in this discovery which is
not comforting, and is apt to shake the foundations of religious belief.

Some minds are led to doubt if there be a supreme
reality at all, and so to question the existence of any binding
rule of life. They are tempted to think that, through a

B

series of phantastic impressions, our race is being lured onward to the 'dark tower' of nonentity. Others would tell us that God teaches through illusion, that error leads the way to Truth : but the 'husk' has no meaning unless the 'kernel' is already there in germ. The words of St. Paul at Athens, 'that they should seek the Lord if haply they might feel after him and find him,' suggest a more satisfactory solution. In the wildest aberrations of the religious consciousness there is yet a groping after the supreme, a craving desire to realise what is more and mightier than man, and to find a support whereon his weakness may rely. There would be no progress if there were no shadows to be done away. Our aim should be to bring out from amidst their grosser surroundings those broken lights of higher things which come to us refracted through the thoughts of men :

> Which all touch upon nobleness despite
> Their error, all tend upwardly, though weak,
> Like plants in mines which never saw the sun,
> But dream of him, and guess where he may be,
> And do their best to climb and get to him.

The late Dr. Hatch, in his able course of Hibbert Lectures, unfortunately posthumous, has drawn out in detail what has long been known, the fact that historical Christianity owes much of its intellectual form to Greek traditions ; as it is no less certain that its ecclesiastical organisation is largely due to the influence of Imperial Rome. But it is not to be supposed that the value of the ideas thus historically assimilated has been exhausted in a process which was to a great extent accidental. It is at least worth while to trace the course of the stream from which so much has been derived. The Hellenism which became absorbed into Christian theology was Hellenism already in its decline : a form of culture from which, in the endeavour to systematise it, and to reconcile tradition with contemporary thought, much of what was originally essential had disappeared, or had been modified by a fresh influx of Orientalism. The knowledge that an Hellenic element enters into our actual inheritance should rather stimulate us to look back upon the times from whence that element came down, to study it as it was in its prime, and try to understand the living minds in which the conceptions that were essential to it first arose.

If in the earliest articulate utterance of the Hellenic spirit we discern a profound conviction that the Power which is supreme sends down inevitable redress of wrong, guards jealously the family bond, protects the suppliant and the stranger, and tempers even just vengeance with deep human pity; if as history advances the conviction of the divinity of justice and of the nobleness of self-devotion clears and widens more and more ; if a yearning after religious purity springs up unbidden, and suggests a brightening hope of future blessedness; if, as thought awakens, the human spirit, weary of the play of imagination, and prompted by some divinely kindled spark, begins consciously to reach after ' the One,' ' the Whole,' ' the True ' ;—even if we stopped here and went no further, shall we be told that this struggling of noble hearts and minds to live and think aright is all in vain, that they were pressing towards no goal ; or that because about the same time, or a little earlier, another race of whom the Greeks knew nothing, by a sort of parallel evolution, were developing out of an old tribal worship other modes of consciousness, under holier inspirations and amidst a fiercer furnace of affliction, can we therefore afford to discard the ' thoughts that breathe and words that burn ' of the Hellenic race, or rest contented with some feeble and distorted imitation of their works of decorative art, and not rather accept as part of our inheritance, to be inwrought into the Christianity of the future, ' whatsoever things are venerable, whatsoever things are just, whatsoever things are pure, whatsoever things are lovely, whatsoever things are of good report ; if there be any virtue and if there be any praise ' ? In that familiar catalogue, which is correctly rendered on the margin of the Authorised Version, the Apostle, for once at least, is not hebraizing, but is employing terms which are characteristically Greek.

' There is a spirit in man ; and the inspiration of the Almighty giveth them understanding.'

That does not mean that progress is by any means con-

tinuous. All growth is liable to interruption and temporary
declension; and the question, what is the culminating point,
is not always easy to determine. Every forward step leaves
something fair and good behind it, not to be recaptured.
The history of religion, to be at all faithful, must take
account of checks and drawbacks. For nations, as for individuals, there are moments when custom presses on them
with a weight

> Heavy as frost and deep almost as life.

The stream while growing fuller does not always become
clearer as it advances; but it would be in the highest degree
irrational to infer that there is no goal of perfection towards
which aspiration, enlightened by experience, tends. If this
were denied, the task we propose to ourselves would be impossible; any record that covers a long period makes it
manifest that the path of human development is onward on
the whole. This 'weight of custom' presses deep, but
life is deeper yet—*eppur si muove*. And the later stages
may often throw back light upon the earlier, and win for
them a more favourable interpretation. Thus the worship
of a cruel deity may be interpreted as a sort of dumb
pleading with a severe but merciful creator, and in the
deepening gloom of the Greek Hades there is an earnest
of something better in reserve than that other world, a
faded duplicate of this, which to the men of the stone age
had been a vivid and satisfying reality.

The 'new definition' still awaits the hour and the man.
The present generation can only prepare the way for it; and
to have done so in however humble a degree will be the
chief honour of Lord Gifford's bequest. My predecessor in
the Gifford Lectureship, Professor Caird, now Master of
Balliol, has put forth a comprehensive survey of the Evolution of Religion in universal history. Professor Tiele,
from a different point of view, has expounded, with equal
knowledge and ability, the elements of a Science of Religion.
And Mr. Andrew Lang, the first St. Andrews Gifford lecturer,
in his recent volume on 'The Making of Religion,' has put
forth an independent hypothesis, supported by his extensive

study of savage tribes. But in every such widely sweeping theory some things must inevitably be left out of view, and while the comparative treatment of religions is pregnant with important results, it is necessary as a previous condition that the religious development of the chief races of mankind should have been separately studied and delineated.

I do not propose, however, in the present volume to give anything like a complete account of Greek religion. Mr. Farnell's learned work on the 'Cults of the Greek States' supplies a want which has long been felt in England, and deals with the subject of Hellenic worship on lines that are more rational than those followed by many Continental writers. But there is still room for an attempt to exhibit in a continuous treatise the way in which the ritual and mythology reacted upon the higher minds in Hellas, as this is clearly reflected in classical Greek literature. The aim of my endeavour is to trace, not origins chiefly, but rather tendencies—not whence, but rather how and whitherward the religious consciousness in Greece was moving. What were the ruling thoughts in each successive age respecting that which was conceived as higher than man? How were those thoughts limited or frustrated, and what germs of further development were contained in them? What in the most general outline was the Hellenic contribution to the spiritual inheritance of humanity?

If in order to strengthen the foundations of religion and morality, we are to gather out of every civilisation what it contains of good, it is necessary in each case to go back to the period, not of crude beginnings (which explain little), but of originality and bloom—to learn the secret of the great masters from themselves. This is not less true of Greek culture than of Hebrew prophecy or of the great Oriental religions. But the attempt in this case is in some ways more difficult; partly because of the comparatively slight predominance obtained in Hellas by the priesthood, who, being mostly elective, and in any case local and unorganised, formed no separate caste, and had no interests apart from the other citizens. Freedom and consequent variation in development are marked characteristics of spiritual life in

Greece. Hence the phenomena to be studied are extremely diverse, and a process of distillation is needed in order to bring out any clear result. Opinions thus obtained must always be given with an understood reservation. In speaking of the forms of thought, feeling or imagination belonging to an age, it is impossible to avoid giving to them a distinctness which they could not have for those who were under their immediate sway. Such statements, therefore, so far as they are justified, must be accepted as affording an incitement to the fresh study of the literature in itself, else they are apt to become a sort of *caput mortuum*, and to lose all suggestiveness and value.

In what follows I shall refer but rarely and from a distance to other religions. 'Analogy,' it has been said, 'is a broken reed, which may often serve to point the way, but should not be used as a staff to lean upon.' The air is full of generalisations gathered from a wide and various field, many of which may serve to guide and enlighten observation, but none of them can be regarded as exhaustive. The student of a particular culture may be grateful for their help and guidance, but to bring them prominently forward would only lead to confusion.

It is unavoidable, however, to refer briefly at the outset to recent speculations concerning prehistoric religion. For in all religions there are survivals from primitive times, and Greece is no exception to the rule. But in considering these, our desire will be to distinguish what is characteristic of the Greeks, as we know them, from the accidents of their inheritance, and to appreciate the fertile ingenuity of the Hellenic genius in adapting obsolete elements, whose meaning had faded, not only to new forms of beauty, but to the expression of deep thoughts of undying significance.

1. Primitive man, they tell us, felt himself to be surrounded by living powers akin to him yet other than himself, and fearing harm or seeking help from these, looked wistfully to inanimate objects which he endowed with life as having struck his fancy or inspired him with terror. There are not wanting traces of this, the simplest of all forms of worship, in Greek ritual and mythology.

Whether it were really the earliest form or a subsequent undergrowth fortunately does not concern us.

2. A further stage hardly less strange to us, which the Greek of historic times had largely outgrown, is the worship of plants and animals. Of this there are many traces in Greek culture, yet hardly in the primeval forms of which our generation has heard and read so much. Some isolated phenomena (the names of the Sicyonian tribes for instance) have been thus explained, but such a mode of interpretation is apt to be extended too far. The absence of any clear remains of ' totemism ' may be due to the fact that the tribal system had long since been supplanted by larger organisations, or to the original prevalence of patriarchal government. But it is still open to doubt whether the attribution of a mystic power to animals must of necessity in every case be associated with the assumption of blood relationship between the animal and the tribe.

In another sense the theory here referred to is suggestive of an important truth which has been recently made popular through the writings of the late Mr. Robertson-Smith. That man in society, whether the unit were the family or the tribe, was not moved to religious rites by fear alone, but that amongst the powers with which he imagined himself to be surrounded he selected one in whom he placed his confidence and hope, claiming him as an ally ; that this power became to him the symbol of a common life, a rule of conduct, a preserver from the public enemy ; and that his most solemn act was one of communion with his god and with his kindred,—is a conception which throws a flood of light on the inmost spirit of early worship. It explains the joyousness which attended every act of sacrifice, and reminds us that even in the earliest religion, which is thus distinguished from magic and superstition, there is an element not of fear only but of hope and love.

But to return to animal worship. That either in the hunting or the pastoral stage of culture, an intense interest should be felt in the animal life with which the people were associated for good or evil, is easily intelligible, and when no abstract expression has been found for ideas and attributes whose importance is notwithstanding felt, a rude symbolism is the most obvious vehicle of expression. The very simplicity of such symbolism, lending itself to various interpretations, is a fruitful source of misunderstanding. So with regard to tree worship, which may either be referred to the time when men lived on acorns or beech nuts, and so literally depended on the bounty of the tree, or may be connected, as it has often been, with another set of notions altogether (see below, section 3). Some instances, however, are too obvious to be mistaken. The power of water permeating all things, now as a torrent coming down with destructive force, now renewing the face of nature with generative influence, found its concentrated symbol in the bull, whose onset was irresistible, while he was the father of the herd. Earth, the genial mother of all living, whose kindly produce nourished youth and age, was thought of by an agricultural people as the sacred Cow : the god of light, in the imagination of a nomadic people, on similar grounds might take the form of a ram, and so on. On the other hand, those creatures who are the enemies of mankind, or of their works, the wolf that ravages the flocks, the boar that wastes the produce of the ground, would be sometimes propitiated as divine powers and sometimes sacrificed to the protecting deity. There were other ways in which wild animals had impressed the human imagination. Thus the lion, as the type of strength and courage, was the favourite symbol when these virtues, so important to a primitive race, could not otherwise find an adequate expression. However this may be, it is clear that the worship of animals and the strange rites attending it had an important influence on the growth of religion. There appear to have been acts of faith in which the worshippers sought to identify themselves with their god and to partake of his attributes, by donning the skins of lions, bulls, foxes, goats, and even asses. Such rites as these, whether indigenous or imported, left undoubted traces on Greek culture.

3. But animal worship is only one of many concurrent sources of religion in Greece ; another is that strange phase of enthusiasm which appeared early at so many centres, and

became so ineradicable, which arose from a sense of the mystery of continuous life, or, as Professor Jowett expressed it, 'from man's wonder at his power of producing another in his likeness.' Whether this came in from the north, south, east, or west, from Thrace, Syria, Egypt (as Herodotus thinks), or Libya (as Mr. Flinders Petrie suggests), makes little difference to our study of it in historic times. There are yet other forms of worship closely akin to this, involving the idea of sex and procreation, such as those which assume the opposition or parallelism of male and female powers, the primitive philosophy of a marriage between Heaven and Earth, and all its consequences. There is the whole range of phenomena having to do with the productiveness of cattle and of the ground, with seedtime and harvest, with the vintage and the winepress; all these are inevitable factors in early religion, and enter largely into the foundation of which Greek religion is the superstructure. The worship of Demeter, of Dionysus, and of Cybele, though coming from different centres, yet if traced back far enough seem to intertwine their roots in the tendencies thus arising, and were accordingly amalgamated in later times.

4. A higher influence also enters in, perhaps from the east, but yet to some extent probably operative in prehistoric times, the worship of the elements : the over-arching sky, the sun and moon, the constellations, the dawn, the cloud, the storm, the wind, the sea. Solar mythology has been somewhat discredited of late, and there is perhaps a danger of this factor being too much ignored. It is creeping in again, however, at another entrance, through speculations on Babylonian and Egyptian influence. In actual worship attributes derived from various sources were combined. Apollo is certainly a god of flocks and herds, but is not the shepherd also a watcher of the sky? Who is to assure us that a nomad people were insensible to skyey influences? Artemis is the patron of all wild creatures and of the chase. But may not the imagination of a tribe of hunters have been stirred by the sight of the moon, walking in brightness among the trees of the forest? Even if we must travel back to Chaldea for the origin of such impressions, are we

not daily finding more evidence of very early contact between distant peoples ?

A theory has been maintained according to which not only the orientation of Greek temples, but many features of Greek mythological tradition are due to the existence among the priestly caste of a knowledge of stellar pheno-mena, derived ultimately from Chaldea. These notions appear to me as yet to be very imperfectly substantiated, and, if the fact were so, it has had little perceptible influence on religion in Greek literature. This religion was not made by any priesthood, but by the singer whose motive was poetical and artistic, and the question for us is, not what traditions about the stars may have been held in a mystery by those who built the temples and fixed the seasons of great festivals, or impressed various emblems upon coins, but what thoughts, imaginations, and emotions were awakened in the minds of those who worshipped and who went their way relying on the priestly arrangement of the ceremonial, but thinking their own thoughts, and guided by the imagination of their poets. It must be owned that the priesthood kept their supposed secret well. The names of certain constellations are known to Hesiod and even to Homer, and the Prometheus of Aeschylus is said to have taught mankind the risings and setting of the stars. Arc-turus and the Pleiads were allowed to mark certain seasons of the year; but it is strange—if astronomy and practical religion were from the first combined—that it should have been left for Aratus in the Alexandrian time to divulge the fact, in versifying the science of Eudoxus ; and that the Lion Gate of Mycenae, if it symbolised the sun in Leo, should have faced north-west. It may be questioned whether the belief in stellar transformations, which became rife in Alexandrian times, is at all clearly traceable in Greek literature before Euripides ('Helena' 140).

5. Some persons find the origin of all religion in the worship of ancestors or of great men, who in their lifetime, for good or evil, had dominated a family or a tribe. There can be no doubt whatever that this element entered largely into Greek religion, although strangely enough there is hardly

a vestige of it in Homer. But neither can this be taken as an exclusive principle from which everything can be deduced. Mr. Lang, in the volume above mentioned, has argued with considerable force, that the conception of a supreme creator, the author of good and redresser of wrong, arises quite independently of animism and ghost worship, at a very early stage of human culture.

All the factors I have mentioned are really present; they are all true causes, and they have acted and reacted on one another. It requires great caution, in dealing with phenomena so complex, to avoid tracing each of them to one of these various sources, and also—when we consider the sameness of human nature—not unduly to connect developments on Grecian soil with similar appearances in Babylonia, Phrygia or Egypt. There is a weighing of souls in the Egyptian ' Book of the Dead,' and there is a weighing of destinies in Homer. A favourite vein of speculation would regard the image of the balance in the Iliad as derived by tradition from the sacred writing of another people, some thousand years or so before. But it is surely conceivable that so natural a figure may have occurred independently at long intervals to different minds. The study of savage races is very useful as a caution against the rash identification of similar phenomena. But this caution also may be pushed too far, and we still wait for clearer evidence upon the subject.

The fascinating study of ' origins ' is made more difficult, as I have hinted above, by the freedom of the growth of religious ideas in Hellas as compared with Egypt, or Palestine, or Persia, or any other land in which the priesthood obtained a dominant ascendency, and succeeded in stereotyping tradition. But this only renders the progress of religious ideas in Greece more interesting. No doubt if we could interview the priests of Delphi or Eleusis, as Herodotus professes to have conversed with the priests of Memphis, we should learn many things which neither poet nor philosopher has cared to record. But what we should gain by this would be less to our immediate purpose than what lies actually before us. For Greek religion as an

historical fact—the contribution of Hellas to the spiritual
life of humanity—has been transmitted, not through priestly
tradition, but by the living voices of poets, historians, orators,
philosophers.   This is itself, of all the facts, the most characteristic.   Greece was from first to last, beginning with the
fathers of epic poetry, the home of spiritual freedom.   The
singer was himself a sacred person, owing allegiance principally to the muse and comparatively independent of other
observances.   Priest, soothsayer, king, herald, and warrior,
were all contemplated by him with disinterested objectivity.
He reflects the mind of his age ; he has also inspirations
which reach far beyond it.   Homer, in point of human
feeling, was as untrammelled as Plato in philosophic thought.
The Greeks had no period in their historical development
corresponding to the age of Ezra among the Hebrews, or to
the predominance of the Theban priesthood in Egypt, or to
Indian Brahmanism, or the late revival of Zoroastrian ritual
in Persia.   Such periods have given to those civilisations an
appearance of immovable uniformity, which is probably very
different from the reality if the whole were known.

But if the scope of the present work forbids our dwelling
at any length on questions which absorb the interest of
Hellenic archaeologists, or on the discoveries of Egyptology
and Assyriology, the importance of these studies is not for
a moment to be ignored.   So much at least is gained from
such discoveries, that we are not burdened at the outset
with a body of speculative disquisition which the investigations of our contemporaries have proved to be baseless.   The
background recedes into greater distance, the whole is
seen in more just proportions, and while many new possibilities have been suggested, experience warns us against
making too rash use of them.   One general truth seems to
result from the inquiries which have made such rapid
progress of late years—namely, that in their primitive forms
all the religions of mankind are strangely alike.   To express
it in the terms of a current philosophy, *homogeneity* attends
the earliest phases ; *evolution* brings *differentiation*, and
this again inevitably precedes the final *integration*.   It is
with growth that humanity, whether in nation or individual,

assumès its characteristic form. There is much wise suggestiveness in Professor Tiele's distinction between the origin
of religion and its earliest phase. The germ of life is less
apparent in the first green lobe which the seed puts forth
than in the full-grown tree.

There is a widespread fallacy on this subject analogous
to that which has sometimes prevailed about the meaning of
words. It is a common idea that words are sufficiently
explained by their etymology, which is no doubt some help,
but such crude analysis has very little to do with the state
of diction at an advanced period of any language, and still
less with the realities corresponding to it. An extreme
stage of the fallacy to which I refer is reached when it is
imagined that by tracing the verb 'to be' in several
languages, an approach may be made towards unravelling
the secret of existence. The attempt to interpret by means
of etymology has often led to ridiculous mistakes, and the
same is true of attempts to explain the nature of religion by
bringing some advanced phase of it into immediate connection
with real or supposed primitive phenomena, which are illustrated by surviving customs of remote peasantry. Suppose
that a stranger, in describing Scottish religion, were to say
that our temples open generally to the west, though with
less precision than that observed in some other lands ; that
we have abjured hero worship, but still keep the vigil of the
day that was formerly sacred to all the heroes, and that on
this occasion certain rites of divination are maintained, such
as that of burning hazel nuts on the hearthstone and of
dipping a garment in a stream and looking backward, with
other strange observances which are described by the poet
of the nation ; that horse-shoes are hung outside doors as a
protection against evil spirits or the evil eye ; that offerings
are made at sacred wells, to which the sick and infirm are
carried for miraculous cures ; that in some districts if a pig
is met with in the road the person who encounters it must
immediately touch cold iron ; that on the vigil preceding the
first day of the year, a time sacred to a local Bacchus whom
the inhabitants call John Barleycorn, a custom has been
introduced from over seas of lighting up a pine tree on

which offerings are suspended, and round which the children move ; (that this remnant of tree worship should have come from abroad is more remarkable, because fir-trees are so common in the land)—would this be an adequate description of Scottish religion? Would it help us to understand that power which arouses and also calms our passions, controls our energies, purifies our homes—the power that has wrought out our liberties and made us a nation? Such phenomena as those I have alluded to are inseparable, it may be, from what may be roughly described as popular religion ; they afford material for endless investigation on the part of the students of folklore ; but they do not constitute religion in the sense in which the term is here employed. They form rather the leaf-mould out of which it springs, whose quality is indicated by the weeds that grow upon it ; but they have little to do either with the deeper roots or the spreading branches. To suppose, for example, that any light can be thrown upon the spirit and meaning of Euripides by connecting the action of the Bacchae with some ritual of which the traces remain, say, amongst the Russian peasantry—though the process may be ingenious, and some such far-off connection may have a real existence—is a mode of commentary which confuses more than it enlightens. For it ignores a whole history of feeling and reflection, of action and reaction, of thought and imagination, that has come between. Such speculations have an absorbing interest, an indubitable value, but they provide no answer to the questions which concern us here—viz. first, What were the religious motives which actuated the Greeks in historical times? and secondly, What did the Greeks or any of them contribute towards the religious inheritance of humanity? Was Hermes a god of winds or of boundaries, or a Phoenician culture-god? Was Apollo originally the sun-god, or, as Usener thinks, only the warder-off of ill ($\dot{a}\pi o$-$\pi\acute{\epsilon}\lambda\lambda\omega\nu$)? To us it matters little, so long as we know how the Greeks of historic times conceived of them. Athena and Artemis as well as Aphrodite have been traced by some to the Babylonian Ishtar, while others (countenanced by Plato) would identify Athena with the

Egyptian or Libyan goddess Neit. But such speculations have no bearing on what an ordinary Athenian felt or believed. The Christian seasons of Christmas and of Easter have till lately been supposed to have some relation to Pagan festivals of the winter solstice and of the return of spring, and there is no doubt that the orientation of churches is remotely derived from the east. But does it therefore follow that there is a close and vital connection between the religion of Babylon or of Egypt and that of modern Europe? Or because the Feast of Pentecost coincides with the Jewish Feast of Weeks, do Christian worshippers at Whitsuntide remember that it is harvest time in Judaea? A German critic has made the suggestive remark that the complete personification of divine names was only possible when their original meaning had been forgotten.

When the Spartans delayed their coming to meet the Persians on the ground that it was not yet full moon; or when they opposed the Pisistratidae in obedience to the oracle, because as Herodotus expresses it they chose to obey God rather than men; or when they allowed Mardonius to over-run Attica because they were bound to keep the festival of the Hyacinthia, on which they imagined that the safety of Sparta depended; or when at Plataea they refused to move until in answer to the prayer of their king the omens were favourable, they gave evidence of the indubitable reality of one aspect of Greek religion; it was the same clinging to the letter of tradition which led a small minority of the Athenians to trust in the wooden wall on the Acropolis. But the majority of the latter people, who sent their wives and children across to Salamis while they manned their fleet, deserting the family hearths and the public temples alike, and according to Plutarch formally entrusting Athens to the keeping of Athena, evinced a nobler faith and were obedient to a higher law, to which Themistocles gave an expression that still lives on British soil, when he told them that by the wooden wall they must understand their fleet. It is to the consciousness of such higher impulses, and of a divine power directing them—Athena still caring for her people, though her image was destroyed—that the world owes immortal utterances of religious thought which are still working and must ever work for good. The higher mind of Greece was gradually evolved; and although it shone most brightly in dark hours, was never thoroughly recast or moulded anew out of the furnace of a great national affliction, such as the Captivity was to the Hebrews. Hence the Greek cannot be said to have learned the lesson of the blessedness of sorrow, although at moments he came very near to the revelation of a divine being suffering for man. Yet if Greek religion left us nothing so *fusile*, if I may be allowed the expression, so penetrated with the fire of inspiration and of holy zeal as Hebrew prophecy, our religious inheritance would be the poorer if we had not also the serener light of Hellas, in which the heavenly and earthly are blended in one clear vision. The clouds of mythology which imagination had illuminated still hung about their most aspiring thoughts, and blurred their outlines, and yet without relinquishing the past, the Greeks, or rather an exceptional Greek here and there, saw further into divine truth in some directions than men of any other race have seen. In this process of gradual evolution, especially at certain points in it, different strata of religious culture are found existing side by side: traditional observances, new rites and doctrines and speculative ideas. While the national worship was maintained with extreme care, that which was most essential to it was not the understanding of its origin, but the fact that it was national: the expression of a common feeling of piety towards the state, and to the power that upheld the state. But even the popular or national religion was no longer precisely what it had been; for through the influence of successive priests and legislators, the public ritual had undergone many modifications, although these were in a manner disguised by being represented as revivals of the past. Each victory or defeat brought new gods or heroes into prominence; an earthquake or a famine gave fresh stimulus to certain worships, often at the direction of an oracle. The dynastic importance of particular families gave precedence to the deities whom they worshipped, and the struggle between progressive and conservative instincts within the same people resulted at once in the perpetuation of old customs and in their transformation or the infusion into them of a new spirit.

In this secular process, which cannot be followed into minutiae, some inborn tendencies of the race were sure in the long run to make themselves apparent. Thus the observances of a particular age, while they have the appearance of fixity and of being merely a deposit from the past, are really, so far as they are alive, the expression of present needs, desires, emotions, and, like that which they express, are in a state of transition. This continuous growth may be interrupted by some violent convulsion, but when the trouble is past it ' will close and be itself again,' and to the popular consciousness will seem to have been always the same. This appearance of identity is illusory, as I have said ; but that which is really the same and yet not the same, because ever developing, is the mind and spirit of a people, which, while cherishing old traditions because they are national, interprets them according to its own stage of thought and culture. Thus we return again to the same point. The origin of a religious rite or ordinance is one thing, its significance for those who observe it is quite another thing.

What in a religious sense are we to understand by the Greek spirit? That is the question to be solved. And before attempting to answer it through an examination of Greek literature, some superficial generalities and rhetorical commonplaces have to be swept aside. 1. Since the renaissance of art, the Greek has been commonly regarded as purely and simply a worshipper of beauty. Mr. C. H. Pearson sums up what most men think, in saying that modern civilisation owes its principles of beauty to the Greeks, of law to the Romans, and of religion to the Hebrews ; and Mr. William Watson, at once a refined poet and a critic of uncommon insight, says that the Greek race was ' simply intoxicated with beauty.' We shall find that that is after all a partial view, and it is apt to be associated with another impression that is still more misleading. Many persons imagine that the one point in which the Greeks excelled other races was the power of enjoying life ; and it is supposed that the way to imitate them is to take everything lightly and not seriously. It needs not to enter at all deeply into Greek culture, to see that there could not well be a more strange perversion. It is simply ludicrous when applied to the fifth century B.C., and can only be accounted for by supposing that some of those flowers which bloomed around the ruins of Hellenic culture in its decay, such as the epigrams of the Anthology, and the songs of the pseudo-Anacreon, have been mistaken for the original substance.

The Greeks made life beautiful, not because they were self-pleasers, but because they believed in gods who cared for human perfection—for perfect bodies, perfect minds, perfect works, and splendid actions. Not unfrequently the religion of the Greeks, so far as they are credited with religion, is supposed to be identical or co-extensive with the significance of the remains of ancient art. But this supposition leads to impressions which are to some extent misleading. As in the Italy of the Renaissance, where the artist often failed to share in the devotion to which he gave expression, so that the beauty of a work is not always commensurate with its pious intention, while the devotion of the worshipper often rested upon associations quite distinct from artistic perfection (Titian is often less religious than Bellini or Cima da Conegliano), so we cannot doubt that the sculptor of an archaic image, whether in wood or stone, may often have been more simply devoted to the god whom he sought to represent than the great masters who came after him. And when the art of sculpture was at its height, we may well believe that the pious worshipper was often more impressed with the sacredness of some formless wooden idol than with a masterpiece of Pheidias or Ageladas. Religion gave the impulse to art as its handmaid, and the temples which crowned each height, the shrines by the wayside with the altars before them, and the low-reliefs representing mythical scenes, were the monuments of collective or national religious feeling, to which they gave continual nourishment, and which they informed with nobler thoughts and wider conceptions. But the handmaid could not command the mistress, and the sacredness which attached to some square pillar with the head of Hermes by the roadside had not much to do with the beauty of the workmanship. Greek art was rooted in religion, but the unsurpassable height which it attained was due to the independent working of the Greek spirit, freely idealising the human form in association with the conception of the divine. Meanwhile the religion to which it owed its life and to which it ministered had other workings, of which, as Oedipus says of his own destiny, mere beauty were an inadequate exponent.

2. Since the revival of letters the Greeks have been regarded by many thinkers as the type of pure reason : not Pheidias now, or Polycleitus, but Aristotle, is the prominent figure, ' the master of those that know.' But in studying the religious life of Hellas, as shown in the literature from the seventh to the fourth century, we shall find much that is discordant with such a view, and side by side with clear thinking we shall become aware of vague mystical yearnings and unreasoning emotions. In this connection it is to be remembered that Greek literature, as we have it, is but a fragmentary reflex of Greek thought and feeling.

3. Another literary commonplace is that which speaks of the serenity (*Heiterkeit*) of the Greek. In this again more account is taken of the form than of the spirit of Hellenic culture. The conception of *Serenity* gives but a poor account of Aeschylus or of Demosthenes, though it has a true application to Pindar ; and in him, too, there is often an under-current of sadness beneath the persistent euphemism.

4. Once more, the Greek ideal is thought to be summed up in the word 'moderation'—the Delphic μηδὲν ἄγαν, the Aristotelian μεσότης. Moderation is a great word, and enters largely into all that is best in the Greek philosophic temper. But it is not to be forgotten that it is moderation supervening upon intensity, that ' beneath the marble exterior there is a soul thrilling with spiritual emotion.'

The history of religion cannot be separated altogether from secular history—least of all in Hellas. Religious impulses have in all ages and countries been apt to become

c 2

the instruments of policy, and in the case of no people is this more obvious than amongst the Greeks. It is a nice question how far this subordination was conscious or unconscious, and how far in either case it may have been consistent with the sincere acceptance of the religion. The great importance that was attached to Delos in the fifth century was intensified by the necessity of having a centre for the confederacy within reach of Athens, provided with a religious sanction ; and when the Athenians added emphasis to this by cleansing the island, and removing the bones of those who had been buried there, they were guided by a strange combination of sagacious policy with superstitious feeling. When Themistocles restrained the Athenians from the pursuit of Xerxes by saying, ' this deliverance is the work of the gods, whose jealousy would not suffer the pride of an impious man. Let us not provoke them by following our advantage too far, but let us rebuild our ruined temples, and restore our homesteads and our family hearths,'—he availed himself of religious sentiments which were alive in every Athenian breast. But how far did he share them himself while making use of them :—especially if, as Herodotus calmly says, ' he was providing a refuge for himself, in case his countrymen should turn against him, by establishing a claim on the gratitude of Xerxes'? The most obvious answer is that he was not sincere. Yet it may not be the true answer ; and it is only fair to remember that in their earlier forms religion and public life were the same thing.

This case affords an illustration of the mixed condition of human affairs, in which the ideal is blended with the actual so inextricably as to appear unreal. Yet its reality remains when all attendant circumstances have vanished. Human imperfections cannot permanently cloud the aspiration after the divine, and even the shadow of a divine authority may long outlive the faults of its ministers, as in fact the influence of the Delphic oracle survived in spite of acknowledged mystifications and deceptions, and even the well-supported imputation of bribery.

The example of Themistocles may further remind us that in speaking of Athenian religion in the present volume we shall have less to do with the religious attitude of the many than of the few. For it is this last which gives its main importance to the subject, and while it is interesting to know what the average Athenian felt about Ajax or Theseus or Athena, this interest is largely due to the gratitude we owe to those select spirits who soared above the level of their age and have left to succeeding times deep thoughts and great imaginations couched in perfect words, which belong eternally to what is highest in man, and are constituent rays of that harmonious truth which is 'the light of all our seeing.' The Greeks partook of many faults which were prevalent in the ancient world : it is often said, for example, that they were sensual; so were the Hebrews, as their own prophets bear witness; so were other Asiatics in a super-lative degree. But there were men amongst the Greeks, and not one or two only, who learned to govern their own lives for the good of others, to strain after perfection, and to realise in human nature a noble conception of the divine, 'filling up,' as Aristophanes puts it, 'the image of virtue.' It is with these that we concern ourselves, not with the common herd. But it may be truly said of the Greeks as a people, that the sheer activity of mind continually tended to raise and purify those elements of human nature which in less gifted races are left to grovel in the mire. Even their best men long looked indulgently on some things which we have learned to execrate, but about these also their greatest clearly saw the truth at last; and it had been anticipated in the divine silences of Homer.

A distinction to be continually borne in mind is that between religious feeling and mythology : the attitude of the worshipper is often different from that of the hymn-writer or the religious poet. The one is prepossessed and absorbed in the act of worship, the other has a free and unembarrassed mind. The worshipper looks up in all simplicity to the power that is able to help or save, and is anxious to omit no jot of the required ceremonial, as he is instructed in it by the *exegetes* or the priest. If he is a learned man some part of the legend of his god may occur to his imagination, but he will dwell upon it only for immediate edification and with a reverence which precludes wild thoughts or strange inventions. The mythologist, on the other hand, is nothing if not inventive; his *rôle* is to entertain and please. He too is guided by religious feeling: he is eager to engage the minds of his hearers with thoughts about the great being of whom his own imagination is full; and there are limits conventional and spiritual which he may not pass; but in the hour of festival the gods too are imagined as being in a festive mood, and as not disdaining to have told concerning them what in the licence of their divinity they have not been ashamed to do. Thus the religious feelings of men in their moments of distress and difficulty are not to be gauged by the representations of divine action to which in times of ease and festivity it was their delight to listen.

The belief of man in powers that are ready and willing to help him, especially in times of anxiety or suffering, and still more his belief in spiritual enemies, is always liable to be confused with traditional or arbitrary notions imposed upon him from without, to which, in his ignorance and immaturity of thought, he lends too willing an ear. The wonder is, not that so much of blind faith in groundless imaginations should have entered into Greek religion, but that Greeks without ceasing to be religious should have worn so lightly the burden which descended from an immemorial past. Vague spiritual presences, uncertain whether friendly or hostile, had haunted human spirits before the family or even the state was a reality, that is before the existence of religion in any true sense at all. Such influences were only too ready to revive, especially in weaker minds. There was, moreover, the bondage to impressions, words, observances, which had a living reality for some past generation of mankind, but continued to exercise their ascendency over a generation that had lost the clue to them and had outgrown the stage of incipient thought and reasoning in which they originated. Here the fertility of invention native to the Greeks was of great service to them. We sometimes speak of the religion that is learned at a mother's knee, and

Plato in like manner argues that the existence of the gods cannot be doubtful to those who have seen their parents sacrificing and offering libations. The same motive of filial piety gave strength to rites and ideas handed down from primitive ages, accepted without question, and transmitted with less and less of understanding. As thought from time to time awakened, or emotion roused imagination, new meanings were read into the old forms, and in these new meanings the spirit of the age revealed itself. Things which it was impious to question, it became a moral necessity partially to explain.

The following were some of the chief modes in which superstition entered into Greek religion :

1. The notion of divine anger became ultimately the occasion of much that was most valuable in Greek thought. But the crude form of it, which saw in each disaster an outcome of divine revenge, or of the envy of the gods at human prosperity, clung persistently to the popular religion, and effectually overclouded such glimpses as reflection had opened of the nature of God. Even in historical times occasions arose in which the panic or despair of a people could only be appeased by rites of hideous cruelty, which were supposed necessary to pacify the wrath ($\mu\eta\nu\iota\mu\alpha$) of an angry god. (Such recrudescence of disused religious forms in times of stress is found in all religions—see Jeremiah xliv. 15–19.) The ministers of religion in counselling such rites are not to be accused of heartless hypocrisy. They acted under an impulse in which they sincerely shared, or at worst followed the dictates of tradition, in the hope of satisfying the craving for religious peace which seemed otherwise unattainable for their countrymen. Thus the human mind, by its natural working, contributed to its own enslavement. It is hard to say how long the custom of human sacrifice was continued in Arcadia, but it would seem to have still existed in the time of Plato, and there is little reason to doubt that Themistocles, however unwillingly, yielded to the clamour of the Athenian populace for the slaughter of Persian prisoners in honour of Hellenic gods, an act only less barbarous or less inconsistent with general Greek usage

than that of the Persians of the same period, in burying their prisoners alive.

Yet Greek religion in the time of Plato and even of Themistocles was a deep reality, and in the higher minds was already penetrated with moral enlightenment.

2. So far men's thoughts were guided by the natural conviction that the 'curse causeless cannot come.' But the belief in gods suggested not only fear but hope : the hope, namely, of communication between man and God. The powers which closely surrounded human life could not be imagined as altogether silent. Hence the constantly recurring belief in omens and signs, a belief that prevailed especially among women. What is here most noticeable is the persistence of the belief, side by side with an ever-returning scepticism. The scepticism is almost as old as the belief. Penelope is evermore seeking to diviners, but Telemachus is tired of listening to them. The wise Noemon interprets aright the augury of the eagles, in accordance with the secret wish of his heart, while the bold Eurymachus scouts every omen that thwarts his purpose. In this he may be thought to speak out of the naughtiness of his mind, but his disbelief is shared by the patriotism of Hector, who declares that the best augury is to defend one's country.

The diviner is, notwithstanding, a constant figure in Greek life; and his influence, though often suspected of corruption, was none the less important. This general tendency found its main support in the great oracular seats, of which Dodona in the earliest times, and Delphi throughout Greek history, stood out pre-eminent among a host of less important centres. The divining well mentioned by Pausanias, into which you dropped a mirror and took it out and read your fortune, is only a particular instance of a widely spread phenomenon. What led originally to the singular importance attaching to Dodona and Delphi on the mainland, or to Branchidae in Ionia, is a point of great obscurity, in which mere accident may have had a large share. The only thing to be here insisted upon is the fact that the human desire for divine communication in the crises of private or public life maintained the ascendency of those institutions which had the sanction of primeval reverence, and of association with the immediate presence of a god.

The period of Hellenic culture which I propose to consider has five chief culminating points.

1. The prehistoric age, vaguely described as Mycenaean, of which we know very little, but of which scattered hints have lately been gathered by archaeological investigation. It was, in fact, the bloom of an advanced civilisation which had a very real existence, whether to be called Achaean, Danaan, or Pelasgian. It is necessary to refer to this period, but I shall only touch upon it in so far as it appears to me to throw some light on subsequent developments which are manifested in literature.

2. The Homeric age, apparently the product of this Achaean culture transferred to the coasts of Asia Minor, and there again developed in new forms.

3. The growth of the great cities, and the first rise of philosophy in the sixth century before Christ. Side by side with this we shall have to study the main features of the post-Homeric religion, preceding the specially Attic period.

4. The period following the Persian war. In this, while the Attic genius takes the lead, we have also to include the reflection of a wider Hellenism in the histories of Herodotus.

5. The development of philosophy, chiefly on Athenian soil.

But the division of our subject cannot be made to turn thus simply upon considerations of time. We have to consider also, especially in the earlier period, distinctions first of race, and secondly of locality. Throughout Hellenic culture, there is a general community of type underlying all distinctions. But every city, whether small or great, had its own peculiarities (Herodotus tells us that there were four pronounced differences of dialect amongst the Ionians of Asia Minor), and above all, there was a marked diversity between Dorian, or at least Spartan, institutions and those of the rest of Greece. Nor was it a matter of indifference whether the Dorian city was planted at Sparta or in

Rhodes or Crete, at Syracuse, or mingled with Achaean and perhaps barbarian blood at Tarentum or in Cyrene.

These separatist tendencies proved stronger in the end than the nobler impulse to pan-Hellenism. But it is not to be forgotten, that while this last was rooted in an essential community of race, it was also encouraged and supported by great religious institutions. Amongst these the Delphic oracle and the Olympian games were the most prominent.

It is a common observation that religion and morality sometimes move on separate lines, and that in their gradual approximation consists the elevation of humanity. In one sense, of course, religion is ethical always, and never more so than in primitive times, for it is a rule of life which enters into the minutest details of conduct ; but when not enlightened by reason, it is a blind guide, often leading to the most monstrous perversions. The awakening of reason and of true moral feeling has often taken the form of irreligion ; but there is a weakness inherent in such a negative attitude, which prompts a counter movement towards the purifying of religion from within. In each successive stage of the long history, the measure of advance is registered through the free action of individual minds ; and it is because the best minds in Greece could always freely act, that the expression of their inmost thoughts has an imperishable interest for mankind. The form which that expression took was relative to the conditions of popular belief and custom ; this detracts nothing, however, from its charm and freshness, but rather enhances the touch of nature which proves the kinship of the great minds of Greece to the wise and good of other lands and times.

CHAPTER II

ANTECEDENTS AND SURVIVALS

Aryan and Semitic elements—Adumbration of the earliest phases—Preceding civilisations—The Mycenaean age—The Aryan stock—Contact with aborigines—Foreign influences—Survivals—Recapitulation.

ALTHOUGH the subject of this volume is religion in Greek literature, it is necessary to premise some observations on the time before the literature begins. But in the case of Greek religion this is especially difficult. Greek culture stands out before us as an independent fact, self-developed out of previous elements which are imperfectly known. Yet our idea of it is inevitably modified as we gain some fragmentary perception of preceding civilisations, and of the constitution of the races surrounding the Aegean and Ionian seas, in ages before the earliest date that can be assigned to the Homeric poems.

Speculation and enquiry are still active about the prehistoric age in what was afterwards called Hellas. Between those who refer everything to an Aryan or Indo-Germanic origin, and the supporters of some theory of early Semitic elements, whether coming in through Egypt and Libya, in the third millennium B.C., or through Phoenician commerce towards the end of the second millennium, or through Hittite and Phrygian influences at an indefinite time, there is a confused noise of battle that is distracting to the ear. First the discoveries of Schliemann seemed to revolutionise the whole subject. And now those of Mr. Flinders Petrie and Mr. Arthur Evans are threatening to open a new region from which other cross lights enter in. The comparison of late authorities with newly found inscriptions of uncertain date has given rise to a crop of ingenious theories, which it is difficult either to assent to or refute. Another Lobeck seems to be required, who should sift out the more questionable evidence, and determine the residuum of demonstrated fact, however fragmentary it may prove to be. Instead of dogmatising in the present state of knowledge, it may be well to put into the form of queries some considerations which are suggested by recent investigations. Are similar names, traditions, customs, in Arcadia, Boeotia, Thessaly, or in Elis and Aetolia, to be accounted for by a southward or a northward migration, or by common tendencies approaching from east or west? Was the gap which separates Hellenic culture from the remote past now partly known to us, a period of declension or of development? Are the traces of Semitic origin, some of which are indubitable, to be referred to a Libyan infusion in the third millennium B.C. or to Egyptian domination in the second millennium, or to Phoenician enterprise, or to contact with Phrygia by way of Thrace or across the Aegean? And are we to suppose that ideas, symbols, or rites, which came in from the east, retained much anywhere of their original meaning? The persistence of tradition under all changes is indeed surprising, and there is something disquieting in the circumstance (if Pausanias was rightly informed) that a shape so un-Hellenic as that of the Phigalian Demeter should have lasted into Roman times. But that which is at once difficult and desirable to ascertain in the study of Greek origins, is the blend of diverse influences meeting in one wide channel. How strangely composite, for example, was the religion of Delphi : the navel of the earth, the grave of Dionysus, and his nocturnal haunt, the seat of magic rites analogous to those of South Sea Islanders, yet under the Apolline priesthood a source of mental and moral illumination spreading far and wide ! As we look steadily at the welter of facts and opinions still awaiting settlement, some dim forms begin to look forth upon us from the backward abysm of time.

1. Out of the vagueness of Polydaemonism, there emerges here and there the conception of a male and female power, supreme over all—at first unnamed : it is enough to specify the god and goddess mentioned amongst more recent

deities in the Eleusinian rites : also the powers worshipped as Pan and Selene in Arcadia, and at Dodona the mysterious divinities who in historic times assumed the names of Zeus and Dione.

2. There is the power of Earth, beneficent, mysterious, associated with the nether gloom. She is the author of fruitfulness and barrenness ; she is the Great Mother—hence identified with Rhea and with Cybele ; she has a child who appears and disappears—hence the twofold image of the Great Goddesses, recognised in later times as Demeter and Persephone, Damia and Auxesia, or the like. Earth worship passes readily on the one hand into Chthonian religion, and on the other into the power of divination.

3. Sometimes pairing with the Earth, there is a god of the great deep : known in historic times chiefly as Poseidon. And it is observable that his earliest seats are not upon the seashore, except at Corinth and Troezen, but far inland : at Mantinea, at the Minyan Orchomenos, and in the hollows of Thessalian hills.

4. There is also the power that rules in high places, identified sometimes with Cronos, more commonly with Zeus. He gives the rain, he rules the clouds, he wields the lightning, and lives amidst the brightness of the sky. If 2 and 3 remind us of some Babylonian worships, in Zeus (Dyaus, the bright one) we confidently recognise the Aryan stock.

5. Again there comes in the eternal Feminine in various forms : Aphrodite, Urania, Hera, Artemis. In some regions this class of worship becomes confused, but it is throughout associated with marriage or virginity, with childbirth or widowhood and bereavement. Aphrodite has Phoenician affinities, while Artemis sometimes passes into an almost Phrygian phase, and sometimes assumes the attributes of Persephone.

6. Less mysterious and remote, more familiar but not less reverenced, are sons and daughters of the highest who are also comrades and helpers of mankind. Some of these are ever immortal ; others die and are lamented, they are born again and men rejoice. The chief among them are

Apollo and Athena, the enlighteners, guides, and defenders of the race who pray to them. Attending on them are various 'culture deities,' patrons of the arts of life: Hephaestus, Triptolemus, Asclepius, the Graces and the Muses, the Dioscuri, Hermes, Dionysus, Herakles. That in some regions, as in Thrace or Crete, Dionysus was originally the supreme god, or that the universal hero to whom the name of Herakles was attached came to be identified with a Semitic sun-god, need not trouble us in this general survey.

7. Rumours of contention between divine powers, as between Apollo and Herakles at Delphi, Athena and Poseidon in Attica and elsewhere, have been variously accounted for ; the most plausible explanation on the whole, though not universally applicable, is the introduction of a new worship by a conquering race. Tales of contention of the human with the divine, always ending in disaster, may sometimes be mere moral apologues, but may also indicate the gradual triumph of an unfamiliar worship, as in the legends of Lycurgus and Pentheus, of Niobe and of the daughters of Proetus.

8. Persistent amidst all changes in lands which can be called Hellenic, was the sacredness of Hestia, the family hearth. And here at all events, whatever may be thought of other religious phenomena, we are on the firm ground of Aryan tradition. Both word and thing belong to the *peculium* of the Indo-Germanic race.

The tribes that in historic times inhabited the region, and tended gradually to become one people, had probably never been quite homogeneous, and their civilisation, including their religious rites, was composed of elements derived from different quarters. The extended seaboard, especially of the Peloponnesus and the neighbouring islands, gave large opportunity for contact with foreign influences. To what extent these had been operative in the earliest times is a question as yet undetermined. We know for example that Cyprus was successively occupied by Egyptian and Assyrian conquerors and became an important centre for the wide ramifications of Phoenician trade. In the reign of the Egyptian king Akhenaten about 1400 B.C., it was already, as a dependency of Egypt, the main source from which copper was imported. A small carved work in ivory, found in that island by Professor A. S. Murray and assigned by him to the eighth century B.C., affords a striking example of the effect of mutual contact. The subject, a griffon overcome by a god in human form, is identical with that of a similar work in the Assyrian collection, but the spirit of the execution, conveying so powerfully the dominance of human over brute nature—the same motive, by the way, as that in Botticelli's Minerva and the Centaur—is essentially Greek, and not less so is the perfection of naturalistic art with which the chase of the wild bull and the disasters attending it are represented on the Vaphio gold cups, to which a much earlier date has been assigned. The discoveries of Mr. Arthur Evans go far to prove that well-nigh 2000 years before our era religious rites closely akin to the Egyptian had found their way to the south-eastern coast of Crete. And the dominance of Crete in early times over the islands of the Aegean, asserted by Thucydides, receives a striking confirmation from the recently discovered poems of Bacchylides, from which it appears that the island Ceos, no less than the city of Miletus, claimed to have been colonised by Ecphantus, a descendant of Minos. Such isolated points do not warrant deductive inferences, but they are very suggestive.

It may therefore be worth while to resume, in the merest outline, what we may take for known about these earlier civilisations. At a time not far removed from the date which used to be fixed for the creation of the world, the Semitic power of Babylon had risen and subdued an earlier race, known to archaeologists as Sumerians, whose religious ideas became incorporated with those of the conquering people. The original seat of this religion was Ur of the Chaldees, near the mouth of the Euphrates, on the Persian Gulf. About the middle of the second millennium (1500 B.C.) the power of Babylon was held in check by the dominance of Egypt to the south-west and by the rival power of the Hittites to the west. After the victories of Thothmes III., the king of Egypt was suzerain over parts of Syria, and governed them through native princes with whom he held

communication in the Babylonian language.   Before 1200
B.C., if we may trust Egyptologists, the inhabitants of the
shores of the Aegean and of the Mediterranean were known
to the Egyptians under names which are perhaps equivalent
to Achaean, Ionian, Sardinian, Tyrrhenian, Danaan, Carian,
Lycian.   These last are believed by some to be included
amongst the allies of the Hittite power gathered together at
the great battle of Kadesh in the fourteenth century B.C.
From about the year 1300 B.C. the Assyrian power is
extending, while that of Egypt is shrinking.   A strangely
vivid light has been thrown on its decline by the famous
Tel-el-Amarna letters which are condensed in Mr. Flinders
Petrie's 'Syria and Egypt.'[1]   If the Khabiri, there associated
with the Amorite and Hittite powers, were the stock of the
people afterwards known as Phoenicians, we have here the
first clear indication of their arrival on the north Syrian
seaboard.   Sidon, Tyre, and Byblos are wrested by them
from the suzerainty of Egypt in the later fourteenth century.
We should therefore be justified in placing the period of the
Phoenician sea power in the five centuries between 1300
and the end of the eighth century B.C.   Those who
have raised a doubt as to the existence of Phoenician

---

[1] These letters afford some curious indications of the international workings of religion in an early time.

1. A Babylonian viceroy asks the king of Egypt for 'much gold' for the
decoration of a great temple which he is building (to a Babylonian god?)

2. A Babylonian princess writes to her sister who is dwelling at the Egyptian
court, ' May the gods of Burraburiash (Babylon) go with you ! '

3. The king of Alashia (Cyprus) sends a vial of sacred oil for the anointing
of the king of Egypt on his accession.

4. The governor of a city near Damascus complains that the Hittites have
carried off *Shamash, his father's god*.   He asks the king of Egypt for gold to
ransom him.

5. Dushratta of Mitanni (Northern Mesopotamia), in writing to his son-in-
law Amenhotep III., not only says, ' May Istar bless you ! ' but sends a statue
of Istar, goddess of Nina (Nineveh ?), to be worshipped by Amenhotep and
returned.

6. Similarly Ribaddi, the faithful tributary, writing from Gubla (Byblos)
says : ' May the goddess of Gubla give power to the king ! '

7. On the other hand the people of Dunip in their touching appeal for help
say : ' The gods of Egypt dwell in Dunip ; but we no more belong to Egypt.'

8. And, similarly, the treacherous Akiyyi, in asseverating his loyalty, appeals
' to the king's gods, and the Sun.'

domination object to it on the ground that the Greeks borrowed no terms of navigation from that people ; but it now appears that Mediterranean shipping had a much longer history, and that the Lycians were a sea-going people at a still earlier time. The great conquerors Sennacherib, Sargon and Assurbanipal swept over the Asiatic continent during the eighth century before Christ, leaving traces of their power even in Cilicia and Cyprus. Soon afterwards there intervened that strange incursion of Cimmerians and Scythians from the north, reaching as far as Ascalon, and resulting in a temporary alliance between the Lydian and Assyrian kingdoms. Assyria fell before the Mede, through the conquest of Nineveh, 605 B.C. About this time the power of Egypt again asserts itself under Psammetichus and his son Necho, the conqueror of Jerusalem ; but the military strength of Egypt was now decaying and they employed Greek mercenaries. The intercourse of Greece with Egypt, hitherto indirect and intermittent, is from this time constant and increasing. The settlement at Naucratis, which had succeeded to the camp at Daphne, was now completely recognised, and a race of half-breeds called the 'interpreters' became intermediaries between the two peoples.

After the fall of Nineveh, Babylon again comes to the front under Nebuchadnezzar, and the Mede who had destroyed Nineveh was in his turn supplanted by the Persian under Cyrus the Great ; but the religion of all these peoples retained an influence from Chaldean tradition, latterly modified, to what extent is not yet clear, by the great mind of Zoroaster.

It appears to be very doubtful whether the direct predominance of Egypt ever passed effectively beyond Cyprus and the southern coast of Crete. The assumption of Foucart that Minos was an Egyptian viceroy has no confirmation in Hellenic traditions, which represent him as the son of Europa, a Phoenician princess. And the Argolic legends which make Danaus the brother of Aegyptus may have grown up in times long subsequent to the eighteenth dynasty. The rapid growth of legend is sufficiently exemplified by the myth concerning the end of Croesus, which in little more than a century assumed for Bacchylides and Herodotus two wholly different forms. The belief of Herodotus that the Thesmophoria were introduced by the daughters of Danaus is contradicted by the association of this village festival with marriage rites, which have more an Aryan than an Egyptian complexion. The references to Egypt in the Homeric poems imply only such acquaintance as would come from distant rumour, and rank with the mention of Libya and other regions having no proved contact with Greek life. The Assyrian did not force his own religion upon those he conquered, but took tribute from them and left them to themselves. Thus from the sixteenth to the seventh century B.C. there was ample room for the separate growth of tribes inhabiting the region afterwards called Hellas, whether Achaean, Danaan, or Carian. At two centres, one on the mainland of Greece and one in Peloponnesus, arose the great kingdoms of Orchomenos and Mycenae. But during the greater part of this period they could only have a limited command of the sea. For until the eighth century, the Phoenicians, a Semitic people, pioneers of adventure, commerce, and manufacture, were practically the only sea power, and became the natural channel through which the lands between the Aegean and Ionian seas must have received most of the influences which reached them from without. The decline of this maritime empire is nearly as obscure as its rise, but may be accounted for by the loss of its principal base of operations, through the weakening of the power of Tyre by Assyria.

Phoenician factories studded the seaboard of the Levant and the Aegean and the other shores of the Mediterranean, as far as Gades and beyond it. Wherever there was mineral wealth they came, and came to stay—as in Cyprus, Thasos, and Euboea; wherever there were purple fisheries—in south Laconia and the Corinthian Gulf, at the Euripus—they established themselves. If M. Bérard is right in a tenth part of his conjectures, they penetrated far inland. But according to Mr. Arthur Evans 'Semitic' influence in

Greece had dated from a much earlier period, coming in from Egypt by way of Libya. These and similar theories, if once established, might help to explain the readiness with which, in later times, oriental symbolism and magic obtained so wide a hold on the Hellenic mind. But the disappearance of the Phoenician power, as I have said, is not less remarkable than the proofs of its existence. This people seems to have withdrawn gradually from the Aegean, as Greek mariners from Samos, Thera, and elsewhere became more adventurous; and as Tyre declined. They left their mark, however, in Cyprus, over which they long retained some hold ; in Crete, where the legends of Minos and Daedalus indicate their presence ; at Cythera, Thasos, Samothrace, and even at Rhodes, which appears as Rodanim amongst the sons of Javan in the genealogy of Genesis X. German antiquarians have lately thrown doubt upon the constant Greek tradition of a Phoenician settlement in Thebes. 'Was ever a Phoenician settlement so far from the coast ? ' asks one of them. But Thebes is not further from the coast than Tamasus in Cyprus, the town of Thammuz, where the Phoenicians certainly had lodged. The name of Chalcis, 'Copper Town,' suggests Phoenician occupation whether as a commercial depot or for mining purposes, in Euboea ; and as the power of Orchomenos increased, the Phoenicians, to secure their hold on Chalcis, might naturally plant a strong fortress, the Cadmeia, on the slopes of Onchestus, somewhat further from the sea. It is perhaps significant that there was a Chalcis also on the Aetolian coast. The fact that the Phoenician alphabet was differently adapted in different parts of Hellas shows that Thebes was not the only centre where such learning was obtained, but does not prove the Greeks to be wrong in asserting that Cadmus brought the alphabet to Thebes. Herodotus says expressly that Membliareus, a companion of Cadmus, remained at Thera ; and that the Phoenicians mingled with the Greek population there. The question is an important one, for if the Phoenicians brought with them any seeds of Chaldean worship or mythology, the way from Thebes to Delphi would afford one obvious inlet for these. The Delphic fable of a contest between Herakles and Apollo is especially significant in this regard. It is interesting at least to speculate on the possible connection between a Semitic strain thus insinuated into Hellenic life, and the presence here and there of an intensity of personal feeling, a fiery earnestness of mood, more in keeping with our conception of Semitic than of Aryan life—as in the motive for the attempt of Aristogeiton, and the persistent vindictiveness of Pheretime.

Another people who early found their way into the Aegean were the Tyrrhenians, who made a settlement at Lemnos, and whom Herodotus identified with the Pelasgians.

Thus there are several channels through which foreign, that is mainly oriental, influences might find their way : first the doubtful Libyan infusion; then Phoenician commerce and intercourse, especially where a city once Phoenician was occupied by Greeks ; then Egypt (with which, however, direct intercourse was infrequent, until towards the close of the seventh century B.C.), and lastly Asia Minor, where religious impulses, perhaps reinforced from further east, had taken a determined bent, especially in Phrygia.

The similarity of manufactured articles discovered in tombs ranging over a wide region has led to the inference that a race or races owning common tendencies and elements of civilisation must have occupied the lands round the northern shores of the Mediterranean at a time extending far into the second millennium before Christ. The substantial uniformity of this ancient culture, whether implying identity of race or not, bears witness to the fact that in those early days there was more communication between distant parts of the world than was formerly imagined. The traditional connection of Arcadia with Crete and Cyprus, for example, recalls a state of things which in historic times had passed away. Lines of commerce existed both by land and sea, extending from Mesopotamia to the Atlantic, and from the Delta to the shores of the Baltic.

The previous question naturally returns : What was the main stock that being exposed to all these influences reacted on them so powerfully as to create the complex phenomenon known as Greek culture? The evidence tends to show that the race, whencesoever it came, was mainly Indo-Germanic, or Aryan, although modified through intercourse with aboriginal tribes and with Semitic merchantmen. And it is important to observe that through all modifications it retained its identity. The religion of the family in the patriarchal form was its essential core, which might be overlaid from time to time, but could never be supplanted. The institutions of marriage and of inheritance which had come down from immemorial times were never obliterated ; and the religion of the hearth, appearing for example in the ceremonies following upon birth, persisted through all changes of public ritual. If we now imagine the first arrival of one branch of this Aryan race in what was afterwards called Hellas, we cannot but suppose that its career of conquest was gradual, and that the extermination of the previous holders of the soil would be by no means complete. The conquerors brought with them at least one sacred name (Zeus = Dyaus) which comparative philology has shown to be derived from the old Aryan speech. But to judge from analogy, the religious rites which they found existing amongst the conquered people would naturally react upon the conquerors, and become incorporated with their own ritual. For example, as they over-ran Arcadia they made their way with difficulty to a mountain fastness, perhaps the last refuge of the conquered people ; the summit was occupied by the native god, on whose altars that people had offered human sacrifice in their extremity, with magic ceremonies supposed to bring down the blessing of the rain. Was this a purely savage rite dating from immemorial times, in honour of some wolf-god, himself originally a wolf, and now the protector of the flock ; or had Semitic strangers instituted the rite in worshipping some Baal-Ammon, to whom, like the priests on Mount Carmel, they cried aloud in time of drought ? The form of the precinct and the absence of a statue, two pillars being the only sacred objects, point strongly in the latter direction ; and this hypothesis is also rendered probable by the analogy of the cult of Athamas in Northern

Greece, of Artemis Brauronia on the Attic shore, and of
Artemis Laphria at Calydon, near the opening of the Corinthian Gulf.   However this may have been, the conquerors
accepted the ancient worship under a new name; the altar
was consecrated afresh to Zeus, the god of the sky, to
whom mountain tops were especially dear.   But the new
deity retained the ancient attributes as Zeus Laphystius,
and was worshipped with some part of the old ritual.   By
some such means it came to pass that the same deity had
different attributes in different localities.   Perhaps the most
singular of such survivals was the worship of the Dodonaean
Zeus.   In that highland retreat, the Greek invaders had
found a primitive tree worship combined with veneration
for a male and female deity, whom the newcomers named
Zeus and Dione.   The priests, a sort of Druids, still in
Homer's time lay upon the ground, no doubt watching over
the life of the tree, not taking time even to wash their feet,
and were the objects of a special reverence, which made
Dodona the centre of oracular wisdom.   According to the
fable in Herodotus, the oracle itself was in some way related
to that of Ammon in Africa, and to the Hyperboreans, whose
tokens were annually sent also to Delos.   The sacredness of
Styx (a duplicate of the Arcadian river), of Acheron and
Cocytus found acknowledgment in the same region.   How this
is to be interpreted is obscure; but it seems to imply that the
oracle was at some period, of which a dim tradition remained,
superinduced upon an earlier ritual.   Some secret corre-
spondence between priests and soothsayers at distant centres
is a possibility that is not to be ignored.   What mainly
concerns us here is the conception, without which the
whole subject becomes a hopeless tangle, of what may be
termed the *contamination* of worships.   The Aryan invaders
may be supposed to have given to the nature-deity the
name of their own supreme god, while they did not venture
to disuse the primeval barbarous rite which had engrained
itself in the minds of the inhabitants.

The cult of Artemis presents another example of the
variety superinduced upon Greek worship through the
Hellenic tendency to identify the gods of alien races with

their own. The cruel Artemis of Brauron was identified with a goddess of similar propensities on the Tauric Chersonese; while her namesake at Sparta was satisfied in historic times with the blood of young men effused in scourging—their endurance being thus tested, like that of American Indian braves, on the threshold of manhood. The divine huntress, sister of Apollo, presiding over birth and death and maidenhood, was at Ephesus again identified with a great Phrygian or eastern nature-power which never became completely Hellenised or humanised. And yet how beautifully the Greek spirit shines forth in the work of the artist who has represented the restoration of Alcestis from death, after her self-sacrifice, on one of the pillars of the temple dedicated by Croesus, the first letters of whose name are still upon the basement! Nor could the Athena worshipped at Barca and Cyrene, and associated with the Lake Tritonis in Libya, be more than accidentally connected with the daughter of Zeus, the mistress of Athens. It need therefore not surprise us if when we come to treat more at large of some of the most prominent forms of Greek worship, such as that of Herakles, of Aphrodite, or even of Poseidon, we find Phoenician and other foreign elements inextricably blending with native conceptions.

Many isolated ceremonies noticed by Pausanias as still connected with local cults in his own time have a complexion that recalls primeval religion. For example, at Triteia, an *inland* city of Achaia, he found a sacred place of the 'Greatest Goddesses,' as they were called, probably identified by the Greeks with Demeter and Persephone, whose annual festival was of an orgiastic nature. The images of these holy powers were, as they had always been, of clay, symbolising, perhaps, the fertility of the ground. Such magic symbolism, similar to what Herodotus and Pausanias describe as existing in Aegina and Troezen in the age before the Persian war, where it was thought necessary that the images should be of olive wood from Athens, might, of course, originate afresh at almost any period, but it is natural to suppose that, like the use of white poplar-wood and of the water of the Alpheus at Olympia, it may be a survival of primitive tradition. These examples may suffice to indicate a general phenomenon—namely, the effect produced by the reaction of primeval local ceremonies upon the Aryan deposit. This may be assumed as one of the many causes of an almost infinite variety in the popular worship of deities, who throughout Hellas were called by the same names. From the Great Goddesses of Triteia, or the Troezenian Damia and Auxesia, to the Demeter of Eleusis or of Cnidos, there is a greater gap than can easily be filled by the progress of a purely Hellenic culture.

Mr. Matthew Arnold, in his treatment of the legend of Merope, has shown a fine appreciation of the mode in which the Greek imagination remoulded the fragments of animal worship that survived in their ritual. In alluding to the fable of Callisto, that is, of Artemis transformed into a bear, he beautifully suggests the persistence of human feeling under the rugged disguise.

> But his mother, Callisto,
> In her hiding-place of the thickets
> Of the lentisk and ilex,
> In her rough form, fearing
> The hunter on the outlook,
> Poor changeling! trembled.
> Or the children, plucking
> In the thorn-choked gullies
> Wild gooseberries, scared her,
> The shy mountain bear!
>
> Turning, with piteous,
> Distressful longing,
> Sad, eager eyes,
> Mutely she regarded
> Her well-known enemy.
> Low moans half uttered
> What speech refused her ;
> Tears coursed, tears human,
> Down those disfigured
> Once human cheeks.
> With unutterable foreboding
> Her son, heart-stricken, eyed her.
> The Gods had pity, made them stars.

That is the manner in which Greek poets dealt with the bull Achelôus, the heifer Io, the equine Demeter, Philomela,

Procne and the rest : accounting for what was really the earlier form by a theory of metamorphosis. In like manner they were able to assimilate and to transfigure the monstrous types of griffin, sphinx, chimera, harpy, siren, &c., often giving quite a new significance to the borrowed form.

In trying to imagine the religious condition of any tribe or community within Hellenic limits, in what is vaguely known to us as the Mycenaean age, we have thus to take account not only of Aryan tradition, and of the originality of the Achaean race, but (1) of immemorial usages clinging to each several locality, especially amongst herdsmen and tillers of the soil ; and (2) of foreign influences operating chiefly at great centres, such as Argos or Thebes, which, although their effect was mainly visible in art, yet coloured in a less degree the tissue of religious sentiment and imagination. Many opportunities of dealing with the former point will occur in the sequel. Some remarks upon the latter topic may fitly find place here.

There is good reason to suppose that the dynasties which successively prevailed in Hellas and in the islands, Siphnos, Paros, Naxos, Aegina, Argos, Thebes, imported much not previously existing amongst their countrymen. The islands had the start in civilisation, not to mention Crete and the legendary fleet of Minos, which put down piracy and instituted a reign of comparative peace ; the islanders, even when raiding one another, had more intermission from peril and disturbance than the tribes on the mainland. The wild beasts were more easily subdued; the wealth which the island chief amassed was more securely held, since to pass a boundary and drive a neighbour's cattle was easier than to cross the narrow seas in twenty-oared galleys. Living in comparative tranquillity, the islanders had more opportunity for cultivating the ground, and for developing the special resources of their land. Thus Siphnos in very early times had gold and silver mines which made the island important and envied. The Siphnian treasury at Delphi, if rightly so identified, gives evidence of this. Paros from its marble quarries, and Naxos from its fertility, had each a long career of prosperity. But above the rest Aegina long exercised a predominant power. Her prowess, which Greek tradition dates only from Aeacus, must have had a yet earlier than that imaginary source. The prevalence of the Aeginetan talent before the time of Pheidon leads to the natural inference that the commerce of a very early time was dominated by the Aeginetan power. Some time afterwards the Achaeans of the mainland came under the predominance of the dynasty which Hellenic legend recognises as that of Pelops. According to the story they brought their wealth from Phrygia to Argolis, and found a secure treasure-house for it, not in an island, but amongst the fastnesses of the hills. To Atreus, as to the Kenite, it might be said : ' Strong is thy dwelling place, and thou makest thy nest in a rock.'

Whether they found or brought with them that religion of Hera, which long prevailed in Argolis, is impossible to say. Nor can it be confidently determined whether the association of this worship with that of Epaphus, a Greek form of the Egyptian Apis, and the legend of the daughters of Danaus connected with it, was earlier or later than the seventh century B.C. But it is manifest that here again we have a contamination of cults. The bovine goddess of an agricultural race, the patroness of marriage rites, is identified with the Eastern lady of the sky, while the transparent symbolism of the fable of the wandering moon watched by a thousand cruel eyes, till the watcher is transfixed at dawn, has been superinduced upon the original worship. A still further modification, prevalent at Cyrene in Alexandrian times, was embodied in the ' Aetia ' of Callimachus. One feature in the Perseid legend is singular, and points to some early conflict between endogamous and exogamous customs. The daughters of Danaus, instructed by their father, regard as unholy and unnatural the proposed marriage with the sons of their uncle Aegyptus. Perhaps a distant light is cast on this obscurity by a sentence of Sir Richard Burton's : ' From the very beginning of his history the Jew, like his half-brother the Arab, always married, or was expected to marry, his first cousin.'

To recapitulate briefly some of the views advanced in the

preceding pages. Our materials for constructing an image of prehistoric Hellas, although more abundant than what lay before Thucydides, are fragmentary in the extreme. There are no monuments as in Egypt even of isolated periods in a long line of kings ; nor even such obscure accounts as have lately been deciphered respecting Babylonian conquests and achievements in culture : little more indeed than bits of decoration on broken potsherds, personal adornments—chiefly of gold and bearing marks of foreign influence, and the structure of their tombs. The most definite clue to such knowledge as is still attainable is afforded by the evidence which archaeologists have collected of the widespread prevalence of a uniform scale of weights and measures, some of which have been identified with those of Babylon. Recent discoveries have inevitably awakened curiosity, and imagination is stimulated to fill in the outlines with some help from comparison and conjecture.

The tribes who lived about the shores of the Aegean seem to have been of the same kindred and much of the same stage of culture with those who lined the coast of the Mediterranean, as far westwards as the Gulf of Lions. They belonged to what is designated the Neolithic age, or are in transition from this to the age of bronze. The prevailing race was Aryan, mingled with some inferior aboriginal stock. Phoenician settlements were scattered along the seaboard, but few of them (unless Tiryns is Phoenician) remained so distinctively Semitic as those at Carthage, Eryx, or Panormos. What religious elements distinguished the communities or the sparse and scattered populations thus circumstanced we can only conjecture, but we may be confident as to some isolated points. It is fairly certain, for example, that to the Aryan race in all their wanderings the fire of the central hearth, with the enclosure surrounding it, was permanently sacred.

In the Homeric 'Hymn to Aphrodite,' Hestia is the daughter of Kronos, i.e. the sister and contemporary of Zeus. And in the 'Laws' of Plato, Hestia, Zeus and Apollo guard the citadel. A striking survival of the primitive tradition is the Spartan custom mentioned by Xenophon, or whoever

is the author of the treatise 'de Rep. Lac.,' to the effect
(xiii. cc. 2, 3) that whenever the king went forth to war he
performed a sacrifice in his own house, and the fire from
that altar was carried with him to the frontier. There he
sacrificed anew, and the fire of this second sacrifice went
on before him, and was never extinguished until his safe
return.

Nor can there have been absent some recognition of the
sacredness of other elemental powers. The fruitfulness of
earth, the force of the winds, the incalculable movements of
the sea must have demanded worship even apart from
foreign intercourse. Some cave whose dark profundity men
feared to penetrate lest it might usher them into the lower
world, or some deep well whose crystal clearness imaged the
sky and the surrounding scenery as in a Camera Lucida,
stimulated imagination to suggest means for communicating
with the divine. Nor could the race have entirely lost that
reverence for the supreme brilliance of the sky (Uranus=
Varuna)or for the sun in his strength, and the moon walking
in brightness, which are among the oldest inheritances of
Indo-Germanic peoples. The name of Zeus, the giver of
light, came with them from their first abodes, and was
identified with the local god who was generally imagined
as inhabiting the summit of some lofty mountain. The
path of migration from Thessaly to Boeotia, from Boeotia
and Aetolia to Arcadia and Elis, is marked by similarities
of worship and of divine attributes which permanently
remained, as for example those of the Itonian Athena.
That kings and chiefs at least were worshipped after
death we learn from the construction of the beehive
tombs, in which the ante-chamber was clearly intended
for the commemorative feast. But neither Zeus nor the
forefathers of the conquering race could supplant or ex-
tinguish local sanctities, native to each region. The
depth of the forest, the darkness of the cave, the living
waters of springs and rivers, the fire of the volcano, were
animated with airy superhuman presences which from time
immemorial had been feared and propitiated.

We have further to imagine the effect on an impressionable, keen-witted people of casual intercourse with strangers. Before they had themselves learned to go in quest of merchandise the Phoenicians came and brought commodities from alien shores. If we suppose a crew of those eager adventurers, storm-stayed in some port amongst the Cyclades, compelled to fraternise for a while with those who bartered with them, what tales of wonder might they not pour into the all-receptive mind of the Achaeans? Through some such channel Babylonian and Egyptian elements may have entered even into primitive Greek religion, although the factors were probably reinforced through the actual fusion of Semitic and Aryan elements at Thebes, and perhaps at Tiryns. The bright Achaean intelligence may have thus early received a tinge of oriental sadness as in borrowing the Linus-song, and learned to conceive dimly of a world beyond the grave, in which the perjurer and the parricide would be punished for their sins, or even of a judgment of souls, of which the rumour reached them out of the 'Book of the Dead.' They learned to name the constellations, the Bear, Arcturus, Orion, and the Pleiades and Hyades, so important for mariners. (The name Sirius, however, is undoubtedly Aryan.) We know not how early they may have been taught to conceive of a superhuman conflict between good and evil powers, of the rebellious Typhon, of dragons subdued by gods in human shape. The mystic power of prophecy so prominent in Babylonian worship might also thus impress itself from afar off in echoes borne from distant shrines, such as that of Branchidae, which some adventurous chieftain might visit with gifts in the hope of gaining further advantage. The oracle of Dionysus in Thrace, of Zeus at Dodona, of Apollo at Pytho, became established in places which had probably been held sacred from a still more remote antiquity, but those who worked the oracles borrowed some of their methods from elsewhere.

Social relations between individuals and families, and even between tribe and tribe, were in process of formation. Some kind of patriarchal bond held together their village communities, while here and there, as in Lycia, some trace of a quite different phase of family life, holding not of the father but of the mother, seems to have survived. A sense of kinship, even with strangers, must have sprung up between men who understood each other's speech. They would compare worships and recognise the same divinities under different names. Civic life was not as yet, unless that were to be called a city where some great and wealthy lord had built his fastness, round which his retainers clustered; still less can many villages have been united under one settled government. They might combine for purposes of defence or even aggression : the inhabitants of the plain to resist the mountaineers, and the like. Or many tribes might temporarily coalesce to repel the advance of some great conqueror. But we can hardly suppose that there were great assemblies to which many tribes resorted at once, as at the Delian festival in later times. Yet this is not impossible. What an opportunity it would be for the display of such ornaments as those lately discovered in Aegina, as well as for feats of strength and speed ! The fact that Troezen and the Boeotian Orchomenos both belonged to the Amphictiony of Calauria, worshipping Poseidon, seems to carry us back to a very early time. All is conjectural, but to let one's fancy play about the chasm of ignorance may at least serve to counteract the fallacy of supposing that times of which we know nothing were necessarily vacant of activity or altogether rude.

External influences, however, do not act equally upon art and on religion. People at an early stage of culture, however receptive, are too entirely steeped in the awe and reverence which has descended to them from their forefathers to adopt heartily or entirely a system of worship coming from abroad. The imitative faculty may be active in grafting foreign features on native religion, but the inherent force of that religion will always prevail over such adjuncts, which to begin with are but imperfectly understood. The art itself appears principally at a few centres where it was encouraged by reigning dynasties ; and here a fresh element of uncertainty comes in. Were the beehive tombs at Mycenae and Orchomenos, for example, the genuine products of Achaean or Pelasgian invention, or did some wealthy chieftain, to begin with, bring over architects and master-masons from abroad? However this may have been, the burial custom, which is here involved, implying the worship of ancestors, was of native growth. The minor remains bear evidence, not merely of imitation, but of the independent originality of the Achaean race, and evince a keener interest in reproducing the forms of the surrounding world and the activities in which men took delight, than in expressing religious feeling or adumbrating a world unrealised. Incidents of war and the chase have more fascination for the Mycenaean artist than traditions of the past or the conventional reproduction of foreign prototypes. And to speak more generally, had Egyptian or Assyrian priests been never so generous in communication, it was impossible for a Greek of any age simply to assimilate Egyptian or Chaldaean ideas.

That Cadmus brought letters with him to Thebes, and with letters perhaps the elements of arithmetic, or even the signs of the Zodiac and other secrets of navigation, or that—as Aristotle maintains—the elements of geometry were first known in Egypt and communicated to some enquiring Greek, are important statements and may possibly be true. But except in so far as these scientific principles may have been necessary to the mechanical training of the architects of the early temples, or the sculptors of archaic statues, they have little direct bearing upon the growth of Hellenic religion. Art reacts on ideas but does not create them. Those who have seen both Egyptian and Hellenic monuments are aware that the religious sentiment which guided the hand of the artist in either land was largely different. The pious Egyptian thought less of the present world than of a future state of being; his principal gods were judges of the dead rather than guides of the living. His highest skill was spent in the adornment of colossal tombs. The divine powers whom the Greek chiefly worshipped were the sources of Life and of Light, to whom the tribe, the household, or the village owed its yearly prosperity, and on whom depended its greatness or its decay. The noblest temples were built in token of thanksgiving for some signal mercy and declared the people's sense of the actual presence of their god, whom they delighted to represent in a form of perfected humanity, not only in eye and brow immortal, but in every lineament, joint, shape, and limb. The tombs of great men were worshipped, because the dead man was imagined as having power over the life of his successor; but although burial was so important, no man, however wealthy, in times characteristically Hellenic and in central Greece, thought of spending elaborately on the preparation of his tomb. Greek law-givers expressly forbade great pomp in funerals. The Mausoleum in Lycia, though adorned with splendid works of Greek art, had an essentially barbarian cast. Another difference here comes in : from an early time a sense of equality, or at least of moderation, went hand in hand with the idealism which was the inalienable portion of the Greek. The Assyrian sought to deify the individual conqueror, whom he represented of colossal stature, and perhaps with wings, but otherwise with realistic fidelity in form and habit as he lived, surrounded as in life with servants and tributaries, each bringing his appropriate offering. Notwithstanding hieroglyphic symbolism, something of the same kind is true of the Egyptian monuments : they also sought to deify man ; the instinct of the Grecian worshipper was to humanise deity. The image of Pausanias, king of Sparta, that stood by the altar of Athena of the brazen house, forms an apparent exception. But the fall of Pausanias, not long after this act of Asiatic pride, proved him tainted with barbarism, and it will be remembered that his attempt to inscribe his own name at Plataea was frustrated by what may be described either as the jealousy or the sense of equality that prevailed amongst his allies. That his image should have remained *in situ* is a characteristic touch of Greek moderation and conservatism. The Roman senate would have abolished it. The Persian porch at Athens, in which the historian Pausanias saw the marble forms of distinguished Persians, including Mardonius and Queen Artemisia, may perhaps be cited as an instance of Athenian pride, but it is a pride which finds expression, as in the 'Persae' of Aeschylus, in honour done to vanquished enemies.

To return once more to prehistoric times. Whether they had anything corresponding to the temples of the historic period, or a class of priests employed in taking care of them, or images of wood or stone carved curiously to represent the deity, is still an open question. It is impossible to say how far back such rude approximations to the human form as have been found at Amorgos and in other islands may be supposed to carry us. But it is possible that Xoana of wood or marble, which were afterwards regarded with peculiar reverence, may have come down from a period far remote. Dr. Waldstein discovered at the Argive Heraeum an upright stone which seems to have been an object of worship, and may be the very unhewn pillar which Pausanias describes as symbolising the goddess. Grotesque and terrific shapes, such as the Gorgon head derived from the Arabian Bes, or such monstrous combinations of the human and serpentine as the figure of Erichthonios on the pediment preserved in the Acropolis, belong in all probability to the period following upon the bloom of Mycenaean art. And some aniconic symbols (such as the conical form of Aphrodite) may reflect Phoenician worship.

Some questions may be suggested to which there is no certain answer.

1. Are the gods of Greece originally those of a hunting or a pastoral or an agricultural people? All elements appear to have been present, but in what degrees it is extremely difficult to say.

2. Were those rites which have less to do with patriarchal life or with the religion of the family, such as the worship of Demeter and Dionysus, inherent in Greek religion from the first, or brought in afterwards? With regard to Demeter, the answer seems to be that her worship grew naturally out of primitive village festivals, but was greatly modified in historic times by external influences. These, however, for reasons given above, can hardly have had much force before the seventh century : the Thesmophoria was associated with marriage customs, and the cult of Demeter in this respect resembled that of Hera. And if the Argolic empire of Pheidon belongs, as recent historians maintain, to the seventh century, when Greeks were settling at Daphne or Naucratis, and Amasis sent offerings to Delphi, the attribu-

E

tion of the Thesmophoria to the Danaides—indeed, the whole legend of the Perseidae—may well have taken shape about that time. As to Dionysus, it is better to reserve our discussion of him for a subsequent chapter.

One more consideration may be added here. It is often said that for the understanding of a religion, one should look not at what people feel or think, but at what they do. This is perfectly true where origins are in question. But in studying the development of religion, it must be always borne in mind that many things are reverently observed of which the original significance is utterly lost ; an often blind conservatism, and clinging to continuity, is a constant attribute of religious feeling. The point really in question is, not what they do, but in what spirit they do it. Shakespeare, in his beautiful delineation of the natural religion of Imogen's brothers, who had been brought up in the cave, away from the court, has finely touched this point. In laying out Fidele, whom they suppose to be dead, the elder says to the younger :

> We must lay his head to the East,
> My Father hath a reason for 't.

That is all, and that is enough.

We are now prepared to enter on the proper subject of this volume : ' Religion in Greek Literature from Homer to Plato.' And to prevent disappointment it may be well to premise that I do not profess to deal, except incidentally, with the religion of the common folk, which, varying as it did in different localities, and in many places continuing without substantial change down to Christian times — (Demeter, Persephone, the Nereïdes, Olympus, Charon, &c., are recognisable at the present day)—affords a fascinating subject for endless investigation. Had I undertaken such a task after a few years of study, I might well be deterred from the attempt to execute it, when such admirable and extensive treatises as Mr. Farnell's ' Cults of the Greek States ' and Mr. Frazer's ' Pausanias ' are accessible to English readers. As it is, the fact that some ' survival ' in ritual or mythology belongs to the common stock of universal folk-lore will rather be made the excuse for passing lightly over it in the present work, except where it has manifestly contributed to some higher or more characteristic development.

And yet one curious survival, pointing backward to a phase of tribal religion, may be here described. The Zeus of the Athenian citadel, whose worship was to a great extent overshadowed by that of Athena, had one great festival, the Dipolia, at which a ceremony called the Buphonia, ' the murder of an ox,' was continued down to the time of Theophrastus. 'Stalks of barley and wheat were placed on the altar, and an ox which was kept in readiness approached and ate some of the offering, whereupon it was slain by a priest who was called "the murderer of the ox," and who immediately threw down the axe and then fled, as though the guilt of homicide were on him ; the people pretended not to know who the slayer was, but arrested the axe and brought it to judgment.' So much is told by Pausanias, but more particulars are given by Porphyry, quoting Theophrastus : ' Maidens called water-carriers were appointed to bring water to sharpen the axe and the knife ; one man handed the axe to another, who then smote that one among the oxen, which were driven round the altar, that tasted the cereal offerings laid upon it ; another ministrant cut the throat of the fallen victim, and the others flayed it, and all partook of the flesh. The next act in this strange drama was to stuff the hide with grass, and sewing it together to fashion the semblance of a live ox, and to yoke it to the plough. A trial was at once instituted, and the various agents in the crime were charged with ox-murder. Each thrust the blame upon the other until the guilt was at last allowed to rest on the axe, which was then solemnly tried and condemned, and cast into the sea.' [1] To discuss the origin of such a rite is beyond the scope of the present work, but its primitive character is manifest. Compare the sacredness of the kine in the Persian Gathas, and in India to this day. And yet, strangely enough, the trial of the inanimate instrument reappears in Plato's ' Laws ' (ix. 873 E) : ' If any lifeless thing deprive a man of life, except in the case of a thunderbolt or other fatal

[1] Quoted in Mr. Farnell's *Cults of the Greek States.*

dart sent from the gods,—whether a man is killed by lifeless objects falling upon him, or by his falling upon them, the nearest of kin shall appoint the nearest neighbour to be a judge, and thereby acquit himself and the whole family of guilt.   And he shall cast the guilty thing beyond the border.' (See Farnell's ' Cults.')

CHAPTER III

RELIGION IN THE ILIAD

From central Greece to Asia Minor—The religion of a conquering race—
Different aspects of the Divine—The Homeric pantheon—Hero-
worship absent, why ?—Limitation and extension of polytheism—
Zeus and Fate—The Homeric Hades—Custom and morality—
Inevitable inconsistencies.

THE Homeric poems are the earliest as they are in some
ways the greatest expression of the Hellenic spirit which has
come down to us in a connected form. But many difficulties
stand in the way of taking their evidence for the purpose of
the present enquiry.

1. The legends on which the Iliad and Odyssey were
based had probably been brought across by emigrants from
the mainland of Hellas to the seaboard of Asia Minor,
where they were developed, recast, or embroidered and finally
shaped. Not only therefore do the poems contain the
reminiscence of a former age, but a reminiscence crossed
with later associations which had been gathered upon a
different soil. It cannot therefore be inferred that the picture
of religious ritual and emotion which appears in the Iliad
represents what really existed in Phthia or at Orchomenos
or Mycenae in the preceding age, and not rather what was
familiarly known to the poet at Cyme in Aeolia, or at
Smyrna, or in the island of Chios.

2. The singer, although he claimed a sacred office and
was conscious of the inspiration of the Muse, was not a priest,
or an expositor, whose business was to initiate his hearers
into religious mysteries. His motive was practical and
artistic rather than religious, and his work had less to do

with religion than that of the lyric or tragic poet of the fifth century.

3. The audience of the epic poet were not the common people, but members of an aristocracy, warlike chieftains, who listened to his lays after a day of hunting or of battle. Many rites and beliefs may have existed, and deeply influenced the mind of the people, for which the hearers of an Homeric rhapsody cared little.

4. It follows from what is said above that the poems throw no light at all on the contemporary civilisation of central Greece. In Thessaly, Boeotia, Attica, Laconia, many germs may have been already ripening which had great influence on the after history of religion, but of which the gilded youth of Aeolian or Ionian cities knew nothing.

5. The Ionic poet, however scrupulous in maintaining an antique colour, drew much of his illustrative and decorative detail from circumstances nearer home. He presents us therefore with a combination of old memories and recent impressions ; so that in speaking of the heroic age as described by him, we have in view, not a single object, but several blended in one atmosphere ; as when we look on a succession of ridges of some mountain chain which distance and the effect of light make indistinguishable. The poems are a treasure-house of things new and old, preserving some relics of an immemorial past like flies in amber, while bearing on their surface all the gloss of novelty. Thus they contain at once too much and too little : too much in so far as they reflect the consciousness of a cultivated Ionian of the ninth or eighth century B.C. ; too little in so far as the poet ignores or deliberately rejects what is beside his purpose or alien to the spirit of his art.

All these considerations must be borne in mind as a sort of running commentary on what is now to be said. And what is specially to be remembered is the restricted scope of the poems as religious documents. In approaching them with a view to learning something of the religious mind of the heroic age, we have to contract our view and fix it almost exclusively on the chieftains of the conquering race. Allusions to the life of the common people occur very rarely, although they are the more affecting on account of their scarcity, like Milton's comparison of Eve in Paradise to a village maiden.

In certain regions of the land afterwards known as Hellas a comparatively stable condition of society seems for a time to have been attained. We hear of forays and reprisals, of wars between Pylos and Elis, or between Argos and Thebes, of dynastic troubles in Aetolia, and the like ; but these are matters of ancient history. The race of kings tracing their origin from a divine source have their mutual jealousies and private quarrels, but on the whole have learned to respect one another's rights, while they alternately protect and oppress the people, who labour, fight and foray under shadow of their power. Individuals of the ruling class have by force of character, by the wealth they have amassed, and by personal prowess, established an ascendency that is more or less widely acknowledged. The disturbing force of commerce has not yet crossed the simple classification of chiefs, retainers and common labourers. War, hunting, pasturage, and a modicum of agriculture are the principal industries. The king, while outwardly paying reverence to sacred persons such as heralds, prophets, and ministers of holy shrines, is little inclined to acknowledge any intermediary between himself and deity. He sacrifices, not as combining priestly with regal functions, but as the natural head of his family and clan, or of the army which he leads ; and while strictly observing a simple ritual, he is assisted in it not only by the heralds, but by his sons or comrades, especially by unmarried youths, whose fresh age marks them out as acceptable to the gods. If the horns of the victim have to be gilded, it is not the priest but the goldsmith who is employed. It is sometimes imagined that the Iliad merely describes the rough life of a camp, in which things are done irregularly, as emergencies permit, but in turning to the Odyssey we find no difference in this respect.

Speaking for the present of the Iliad by itself, I proceed to remark (1) on the relation of the poet and his audience to religious tradition ; (2) on what may be called the personnel of the Olympian dynasty ; (3) on the notions of fate, the Erinnyes, and the world of the dead ; (4) on the moral elements in the poem, and the traces of incipient ethical reflection ; (5) on the inevitable inconsistency in the Homeric presentation of divine things.

1. The gods in Homer are regarded in two wholly different aspects. On the one hand, they are conceived as powers having a sort of vague omnipresence and ruling over their several provinces in the world of nature and of men ; thus Zeus, the lord of the sky, is thought of as the immediate agent in sending rain or snow ; Poseidon commands the sea ; Ares is identified with battle, even to such minute details as the flight of a spear ; such attributes of super-human powers have entered into the language, and are introduced without special purpose or premeditation. But again, the same gods are thought of as magnified human personalities, having their separate homes on the summit of a great mountain, hidden by clouds from human sight. As thus conceived of, the wills of the gods are swayed by varying inclinations, which are sometimes only accidentally associated with their special functions as divine powers. They favour and protect their worshippers ; they take part with this or that warrior ; they resent the death of their sons, and in other ways are moved by passion and desire. Zeus exercises a sort of limited monarchy over this distracted realm ; in the long run he controls it absolutely, for his will and the determination of fate are one : this is both a religious belief and a requirement of artistic unity ; but on the other hand he shows from time to time all the caprice and inconsistency of an earthly ruler. His tenderness for Thetis forms the hinge of the whole action of the Iliad, in which, to avenge the honour of Achilles, the Trojans and Achaeans suffer all the extremities of war.

It is to some extent matter of conjecture how far the audience of the poet were expected at every moment to realise for themselves the divine machinery which outwardly binds the action together. Mr. Leaf in his ' Companion to the Iliad,' page 355, observes that the brutal ferocity of Achilles to Hector would be softened for the ancient hearers by feeling that the gods were on his side ; and that this fact, far from detracting from his personal heroism, would rather exalt it in their eyes. 'To them the presence of the gods on Achilles' side was not so much a mere extraneous aid as a tangible sign that Achilles was after all fighting the great fight of Hellenism against barbarism; it is a reminder that the action on earth is but a reflection of the will of Heaven, and exalts rather than belittles those to whom the help is given. The moral superiority of Achilles being thus warranted from the point of view of national and religious feeling, to him redounds all the exaltation of his adversary.' With all deference to one who has entered so deeply into Homeric criticism, I cannot think that this was really the meaning of the great poet, perhaps the greatest of the world, whom we imagine as standing behind the action of the Iliad. It is true, of course, that all sense of human obligation towards an enemy is absent here, except so far as the poet himself implicitly condemns the excess of fierceness which he depicts. It is felt as excessive, but not as ignoble. The impression, however, which he intends to emphasise, and which was no doubt produced upon the hearer who was in sympathy with him, was not, 'how the gods protect Achilles!' 'how mightily the power of Zeus is working!' although that is also present as a circumstance of awe; it was much rather, 'how intensely Achilles loved his friend!' This cardinal motive was not obscured for them by the savagery of the action, as it is for the sensitive consciousness of the modern reader: the ferocity was the measure of the affection.

2. The theology of Homer is considerably advanced beyond that stage of polytheism in which the varied aspects of earth, sea, and sky, of woods and rivers, of light and darkness, are simply personified. Even the highest gods retain many reminiscences of their functions as nature-deities: perhaps also some attributes adopted from more primitive worships; but each of them severally is invested with a character distinctly human, and is moreover associated rather with the place or nation whom he protects, or with the dangers from which he delivers his worshippers, than with his antecedents as an elemental power. It may

also be said that in the Iliad the Olympian gods are partly leaving behind them the local and particular stage, and becoming organised into a Pantheon. The heroic world lives in close intercommunion with the deities from whom the kings derive their race. At rare intervals some allusion occurs to yet more ancient powers whom Zeus, Hades, and Poseidon have supplanted. Zeus is now supreme within the realm of light. Cronos and the Titans and old Iapetus are bound in some dungeon far beneath. Whether in this we recognise a religion of the conquered peoples, or some infusion from the east, or the outcome of a dim consciousness that the visible universe is not all, the fact of these allusions in the Iliad interests us from its connection with subsequent developments in Hesiod, Aeschylus, and elsewhere, which are thus proved to have had their antecedents in pre-Homeric times. Meanwhile, for the epic poet, the Olympic dynasty fills the celestial scene. Olympus in the Iliad is still localised, and is probably, at least in the original legend, the cloud-capped mountain in Thessaly, exalted and beautified by poetic imagination. Here Zeus holds his court, and in the winding glens between the summits are the homes of his children. His will may be thwarted or eluded for a time, but is ultimately irresistible. His supremacy, sometimes hardly distinguishable from destiny, is the most definite theological conception in the Iliad. No passages of ancient poetry are more impressive than those in which the nod of Zeus is described as compelling the world ; and the opening of Book viii. in which he challenges all other powers to pull against him, although crudely expressed, carries with it a profound conviction. The simple faith in Zeus as the almighty disposer, and even as the guardian of justice, appears in the prayer of the Achaeans to him, that in the trial by combat between Paris and Menelaus the wrongdoer may fall. But the prayer is unfulfilled, else the poem could not have been continued. The son of Cronos does not perform it for them ; and as mythologically conceived the supreme deity is full of human weaknesses. He and Hera have their several favourites to whom they show kindness within the bounds of fate ; he is cajoled by his consort with the aid of Aphrodite and Sleep ; he grieves with paternal fondness when it is fated that his son Sarpedon must fall.   Even when honouring Achilles, he pities Agamemnon's tears.   He pities the Trojans, who have done him faithful sacrifice, but acts against them.   In all this we find only human feelings magnified, which stand in unconscious contradiction to the universality which is already attached to the notion of the supreme god.   Nor is the Dodonean, Pelasgian Zeus, to whom Achilles prays, the same whom Hector entreats to protect his son.   It is observable that the Achaeans think of Zeus as the dispenser of battle more seriously than the poet does ; also that Zeus in Homer never makes himself visible to mortal eyes.

Hera, the Argive goddess, appears now as the protectress of her chief worshippers, and now as the consort of Zeus. She and Athena are at the head of a small faction, including Poseidon, who oppose themselves as far as they durst to the caprice of the supreme god in honouring the son of Thetis by afflicting the Greeks.   Her standing epithet, Hera ' of bovine looks,' is regarded by Dr. Schliemann and others as originally having reference to the pristine worship of the goddess under the form of a cow, a cult akin to that of the Egyptian Hathor.   The fact of such early symbolism, retained it may be from the primeval worship of a pastoral people, has been confirmed by further discoveries, but it need hardly be said that no consciousness of this is present in Homer.   The relation of Zeus to Hera no doubt recalls some early contrast between male and female powers, conceived as creating and ruling the world ; according to Tiele it results from an imperfect blending of a patriarchal with a matriarchal deity.   Neither of this, however, has the poet any distinct idea.   Such primitive nature-worship is to him already a ' creed outworn.'   The Muses and the Graces, givers of glad impulses, have left their native seats in Thessaly and Boeotia, and are thought of simply as divine powers.

The position of Apollo in the Iliad is rather singular. His epithet, the far-darter, reveals him manifestly as a solar deity, and in an oft-repeated formula he makes one of what has been called the Homeric trinity with Zeus and Athena. The pastoral attributes, so prominent in later mythology, are present only here and there in the Iliad. His love of song already appears in the first Iliad, when the Greeks celebrate him by singing a beautiful paean, to which he gladly listens ; and in the picture of Olympus, at the end of the same book, he wields the lyre to which the Muses sing. In the ninth Iliad Achilles instances the wealth of Apollo's Pythian shrine. But in his poetic function, as a part of the celestial machinery, Apollo is rather a Trojan and Asiatic than a Grecian deity. The poem opens with the offence done to him in the person of his minister, and with his vengeance, on which the subsequent action turns. He interposes many times on the Trojan behalf, he is the patron of Pandarus, and the rescuer of Aeneas. He borrows the Aegis to terrify the Greeks withal. He stands constantly beside Hector, whom he heals of his wound. He disarms Patroclus, he checks Achilles ; and if at last he betrays Hector, he does so under the compulsion of destiny. His seat at Chryse was one of many belonging to him on the Asiatic shore.[1] Apollo was the god of the Lycians, he had a shrine at Tenedos, and we know from independent sources that he had an oracle of time-honoured antiquity at Branchidae. With Poseidon he builds the Trojan wall, and he becomes the shepherd of Laomedon. Here for once we have a trace of his pastoral character. He again assists Poseidon in destroying the rampart of the Achaeans. To whatever source or sources the conception of him is to be ascribed, Apollo has long since assumed a quasi-human personality quite distinct from the sun-god, and he is not yet identified with the god of healing. Except that he naturally protects and heals his worshippers, his office is rather to destroy. He is the son of Latona, and brother of Artemis, but his birth at Delos is not mentioned either in the Iliad or the Odyssey, although his altar at Delos is once mentioned in the latter poem (vi. 162).

Artemis is the female counterpart of Apollo, and is fre-

[1] The local deity there, Chryse 'the golden,' has been identified with Theia, the goddess of gold in Pindar.

quently mentioned as the author of sudden and painless deaths, especially to women, a trait which anticipates her later worship as Eilithyia, goddess of childbirth. She is the huntress with the golden arrow's of the certain aim, bright, crowned, enthroned on gold, the mistress of wild creatures. She has no prominent place in the action of the poem, but in the battle of the gods, probably a late passage, she assists Apollo against the Greeks, and is treated ignominiously by Hera. Except the slaughter of the children of Niobe, and the sending of the Calydonian boar, hardly any of the legends which afterwards grew around her find a place in the poem. She is regarded as a type of austere beauty, and she is already worshipped with choral dances of virgins, but her own virginity is less dwelt upon than it is elsewhere in Greek poetry.

The story of the Iliad gives a curiously divided aspect to the person of Athena. Her temple stands upon the citadel at Troy, under the attribute of 'defender of the city.' Yet she has her native home at Athens, in the house of Erechtheus. One of the best remembered scenes in the poem is that in which, at the bidding of Hector, his mother Hecuba and the other Trojan matrons make their solemn offering to her of the largest and fairest garment (Peplos) they can find, and pray for the deliverance of their sons and people, and the goddess denies their petition. At the same time she is actively employed in passing to and from Olympus in the interest of the Greeks. She descends to moderate the action of Achilles, beside whom she is said to move continually; she steadily befriends Odysseus and Diomedes, and other heroes of the Achaeans, and is joined with Hera in support of the Achaean and particularly the Argive cause. Although universally acknowledged as an Achaean goddess, she is already to some extent identified with Athens; though she inhabits Olympus, she is content to dwell in the close-built house of Erechtheus; and in the second book, which, however, may possibly be later than the main body of the poem, she is mentioned as the nurse of Erechtheus, whom the earth brought forth, and whom she established in her own rich temple there, where the sons of the Athenians year after year propitiate her with bulls and rams. She is, in a special sense, the daughter of Zeus, the supreme god, and is quite as much the patroness of action as of counsel, the helper of Herakles and Diomedes as well as of Odysseus. Her maidenhood is not described, but is implied in the sacrifice to her of the heifer (vi. 94, 275, 308, x. 292, xi. 729). She inspires the charge of battle, she is the defender of cities ; she is called by the name of Alalcomene, said to be a city of Boeotia, which itself signifies *defence*. She is the invincible one, the unsubdued. If Hera is bovine, Athena has ' the look of an owl,' but the derivation of the epithet is uncertain, and to Homer it certainly meant either ' grey-eyed ' or ' keen-eyed.' She remonstrates with her father, and even goes forth with Hera to the aid of the Achaeans against his express desire, until warned to return. The attribute of wisdom comes out most distinctly in the passage of Book i. where she moderates the wrath of Achilles (cp. x. 245). Her function as the patroness of arts and crafts (Ergane) appears only at v. 61, 735, where she is credited with having adorned the garment worn by Hera, and at xiv. 278, where she is the patroness of the Trojan craftsman Harmonides.

Poseidon acts chiefly as a disturbing and retarding force in the machinery of the poem.   He has a grudge at the Trojans, and supports the Greeks ; except in what is called the ' Little Aeneid ' (Book xxii.), where he inconsistently appears in the interest of Aeneas.   His rebellious spirit strives to break the bounds which Zeus and fate have set to his limited empire.   He is more visibly associated with the element which he rules than the deities previously described ; and as a consequence of this, he is seldom found upon Olympus. His favourite haunts are Helice and Aegae on the Corinthian Gulf, and he has a convenient watch-tower on the top of Samothrace.   His ancient shrine upon Onchestus is not mentioned.   He has locks of blue-black or seagreen hair, and is worshipped with sacrifices of bulls, the appropriate victim also for river-gods.   In speaking of him as the encircler of the earth, or in comparing his shout to that of ten thousand men, the poet obviously associates him with the sea, no less than in attributing to him the disappearance of the Grecian rampart. But the conception of his deity is not clearly consistent. He is not only the encircler but the shaker of the earth, and there may be a natural association between the raging·billows and the earthquake by which, as in the 'Prometheus' of Aeschylus, the earth is rolled in surges to and fro. But Poseidon is also the giver of the horse, and there are traces of this already in the Iliad. He gave to Peleus the immortal steeds. To him as patron of horsemanship Antilochus prays, and is bidden by Menelaus to swear by the same god that he had not played foully in the race. These hints occur in Book xxiii., which is considered late, but we may also observe that in viii. 440 Poseidon is employed in loosing the horses from the chariot of Zeus.

Except in late and doubtful passages, Hermes appears only incidentally in the Iliad. In Book xxiv. he is the safe-conduct of Priam, and he is mentioned amongst the deities who take part in the battle of the gods, as siding with the Trojans, but refusing to fight with Latona. Both these passages, however, belong to what is now commonly regarded as the latest portion of the Iliad. The slight allusions to him in other parts of the poem, for instance, as the father of Eudorus, Book xvi. 180, or as the giver of flocks and herds in Book xiv. 491, suggest the impression that, as a pastoral deity, he is not greatly regarded by the Argive chiefs. His attribute as a cunning deceiver is twice referred to (v. 390, xxiv. 24), and the epithet Argeiphontes dimly alludes to another part of his legend, not mentioned in the Iliad.

There are degrees not only of power but of worth even amongst the Olympian gods. The Ares of Homer still bears some traces of the warrior deity of Thrace, who was his prototype. He is a mighty being, a type of vigorous manhood, and the heroes in their moments of highest valour are compared to him. He is gigantic, brazen, of astounding voice, irrepressible, swift, shield-piercing, rousing to the fray; but he is insatiable of battle, the destroyer of men, ever favouring one side, namely that which happens to be the stronger. When wounded he covers seven roods of ground. Zeus, in speaking his true mind, declares that Ares is the most hateful to him of all the gods. He is the enemy of the Achaeans, for the most part favouring the Trojans in the war, and in this there may be something of the same feeling with which the author of the 'Telegonia,' a later epic, represented Ares and Athena as encountering each other in battle. But, just as Zeus, while acting in his own person, is inconsistently associated with ordinary elemental phenomena, so the name of Ares, only half personified, often stands merely for the spirit of war, which gives life to the glancing spear, which is roused by the leaders of the host, and operates in manifold ways, altogether apart from the bodily presence of the god.

Aphrodite, in the Iliad, chiefly impersonates external beauty, sensual charm, and the mutual attraction of the sexes. She is, of course, the friend of Paris, and despotic mistress of Helen, and she is also the mother of Aeneas. She loves laughter and smiles, she is golden and the giver of golden gifts. But in the Iliad she is spoken of on the whole with scant respect. Paris indeed rebukes Hector for scorning her gifts, but Helen, who knows her best of all, reviles her with such bitterness as only a woman can feel, until she is once more overborne by the irresistible spell which subdues the revived recollection of her former home and her longing for her brethren at Lacedaemon. Aphrodite subserves Hera in the unworthy stratagem by which the action of the poem is delayed, and the vigilance of Zeus is hoodwinked for a while. In the battle of the gods, a passage of doubtful antiquity, xxi. 416, she is present on the side of the Trojans, and when Ares is overthrown by Athena, she leads him out of the fray. In Book v. 131 ff. and 352, she is wounded by Diomedes, whom Athena has taught to refrain from attacking any except this weakest of the gods, 'the deceiver of unwarlike women'; and Ares gives her his chariot to return to Olympus, where she falls into the lap of her mother Dione, and is gently rallied by Athena and her father Zeus, who tells her to keep within her sphere, and to preside over the rites of love alone. The two passages last mentioned are the only hints in the

Iliad of the close relation between Ares and Aphrodite, which is the subject of the song of Phemius in the Odyssey, and became prominent in subsequent mythology. Also in Book v. she is called Kypris; cp. Odyssey viii. 362–3, where Aphrodite retires to Paphos in Cyprus, while Ares flies to Thrace. Thus the foreign origin or connection of both deities is suggested.

Hephaestus, on the other hand, is in no way connected with Aphrodite in the Iliad, his consort who receives Thetis in B. xviii. 382 being one of the Graces, who are native Thessalian deities. This god also, like Poseidon, is closely associated with the element which he represents and rules, and as the god of fire he is, like Prometheus afterwards, the supreme artist. His lameness, which moves the laughter of the gods, has been variously accounted for. In the Iliad the cause assigned for it is his fall from heaven, which is also an obscure point in his legend. That Lemnos received him in his fall is an incident suggested by the volcano Mosychlus, which in early times was active in the island, but now seems to have disappeared beneath the sea. Except where, as the god of fire, he resists Achilles, he is simply the divine artificer, as Daedalus is the mortal one.

Hades as a personal deity comes in only incidentally as the receiver of the souls of the departed, the strong gate-keeper who opens not the house of his prisoners. His element is below, but once under the nod of Zeus he starts up from his throne, in fear lest the earth should open above him, and disclose his gloomy realm. Homer's conception of the world of shadows differs from that of savage races only in the more abiding consciousness of its unreality. The change from burial to cremation may have contributed to this. When the early Achaean interred his loved ones, he had positive satisfaction in thinking of the happy hunting ground to which he sent them, and in imagining some real continuation of the being that had been seen and felt so lately throbbing with warm vitality. To Homer this ardent uninstructed faith was a relic of the past. The thought of Hades was repulsive, but there was hardly any hint as yet of anything to take its place.

F

The gods so far described had been established in Hellenic worship long before the Iliad was composed. But the personifying spirit and the mythopoeic faculty were still active, and many minor powers are brought in to reinforce the divine army, even in Olympus where the Muses sing and Ganymede reposes. Apollo having lost his solar character, the sun-god appears in proper person as Helios the all-seeing, or as Hyperion, who was afterwards made the father of the sun. Earth cannot rise to Olympus, but she is not the less a goddess distinguished from Demeter, with whose worship she was afterwards associated; and it is perhaps significant that in striking the truce, while the Achaeans bring a victim for Zeus, the Trojans bring a white lamb for the sun, and a black one for the earth. Elsewhere, however, scarcely any distinction can be made between the Trojan and Hellenic worships. Nor are the powers that rule the spirits of men by any means exhausted. Ares has for companions Eris and Enyalios, or again the war-goddess Enyo : he is accompanied by Terror, and Flight, who is his son. Iris is both the rainbow and a messenger of the gods, hence she is often momentarily present in Olympus. Then there are the sea nymphs, the woodland nymphs, the mountain nymphs, and greater than these, the rivers, of whom Scamander plays such a distinguished part in a crisis of the poem. The Dawn, a separate personality, is the mother of Memnon. And besides these there are Eilithyia and other powers conducive to human life.

Since every act required the immediate co-operation of a god, there was scarcely any limit to the inventive work of imagination. It is obvious upon the whole account, that so far from being the creator or nominator of the Greek Pantheon, as Herodotus supposed, the epic poet accepted it as part of the tradition upon which he worked, though it is manifest that the Homeric selection and representation had a powerful and most important influence in perpetuating particular conceptions. To the Homeric poems it was due that after generations conceived more nobly of divine action than they would otherwise have done.

An important question remains. Were heroes or demi-gods already worshipped in the time of Homer ? The best authorities give a simply negative answer, and there is certainly no distinct trace of anything of the kind. The case of Herakles, of which more will be said in the sequel, is a possible exception, proving the rule, and the immortality or quasi-immortality, miraculously accorded to favourites of gods, such as Tithonus or Ganymede (both belonging to the Trojan legend), is independent of the main stream of current mythology. And if the myth of Erechtheus is admitted as an exception, this occurs in the catalogue of the ships, which is generally referred to a later (Boeotian) source. Yet it would be strange if the worship of ancestors, one of the most primitive forms of religious culture, had been entirely absent from the earliest ages in Hellas, and that it existed in some shape is proved by the construction of the beehive tombs. It has been suggested that the Aeolian emigrants in passing to Asia and exchanging crema- tion for burial may have forgotten their former worship of their fathers' tombs. Living in a perfect climate they only thought occasionally of death. It is, however, worth con- sidering whether in depicting the life of the generation in whose veins the blood of Zeus still flowed, the poet has not deliberately ignored the divine honours paid to them in his own day. The readers of the ' Ajax ' of Sophocles receive no hint of that which the spectators knew, that the prince of Salamis had his image and his shrine amongst the other sons of Aeacus at Aegina, and his altar at Salamis. Orestes was also worshipped (cp. the Oresteion at Tegea), but this does not occur to the student of Aeschylus or Sophocles. And we may observe that it is not to be expected that the Myrmidons at Troy should offer incense to Achilles while yet alive or that Agamemnon should receive divine honours in his lifetime. However this may be, certain notes of preparation for the form of religion which afterwards became so important are observable in several places in the poem. See especially B. xi. 761, where Nestor recalls his past glories, when men prayed to him on earth as to Zeus in heaven, and the frequent reference to the divine prowess of a generation which has passed away. It may well be imagined that while the Iliad reflects the feelings and beliefs of a proud aristocracy, at whose banquets it was originally sung, other traditions may have been passing amongst the subject people—fragments of myth and legend which had not yet found a poet who should give artistic shape to them. Some such hypothesis appears requisite, in order to account for the fact that many survivals of mere nature-worship and of early custom and ritual appear for the first time at a later stage of Greek literature ; so that, as Mr. Leaf broadly puts it, the Homeric civilisation is modern as compared with that of Athens. It does not follow that such fancies ' had long passed out of all remembrance at Mycenae,' but only that the selective art of the poet singing on the coast of Asia avoided them, or that they were unsuited to the fastidious taste of the chiefs before whom he sang, who were more interested in matters of war and honour than in mythology. The legend of Herakles may have been better known than appears from the poem, and even that of the Argonauts is once alluded to (vii. 468 ff.). Elis was already a seat of divination and magic (xi. 740). Chiron, a mysterious being, tutor of Achilles, is mentioned in xi. 831 as the most righteous Centaur (δικαιότατος Κενταύρων).

It remains to speak of two deities, Demeter and Dionysus, who are practically absent from the Iliad, and their absence is significant. In one passage, indeed, Demeter is spoken of as one of the many consorts of Zeus, but the passage, xiv. 326, is one of those legendary lists which were peculiarly subject to interpolation. Elsewhere Demeter is simply the giver of the corn, and is spoken of, and that only twice, in the familiar phrase ' the grain of Demeter.' She is also mentioned incidentally in alluding to a Cretan fable that made her the wife of Iasion. Persephone, in the Iliad, is not her daughter, but only the wife of Hades, and a Chthonian power. Dionysus appears only in two passages, both late or suspected, viz. in the list already spoken of, where Semele his mother is mentioned among the consorts of Zeus, and in the allusion to Lycurgus in the speech of Diomedes, vi. 130 ff., a passage which has sometimes been questioned as contradicting the tenor of Book v. (It may be noted, however, that as Aphrodite's feebleness in war is her chief attribute, so this passage dwells on the cowardice of Dionysus who takes refuge in the lap of Thetis.) Are we to suppose then that the worship of Demeter and of Dionysus had not yet become established in Hellas? or that for some reason the poet has chosen to ignore them? That in many of the islands Dionysus was already worshipped is extremely probable. That a worship of Demeter, although much simpler than in after times, prevailed wherever agriculture flourished, is almost certain; and is, indeed, implied in the phrase which speaks of her as the giver of the grain. But the proud warriors who listened to the epic singer took little account of such village celebrations. These pagan deities, as in a sense they may be termed, had no place in their regard beside Athena and Apollo. It was reserved for Attic literature to immortalise both deities, and spread their glories over the earth for the coming time.

3. But in the theology of the Iliad there is something higher than the traditions of divine action and of warlike achievement; and this is partly due to the genius of the poet.

However lightly Homer may conceive the quarrels between Zeus and Hera, or the laughter of the Immortals at lame Hephaestus, there can be no doubt as to the seriousness with which he regards human destiny as a divine irreversible fact. Fate presides at the birth of each human being and fastens round him the thread which she herself has spun. This regulates his varied fortunes and decides his term. Hence Fate is again associated with Death, the crusher of the spirit, whose power is joined with the might of Destiny. The breath of man goes forth, and his shadow is received by Hades the strong gate-keeper, while he himself, if he escape the dogs and vultures, returns to his earth, with or without the help of devouring fire. Fate is sometimes a separate power, at others can hardly be distinguished from the will of Zeus, or of the gods collectively. Even when personified, the destinies are not yet supplied with a genealogy, nor is their number fixed. Sometimes each man would seem to have a separate destiny, sometimes the lot of all

men would seem to depend upon a single power. The great
conception of Destiny as a supreme divinity, which plays so
large a part afterwards in Greek culture, is present in Homer,
but fitfully, and except in rare passages is not as yet consistently personified. The share, or lot in life, is spoken of in
much the same way as a man's share in the spoils of conquest,
or in a banquet. The thing signified, however, is deeply
inherent in the poem. The dishonour done to Achilles is
felt from the first as the more pathetic because of the early
death to which he is doomed. This unwelcome truth is
clearly understood between Zeus and Thetis in their colloquy
in the first book, and is alluded to by Thetis herself in her
address to her son (Book i. 416 ff.). Erinnys is likewise a
power at once singular and plural. The Erinnys that haunts
the gloom hears out of the nether darkness the curse of Althaea
on her son. On the other hand, the Erinnyes in the plural
are appealed to by the father of Phoenix who had outraged
his feelings, and again it is said that the Erinnyes ever
accompany the elder brother. The Erinnys is a personified
curse which becomes operative against the guilty, especially
for the breach of filial or domestic sanctities, although even
the poor man, when neglected, has his Erinnyes who
vindicate him ; and in the singular passage in which the
horse of Achilles breaks into human speech, he is checked
by the Erinnyes, who seem here to personify a law of
nature. The Erinnys is associated with Hades and Persephone (ix. 457) and with Moira and Zeus in the confession of Agamemnon, who refers his infatuation to their
anger. And this reminds us that Atè, infatuation personified,
is hardly less dreadful than the curse itself. It is enough
to recall in a sentence the famous allegory of Agamemnon,
in which Zeus himself is described as not exempt from her
disastrous influence.

The Homeric conception of Hades, the place of shadows,
is too familiarly known to need description. The epithets
of Hades, ' he of the swift steeds ' hurrying men away, ' of
the strong gateway,' 'of the stern, unrelenting mood,' are
sufficient to bring it back to mind. One point, however,
deserves special mention. The conception of the world of

death is simpler in the Iliad than elsewhere. The soul or shade passes immediately from earth to the unseen. It needs no conduct or extreme unction. The one passage which conflicts with this, when the shade of Patroclus complains that without burial he cannot pass the river, for the other shadows drive him away, belongs to a book which even conservative criticism admits to be later than the main body of the Iliad. Ermin Rohde has remarked that the funeral of Patroclus is performed according to rites which belong to a yet earlier stage of religious culture, implying a more vivid belief in continued existence after death. The poet's aim is to evince the boundless passion of Achilles ; but the *customs* are a survival from a past which believed in a real continuance of being, and also entertained a *fear* of the dead, which survives in our fear of ghosts, but from which Homer is free. The ghost of Patroclus is seen by Achilles in a dream, not with any fear, but with tender pity : on the other hand, there is a pervading sense of the gloom of Hades and of the helplessness of the shadows of the dead. The body which is the man's self is subject to decay. Thence came the temptation to maltreat the dead body of an enemy. But the unsubstantial ghost, which has fled away, is a wretched and feeble being, if it may be said to be at all. The darkness of the invisible world and the misery of mortality are intensified by contrast with the vivid brightness that surrounds the actual energies of the living man, and there is also a strain of dissatisfaction with the primitive belief, which was ultimately to lead to a reconstruction of that belief, on the higher basis of spiritual idealism.

4. In the infancy of reflection the morality of a people is embodied not in words and maxims, but in custom and feeling. In the age represented by the Iliad, settled institutions, νόμοι, were not as yet ; but Themis, or positive obligation, was acknowledged, not only in the command or judgment of the king, but in many rules of life, which although not formulated were universally held sacred and are appealed to as the sanction of conduct. It may be observed in passing that the word signifies both judgment

and the place of judgment (see Book xi. 807) ; also that
Themis as a divine person is employed in summoning the
council of the gods. Even acts which in modern times
would be referred to Nature are in Homer often included
under this term. Of ceremonial obligations we have already
spoken. That in their associations, both with greater and
lesser occasions in life, religious sanctions had a restraining
influence over the violent passions which were subject to no
other control, is sufficiently obvious ; the urbanity of manner,
which so often contrasts with the savagery of military licence,
is largely to be referred to this cause. The habit of euphemism,
that is of avoiding words which might provoke the gods,
was by no means an insignificant feature in the civilisation
of an age in which personal influences were absolute in the
human sphere. It is true that custom carried with it often
only a *positive*, that is a literal obligation. The breach of
the oath once passed awaked a religious terror which the
most outrageous perfidy, without this, could not occasion.
The only reference in the Iliad to a judgment of the dead (a
notion which thousands of years earlier had been a cardinal
point in Egyptian religion) is the appeal of Agamemnon to
Hades and Persephone as those who punish oath-breakers
beneath the ground. But the spirit already stirs beneath
the letter, and the sense of divine presences who regard the
oath, who care for the suppliant and the stranger, has a
power to humanise and refine. However inconsistently and
vaguely, the supreme god is already revered by those who
pray to him as supporting the *just* cause. Another influence
tending in the same direction is the respect for sacred persons :
the ministers of shrines—but these are mostly on the Trojan
side (where the priesthood of Theano is elective, and
Helenus is priest, prince, and warrior in one)—the herald,
who serves not kings only but also the gods, and the prophet,
or interpreter of dreams. Even the wrath of Achilles
softens at the approach of the embassy to which the heralds
lead the way. That the person of Chryses is more respected
by the army than by its commander, when his passions are
roused, takes little from the effect of the gentle reverence
which surrounds the man of prayer and the restraint to

which this gives rise. More universal, and not less potent because unseen, are two powers which throughout Greek life hold equal sway, Respect and Right, αἰδώς τε καὶ δίκη, especially the former. The appeal to αἰδώς is frequent in the Iliad; it is 'Reverence, that angel of the world,' which is the soul of discipline, which gives authority to office, which occasionally prompts mercy to an enemy, and ever compels pity for the suppliant, and together with the fear of Zeus inspires hospitality towards the stranger. The wrath of Achilles is doing violence to this feeling when Athena cautions him in Book i. But in receiving the embassy, and in his treatment of the corpse of Eëtion, king of Thebe, whom he has slain, he shows himself fully sensible of it in his normal mood. The meaning of δίκη (= right) in Homer is less fixed. In the Iliad δίκη is the exercise of jurisdiction in the concrete. It is sometimes almost equal to Themis, implying right sanctioned by custom, sometimes merely what is usual in a person or a class of persons—their customary or appointed 'way.' In this sense it is applied in the Odyssey even to the condition of the dead.

The Greek city, in the later historical sense, did not yet exist. The centres of moral sanction lay in the family and the clan. Domestic duties were profoundly sacred. The acknowledged licence of the camp, or of the roving wayfarer, does not prevent the rule of monogamy from being generally established. Even in the connections which are without this sanction, there is a tone of grace and genuine affection which redeems them from coarseness, but the distinction between legitimate and illegitimate is clearly maintained. When Agamemnon declares that he prefers Chrysêis to his wedded wife at home, that is understood to be the outbreak of a tyrannical disposition. On the other hand, the affection of Achilles for Brisêis, which she returns, is on both sides a true and delicate feeling, although it does not interfere with matrimonial projects, in case of his living to go back to Phthia. And Agamemnon, even in carrying out his harsh caprice, abstains from the last outrage against the rights of his rebellious comrade. Yet unchaste actions even of an infamous kind, although they compel the offender to exile from his own people, do not prevent him from obtaining shelter and protection under a neighbouring chief. The case of Phoenix is an example. Similarly, bloodguiltiness, as a rule, makes flight inevitable ; though, as Agamemnon says, in many cases the avenger of blood may be pacified by a money payment on the part of the homicide, who is then permitted to remain with his own people. The sanctions surrounding human life were not yet deeply fixed. In the Gortyn inscription every offence against the person, as in early England, has a money value estimated according to the dignity of the person injured. Among the many instances of homicide which occur in Homer, there is not one in which any reference is made to the ritual of purification. This was developed afterwards, with the growth of the worship of Apollo, in which a doctrine of atonement became part of the priestly instruction, and also with the creation of something approaching to a system of criminal law. The movement in the religious consciousness, which is implied in passing from the stage represented in Homer to such a theology of guilt and atonement as we find in Aeschylus, is very noteworthy, even if it may be supposed that the purifying rites themselves had an early origin in some Hellenic or non-Hellenic centre of religious culture. The significant fact is, that the feeling of the necessity of atonement or satisfaction for bloodshed became ultimately universal.

The Homeric world has often been censured as un-moral, and it is true that conduct as represented in the Iliad is largely guided by personal impulses, and not by ethical considerations duly formulated. But there is a morality of feeling which in many ways anticipates the most refined ethical determinations, and of this the Iliad is full. The poem does not abound with moral maxims, still less with moral principles ; but human experience in its purest forms is nowhere delineated with greater vividness, subtlety and delicacy, nor with more of penetrating insight. As tried by any modern standard, there are gaps in the moral code. The relations of husband to wife, of brother to brother, and of friend to friend, are nobly conceived, but the laws of humanity and mercy are rudimentary. There is some difference, however, between the views of life and of the world entertained by the average warrior, by persons under the stress of extraordinary passion, and by the poet, and this in two ways, first in constructing his story, and secondly, in his general contemplation of human things.

What is essential in Homer is not always that which has left the most lasting impression on mankind. The beauty of Helen, of the 'face which launched a thousand ships,' has passed into the 'world's desire'; but the remorse of Helen, her misery and feeling of her own condition, on which the poet lays at least equal stress, have been little noticed. The meeting of Paris in the field with the man whom he has wronged, which 'cows his better part of man,' has also a profound significance. It is indeed within the human sphere that the *divine* in Homer is to be found. The humanity of the age (incomplete as it was) had far outgrown its theology. The poet is often more far-seeing than his own Zeus. Impressions of experience and types of human character have sunk deep, and are reproduced with extraordinary distinctness. To the poet, at least, the persons of his story revealed far-reaching truths of which he loses sight when he speaks separately about the gods. Of course no anachronism could be more extravagant than the attempts of philosophers in later times to find all wisdom in Homer. Not to speak of the absurdities involved, the *naïveté* and freshness of epic poetry are thus utterly destroyed. Nor is Colonel Mure altogether justified in drawing out at length all the types of character which he finds in Homer. That is apt to make of the epic poet a sort of modern man of the world. But no delineation of human passion at its height has ever surpassed the Homeric picture of Achilles; nor has any poet of later times reached greater depths of tenderness than appear in the dramatic portraiture of Helen, of Brisêis, or of Andromache. The proud veracity of Achilles anticipates a moral standard belonging rather to modern than to ancient life, and rarely dwelt upon in Greek literature, though the note is repeated more emphatically by Sophocles in the

'Philoctetes.' When the Homer of the Iliad is face to face
with life in its elementary aspects, with the foundations of
character and personality, the limitations of the traditional
theology and of imperfect social conditions are hardly
apparent; it is here that he proves himself indeed immortal :
the sorrows of Andromache, the desolation of Briseis, the
home affections and the manly patriotism of Hector, the
moving appeal of Priam to Achilles, speak not to one age
only but to all time, and penetrate human nature to the core.
Nor should we pass over what may be described as Homer's
ethical good taste, which is unsurpassed both in ancient and
in modern poetry. Those special aberrations of the moral
sense, from which Greece was never wholly exempt, must
have existed before the Iliad. Yet the poems are absolutely
free from any hint of it. In this Homer is superior to Solon,
Aeschylus, Pindar, Sophocles, and all Greek writers down
to the middle of the fourth century, when Plato in his old
age composed the 'Laws'; and in this as in much else the
poet justifies Dante's description of him as one ' who, like an
eagle, soars above the rest.'

In such blending of high feeling with childish fancies,
we are confronted with a state of the human mind which is
hard for us to realise, although a superior intelligence might
not have far to seek for similar contradictions amongst ourselves ; and in the poetry of Dante, and even Milton, there
are inequalities of an analogous kind. The 'affable arch-
angel' communicates to Adam in Paradise, as facts of angelic
experience, what appear to us nowadays nothing better than
ridiculous inanities. The passage in which this occurs is of
a very different order from such flights of genuine poetry as
the complaint of Adam through the still night, the creation
of the birds, the address of Satan to the sun, the lines on
ambition in ' Paradise Regained,' or the apostrophe to light at
the opening of Book iii. of ' Paradise Lost.' The reflection
can hardly fail to occur to the reader of Homer, that the
poet himself takes less seriously the representation of superhuman persons and their actions, than those scenes in which
his principal characters are most deeply involved. The
truth is that before the groundwork of the Iliad had been

laid, the worship of the Olympians on the Asiatic seaboard was already growing old. The poet's impressions 'of man, of nature, and of human life' have a freshness and perfection far surpassing the conceptions of divine beings which he shares with his contemporaries; it does not appear as if he had deliberately modified these, although with the selective power of a great artist he has probably omitted many features on which commoner minds would have been apt to dwell.

The very depth and vividness of the poet's perceptions, combined with the absence of reflection, lead, however, inevitably to glaring inconsistencies which appear strange to a more philosophical age. The moving spring of the Iliad, the intense wrath of Achilles occasioned by an insult which only yields when it is supplanted by the deeper rage for his comrade slain, exhibits the union of tenderness and vindictiveness which is one of the marked characteristics of antiquity. The savagery of Achilles was to the ancient hearer only the measure of his love for his friend. And the tenderness to the aged Priam which succeeds it springs as instinctively from the inmost source of emotion as the outrage on the dead body of Hector. The contrast could not be more strongly marked than in the single line describing Achilles' farewell to his dead friend : 'He groaned as he laid his slaughterous hands upon his comrade's breast.'

Religious and other motives are variously conceived, because the mood in which the world is regarded changes with the change of situation. Intense enjoyment of life may be regarded as the major key which dominates the Iliad ; but the minor note is not less emphasised, and is increasingly heard towards the end. The gods are the givers of good things : that is the simple faith of the Achaean when he prays ; but prayers often cross, and the gods do not hear both sides, but give the victory to one, xiii. 302; though they are not always so scrupulous as in viii. 440, where they refrain from tasting of the sacrifice ; and the hero whom a god opposes breaks out in expostulation as Asius does (xii. 164), though at other times he may have been pious enough. This is very characteristic of an early stage of religion. Again, the gods are interested in human things and care for their worshippers who sacrifice to them, yet they are overheard reproaching one another with the folly of taking mortal affairs too seriously, and Zeus himself remarks that no creature that lives and crawls upon the ground is more miserable than mankind. The view of a situation which commends itself to the persons of the story is often inconsistent with the supposed reality : the treachery of Pandarus, for example, is hailed by the Achaeans as securing victory to them, since there is a fresh act of impiety on the Trojan side ; but it has no apparent effect in the sequel. So in other places the neglect of sacrifice is assigned by popular feeling as a cause of disasters which are otherwise accounted for in the poem. Further the omniscience and omnipresence of the gods is a thought of which the mind of the age has glimpses, yet imagination fails to realise it. Many incidents would be impossible, could the gods be supposed to be conscious of all that passed. Zeus is the ideal of wisdom ; yet he is deceived by a contemptible fraud : Zeus as the god of the sky, who gives the rain, ceases not to work when as Hera's husband he is asleep on Ida ; and though Ares favours the Trojans, yet if the blood of the Trojan Aeneas were spilled by Grecian Diomedes, it would satisfy the valiant god of war.

To the poet it seemed only natural that the gods should combine superhuman powers with human frailty. When Thetis implores Zeus in his almightiness to honour Achilles, he remains silent for a while, and to a thoughtful reader it might seem as if the father of gods and men were meditating on the many deaths and other sorrows for mankind which are involved in his assent ; but, as the sequel proves, he is really thinking of the domestic scene, the quarrel with his wife, which must inevitably follow on his tremendous nod.

When the Iliad and Odyssey became the basis of education for the Athenian youth, the protest of Plato against such inconsistencies might well be justified. And those who thought of Homer as the inventor of Olympus (how falsely we have seen) might accuse him vehemently, as

Xenophanes and Heraclitus did. The age of reflection having once begun, the contrast between heroic nobility and divine imperfection could not fail to be perceived. This led to criticism and scepticism and to allegorical interpretations of mythology.

Yet when the poem is considered on its merits, the point most to be observed is the independent manner in which the poet stands behind his own creations. He is really, as already said, more wide-seeing than his own Zeus, comprehending in one glance the objects of worship and the worshippers, each of whom regards passing events from a particular and subjective point of view. The disinterested objectivity of Greek art is manifest throughout the Iliad.

On the other hand many survivals of primitive mythology appear as patches amidst the tissue of such nobler work, either as incidents of the celestial machinery, or in the way of casual illustration or allusion. One such incident of peculiar interest is the binding of gods by one another, a feature which is familiar to the students of general mythology and folklore. It betrays a dim consciousness of the essential inconsistency of polytheism. Another curious feature of the popular belief, which appears incidentally in the poem, is the vain striving of mortals with immortals, as of Niobe with Latona, of Lycurgus with Dionysus, and of Idas with Apollo.

Perhaps the most childish of such imaginations, next to the deception of Zeus himself by Hera, is the sending of the dream by Zeus to Agamemnon, inspiring a false hope of the immediate fall of Troy; whereon the king sets about to deceive the Achaean host. Both acts are characteristically Greek, but they belong to a *naïve* and early stage of Greek religion. The poetic motive is to interest the hearer, who contrasts the appearance with the fact; it is the same which in a far subtler form enters into the composition of tragedy, and has been described under the somewhat questionable name of 'irony.'

The almost entire absence of abstract reflection in the Iliad at once accounts for and excuses many happy inconsistencies, of which the poet is profoundly unconscious.

It may help us to realise this state of mind, if we consider some of the few proverbial sayings in which the wisdom of life already began to be embodied.

Book i. 216. He who hearkens to the voice of gods is heard by them.
Book v. 530. When men respect each other more are saved than slain ; but when they fly there is neither glory nor defence for them.
Book vii. 282. It is a good thing to obey the influence of night.
Book ix. 256. Kindness is the better part.
Book x. 224. When two advance together, one perceives the way of advantage before the other can ; but one, though he perceive, has still a shorter view, and slender thoughts.
Book xi. 408. I know that only cowards leave the war, but he who hath prowess in the fight must stand stoutly, whether he be wounded or wound others.
Book xiii. 115. The thoughts of good men admit of remedy.
Book xiii. 237. The valour even of sorry wights is something when combined.
Book xix. 155 ff. Where Odysseus advises that the host should dine before the fight.

These simple thoughts are of very different calibre from the feeling of the situation which the poet ever and again displays.

It must be considered also how imperfect was the ethical vocabulary. The word of praise perhaps most expressive of the contemporary ideal was ' blameless ' or ' without reproach.' But this conveyed no moral significance at all ; it simply meant that the person so described had no defect either of birth or personal qualities that could forfeit for him the position of a chief. It is applied for instance to Aegisthus, even in the Odyssey. The word which afterwards was the philosophical equivalent for virtue occurs only a few times, and then in the most simple meaning of manhood, that is, martial valour, or merely strength. Once more, the absence of fixed institutions already referred to, the inchoate condition of social life, must be taken into the account. The primary duty of hospitality is, of course, often dwelt upon, and is deeply inherent in the whole action of the poem ; on the other hand the idea of justice is still irretrievably bound up with revenge. See especially the passage where Menelaus is about to spare his foeman, but is overruled by the righteous counsel of his elder brother.

The idea of Nemesis, afterwards so potent, is only fitfully present in the Iliad, where the word itself has the more simple meaning of natural anger or indignation. Some anticipation of it, however, appears in the last book, where the gods are roused to indignation by the passionate outrage of Achilles, and this indeed is the highest point of ethical development which is attained in the whole course of the poem.

There are incidental touches elsewhere in the Iliad, in which something approaching to the same spirit is revealed : for example, the simple human pathos of Achilles' own comparison of the weeping Patroclus to a little girl who clings to her mother's dress begging to be taken up. Nor is the tragic meaning of the fate of Achilles confined to the last books, although it is naturally there more fully dwelt upon.

It is time to put together succinctly the main characteristics of what may be loosely termed the theological conceptions of the heroic age, and of the poet of the Iliad. (1) The interest in human things was far more vivid than the traditionally accepted notions of things divine. The heart of man was deeply engaged in the former, while the other touched only his imagination or his fear. This is true at least of the poet and his hearers, whatever may have been the reverence for sacred persons amongst the common people. The priest of Apollo might cry to him to avenge his wrong : Achilles, in a supreme hour, might appeal instinctively to the god of his fathers and his house : the Achaeans might lift their voices to heaven in the stress of fight ; but for the poet and his audience, it is the human figure of Chryses or of Achilles that most signifies. (2) The delineation of human things owes part of its unrivalled freshness to the absence of reflection. It has been observed that only two out of innumerable similes are taken from the action of the mind, and then it is the swiftness, not so much of thought, as of imagination, that is in point. (3) The bright distinctness

G

of early horizons in Homer is correlative to the vagueness and gloom of the conception of a future life. The words of Aristotle—' death is terrible, for it is an end '—comprise in a formula what is felt rather than expressed in the Iliad. (4) The poem reflects a stage both of mythology and legend in many ways different from that which is to be found in the literature of the fifth and fourth centuries. The latter, however, undoubtedly contains survivals of a still earlier culture, and it is worth considering whether these were known to Homer, and rejected by him as unsuited to his art, or whether they were altogether of independent growth. It has been already remarked that such a doubt may be raised in regard to hero-worship. On the whole, it seems probable that, as there came to be more intercourse between the various centres of Hellenic life, certain features of ritual, myth, and legend would find their way into the general stream of literary tradition, which at the time when the Iliad was composed were unfamiliar to the poet, or altogether unknown or indifferent to his special audience. (5) It is an uncertain question how far, or in what sense, the will of Zeus in the Iliad is to be regarded as righteous. The notion of Nemesis, as above observed, is occasional rather than pervading. It is even doubtful whether the pathos of Achilles' fate conveyed to the poet's hearers the warning against ' too much ' which it must undoubtedly have carried with it, as read or recited to a contemporary of Herodotus. The essentially Greek thoughts of measure, justice, and equity are not absent from the poem, e.g. in Nestor, Odysseus, and Diomedes, but it is not in Olympus that they are to be found. Themis, the ordinance of authority, is but a shadowy precursor of the idea of law, ' the universal king,' which became so pronounced in subsequent Greek history. The power which vindicated order and punished the breach of social duties is already the Erinnys, a name of doubtful origin, but always associated with the darkness of the under-world. The passion of Althaea when she smites the earth with both her hands in calling up the Fury from beneath brings this association strongly to mind. The thought of a judgment after death occurs incidentally in two isolated passages. But the vagueness of the moral sanction, and the absence of any clear standard of conduct, apart from primitive custom, only enhances the ethical originality of the poet who has represented the self-denying patriotism of Hector, the wifely devotion of Andromache, the self-control of Diomedes, and the pure friendship of Achilles and Patroclus. Two notes are struck by Homer which sound far onwards into Greek literature ; to the modern ear they seem to jar, but in ancient life they are correlative. The precept 'thou shalt love thy friend' is still inseparable from the other precept 'thou shalt hate thine enemy.' However paradoxical it may seem to our Christian sense, the tender affection and the stern inexorableness which show themselves in the same person combined to manifest the freshness and force of unsophisticated nature.

CHAPTER IV

RELIGION IN THE ODYSSEY

Obvious differences from the Iliad—Growing civilisation—Vindication of domestic right—Not sentimental—Modes of worship—Mythology —Heroic legend—Moral principles—Ethical reflection.

NOTWITHSTANDING the imperfect development of society, and the poverty in ethical terminology which marked the heroic age, the Iliad contains clear evidence of the deep hold which had long since been taken by domestic institutions, and of the strong sanctions which surrounded the elementary relations of human beings to one another. These are imagined with such depth and force as to contain the essential substance of all morality under a religious bond. The vindication of the rites of home, and of the rules of hospitality, underlies the action and is never quite lost sight of. The poet's vision ranges far beyond his age, extending to the contemplation of universal humanity. His impressions are conveyed with incomparable vividness, subtlety and delicacy, but always in the form of feeling. The process of reflection and abstract thinking has hardly begun. The picture of the gods, on the other hand, and of their dealings with mankind, although grand and sublime in part, and pathetic on the side of the worshipper, is full of the crudest inconsistencies. The conception of divine power is more developed than the ideas of justice and beneficence. The most universal attribute of the gods is their exemption from death, which places a gulf of absolute separation between them and mortals—even those in whose veins the blood of gods is flowing.

In the Odyssey human things are regarded more comprehensively on the whole, but are touched everywhere with a somewhat lighter hand. The gods, with the exception of

Athena, and perhaps of Poseidon, who is necessary for the machinery of the poem, are less distinctly conceived, and the gap between them and poor mortals is practically filled up for the imagination by a sort of fairy world of semi-human beings. The conception of Elysium, as a place far away upon the earth, to which the sons and sons-in-law of Zeus go after death, strikes a note which is absent from the Iliad ; and in the eleventh book, which, in part at least, is a later addition, the world of the dead is imagined under a different aspect, and there is a distinct reflection of the sacrificial worship of the dead (' blood-drinking ghosts '). The gods are much more frequently spoken of collectively in the plural number, and so far as they intervene to govern human things, they do so with a serious purpose, and mostly with a view to vindicating the right. Life is still the slave of destiny, but men are blamed for their own misfortunes ; in this spirit the crime of Aegisthus is denounced by Athena, at the opening of the poem, and both the companions of Odysseus and the insolent suitors are said to be responsible for their own destruction. These are some of the more obvious differences.

The legend of Odysseus is believed by some authorities to have originally taken shape in Arcadia. Assuming this to be true, the tradition would find its way to Ionia with the emigrants from Pylos, who accompanied the Neleid prince who helped to colonise Miletus. And accordingly, those elements of religious life which came from Phthia or Thessaly are less prominent here ; and as the Ionian settlement was later than the Aeolian, so the Odyssey and even the materials out of which it grew are later than those of the Iliad. The poet, whom we suppose to be an Asiatic Greek, betrays his ignorance of the geography of the Peloponnese and the adjoining coasts. At the same time, the poem shows a greatly extended interest in the habitable world. This is not the place for considering the contradictions of the geography. It has been further confused by the fancy of the later Greeks, who, as they came to know more, seem to have transferred some imaginary features from the mouth of the Black Sea to the coasts of Italy and Sicily. The description, such as it is, could only have come into existence at a time when navigation was extending, and men's imaginations were much exercised with voyages of discovery.

The Iliad is a poem of passion, the Odyssey a poem of endurance; the one moves amongst scenes of battle, the other amongst romantic adventures. Comradeship, rivalry, and vindictiveness are the springs of action in the Iliad; the Odyssey presents us with a persistent will, passing onwards through manifold hindrances towards a purposed good. It is the apotheosis of conduct rather than of personal feeling, but this very fact perhaps involves an advance in reflection; and when we look more closely at the work, we find many other kindred traces.

The dwelling place of the gods is differently conceived. Olympus in the Iliad is still a mountain top with many peaks and ridges, in the hollows of which the gods have their golden houses. In the Odyssey, Olympus is hardly distinguishable from an unseen heaven, not snow-clad and clouded like the mountain in the Iliad, but far withdrawn, exempt from storms and rains and wind and snow. Like the Nysaean hill of Bacchus afterwards, it has no precise locality, but just so much reminiscence of the original mountain as to give a touch of picturesqueness. We shall find a further stage of progress towards a pure abstraction in the Olympus of the Attic poets.

As regards hero-worship, Menelaus is told by Proteus that he is destined to depart to the Elysian plain; the deification of Herakles is alluded to, though in a passage that is probably of later origin than the rest, and Ino (Leucothea) has also been raised to the skies.

Domestic and patriotic virtues form the cardinal interest of the whole action; and it is important to remark that the constancy of Odysseus, Telemachus, and Penelope is entirely without the modern note of personal sentiment. It is not the womanly charm of Penelope that draws Odysseus home: it is the thought of home as such, with all its claims upon him. It is not because Odysseus won her heart, many years ago, that Penelope eludes the suitors, but because he is her lord, the noblest of men, and because she cannot bear to think of leaving the mansion, so full of precious things, and parting from her son, to cheer the spirit of some less noble man. The reserve on both sides, when at last they come together, is extremely remarkable, and essentially Greek. Not that feeling is absent from either of them, but rather that it is profound, and is inseparable from practical aims, extending to a lifetime.

It is even more apparent in the Odyssey than in the Iliad that the poet does not take the gods altogether seriously, but rather handles them with a consciously artistic purpose. Poseidon, for example, affords the chief celestial machinery for the action. He persecutes Odysseus in revenge for Polyphemus, the Cyclops, who is his son ; until Hera interposes, and by permission of Zeus secures the release of her favourite. Still more capricious are the poet's dealings with that fairyland of imagination, in which he has placed such unheroic beings, neither divine nor human, as the giant Laestrygones, the one-eyed Cyclopes, the Sirens, Scylla and Charybdis, the witch Circe, the nymph Calypso ; who diversify the action, and occupy the borderland between . gods and men. It is not to be inferred that these were all unknown to the poet of the Iliad, or to his hearers, but their introduction into a serious poem was probably something new. A taste for the marvellous, for strange experiences and adventures, had supervened together with the progress of navigation. The dwellers on the coast of Asia drank in eagerly the tales which travellers brought them from the outer world ; a sort of mythological geography became the food of their imaginations. At the same time the consciousness of their own civilisation tended to express itself in the supposed contrast between civilised and savage mankind. Hence the account of the Cyclopes, who cared not for one another, nor for the gods, but each commanded his own household, or cavehold : a note that is taken up by Plato and Aristotle.

To the same consciousness—that of a growing civilisation—we owe the very different picture of the Phaeacians who take Odysseus home :—of Nausicaa, the mirror of maidenhood, the courtly Alcinous, the gracious Arête, and the dainty youths of whom Horace speaks as *In cute*

curanda nimium studiosa juventus ('Young men whose care
is to be neat and trim '). This charming episode has been
variously understood. The ancients, perhaps too literally,
identified Phaeacia with Corcyra (where there is a river near
the town and also poplar trees), but the Corcyraeans of
history are most unlike this gentle folk. Some, led by the
alliteration, think that the Phoenicians were in the poet's
eye; but neither is there any resemblance here, except that
both are seafarers. A more plausible explanation has been
started recently—viz. that the poet of the Odyssey brings
his old-world hero into contact with his own contemporaries
under a thin disguise. The scene may be Corcyra, but the
airy, imaginary folk, whose ship became a rock in the sea—
this people with their walled town, their elaborate harbour,
their well-built market-place, their fair temple of Poseidon,
and grove of Athena—are no other than the Ionians of the
eighth century, whose home was the flourishing Miletus or
the fertile Samos.

Thus the visit of Odysseus to Phaeacia is seen to be the
first, as surely it is the most delightful, of a long series of
imaginings, which with various degrees of bitterness or of
gentle irony have reflected some features or some tendencies
of contemporary life, or have embodied a contemporary
ideal, such as More's ' Utopia,' Swift's ' Laputa,' or Johnson's
' Rasselas.' All grosser elements are purged away ; humanity
appears in the most engaging aspect ; and yet in the self-
complacency of this island folk, in their imagined security,
their pride of ships, their boast of nearness to the gods, it
seems allowable to trace some good-humoured persiflage of
the poet's own neighbours, whom, to avoid offending them,
he has purposely located on a distant and imaginary shore.

To return now to the main drift of the poem. The
triumph of Odysseus single-handed, with the aid of Athena,
is the triumph of justice over lawless insolence. There is
nothing like this in the Iliad, though there is something
cognate to it in the main motive for the Trojan war. The
hero is not merely vindicating his own personal honour, as
Achilles was, but the most precious rights of his kingdom and
his home. It is true that the vindication is unmixed with

clemency : execution is unrelentingly wrought, not only on the suitors, but on the poor misguided maid-servants, who are strung up ' like larks upon a line.' The thoroughness of the Greek artist allows of no half-lights or neutral shades ; indeed, there is little of tenderness in the person of Odysseus. His worth, like that of Ajax in Sophocles, is rather accentuated by the devoted attachment of those dependent on him, from Penelope downwards, including Eumaeus the swineherd, and Argus the dog. It is here that the strokes of tenderness come in. And this gives the opportunity for saying that, while the interest of the poem again centres in the royal race, the blood of gods, the Odyssey contains several interesting glimpses of more humble life.

Some points of manners, especially connected with religion, may be further noted. In the Iliad, after a sacrifice, people enjoy themselves to the full, and without stint. Athena, in the person of Mentor, remarks in the Odyssey that it is not well to sit too long at the feasts of the gods : one should return home again. The gods love moderation, even in an act of worship. In the Iliad the gods appear in various disguises, but never for long. The remark that Athena is ever at the side of this or that hero, for instance Diomedes, is said in a tone of conscious hyperbole. There is nothing like the persistent companionship of the disguised Athena, which both Telemachus and his father enjoy. Athena in the Odyssey also exercises a kind of magic, which, except in the case of the dead bodies of Sarpedon and Hector, is hardly present in the Iliad—making Odysseus alternately old and wrinkled, and handsome and young.

Having thus indicated some of the main features of the Odyssey as a religious work, I propose to touch briefly (1) on modes of worship ; (2) on differences of mythology between the Iliad and the Odyssey ; (3) on the legendary elements of the poem, and the traces of incipient hero-worship ; (4) on conceptions of private and public duty ; (5) on the growth of ethical reflection, as shown (a) in proverbial expressions ; (b) in the ideal of human virtue.

1. A beautiful picture of Greek piety is presented in
the third book of the Odyssey, where Telemachus, accompanied by Athena disguised as Mentor, finds Nestor and his
sons at Pylos engaged in holding a great sacrifice to Poseidon.
They are assembled upon the seashore, a place hardly lending
itself to formal consecration, but perpetually in view of the
divine element of which Poseidon was the personification.
They are offering to him black bulls without a spot of white,
a colour probably associated with the darkness of the deep, the
ἔρεβος ὕφαλον of Sophocles; the animal symbolising im-
petuous strength, and for this and other reasons consecrated
also to the gods of rivers. There are nine stations, at each of
which nine bulls are sacrificed; the poet does not say by
whom, but there is no mention of an officiating priest. Each
victim is held with its head towards the sea. The sacred rite,
including the formal tasting of the inward parts, and the roast-
ing of the thigh-bones covered with fat, for a sweet-smelling
savour to the god, is just completed when the visitors arrive.
Athena bids Telemachus approach, and inquire of Nestor
about his father's fortunes; and when the young man
hesitates, she assures him that by the grace of heaven his
own thoughts, which are not contemptible, will be supple-
mented by the suggestion of a god. Nestor is sitting surrounded by his sons. Their comrades are preparing the
sacrificial feast. On seeing the strangers, all come forward
to greet them and to give them room. They are seated on
soft sheepskins upon the sea sand; they taste of the inward
parts, so sharing the communion of the sacred day (this is
noticeable as an indication that burnt sacrifice was not only
offered to the god, but partaken of in communion with him),
and wine is handed to them for libations accompanied with
prayer. It is offered first to Mentor as the elder guest,
whereat Athena is pleased. She, in the person of Mentor,
prays to Poseidon on behalf of Nestor and his sons and people,
and for the prosperous return of Telemachus, when he has
succeeded in his quest. She pours the libation, then hands
the cup to Telemachus, who likewise prays. The feast then
follows, and only after that Nestor thinks meet to ask the
strangers who they are. Next morning, having discovered

overnight that Athena in person had vouchsafed to visit them, Nestor and his sons hold a private sacrifice to Athena. To her is offered a heifer. The horns are gilded by the smith, who brings his tongs to hold the metal, and his hammer and anvil to beat it out; and Athena herself, says the poet, came to accept the sacrifice. Two youths lead in the heifer by her horns, water for the hands is brought from within the house, and barley-meal. Thrasymedes, the eldest son, stands by with an axe; Perseus holds the bowl to receive the blood; Nestor himself pours out the purifying water, and performs the initiatory rite of sprinkling the meal; and while he cuts off a lock of hair from the victim's head and throws it in the fire, he prays aloud and at some length to Athena. Thrasymedes then fells the victim, whereupon Eurydice, the wife of Nestor, his daughter and his daughters-in-law lift their voices in auspicious shouting. Then the head of the creature is raised from the ground, the jugular vein is opened by Pisistratus, the youngest son, and the blood poured out; the body is broken up, the thigh-bones are taken out and covered with two layers of fat, on which bits of raw flesh are placed. Nestor himself burns these on a fire of cleft wood, and pours wine thereon, while the young men stand by with five-pronged forks in their hands; and when the thigh-bones have been burned, the formal tasting of the inwards follows. The joints are then divided and roasted upon spits, which appear to be held at the fire by hand. It is worth while to be thus minute in following this, which is the fullest account of sacrifice in Homer. The details of Greek ritual are imperfectly known, and for the very reason that they were so familiar to the audience are but scantily described. And it is right to add that the swineherd Eumaeus, another model of hospitality and piety in his simpler way, when he entertains Odysseus as a supposed stranger, loses no time in religious formalities, but simply brings two porkers from the sties, and slays them; the word is 'sacrifice,' and this may imply some shadow of a religious act, but there is no mention of any ceremonial details, before the animals are seized, cut up, and roasted, and the hot flesh laid before Odysseus, spits

and all, and then sprinkled over with white barley-meal.
Nor is there any mention of libation of the wine, which
Odysseus drinks in silence beside the meat which he
devours, while planning evil against the suitors. But when
the labouring men come in, bringing the swine from the
pasture, the chief swineherd takes a bolder line, and sacrifices
in honour of the stranger the best boar of the herd ; and he
goes about this with all due ceremony. They place the
victim at the hearth. Eumaeus himself performs the initial
rite by cutting off the hair, and as he throws it in the fire,
he prays to all the gods for his master's safe return. He
has no axe at hand, but fells the animal with a split piece
of oak (this is the village butcher's plan to this day), then
the blood is drawn, and the carcase broken up, whereon the
swineherd performs the religious rite of laying pieces from
all the limbs upon the fat, with which, as we may presume,
the thigh-bones have been covered. These are sprinkled
with meal and thrown on the fire, after which the cooking
process is completed, and this time the joints are drawn
from off the spits and set together upon trays. The swineherd distributes them to all present, reserving the prime
piece for Hermes and the Nymphs, to whom he has prayed,
and honouring Odysseus with the chine. Odysseus admires
this hospitality. Eumaeus bids him eat and leave the future
to the god, who can do all things according to his will.
Once more a portion, probably the same that had been
reserved for Hermes and the Nymphs, is offered to the gods,
and some of the wine is poured out as libation to them, all
by Eumaeus, who then places the goblet in the hands of
Odysseus.

It is clear that the ritual of divine worship was known to
gentle and simple, and might be performed by any head of a
household, without the interference of a priest. Why then
should there have existed separate ministers of religion ?
Chiefly as caretakers of the shrines and offerings, which, at
some few centres, constituted the wealth of the gods,
especially where there was a seat of divination. The
reverence for the priest was, however, already accentuated by
his consequent nearness to the god, to whom he prayed con-

tinually as ἀρητήρ, and stood in a peculiarly intimate relation. The herald also, and the ordinary soothsayer, each forming a separate class, had special sacredness attaching to them in their limited functions.

2. Greek mythology in some ways adhered strictly to tradition, but it had also in every age a fluid and plastic element, which gave it endless adaptability. The differences in this respect between the Iliad and the Odyssey, though it is reasonable to assign them to different authors, and possibly to a different place and time, are less significant of wide divergence than has been often supposed. The most obvious discrepancy is the employment of Iris in the Iliad, and of Hermes in the Odyssey, as the messenger of the gods. The apparent anticipation of this feature in the last book of the Iliad affords one of the arguments by which that book is separated from the rest. But it should be observed that Hermes is there employed not exactly as a messenger but as a conductor. And we may recall the fact that, in the ' Hymn to Demeter,' while Iris carries the message of Zeus to earth, Hermes is his envoy to the shades. Another difference consists in the assignment of Aphrodite as wife to Hephaestus the divine artificer in the Odyssey, a bit of symbolism of the same kind as his marriage to the Grace in the eighteenth Iliad. This occurs, however, only in the song of Phemius, and may have been a special fancy of some minstrel, not a fixed assumption of mythology. She appears under her name of Cythereia both in the eighth book and xviii. 192. This and her association with Ares perhaps reflect that aspect of her worship which was of Phoenician origin.

The attributes of some of the Olympians are altered, perhaps in consequence of the different tone of the whole poem. Athena is more distinctly the goddess of wisdom and good counsel, but her warlike attributes are retained when occasion serves ; in two similes, B. vi. 233, B. xxiii. 160, she is associated with Hephaestus as having taught arts to mankind. Artemis is still the leader of the Nymphs, surpassing all the rest in stature as well as beauty. She retains her other attributes, and in particular is the special patroness of Penelope, as the faithful wife. Poseidon is constantly in evidence, except for the interval during which he is absent amongst the Ethiopians; he is the father of river gods, and also of Polyphemus, Neleus, and Nausithoös the first king of Phaeacia; hence he is the natural guardian of the Phaeacians, being the grandfather of Alcinoös, and his temple stands in the centre of their public place. This last, it is worth observing, is described as built or surrounded with great stones, sunk deep into the ground. But if the theory above suggested (p. 88) is true, the elaborate temple is part of that advanced civilisation in which the Phaeacians are imagined as anticipating the Ionians of the poet's own time. It is not certain, however, whether the 'fair temple' is to be regarded as hypaethral or covered in.

The other Olympians, including Apollo, fall somewhat into the background in the Odyssey; the cause of this probably being that the action is principally at sea. The chief allusion to Apollo is in the mention of a quarrel between Odysseus and Achilles, whereat Agamemnon rejoiced, because the Pythian oracle had told him that the strife between the noblest of the Achaeans would be for his advantage. This is the story of the first lay of Phemius, not reported at length, at which Odysseus veils his face as he sheds tears. The will of Zeus is of course present throughout, but is more often implied than spoken of, except at crises of the poem, when he grants the prayer of Athena, or of the Sun whose oxen have been slain, or sends Hermes upon a mission. The truth is that in the Odyssey the divine action is already often generalised; not only are gods spoken of in the plural more frequently than in the Iliad; but 'god' or 'a god,' in the singular, often occurs where it is uncertain what individual deity is in question.

Amongst the many minor powers in which the Odyssey abounds, the Harpies deserve special mention. The word appears in the Iliad, but only as an epithet of the mythological mare, out of whom by Zephyrus as sire the horses of Achilles came. There it means simply swift, or possibly swift as a storm wind; in two of the three places in the Odyssey it appears accordingly as a personification of tempest

—snatching men away. But in the prayer of Penelope to Artemis, in the twentieth Odyssey, where she recalls the fate of the daughters of Pandareus, the Harpies, though still identified with storm wind, appear more distinctly as mythological personages, and it becomes more easy to conceive of the after-development of the legend concerning them, in which they snatch away the supper of Phineus, and play other tricks familiar in comparative folklore.

3. Although silence in the Iliad is not always to be interpreted as implying ignorance, it is tolerably clear that the legends of cities and of great houses were already in a state of growth when the Odyssey was written. The version given of them differs from that in the Iliad as well as from the later literature, and is not everywhere consistent. Take first the story of Agamemnon. In this, although none of the incidents could be anticipated in the action of the former poem, some modifications may be traced within the Odyssey itself. In the story as told by Menelaus, or by Athena in Olympus, the guilt of Clytemnestra is implied, but she is not represented as having imbrued her hands in blood. But Agamemnon himself in Hades, or his shade rather, tells how, after he had received his death wound, Clytemnestra herself slew Cassandra over him, and left him without even closing his eyes. In other respects the stories differ : Agamemnon implies that he and his companions at the banquet given by Aegisthus were surprised and slain. In the account given by Proteus to Menelaus, Agamemnon is compelled to land near the abode of Aegisthus, and afterwards finds his way to Mycenae, where the banquet is held, but his companions are not slain. In neither passage is it implied that Orestes, in avenging his father, had killed his mother ; unless this may be inferred from the story of Menelaus, who speaks of him as celebrating the funeral feast both of Aegisthus and Clytemnestra. One point which has raised some confusion is the mention of the storm that caught Agamemnon at Cape Malea. It is probable that the poet, who elsewhere shows himself ignorant of the geography of the Peloponnesus, mistakes the point of Laconia for the point of Argolis. The story of Herakles also is more advanced in the later

poem. In the Iliad he is merely the strong man, who like other heroes is the son of Zeus, but in no wise immortal, though he had taken part in some battle of the gods, in which he wounded Hera ; and on another occasion he had wounded Hades in some obscure contest, described as having taken place at Pylos (also alluded to by Pindar). The encounter of Herakles with Hera and with Hades is touched upon in the speech of Dione (Iliad vi. 130 ff.). Many other points of his legend are referred to, especially that of his birth, in which Hera contrived that Eurystheus should have dominion over him. But his immortality appears only in Odyssey xi. 626, probably a late passage. His ghost is found in Hades, while he himself is feasting amongst the immortal gods, and holding beauteous Hebe. The shade compares his own fortune when on earth with the trials of Odysseus, and recalls the labours he had suffered at the bidding of Eurystheus, although he was the son of Zeus ; above all the hardest of them, that of bringing the hound of Hades (not yet named Cerberus) to the light of day. Herakles, then, has been raised to the skies ; Menelaus, on the other hand, is promised a future life on the Elysian plain, which is described in language nearly resembling that in which Olympus itself is elsewhere spoken of. The gods are to grant him this because he is the son-in-law of Zeus. No reason is given why he and Rhadamanthus are thus preferred to many others, who are of the same divine lineage. But in the eleventh Odyssey Minos is already represented as a judge amongst the dead. The worship of heroes, in later times, did not imply immortality in the sense of being raised to heaven with Herakles, or sent to Elysium with Menelaus, although the latter, or something like it, seems to have been the belief of Pindar. They were imagined as having exceptional privileges in Hades, and as exercising an important influence over the fortunes of their descendants, being mysteriously present in the neighbourhood of their tombs. There is no trace of this peculiar worship even in the Odyssey. It acquired fresh strength and prevalence after the troubles of which the Odyssey shows us the beginning, when a feebler race longed for the protection of the heroic chiefs, who had been either driven out or slain during a time of anarchy. But to this we shall return. Meanwhile one more passage of the Nekyia must be adduced to illustrate the tendency in the Odyssey to extend the privilege of immortality in a modified shape to some exceptionally favoured men. The sons of Leda, wife of Tyndareus, who are here spoken of as his sons, and not the sons of Zeus, have both gone beneath the ground, but there below are permitted on alternate days to be alive. That is their divine privilege. We have here in its simplest form a legend which was afterwards much elaborated. In the third Iliad it had not yet been thought of.

4. The time represented in the Odyssey is the commencement of a period of disturbance and unsettlement; yet there is more evidence than in the Iliad of conceptions belonging to a comparatively settled state of society. In this, as we have seen, there may be some reflection of the poet's own time. The picture of Cyclopian and Laestrygonian life betokens a consciousness of the value of civilisation and the arts of peace. The repose of Menelaus in his own hall, more rich and splendid than that which he had left in desolation, and the tranquil life of Nestor and his sons, are contrasted with the troubled state of Ithaca in the continual absence of Odysseus; the 'confusion in the little isle,' which Telemachus is not yet old and experienced enough to remedy. There is a trace of something like oriental despotism in the promise of Menelaus to give Telemachus possession of a town, from which his friend engages to evict the population; so Agamemnon in the ninth Iliad offers to his offended comrade seven towns on the borderland between Argos and Pylos, which had to be kept under by the sword in order to secure the tribute which the master was to exact. But Odysseus in Ithaca before the Trojan war is supposed to have held his ascendency over the neighbouring chieftains and their retainers without violence, exercising a gentle sway. We find little, however, as yet of anything corresponding to civic life. There is a public place to which the people assemble for sacrifice and festival and to hear the edict of the king, who may have

H

previously made known his will to his privy council. But loyalty, when not compelled by *force majeure*, depended wholly upon personal qualities. It was otherwise with the family and the immediate household, whether of kings or private men. They were bound together not only by the pressure of necessity or the force of affection, but by a religious constraint, which had in it an obligation to which we should give the name of duty. The solidarity of the family was already an immemorial tradition. The filial piety of Telemachus towards the father whom since early childhood he has never seen ; the grief of Laertes, which is comparable to that of Wordsworth's Michael, have a deeper source than mere fondness for a person beloved. The attachment of Eumaeus to his lord is a mingled feeling, consisting partly of loyalty to a master, and partly of affection for one who has treated him well when he was in his power. There is in it a sort of dumb faithfulness like that of Argus the dog ; but it finds expression in the care which he spends daily upon the herd, and his grief at the exactions from which it suffers. The endurance of Odysseus and his control over his feelings is nowhere more tried, not even in his meeting with Penelope, than in the hut of the swineherd. Here again the ideal is accentuated by contrast. The faithfulness of Eumaeus and Eurycleia is opposed to the greed and self-seeking of the goatherd Melanthius and the frivolity of the maid-servants.

The action of the Iliad turns primarily upon the breach of the rites of hospitality, but it is in the Odyssey that we find the exercise of that virtue fully set forth. Once more in this regard we turn to Nestor, Menelaus, Helen and Eumaeus. The courtliness of Helen, who from her experience of life has acquired a quickness of observation in social matters far greater than is shared by her phlegmatic lord, is shown by her discovery of the likeness between Telemachus and his father and her suspicion of the young man's identity. Very charming also is the magic spell by which she soothes the stranger into simple enjoyment of the evening's entertainment, leaving all thoughts of business cares until the following morning. This is expressed symbolically by an Egyptian drug which she instils into the wine-cup, but the reader dwells more on her personal charm. The picture of manners would be incomplete without the mention of youthful comradeship so finely exemplified in the intercourse of Telemachus with Pisistratus. The respect for age is also gracefully portrayed,—for example, when the inspired man hands the bowl for libation to the supposed Mentor first.

5. Proverbial maxims in the Odyssey, though still naïve and childlike, are both more frequent and more reflective than in the Iliad. For example, 'All men have need of the gods' is given as a reason for prayer. 'The mind of the eternal gods is not quickly changed.' 'A god, if he so will, may save even from afar.' 'Not even the gods can ward off death from those they love.' 'A courageous heart has always the best chance among strangers.' 'The gods love not harsh deeds, but honour justice and considerate conduct.' Odysseus wishes for the maiden who has shown him friendship 'a husband and a house and unanimity at home, than which nothing is better or more precious.' Several of these wise sayings are placed by the poet in the mouth of the disguised Athena.

The ethical vocabulary is not much enlarged (except in the use of certain epithets, such as περίφρων), but partly from the nature of the poem, the ideal of humanity held up to admiration has far more in it of justice and of self-control. Odysseus escapes from countless dangers to which not his own imprudence, but the rashness and wilfulness of his companions have exposed him, to their own ruin. They disregard express warnings and commands from the gods, but in doing so they exhibit the unrighteousness and irregular impulses of their nature. Odysseus is saved by the friendship of the gods, notwithstanding the revenge of Poseidon for the condign punishment which the mortal had inflicted on the wild son of a tempestuous god. We are not merely reading between the lines when we interpret this to mean that faithfulness, patience, endurance, temperance are sure of their reward. This is not to allegorise

H 2

Homer; and even Horace is not far from the mark when he speaks of the poet of the Odyssey as a teacher of Justice and Truth, though in following his Stoic authorities he has carried the fancy to excess. And the impressive scene in which the returned Odysseus leaps on the great threshold, bow in hand, with Athena and Telemachus beside him, is no mere climax of a romantic story, but the revelation of a day of judgment.

Throughout the period which we have now reviewed there is observable a strain of pure religious feeling, combined with deep and penetrating impressions of an essentially moral order, but hampered with the inevitable inconsistencies of polytheism, with popular superstitions, and with a backward or inefficient stage of social institutions and of ethical reflection.   We have to imagine a state of mind in which chance words striking upon the ear, in moments of mental tension, had an acknowledged power to encourage or to depress; when it mattered seriously whether a great bird flew on the right hand or on the left, yet in which prayer was offered to the immortals in the simplest faith, and the devotion of child to parent and a man's care for those of his own household were as perfect as at any subsequent time; when divine and superhuman powers were imagined as in perpetual conflict, revenging unintended slights or insults with inordinate vehemence, and yet the supreme will of Zeus, and the final determination of destiny, was believed to be in harmony with eternal right; when gods were imagined as living 'at ease,' and yet as caring for mankind, and visiting them, to judge between the righteous and the wicked; when fate was thought of as absolute, and yet men were held responsible for their own misdoings. The difficulty of reconciling such thoughts to the facts of life was perhaps not greater than other ages have experienced, but it was not felt or thought of. The same person in a moment of disappointment would accuse the gods of envious cruelty, and in a time of need approach them with a simple feeling of dependence and a sincere hope that they would answer prayer and accept the offerings made to them in accordance with the ancient ritual. However difficult it is for us to enter into such a condition of the human spirit, it is necessary to do so if we would understand the subsequent development of religious conceptions amongst the ancient Greeks.

CHAPTER V

CENTRAL GREECE—HESIOD : 'WORKS AND DAYS ' ; 'THEOGONY '—
THEOGNIS—ELEGIAC AND LYRIC POETRY—HOMERIC HYMNS

THE brilliant era of Mycenean or Achaean civilisation, in which
at a few great centres powerful chiefs overawed the surrounding population, had been swept away before successive in-
roads, the chief of which was spoken of in after times as the
Dorian migration.   The resources of the heroic kings may
have been exhausted by some such combined effort as the expedition to Troy.   There followed a long period of unsettlement
and misery, which is partly reflected for us in the poetry of
Hesiod : a time no longer of frank enjoyment, as when the
minstrel sang in the hall of the chief, but one of conscious
distress ;   when peaceful industries were insecure and the
civilisation of many years was broken up or had been
banished to find a richer development upon the shores of
Asia ; when first the Aeolians from the north, and afterwards
the Ionians, headed according to tradition by the Neleid sons of
Codrus, had fled before the advance of alien conquerors.   Yet
in the intervals of turmoil we are led to infer a silent growth
of religion, morality, and imagination.   Then and always
there were religious influences in Greece which tended
towards the unification or grouping of particular tribes, so
creating the outlines of a nation which counter-tendencies
prevented from being fully formed.   The organisation of the
Amphictionic council in northern Hellas, the institution of
the Olympic games in the Peloponnese, are two great evidences of this general truth.   Of these the Amphictionic
influence was gradually supplanted by the predominance of
Sparta and of Athens alternately, under the favour of the
priesthood of Apollo at Delphi ; but the Olympian festival,

when once it had eclipsed the games on Mount Lycaeus, became more and more important for the whole of Hellas. The mention of the Panhellenes in Hesiod and in the (Boeotian) catalogue of ships implies that some union of Hellenic tribes existed in that early time when Hellas was a district in Phthia, just as already in the Iliad the tribes gathered before Troy are called Παναχαιοί.

We return then to central Greece and come down to the time when Ionia was flourishing, and the Homeric poems had assumed something approaching to their final shape. Meanwhile an independent growth of religious thought and feeling had been spreading silently in Boeotia. The race of kings, of whom the epic poet sang from memory, had passed away. Great changes had intervened. An internecine war between Orchomenos and Thebes had weakened both powers, but ended in the triumph of the Cadmeians. Then came incursions from the north and west. The Boeotians descending from Thessaly overran Boeotia, and what had been Cadmeia was now Thebes; Orchomenos was no longer of any account, but echoes of her broken civilisation still remained, as for instance in the worship of Athena Itonia. The great Dorian migration had occupied the Peloponnese, where the rival powers of Argos and of Sparta were slowly establishing themselves, and the mettle of Sparta was being tested by the first Messenian war. Attica remained unravaged, and had already its sanctuary of Athena in the house of Erechtheus. It was in some such condition of things that the father of Hesiod (for some unknown reason) came across the Aegean from Cyme, and settled in the old country of the Aeolians at Askra in Boeotia. We know this from Hesiod himself. Possessing an imperfect mastery of the art of hexameter verse which had so long flourished on the other side, Hesiod found the worship of the Muses still alive upon the slopes of Helicon. His poetry reflects for us the altered state of central Hellas, when the life of the chieftains at once recorded and idealised in the Iliad was no longer in being, and new thoughts and feelings were awakened amongst those who had remained behind. The warlike incursions that had swept away the reigning dynasties passed over the heads of the humbler population, who were bound to the soil, and either suffered an exchange of masters, or according to the terms proposed to Sicyon, as we learn from Pausanias, submitted to the conqueror on condition of a fresh division of the land. These small peasant-proprietors, as we may term them, were not deserted by the Muse whom they annually worshipped, and in the ' Works and Days ' of Hesiod we have a welcome glimpse of the imagination about higher things with which they sought to enliven the dreariness of their lot. They are haunted, as one might expect, with superstitious fancies about lucky and unlucky days and the like ; they dream of a golden age which has unhappily receded far into the past, and there are those amongst them who meditate more deeply on the things which they have heard concerning gods and children of the gods, and who also seek by simple precepts and pithy sayings to instruct and warn their fellows about the life which they must live. From Hesiod come the famous lines which Aristotle quotes more than once : ' The man who thinks for himself aright is best of all ; he who follows another's rightful thought is also good ; but he who neither thinks aright nor listens to another's thought, that man is nothing worth.' In Hesiod, too, the goddess of Right is for the first time personified as Dikè :—' A noise is heard, it is the cry of Justice whom men greedy of bribes are hustling. She weeping comes to visit the abodes of men, bringing evil to her enemies.' ' Thirty thousand deathless beings on the Earth are watching over mortal men : unseen they watch where right is done, where cruelty prevails. Moreover Zeus has a virgin daughter, Justice, revered by the Olympian gods. When any does her wrong, she sits by her father Zeus and tells of it, and then the people suffer for the wrongdoing of their overlords.' ' The man who wrongs another harms himself.' Such *naïve* enforcement of the religion of life is scattered here and there amongst minor precepts about the seasons for ploughing, sowing, and reaping, and the observance for various purposes of lucky and unlucky days.

The idea of a detailed theogony now first appears ;

in which, as we find it in Hesiod, there are many traces of a more primitive and also of a darker tradition than that which Homer has chosen to perpetuate. The dim allusions to the conflict of Zeus with the Titans and with his father Cronos, which are scattered up and down the Iliad, are here explained, and the succession of generations amongst the children of the earth and sky is elaborately set forth. It would be tedious and unprofitable to enter fully into the details of the mythology, and it would be too long to draw out distinctly the elements of primitive reasoning which in this strange web are interwoven with accidental associations and idle fancies. It must suffice to mark the stage of incipient thought about divine things, which is here registered. The question has occurred to the mind of the age, How did the gods come to be? and this was a first step towards universal speculation about nature and its cause or author.

The line in Homer, whether belonging to the earliest portion of the work or not, 'ocean the original of gods and Tethys their mother,' shows already the faint beginnings of such a tendency. The thought of Hesiod, who refers the origin of all things to desire (ἔρως), goes considerably deeper; and it was adopted as a necessary link in the chain of Platonic speculation. But on the whole, the theogony of Hesiod contains few elements of profound or generative thought. It is largely made up out of fragments of primitive reasoning, such as are now familiar to all students of early mythologies. It contains scraps of Eastern tradition, and also indicates the prominence given to certain worships by the importance of the towns in which they were mostly celebrated.

The demi-gods in Hesiod are identified with the kings of the former age, who are now called blessed, and are still looked up to as guardians of mankind. The attempt of some critics to find an historical meaning in the succession of the gold, silver, and iron has no real foundation. The meaning is that things were better and better the further back you went. Some of the more prominent legends concerning the heroic world were accumulated in a poem attributed to Hesiod, and at all events belonging to the same school, the only extant portion of which of any extent is a description of the shield of Herakles, a manifest imitation of the shield of Achilles in the eighteenth Iliad. The chief difference consists in the substitution of legendary and mythological details for the realistic presentation of scenes from ordinary life.

To dwell now a little more particularly on certain points suggested by the body of poetry which has thus been generally described.

1. The aspect of mythology which appears in Hesiod occurs in Homer only in scattered allusions. These allusions, however, cannot without violence be separated from their context and assumed to be later interpolations. The primeval struggles which ended in the conquest of Zeus are implied in the occasional references to the distant place (as far from earth as earth is from the sky) in which Cronos, Iapetus, and the Titans were confined, and where the powers who punish perjury have their seat (cp. Hesiod, 'Theogony' 720-725). The passing mention of Typhoeus (for whom see 'Theogony' 821-868) occurs, indeed, in the catalogue of ships, which is otherwise thought to have affinities with the Boeotian school; but it is, notwithstanding, a striking fact that such an allusion should be admitted, not only in the 'Hymn to Apollo,' but in the canonical text of the Iliad. And certainly, if we glance for a moment at the general features of primitive religion, it must be admitted that the opposition between light and darkness, and the victory of the powers of light, is less likely to have been a secondary than a primary element of mythology.

2. But in the 'Theogony' of Hesiod we trace an endeavour, which, whether earlier or not, is certainly other than the effort of the minstrel to realise in a connected narrative the life of an heroic age. The work is a strange conglomerate in which, together with many childish fancies, which it is idle to account for except by the simple love of story-telling that grows out of personification, the working of dimly conscious ideas is notwithstanding to be traced. Some of these fancies are probably due to primitive tradition, and

some to more recent or contemporary symbolism. Thus the story by which the separation of earth and heaven and the fertilisation of the ground is accounted for is on a par with the mythology of savage races (cp. Iliad xiv. 97–210). On the other hand, the notion of Cronos, the offspring of earth and heaven, devouring his children, until arrested and subdued by his son and conqueror Zeus, is of a higher but still primitive order. Once more, that Zeus should have Metis (Wisdom) for his first consort, and Themis (Justice) for his second, comes of later reflection, and many points of genealogy such as the description of the progeny of Styx, or that of Night, are of a distinctly allegorical character, in which fanciful etymology also plays a part. This does not justify the allegorising interpretation of the Stoics, or of Bacon's ' Wisdom of the Ancients,' which robs primitive symbolism of its native unconsciousness, and ignores its intermittent, accidental working. Yet it is foolish to refuse to see the allegory when it is written in large letters. Hesiod is like his own men of the silver age, remaining a child in his own house, for a hundred years. Yet the child of a hundred years cannot but have thoughts mingling with his childish fancies or shining through them. For example, when Zeus, in order to subdue the Titans, releases the hundred-handed monsters whom he had bound, it is plainly implied that force cannot be subdued by mind alone without the help of power, and the whole conception of a conflict amongst the gods may be regarded as anticipating the leading thought of Heraclitus, that ' war is the father of the world.' The problem of the origin of evil is dimly adumbrated in the story of Pandora.

3. It is an obscure question, yet one we can hardly abstain from raising, how far the theology which in Hesiod seems to be localised in Boeotia had a Cadmeian, that is to say, a Phoenician origin. It would be easy to find parallels between the peculiar complexion of the ' Theogony ' and some phases of Babylonian tradition. The importance attached in 'Works and Days' to the rising and setting of the stars (not, it is to be observed, at all in connection with temple worship, but with agricultural pursuits), or to the *sacredness of the seventh day*, does read like a reminiscence of Chaldea. It is

not a little remarkable that Ketô, the prolific mother of so many strange unnatural forms, of which the sea-god Pontus is sire, is, as her name denotes, a monster of the deep, and thus analogous to the fish gods of early Babylonia. On this, and many cognate subjects, it is necessary to suspend our judgment until we have more light, and to rely only upon the facts that are clearly known.

4. In Hesiod, for the first time, the divinity of heroes as the sons of gods is definitely asserted. This would be more clearly apparent if the sequel of the ' Theogony ' had been completely preserved to us. The legend of Herakles in particular is much more fully developed than in Homer, although, here again, it is not quite safe to rely on the evidence of silence. The hero's crossing the ocean after the oxen of Geryon (' Th.' 291–4) has an especially Phoenician air. The allusion in the Iliad to the wounding of Hades by Herakles, in Pylos amongst the dead, is illustrated by the mention in the ' Shield of Herakles ' of an encounter between the hero and the god of war. Cp. the words of Hera in the fifth Iliad, 385, τλῆ μὲν ῎Αρης κ.τ.λ.

5. The description of the shield of Herakles deserves attention on other grounds. As compared with the shield of Achilles on the one hand, and with the great period of Greek sculpture on the other, it reveals to us an intermediate phase in which art was not dominated either by naturalism or as yet by an ideal of beauty. The images of war represented on the shield are inspired by a sort of ghoulish imagination. The Kêres, or spirits of Doom, digging their huge nails into the corpses of the dead, like the earliest sculptures of Selinus or the monstrous form of Erichthonius on some of the monuments found on the Acropolis at Athens, would be censured as un-Greek, did they not occur in a Greek poem.

The imagery of the poem, apart from such descriptions, has certain features suggestive of a time when the mainland of Hellas was liable to frequent shocks of earthquake. The recurring metaphors drawn from landslips and rocks dislodged from mountains vividly recall the description in Herodotus of the manner in which Apollo defended Delphi from the Mede. (This may remind us of the theory held by some that Hesiod was a poet of Delphi.) The ' Shield of Herakles,' even more distinctly than the rest of Hesiodic poetry, shows an undoubted acquaintance with the Iliad, yet is full of rhythmical defects of which neither Homer nor an Homerid could have been guilty. In this connection, the poet's own assertion that his father came from Cyme in Aeolia is not without significance.

6. The 'Works and Days,' while reflecting in an interesting manner the personal feeling of the poet, no longer a court minstrel, but a rustic bard, contain a mixture of moral, religious, and prudential aphorisms embodying an ethical ideal, at once different from, and in some ways more advanced than, that of the Iliad and Odyssey. The simple fact that didactic poetry here for the first time takes the place of narrative is most significant. Hesiod is in fact an ἐξηγητής or religious expositor. The Muses say to him ' We can discourse in lies that look like Truth : But, if we list, we can tell true tales too.' The Homeric poems reflect the life of the Achaean chieftains in the camp and in the hall—a life abounding in bright energy and in a joyousness which is rather accentuated than overclouded by the darkness which awaits men after death. We are now to look at life from the other side. Not princely birth or accomplishments but honest industry is regarded as the secret of such limited satisfaction as life affords. The idea of Justice (δίκη) is for the first time clearly developed, and is correlative to the sense of injustice which the people suffer under their new masters, the grasping overlords. The feeling of the misery inseparable from life is deepened, and the longing for a lost ideal is expressed in the fable of the five ages, in the course of which honour (αἰδώς) and right feeling (νέμεσις) are represented as having left the world. Virtue and vice are also clearly opposed ; yet power is irresistible—the nightingale must go where the hawk carries him ; the singer may not contend with the judge. Not that wealth is despised if got by labour : it is said (line 311) to be accompanied by virtue and glory, while poverty is also the gift of God ; nor are the gods as yet exempt from caprice. Though one observe the

seasons, yet if Poseidon or Zeus be angry, the ship, even in summer time, is not safe. Superstition and proverbial wisdom are inextricably interwoven : idleness must be avoided, moderation observed,—and the thigh-bones must be duly burned. This implies, however, that every man might still be his own priest. There is little evidence as yet of a temple worship: see for instance the altar to Zeus on Helicon (Hesiod, 'Theogony' 4). Reciprocity is one of the laws of human life, but *to give is nobler than to receive* ; in that saying, prudential morality seems to pass out of itself. Yet amongst the moral maxims instead of ' Bear it that the opposed may beware of thee,' a twofold recompense of evil is enjoined. The superstitious observances required at line 722 ff. of ' Works and Days ' have a very primitive look, and the abstinences there enjoined out of reverence for the sun, the open air, Night, and above all the family hearth, have a distinctly Aryan complexion. Some picturesque touches may be noted in passing, such as the indication of the beginning of spring, ' when a (plane) leaf on the topmost bough is as large as a crow's foot-mark.' Some prudential aphorisms are probably of immemorial age, and may be expected to outlast our race, such as that ' every pickle maks a mickle ' (line 360), and ' it's a poor thrift that spares the dregs ' (line 369) (cf. Plat. ' Phaedo '), ' at lovers' perjuries, they say, Jove laughs.' The word νόμος is acquiring the sense which it afterwards obtained (' Works and Days ' 386). Maxims are still simple, but contain more of the wisdom of life : ' a good neighbour is a good thing ' ; ' a bad wife roasts a man without the help of fire ' ; ' fools grasp at pelf, knowing not that half is more than the whole, nor how much comfort there is in a dinner of herbs.' The feeling of dependence on superhuman agencies is more constant in Hesiod than in Homer. But the intensifying of religious fear and even of superstition in Hesiod cannot be shown to be associated with any marked increase in the power of the priesthood.

7. One or two points of mythology may be touched upon in conclusion. The circumstances of the birth of Athena (l. 888) are different from what was later the orthodox tradition. Probably the more refined poets of a later age

shrank from the *naïve* conception of Zeus swallowing his wife Metis at a gulp. Demeter is as yet simply the goddess of harvest, apparently without mystic attributes, the consort of Zeus, and mother of Persephone and of Plutus. She is associated, however, with Zeus Chthonios, who is sometimes identified with Hades, but here and probably elsewhere is to be distinguished from him. The seventh day is sacred because it is the birthday of Apollo (l. 769). The fifth day is haunted by the Erinnyes (l. 801). In the 'Theogony' as it stands, there is no clear trace of an attempt to arrange the greater gods in groups of twelve or eight or three. It is manifest that in very early times the tract of territory afterwards occupied by Boeotia and Phocis had been the scene of many cross-currents of religious influence. Invaders from the north and north-west brought in the worship of the Muses and Graces, originally nature-deities, from Pieria to Helicon ; of Dionysus from Thrace to Thebes and Delphi ; of Ares from Thrace to Thebes ; while the Phoenicians, entering from the seaboard, engrafted on some native worships the religion of Herakles at Thebes, and of Poseidon on Mount Onchestos, and had possibly established an earth-oracle at Delphi before the arrival there of Apollo or even of Dionysus. The strangely blended attributes of Poseidon, the earth-shaker, the lord of the deep, the bringer of the steed, are best accounted for by some contact with a Phoenician source. Whether or not Thebes is to be regarded as the centre from which this influence spread, its reality is unquestionable : the associations surrounding Cadmus, Europa, Melicertes, Aphrodite, Herakles, Daedalus, leave no room for doubt.

With Hesiod begins the personal or subjective note, which is a new thing in literature, and sounds onward through the succeeding age of lyric and gnomic poetry.

The didactic form, which meets us as a new phenomenon in the 'Works and Days,' appears also in the body of elegiac verse which passes under the name of Theognis of Megara. It is certain that he belonged originally to Megara in central Greece, although Plato and others connected him, whether rightly or not, with the newer Megara in Sicily. These poems reflect the experience, not so much of another age, as of another class, who during the period of unsettlement on the Hellenic mainland had suffered the consequences of political reaction. In the neighbourhood of the isthmus, the old aristocracy were being supplanted, through the growing importance of industry and commerce, by new men whom they despised. Hence a mode of discontent, and of conscious misery, very different from that of the Boeotian peasant, but expressed in precepts into which ethical reflection enters in a somewhat similar way. The poets of the *noblesse* complain aloud that 'money makes the man.' While he glorifies justice as the sum of human excellence, Theognis identifies goodness with high birth, and badness with vulgarity. He commences his poem with an invocation of the Delian—not the Delphian—Apollo, of his sister Artemis, and of the Muses and Graces, who at the marriage of Cadmus had sung this strain : ' what is beautiful is dear, what is unbeautiful is not beloved.' He boasts of being famous in the world, but complains that he cannot please his neighbours. They are not without sense, but are led astray by the enemies of ' the good,' that is, of the men formerly in power. Those who once were poor men and despised now claim to be ' the good.' He longs in vain to find a comrade whom he can trust ; such a partisan is worth more than gold and silver. An open enemy is better than a dissembling friend. With such intermingling of political prejudice and moral wisdom, the poem proceeds, rising here and there into genuine religious fervour, and appeals to Zeus and to Apollo to protect the state from the insolence of upstarts and false friends. The poet has travelled far, but finds no country to please him like his own, not Sicily, not vine-clad Euboea, not Sparta amongst the reed-beds of Eurotas. But somewhat inconsistently he deprecates the spirit of faction, and though at the opening he worships the Delian Apollo, he specially reveres the sacredness of the Delphian oracle. He loves not war, but it is shameful not to fight for one's own state. Amongst many echoes of contemporary thought, this poet gives, perhaps the first clear utterance to the pessimistic strain, of which more will have to be said by and by : 'best of all for creatures of earth not to be born, or see the sun's keen rays ; but when born, it is best most swiftly to pass the gates of Hades, and to lie low with the mould heaped over one.' 'Hope alone of kindly powers remains with men, the rest have abandoned us, and gone to heaven. Good faith, a mighty deity, is gone, sobriety hath left mankind, and the Graces have deserted earth ; oaths are no longer truly kept amongst men, and no one hath any reverence for the immortals. The race of pious men hath perished. They no longer recognise just ways or piety, yet while one lives and sees the light of day, let him show piety to the gods and wait on hope. Let him pray to heaven, and while he burns the splendid thigh-bones, let him sacrifice first and last of all to the goddess of hope.'

Theognis marks the transition towards the age of Solon, as darkness precedes the dawn. I have brought in the consideration of Theognis here, because, although somewhat later as a whole than the Hesiodic poetry, and more in line with the direct succession from Homer, this body of verse contains, probably with later interpolations, some unmistakable echoes of a distinct aspect of the period of unsettlement in central Hellas. Meanwhile, a different phase both of political and intellectual life had been developed in the islands of the Aegean and on the shores of Ionia, some part of which had contributed to the form rather than the spirit of the poems just described. The island centres had been exempt from the immediate influence of great changes to which the Hellenes of the continent on either side had been subjected in the seventh century. They had their quarrels amongst themselves, as one or another island, and one or another powerful individual, had predominated. But there appears to have been more scope than could be found elsewhere, either at this time or afterwards, for the prevalence of personal emotion and intensity of private social life. The lyric poetry which formed the bloom of this civilisation remains to us only in tantalising fragments, which suggest that the loss of such a literature is even more to be deplored than that

I

of the comedies of Menander. But it may be questioned whether, if it had been extant as a whole, it could have been regarded as an important factor in the development of religion in the sense in which the term is understood for the purpose of the present volume. We gather that the worships of Dionysus, Demeter, and Aphrodite were more vividly present to these people than that of the Olympian gods. Archilochus glories in the power with which he can improvise the dithyramb of royal Dionysus, when the wine is flashing through him. Sappho's invocation to Aphrodite is the most intense religious utterance of this individual and subjective poetry, and Anacreon similarly glorified the power of love. The most important in a literary sense, as well as the earliest, of these creative minds was undoubtedly Archilochus of Paros. In him the personal note above adverted to comes into sudden and startling prominence. His was a strong and turbulent spirit, that amidst many outward changes, during an adventurous life, found utterance for its intense passionateness and savage indignation; moved at one time by personal injuries, at another by sympathy with great misfortunes such as those of the Thasians. His apostrophe to his own spirit ' confused with hopeless cares ' is more characteristic of him than the awe he felt at the eclipse, which suggested the familiar thought that nothing is to be accounted strange, not even if the course of nature should be interrupted or reversed. Yet the strain of moral reflection having a religious association is not absent. The decision of victory is with the gods, to whom all things are to be ascribed : ' oftentimes when men are lying on the dark ground in misery they raise them up, and often when most prosperous, they overthrow them and lay them flat ; thence many woes arise, and the man wanders in a life of want, and with thoughts disabled.' ' O father Zeus, thou rulest the sky, thou seest what is done whether villanous or righteous amongst men, thou carest for the insolence and right conduct even of the lower animals.' His prayer to Hephaestus for such gifts as that deity is wont to give breaks off unluckily before we have learned its occasion or its object, whether this be skill in craftsmanship or the fiery destruction of his foes.

Like other poets, he is ready to sing at religious ceremonies, and to lead up the Lesbian paean to the flute. As in all the poetry discussed in the present chapter, the religion of the Muses and of the Graces is a pervading spirit more consciously present than in Homer. The general impression derived from the fragments of lyric poetry of the seventh century is, that in the life of the islanders at this time, before the disastrous consequences of the Ionian revolt, individuals enjoyed a larger extent of social freedom than at any other period of Greek history. But the fear of the gods seems to have sat lightly on them, and the sunny vividness of their mental life can hardly be regarded as a positive moment in the evolution of religion. Yet we take note, in passing from them, of the general fact that in their hours of most intense consciousness and passionate emotion, the appeal to powers above themselves, Zeus, Apollo, Demeter, Dionysus, Aphrodite, Eros, breaks forth instinctively, as from a source of inexhaustible fulness from which they draw a momentary inspiration.

Among the inhabitants of the Asiatic seaboard, of which Miletus was the most important centre, amidst great varieties of social life and culture, there was far more of continuity in intellectual development. It was hereabout that the Homeric poems had attained their final shape, and it was here that elegiac poetry took its rise. Of this, so far as we know, Callinus was the earliest exponent. He lived in stirring days when the host of the Cimmerians was overrunning Asia and threatening the Ionic seaboard. A fragment of his appeal to Zeus to spare the Smyrneans has been preserved, in which he ' casts up to him ' the many fair thighbones of oxen that had been offered in burnt sacrifice. His elegiacs have an heroic ring. Mimnermus is a softer spirit, but he also has some warlike lines referring to the struggle with Lydia, in which Pallas Athena figures as the patroness of warriors. To speak more generally, in the Ionian poetry of this age we trace two principal effects: the love of pleasure, arising partly from the growth of luxury that was due to prosperity and the contagion of Lydia ; and at the same time a pessimistic reaction, which may be ascribed partly to the sense of insecurity of a people dwelling at ease, but under the shadow, first of Lydian, and afterwards of Persian supremacy. The keenness of enjoyment passing over into regret for its transitoriness prompts reflection on 'some undercurrent woe.' Mimnermus singing in this minor key dwells at length upon the note lightly struck by Homer, in comparing human life to that of leaves, so anticipating the philosophy of change of which Heraclitus became the great exponent. Hecataeus and other chroniclers now sought to consolidate and arrange in prose writing historical and legendary tradition, while Pherecydes of Syros, also in prose, continued the effort of Hesiod by attempting a more consistent theogony and cosmogony. The Homeridae, at Chios and elsewhere, besides those additions to the Iliad and Odyssey which modern criticism has attributed to them, not only preserved the Homeric deposit, but individuals amongst them such as Lesches and Arctinus became the authors of new epics dealing with the various portions of the Trojan cycle, such as the 'Cypria,' the 'return of the heroes,' and the 'lesser Iliad.' The 'Thebais 'and the 'taking of Oechalia' belonging to the same period were based on other legends brought from central Greece.

To the same line of tradition belongs the rise of a class of poems of uncertain and probably of various ages. The habit of invoking some great deity on the occasion of his festival, before reciting a selected portion of Homeric poetry, had become usual with the rhapsodists, whose preludes were sometimes of considerable length, and some of these have been preserved to us, under the name of the 'Homeric Hymns.' The present chapter may not unfitly be concluded with a brief reference to the most important of these.

The brightness of Ionian civilisation is pleasingly reflected in the 'Hymn to Apollo.' The birth at Delos is the principal subject, and the hymn itself was probably sung or recited at the Delian festival, which is in fact described in the well-known passage referred to by Thucydides. The exaltation of Delos as a sort of Bethlehem confessing her unworthiness at the unlooked-for annunciation is a prominent feature of the strain ; another is the description of

Apollo Citharoedus when he first appears in Olympus; and not less interesting, although more obscure, is the digression, perhaps interpolated, in which an attempt is made to connect the Delian with the Delphian Apollo, and at the same time to account for the comparative neglect of Telphussa as a seat of Apollonian worship. Edward Meyer has called attention to the comparative depreciation of Delphi, which he interprets as betraying a desire to exalt Delos at its expense, and supposes some connection with the rivalry of Athens with Sparta; but the description of the Delian festival is surely too early to admit of such a motive. The truth rather seems to be that the poet, or poets, belonged to the islands or to the Ionian seaboard and knew of Delphi only by report. Another proof of the absence of Delphian doctrine is that in the account of the slaying of the dragon, otherwise orthodox enough, there is no hint that Apollo needs any atonement for that act of bloodshed. The list of places visited by the god, both in Greece proper and in Asia Minor, beginning with Lycia, Maeonia, and Miletus, is unfortunately broken off by a lacuna in the text, else we might know more of the Delian amphictiony, whose importance survived Athenian ascendency. The effort of the poet, here as elsewhere, is to bring into harmony various local beliefs, not directly deducible from the general attributes of the god. The hymn has a touch of gentle pathos in the personal reference to the singer himself, so long identified with Homer in general tradition, 'the blind old man of Scio's rocky isle.' The golden sheen overspreading the isle in the day of her visitation may suggest a possible origin for the choice of Delos as the birthplace of a solar deity. Some pious soul, perhaps a pirate withal, may have seen some glory of sunrise on the rocky cliff and wondered.

The remainder of the hymn, sometimes regarded as a wholly separate composition, besides the curious episode about Telphussa, contains a minute account of the god's first arrival at Delphi, with a wholly different legend about the birth of Typhon from that which we read in Hesiod, and a very singular myth about the origin of the Delphians founded on the combination of two fanciful derivations of

Crisa from Crete, and of Delphinium from Delphis, a dolphin. These are preceded by the beautiful description of the first arrival of Apollo in Olympus, which forms the conclusion of the first and finest portion of the Hymn. 'As swift as thought he goes from earth to Olympus to the home of Zeus to join the festive gathering of the gods. And straightway on his coming the Immortals are engaged with song and with the lyre, and all the Muses in a throng, alternating with their bright voices, hymn the immortal gifts of gods, and the miseries of men, which they suffer at the hands of the immortal gods, as they live without knowledge or device. Nor can they find a cure for death, or a bulwark against old age. But the Graces with fair locks, and the cheerful Hours, and Harmonia and Hebe and Aphrodite, daughter of the highest, join in the dance, each holding her fellow by the wrist. And there pre-eminent in beauty and in stature, the sister of Apollo brought up together with him, Artemis that showers her arrows, is conspicuous amongst that choir. There too with them are sporting Ares and clear-sighted Hermes, and Phoebus Apollo meanwhile plays the lyre amongst them, stepping loftily with a noble air. And about him shines bright radiance from his glancing feet and from his garment of immortal woof, while Latona of the golden locks and counsellor Zeus delight their divine souls with the spectacle, beholding their own son at play amongst the immortal gods.'

The 'Hymn to Hermes,' of uncertain date, continues the same serene and cheerful strain, passing over into mirth and humour. Hermes, of all the gods, is the most familiar comrade of mankind. He gives them unexpected wealth, and helps them in their enterprises, honest or dishonest, a very St. Nicolas to thieves; the average Greek mind obviously delighted in listening to the story of his tricksy ways. The hymn expatiates on his birth and infancy, which is marked by two great feats—his theft of the oxen of Apollo and his invention of the lyre. His brother Apollo is pacified for the first escapade, by the charm of the invention. This hymn supplies the firmest ground for the theory that would derive the name of Hermes from the Sanskrit, and identify his deity with the breeze of morning which drives away the cows of the sun, that is the clouds, that go before him, and makes them disappear, while the luminary laughs at his young brother's theft and listens gladly to the music of the dawn. But hearers of the hymn had no conception of the solar myth which is suggested by the comparison of Vedic hymns. The spirit of the whole performance has been admirably rendered for English readers by the kindred and sympathetic genius of Shelley. In another hymn addressed to Hestia, Hermes, probably as the god of boundaries, is associated with the goddess of the hearth.

The 'Hymn to Demeter' reflects a wholly different strain of feeling, inspired by a worship which as early at least as the sixth century had obtained a widespread importance on both sides of the Aegean. It was suggested in a former chapter that local village ceremonies and beliefs probably survived the most abrupt political changes, remaining as an undergrowth when the tall trees of the forest were felled; many instances in illustration of this remark may be quoted from Pausanias, and they are mostly connected with the worship of Demeter. Just as in the hymn before us she nurses the child of Celeus at Eleusis, so in the Sicyonic legend she is the nurse of Orthopolis, and it is significant that the cult of Demeter and Persephone is associated with that of the Eumenides and the Fates. The burden of the hymn, embodying the Eleusinian myth, is the blindness of mortals to their blessings, whereby they reject an offered immortality. The main theme is finely exemplified in the low relief discovered at Eleusis, representing Demeter and Persephone and between them the boy Triptolemus (or Zagreus), the child of Hades and Persephone. Persephone is carried off by Pluto and calls in vain on her mother, who hears of her loss from Hecate and from the Sun. Demeter then leaves Olympus, and is found by the daughters of Celeus sitting by the well, like an elderly woman in widow's weeds. She undertakes to nurse Demophoön, the son of Celeus and Metaneira, and would have made him immortal by putting him to rest amongst the embers of the hearth, had not his mother one night seen her doing this and not unnaturally taken alarm. The sorrow of the Great Goddess, in which earth sympathises, issuing in the destruction of the works of men ; her joy in the restoration of her lost child, making earth to flourish again ; the secret wile of Hades, giving Persephone the pomegranate seed which secured her return to the realms below, sustain the human interest of the poem. The promise of immortality, in a larger sense than that which the poet of the hymn could have conceived, has been drawn from the original in a well-known poem by the alchemy of which Tennyson was so great a master, reading modern thoughts into ancient forms of imagination. We shall have to refer again to this hymn in speaking of the mysteries at Eleusis. At present it is enough to say that it belongs to a time when the worship of Demeter at Eleusis had not yet been ' contaminated ' with that of Dionysus.

Three hymns to Dionysus are included in the collection. Two of these are exceedingly short, one of them a mere fragment. In all of them he is the son of Zeus and Semele, and in the two brief hymns the mountain Nysa is mentioned as the place of his nurture. In the fragmentary hymn this is described as a lofty mountain, well-wooded, far from Phoenicia and near the stream of Nile. Thyône is also mentioned as another name for Semele. The longer hymn describes the first epiphany of the god. He is found by Tyrrhenian pirates on the seashore, like a beardless youth, with long dark hair. They bind him with withes, but he bursts them as Samson did ; the pilot then proposes to leave him on the shore, but the captain will not hear of it. They begin their voyage, when suddenly wine flows in runnels about the ship, with poignant fragrance, and over the sail there sprouts a trailing vine, hung over with clusters.[1] Dark ivy winds about the mast, with flowers and berries, and on the rowlocks wreaths are hung. The sailors turn towards

[1] See the ship of Dionysus, on the well-known vase, reproduced in Frazer's *Pausanias.*

shore, when the youth changes to a lion, and threatens them with roaring from the deck. A bear breaks out amidships, and sits up with threats. The sailors crowd in terror round the pilot, the lion seizes the captain, the mariners all leap into the sea and are changed into dolphins. The pilot alone is spared and made a wealthy man.

CHAPTER VI

PERIOD OF TRANSITION—HERO-WORSHIP

ALLUSION has already been made in speaking of Theognis to the way in which the growth of commerce and industry disturbed the simple relations which formerly existed between the members of each tribe. The people became more important, slaves were multiplied, and cities were consolidated. The right of primogeniture was impaired, inheritances were divided, and some powers of adoption and bequest were acknowledged. State prosecution, accompanied with religious ceremonies, at once regulated and attempered the old rough obligation of the avenger of blood. For the gentile name—Alcmaeonid, Eumolpid, Lakiad—came to be substituted first the national appellation—'Aeschylus, son of Euphorion, of Athens,' and by and by the name of the deme or district—'Sophocles, son of Sophillus, from Colonus.' The spiritual centre of gravity was passing from the family to the state, from the hearth to the high altar. And those deities acquired a special prominence who had most to do with civic life : Athena at Athens, Hera at Argos, Poseidon at Corinth. Above them all stands the Delphian Apollo, whose authority reached to all Hellenic cities. But the family, especially in the extended form of the clan, had at the same time an influence which grew with the growth of settled institutions ; and the heroes to whom each group assigned its origin became more and more the objects of ceremonial reverence. Their real presence in the neighbourhood of their tombs or sanctuaries was increasingly believed in, and the worship of ancestors, which had never died out, was more and more fostered as assuring the stability of the community. The early stages of this movement are of course obscure, but half-forgotten struggles left a lasting impress on religious feeling through signal examples of self-devotion in the cause of the fatherland (Codrus, Erechtheus, Menoeceus, Megareus, Aristodemus, Aristomenes), which, whether legendary or historical, are equally important in their effects upon religion.

The steps of this process of consolidation in the case of Athens in the sixth century are known with tolerable clearness, many points having been made more distinct by the recent discovery of Aristotle's treatise on the ' Constitution of the Athenians.' It is no longer possible, as has sometimes been attempted, to deduce such development in a direct line from the family to the clan, from the clan to the tribe, and from the tribe to the city. New divisions required by political exigencies were deliberately made to cross the former division, which was, notwithstanding, continued for social and religious and to some extent for military purposes. The ascendency of the great families, especially where they have the wit to amass wealth and court popularity, dies very hard. Great and small families alike maintained their peculiar sacred rites, except where many joined in a common celebration as in the Apaturia. The Phratry, an old military division, continues to subsist, but the tribe, Phyle, is the *political* unit, which is again subdivided on principles of political convenience. For all these changes religious sanctions have to be found. For example, the ten tribes, which were substituted in the constitution of Cleisthenes for the four previously existing, must each have an eponymous hero, who comes gradually to be regarded as the ancestor of every member of the tribe. This implied a sort of legal figment analogous to the law of adoption, but with less of illusion about it. How purely conventional this came to be appears from the inscription towards the end of the fifth century awarding a crown to Thrasybulus at the restoration of the democracy, in which the privilege is accorded to him of belonging to any tribe or deme at his pleasure. But the case was very different at the time of the former revolution, when the national spirit rose to meet the legislator who found in time-honoured names a sanction for the liberties which he conferred. The

Ten Eponymi were selected by the Pythia from a hundred native heroes whose names were presented to her. In this whole process two divine powers came into increasing prominence, *Apollo* and *Athena* : Apollo as the high authority revealing to mankind the supreme will of Zeus ; Athena as the guardian of the city, which is henceforth one, and is sheltered under her protecting wings. ' Our city shall never perish by the will of Zeus, and the care of the immortal gods ; so high-souled is her patroness, Pallas Athena, of the mighty sire, who watches over her and holds her arms above. It is her own citizens who, under the influence of wealth, seek to ruin the great city by their folly.' These words of Solon are very significant of the spirit of the higher minds of Attica in the early sixth century. The lawgiver's appeal to justice is not less solemn than that of Hesiod, and even more convincing, because more hopeful : ' Her dread foundations may not be neglected' ; 'though she keep silence, she knows what acts are done and what hath been, and in time she comes inevitably, bringing the reward.' Such utterances help us to realise the greatness of Solon's achievement. What figures in history as a political reform was nothing less than the infusion of a new religious principle, affecting, not modes of worship, but the minds of the worshippers.

The reign of law is gradually taking the place of mere customary tradition or the decision of the magistrate. Towards the end of the seventh century, in various parts of Greece, beginning with the shores of Italy, prominent citizens had been entrusted with the duty of preparing codes of law. Zaleucus at Locri in Italy, Charondas at Catana in Sicily, are specially known ; but they are only examples of what was taking place elsewhere. Lycurgus is credited with the Spartan institutions, but he seems to be a legendary figure, in whom some much earlier and some later tradition was concentrated by the popular imagination. At least he cannot have left a written code. For amongst other innovations which the conservative Spartans refused to adopt were walled fortifications and written laws. Their ῥῆτραι were preserved by oral tradition. The Cretan Dorians, on the other hand, had very early an accepted code of family law, which at Gortyn was engraved on the walls of an ancient building, of which the stones have been transferred to the theatre, itself ancient, in which they were found. Draco is the corresponding figure at Athens; he is a real person, and some of his enactments are clearly known. The famous legislation of Solon aimed at meeting a special exigency, and was social and economical, more than constitutional. It is interesting to reflect that his wisdom, which had so much of reason and experience in it, and was quite free from the pessimism which Herodotus attributes to him, was allied with the work of Epimenides, a religious enthusiast, and a sort of medicine man, whose reputation as an exorcist led the Athenians, in their extremity, to invite him from Crete. Plato and Aristotle agree in giving this account of him. According to other authorities he was a native Athenian. Here we find in the Athenian people an interesting combination of native shrewdness with the same simplicity which led them afterwards to be willingly imposed upon by the mummery with which Pisistratus returned, led home by a living image of Athena. It may perhaps be asked whether religious forms and practices, thus conventionally modified to suit political convenience, must not have lost something of their reality, but for the popular mind it was not so : a people of lively imagination, who read little, converse much, and live in the present, are easily capable of new impressions; and new forms which express or satisfy existing emotions soon acquire for them the sanction of antiquity. The worships which gave expression to the growing sense of common civic life were profoundly congenial to the advancing consciousness of each limited nationality. What rather moves one's wonder is, as Plato says, the native strength of the civic bond, which held together under the stress of factions that seemed likely to tear the state in sunder, amidst the contradictory interests of old families, novel claims, and restless ambitions. The love of power did not altogether supplant the love of country. Both often burned together in the same breast.

That individuals of exceptional originality and force had

much to do in moulding the strong fabric of the Hellenic communities is indisputable. But it does not follow that in referring the rules of life, to which they clung tenaciously, to one original source in the person of the lawgiver, they were not following the same natural tendency which led to the creation of the eponymous hero or of the legendary founder of the mysteries. It is also important to observe that it was mostly under the presidency of one strong man, such as Pisistratus, and in connection with the process of consolidation here spoken of, that the arts of architecture and of sculpture attained to such magnificence in their association with religious functions. The buildings on the Acropolis, for example, mark the complete centralisation of religious and civic life at Athens. There is hardly any trace of temple-worship amongst the Greeks of the Homeric time. The kings of the Mycenaean period had been more solicitous to fortify their castles, and to prepare their own beehive tombs, than to raise temples in honour of the people's gods. Such shrines as that which Chryses constructed for his rude image of Apollo were more frequent on the shores of Asia than in Hellas proper. The temple of Apollo at Branchidae, near Miletus, was of ancient renown; but like that of Delphi, which already existed in the eighth century B.C., it owed its grandeur to the offerings of foreign kings, which required a spacious building to hold them. It was when the race of kings had departed, and cities became conscious of a corporate existence, that they built houses for their gods, and supported priests to care for them and to conduct the ceremonies which symbolised the continuity of civic life; and just as the monarch of Tiryns and Mycenae might summon an architect from over seas to build him a palace or a tomb, so the city, which sought to enhance the glory of the house which secured the presence of its god, might send for some one skilled in arts that were not yet fully developed upon Greek soil. It is to be observed, moreover, that the city rather than the priesthood had the initiative in all this course of change. No doubt the priestly caste, for instance the Eteo-Butadae on the Acropolis, had their interests to serve, and well knew how to. work the oracle of the conservative party ; but statesmen such as Solon, Pisistratus, or Pericles were too hard for them, and would not suffer the religion of the people to be made a hindrance to the growth of the state. Thus the safety and glory of the community were indissolubly associated with the present favour of the gods and heroes whom their fathers worshipped, and in whose actual presence, so long as their ritual was duly performed, the people implicitly believed.

The peaked roof of a Greek temple, with the gable end or pediment which gave such grand opportunities for the sculptor's art, is ascribed by Pindar, together with other notable inventions, to Corinth, whose wealth derived from commerce gave her an influence on the progress of the arts, of which the decorated vases of this period afford abundant evidence.

Thus although it is undeniable that the arts of architecture and of sculpture, ever closely associated, were originally derived in some measure from the Egyptians, in so far as mechanical accomplishments were concerned, yet as their increasing splendour reacted on religious feeling, and awakened the native imagination, these arts became, under the influence of Greek genius, a new creation and birth of time. The Greek so invariably transformed what he received into shapes congenial to the Hellenic spirit, that it is at once futile and unimportant, when a few obvious resemblances and differences have been observed, to disentangle further the foreign threads from the whole complex web.

A similar uncertainty attends the far deeper movement which, while these popular rites were hardening into permanent shape, was in progress among a few more aspiring minds, and was ultimately to prove a solvent for the ceremonial conventions that seemed so irremovable. The sixth century B.C. is one of those epochs in the history of our race which mark a widespread access of spiritual vitality. In the case of Hellas it is still a moot question how far some fresh impact from Egypt or from further east had to do with this. But a sort of pantheistic awakening at once intellectual and religious, beginning from many centres, of which the names of Pythagoras, Heraclitus, Parmenides, and the mythical Orpheus may serve to remind us, had set going a wave of mingled speculation and aspiration, which at one time threatened to destroy mythology, at another to transmute it into novel forms. Wants hitherto unfelt were met in various ways. Individuals were not satisfied with the traditional and conventional worships of the family or of the state. There was a deepening sense, we know not how infused, of guilt requiring atonement, of pollution crying for purgation, a feeling which had its roots in very early times, but was now becoming universal. Meditation upon life and death brought into a glaring light the inadequacy of the Homeric conception of a future life, and a craving for some assurance of blessedness hereafter. These desires combining with the primeval village festival gave new importance to mystic ceremonies, especially those of Eleusis, and had considerable influence in shaping the religion of Orphism, with its novel features of mythology, ritual, and discipline. The worship of the Erinnyes or Furies, in which the power of the curse was personified, also assumed novel forms, and was blended with that of other Chthonian powers.

The philosophic aspect of this wide movement will be more conveniently considered in treating of the subsequent growth of philosophy. But it is necessary before passing from it to remember that this also must be reckoned with in estimating the changes in poetry and general literature which emerged about the end of the sixth century. Now, too, the Homeric poems and the lyric poetry which had succeeded them began to exercise a powerful influence upon religion and the arts that ministered to it. The worshipper who had listened to an epic rhapsody, or to some outburst of choral song, could no longer think of the god to whom he paid his vows after the old crude and scarcely human fashion. A refined anthropomorphism tended to obliterate the last surviving relics of animal-worship and of savage rites. A blind reverence still clung to the rude square pillar that merely indicated the characteristics of the human form, but feeling and imagination craved for something more. And this the artist tried to satisfy and to supply. Thence gradually the plastic arts, following in the wake of poetry, set before the eyes of those who came to worship the shapes and the expressive grouping which might render outwardly the forms of fancy. The thoughts of the poet also took a new direction. He chose his subjects more immediately from the experience of life: maxims, apothegms, and apologues became more frequent with him ; he aimed more at suggesting food for reflection, and in speaking of the gods avoided what seemed ugly or repellent. Man began to think of the power on whom his life depended more distinctly as the fountain of justice, and as civic relations were more and more developed, these higher thoughts began to find their centre in some one or other of the Olympian deities, especially in Athena and Apollo. Athena was looked up to by the Athenians as their protectress ; she was also their instructor. Intermittently and to a less degree the Pythian Apollo stood in this relation to the whole Grecian world and to Lacedaemon above all.

The most noted change in this respect was the new consciousness about the guilt of homicide which overspread the whole Grecian world, and was immediately associated with the Delphian worship of Apollo. The only forms of purification known to Homer are fumigation with sulphur, as in the Odyssey, and washing with sea-water, as in the first Iliad. The latter process survived in such ceremonies as the annual washing of the Palladium at Phalerum, and the rush to the sea with which the Eleusinian rites began. But there is no hint in Homer of expiation through the blood of swine (sacrificed to Demeter), or of other forms of ceremonial purgation which afterwards became universal. We have an interesting glimpse of one stage in this process in the visit of Epimenides to Athens, when after a long period of misery the people had called him in to heal them. After inquiry, he declared that this came on them for the blood of Cylon's partisans whom the Alkmaeonidae had slain, when suppliant at the altar of Athena. To purge this guilt, the Alkmaeonidae were banished, and the bones of their dead taken out of their graves and cast beyond the borders of the land. This feeling of blood-

K

guiltiness was in the first instance positive and ceremonial, and was afterwards abused, becoming a superstition and an instrument of unscrupulous policy. But it contained in it the germ of a profoundly moral feeling, and of that consciousness of sin which is the beginning of a deeper religious life. Apollo and Athena thus became vicegerents of their father Zeus on earth, Apollo as the author of religious purity, Athena as the patroness of justice and equity.

The worship of the dead is by some thought to be the origin of all religion. It is at all events a phase through which all races of mankind who have attained to any historical importance have at some time passed. In the propitiation of the Manes it survived the latest period of Latin culture, and was continued by the Greek and Roman Churches in the invocation of saints. In the Cyclades Charon still gets his coin from the mouth of the dead as he did of old. To be without this element of religious life would therefore seem to be indicative either of primitive immaturity or of a late and advanced stage in the growth of the human mind. But the apparent exceptions to this rule are startling enough. Herodotus says that the Egyptians have no such custom ; Hebrew religion presents few traces of it, unless in Saul at Endor ; and in Homer, as before remarked, hardly any vestige of it is to be found. The statement of Herodotus, however, about Egypt is obviously based on a misconception. The departed kings, buried with such pomp, whose pyramids were maintained with great endowments providing for the unending performance of an elaborate ritual, were to all intents and purposes the objects of such worship. If the priest endeavoured to explain to his Greek interviewer that the worship was not paid to Rameses or Necho as such, but to the god with whom the spirit of either was identified, the historian's mystification might easily be as complete as when, relying on appearances, he had identified Osiris with Dionysus. Or it might be meant that the being so worshipped was not a hero but a god. The Egyptian Ka or spirit of the dead was in the case of a king more essentially divine than the shade of Ajax or Orestes. As to hero-worship in the heroic age, I may refer to what I have said above, p. 67. The blood which Odysseus pours into the narrow pit, by the advice of Circe, is precisely such an offering as in central Greece was made at every great man's tomb. The custom of providing the national hero or patron saint with a sacred precinct, such as had once been the privilege of the king, became universal in Hellas before the seventh century B.C. There is no reason to doubt that the hero so worshipped was often a real member of some family, who had impressed himself upon the people's imagination, either by founding a dynasty, or repelling an invader, or by his misfortunes, or in some other way. But political exigencies also gave rise to the invention of what are called eponymous heroes, the supposed ancestors of a family or clan, whose blood-relationship was largely supposititious. Instead of giving his name to the clan, such a hero was often named after it. Semi-divine honours were also paid to the mythical originators of certain forms of ritual. Eumolpus, for example, was the father of those who conducted the Eleusinian mysteries. Another true cause of hero-worship arose when a god of former days had been supplanted by a more important deity, whose son or servant he was now supposed to be. Asclepius, Castor, Polydeuces, and others, whom Homer speaks of as mortals, may have been gods before his time.

The strength of the impulse to worship the dead may be measured by the number and variety of the grounds which made a man a hero. First comes the claim of the head of a family descending from patriarchal times. As many families coalesced into one clan, the common ancestor of the clan must either be found or invented, and every tribe or district which came under a common government had its epony-mous hero, whose worship symbolised the bond of union. As these units again coalesced into a greater whole in forming the city, the many festivals in honour of these ancestors, real or supposed, were sometimes united into one, as in the Athenian or rather Ionian feast of the Apaturia. The founder of a colony, who carried with him the sacred fire from the mother-city, invariably received such honours after death ; and other sacred associations led to the multiplication of such rites, as, for example, the worship of Pelops at Olympia.

This tendency remained a living power in Greece far on into historical times; we know that Hagnon and Brasidas were so worshipped successively at Amphipolis, and the power of the local hero was the object of such vivid belief that the presence even of his image with the army was regarded as conducive to victory. In the same region the people had raised an altar to a Persian governor after his death, because of his extraordinary stature. Such faith must have often been severely tried, yet it survived. We can only point to one instance where it appears to have been shaken, and in this case it is not the native hero who proved so disappointing. When Thebes appealed to Aegina for help, the Aeginetans in all good faith sent the images of the sons of Aeacus, and when defeat followed, the Thebans returned the images, and asked for men. But this failure was not thought of when the presence of the same images at the battle of Salamis was believed to have been decisive.

The hero present at his tomb was supposed to have all the human feelings of a living citizen. The vicissitudes of war, alliance, and colonisation affected the fortunes of heroes as well as of living men. There were many tombs of Oedipus in many parts of Greece : for the Athenian he was buried at Colonus ; for the Boeotian, at Potniae ; for the Corinthian at Sicyon. There was a tomb of Cassandra both at Argos and at Sparta ; of Talthybius, both at Sparta and in Aegina. Orestes, although not a Dorian, was a powerful factor in the Spartan state, and not until his bones had been laid within Spartan ground, and a temple raised over them, could the Lacedaemonians be secure of supremacy in the Peloponnesus. A less fortunate policy was pursued by Cleisthenes, the tyrant of Sicyon, who being at war with Argos, sought to exile Adrastus the Argive hero worshipped at Sicyon. When the Pythoness forbade this in words of contumely, he instituted the worship of Melanippus, of whom legend spoke as the greatest enemy of Adrastus in his lifetime. This, however, was the action not of the people, but of a tyrant. Many cases are recorded in which an enemy received divine honours after death. The tomb of Mardonius in the Plataean territory was respected down to the time of Pausanias.

Onesilas, the Cyprian tyrant who besieged Amathus, having been slain in conflict with the Persians, the Amathusians maltreated his remains, but because of a portent (a swarm of bees having settled in the hollow of his skull) and a consequent oracle, they instituted an annual sacrifice to him, which was continued for more than one generation. On the other hand, it is equally instructive to observe that in removing all traces of the worship of Hagnon the Athenian general, the Potidaeans felt, as Thucydides tells us, that it could not be pleasant for *him* to receive their offerings side by side with the worship of his adversary. Philip of Crotona, the most beautiful man of his time, who was disappointed of his promised bride, the daughter of his country's enemy, and joined the fatal expedition of Dorieus, is said by Herodotus to be the only mortal to whom the people of Egesta ever paid divine honours. They raised a herôon over his tomb and continued to propitiate him with sacrifices. Yet his coming amongst them must have been a serious danger to their state.

Pausanias mentions (iii. 13 § 1) that a tomb of Idas and Lynceus was shown near the tomb of Castor in the neighbourhood of Sparta. The historian thinks it unlikely that such bitter enemies should be buried so near together, but the association is characteristic of the impartiality with which Greek religion accorded reverence to those, although opposed in life, who had in any way impressed the popular imagination. Similarly in Mysia, whether amongst a pure Greek race or not, Thersander who was slain by Telephus was honoured together with that hero in connection with the worship of Asclepius. In the same connection another feature of this branch of ritual appears ; for in the popular imagination, by all except such rare spirits as Antigone, resentment was supposed to continue after death : thus in the 'Ajax' of Sophocles, Odysseus although friendly is not invited to take part in the sepulture of Ajax whom he had offended ; and in the temple of Asclepius just spoken of, the worshippers of Telephus were not permitted to approach Asclepius, until they had purified themselves. The reason was that Machaon the son of Asclepius was slain by Eurypylus the son of Telephus, and for the same reason the songs in praise of Telephus that were chanted there made no mention of Eurypylus, his warrior son.

The act of Cleisthenes above mentioned is a strong instance of the early prevalence of the same belief. Solon, and after him Pisistratus, had appealed from the religion of the Eupatridae, which centred in various local cults, to the universal sanctity of Zeus and Athena, of the Earth and of supreme Justice. But the power of the local gods was not extinct, and when making the people his ally, as Herodotus puts it, Cleisthenes sought for the patronage of great heroes acknowledged by general consent and approved by the Delphic oracle, to counterbalance the influence of great families whose patron saints were still so strong. Each tribe in the new democracy must have its own Attic hero.

The ritual of hero-worship was distinguished from that of the Olympian gods in several ways. Whatever may be the result, either in Greece or Egypt, of the minute investigations which have been of late pursued on the subject of temple orientation, the general fact is indisputable : the temples of the gods in Greece were so contrived that the statue in the main shrine should face the rising sun upon the day of festival. The temple of the hero on the other hand opened to the west, and looked towards Erebus and the region of gloom. This is strikingly exemplified by what Pausanias tells us (confirmed by recent investigation) of the temples at Olympia. The entrance to the Pelopeum, he says, is towards the setting of the sun, whereas the temple of Zeus, as a matter of course, faced eastwards. The same historian's account of the ritual of sacrifice in the Pelopeum is further suggestive. It was performed by the rulers for the year, and the victim was a black ram. Such sacrifice to those below was not followed by a feast. The worshippers did not taste of the victim. The soothsayers had no share in the victim, but an officer known as the woodsman, who supplied the wood for sacrifice, got the neck and nothing more. His business was to supply both states and individuals with wood of an appointed kind in due measure for the purpose of the sacrifice. White poplar was the only wood allowed, and it is very noticeable that whosoever, whether native or foreigner, shared in that sacrifice was not allowed to enter the temple of Zeus on the same day. So true is the saying of Aeschylus, that the honours of the highest gods are kept apart from those of powers below. The exact differences of ritual in minute points between the worship of gods and that of heroes is nowhere clearly stated, except the essential point that in the act of hero-worship the blood was poured through an opening into the ground. But that there were such differences, and that they were very clearly marked, appears from the fact that a special word (ἐναγίζειν) is used for sacrificing to a hero, in contradistinction to the more general term (θύειν), which applies to all sacrifice, but also in a special sense to offerings made to the Olympian gods.[1]

The worship of heroes from whom the race derived its origin was continued with little abatement in democratic times, but there can be little doubt that it was for many generations one of the strongholds of oligarchy. No one can read Pindar without a keen sense of the inordinate family pride with which he regards his own lineage from the Aegeidae as at least equal to that of the Heracleid kings of Sparta. The theme of every Epinikian ode is that the brave are born from the brave, the noble from the noble, and no motive is more operative in his morality than that *noblesse oblige.* Such notions might be consistent with beneficent despotism, but not with any real sympathy with the people. The Athenian tragic poets sought to popularise the native heroes, and to make of them an ideal for the admiration of mankind; but while in doing so they yielded something to the strong current of rising democracy, they also ministered to the

---

[1] A third term for religious offering, ὀργιάζεσθαι, is used by Plato in *Laws* iv. 717 B, and is apparently applied to the worship of heroes and other divine beings (δαίμονες, θεοὶ πατρῷοι) below the rank of Olympian gods.

pride of the tyrant city, and encouraged her in her career of arrogance towards subjects and allies. Yet the existence of such legendary ideals in the past was not the less an indescribable boon, binding together a whole community in indissoluble brotherhood, and bowing the pride of individuals under a deep sense of the hereditary glories and the indefeasible destiny of the race.

The question has been raised of late whether the hero was not in every case a degraded god. That this was not always so is clearly proved by the cases of Hagnon, Brasidas, Artachaeus, and Philip of Croton. That the original occupant of a sacred shrine was often deposed in the interest of a greater deity, whose servant he became, is a familiar phenomenon in religious evolution, and may be acknowledged as the source of much hero-worship. But it matters little in this connection whether the fact were so in any particular case or not. The hero was equally regarded as a mortal who had obtained divine honours after death, and was the object of filial or patriotic adoration.

So much of heroes generally, but an important and very difficult question remains behind. Is Herakles to be regarded as a hero or as a god? The difficulty is one which the Greeks themselves felt, sometimes acutely. In the Odyssey he is already both at once : as a hero who had died his shade is underground, but he himself is in Olympus and is married to fair-ankled Hebe. Pausanias tells us how the people of Sicyon had worshipped Herakles with heroic honours, until Phaestus, son of Herakles, arrived and instructed them to sacrifice to his father as to a god : since when they sacrifice a lamb as formerly, but burn the thigh-bones on the altar and taste of the sacrifice as holding communion with the god ; while other parts of the victim are offered after the manner of hero-worship. Some found a solution in the hypothesis of two persons of the name : one the son of Alcmena, who died on Mount Oeta; the other one of the Idaei Dactyli, more ancient than the former, who had shared with his brothers the guardianship of the infant Zeus and had founded the Olympian games. Something of this kind is said by

Herodotus (Book ii. chapters 42–45). A possible hypothesis is that the belief in Herakles was indigenous in Greek soil, but as the legend grew, it took on foreign attributes and became confused through the ambition of great families to show connection with him, and especially from his being made the ancestor of the royal family of Sparta. Apart from the tale about Olympia, there are not many traces of him on the western side of Hellas (only the obscure battle at Pylos, and the Augean stable); in Aetolia, for example, Meleager seems to take his place, as Theseus did to some extent in Attica. And yet his fame as the founder of the Olympian games, and his connection with Aetolia as the brother-in-law of Meleager, would seem to be older than the time of Spartan supremacy. The type of the strong man, the ideal of a conquering warrior race, is probably more inseparable from Hellenic nature than the Hellenic name itself, and is rooted in immemorial antiquity. As Wilamowitz-Möllendorf has suggested, it may have come with the first conquerors in their descent from the highlands of Thessaly. While holding to his Hellenic origin, I venture to doubt whether in early times he could be said to be exclusively associated with the Dorian name. Two of the earliest seats of his worship were at Marathon and at Thermopylae; the latter is not far from Doris and immediately below the range of Oeta, but Marathon is in no sense Dorian, and there are good reasons for supposing that it had once been a Phoenician settlement.

The Cean muse of Bacchylides in the poems recently discovered, which were sung by choruses from Ceos, not a Dorian island, celebrates impartially the Attic legend of Theseus and that of Herakles in its connection with Aetolia. Herakles then is Hellenic and not Dorian merely. How comes it that so many of his attributes have an eastern complexion, lending colour to the supposition that, like the Hebrew Samson, he is an impersonation of the sun-god? That is probably due to some 'contamination' with the Phoenician Melkarth. The Greek mariner who boasted of his Herakles found that the Phoenician likewise had his patron in a god with similar attributes, of whom Herodotus speaks as the Tyrian and Thasian Herakles—the adventurous wanderer, the cleanser of the earth, the indefatigable labourer. The twelve labours have an unmistakable solar meaning ; the legend of Atlas and of the pillars of Herakles, of the garden of the Hesperides and the golden apples, all seem in different ways to reflect Phoenician culture. It is perhaps not without significance in this regard that Pindar speaks of Herakles as not having that commanding stature which the Greeks admired. The writer of the article Herakles in Roscher's 'Lexicon of Mythology' has shown by an examination of the early monuments that the lion-skin was not always an inseparable badge of Herakles, and makes it probable that it was derived from the east, where a lion was the frequent symbol for the sun. Various fables about the same hero, which are not indigenous to Hellenic soil, such as the stories of Cacus and Antaeus and the oxen of Geryon, also bear some traces of a Phoenician origin. Some of these may have been fixed in Greek mythology by Stesichorus, whose well-known fragment describing Herakles borrowing the sun-boat for his journey to the west is the most distinct evidence of the solar connection. The lion of Nemea is in all probability a mythical being. Lastly, to revert to the question from which we started : the Greek Herakles from the universality of his worship cannot be regarded in the ordinary sense as a hero, but rather, notwithstanding his career of mortality, as a genuine god.

The communities which gradually formed the somewhat heterogeneous aggregate to which we give the name of Hellas were exceedingly numerous and were frequently at war with one another. The Athenians, who thought themselves aboriginal, with an infusion of Achaeans from Troezen and elsewhere, were of a distinctly different race from the Dorians, who apparently came from the far north-west. But there were two great influences which counteracted separatist tendencies, the oracles and the games. Of the latter we see the beginnings in the Iliad in the funeral contests and in the allusion of Agamemnon to the prizes which his steeds had won ; also in the famous simile in which Achilles pursues Hector not for a cup or a cauldron, but for his life. It is manifest that there already existed such local competitions, perhaps imperfectly organised, as are repeatedly referred to by Pindar and Bacchylides, in celebrating some greater victory. Such competitions took place first amongst the members of the same community, and secondly amongst those dwelling within a certain range, the Perictiones. For these minor contests the prize of a brazen cauldron or a silver bowl was still offered, as for example at Sicyon. But at Olympia the gilded crown of wild olive was all the victor had to show, and the great centres at Nemea, Corinth, and Delphi followed suit with the parsley, oak, and pine. The honour of the victory against all comers from the whole of Hellas was satisfaction enough. If we imagine the immense impression made upon each visitor at Olympia or at Crissa by the excitement of the contest; the intercourse with strangers, who, though they spoke another dialect, were easily understood; the common sacrifices, the procession in honour of the victor, and above all, the processional hymn ; we can easily understand that not only for the time being there was a truce of God, but that in spite of jarring interests and ambitions, there must have sunk deeply into the hearts of many individuals a feeling of Hellenic brotherhood and of pride in the Hellenic name. The rich men who had made the voyage from Syracuse, Agrigentum, Rhodes, Cyrene, for the sake of an Olympian crown and had their glory celebrated by the poet both at Olympia and at home on their triumphant return, felt themselves grafted afresh into the Hellenic stock and must in turn have excited in the breasts of the spectators new thoughts of the wide range of Hellenic life. Both impressions were confirmed by the inspired poet, who traced the genealogy of each from Herakles or Aeacus, and recited the noble deeds of ancestors who had come between. The feeling of community of race and worship could not be more effectually impressed.

In the earliest times, the small communities continually at feud with one another would often combine in the presence of a common danger. Having thus served together in war, they would entertain an intermittent neighbourliness and meet at annual festivals, where the elders of each might occasionally sit together in council and confer upon their common interests. Thus Amphictionies were formed, the most remarkable of which, so far as known to us, were those whose centres were at Thermopylae and Calauria. The Cyclades and neighbouring islands similarly regarded Delos as a centre; the Dorians of Asia Minor met at Triopium, the Ionians at Pan-Ionion. The authority of such federations, like that of the early kings, gave way before the circumstances of later times, when they were overshadowed by the ascendency of powerful states ; but they retained many of their associations, and the Amphictions of Thermopylae could even exercise some actual influence when the sanctity of Delphi was threatened. Their power, however, was little more than that of the diet of Frankfort when Germany was united under the military ascendency of Prussia. The importance of Delos was acknowledged by the Athenians when they made it the cardinal point of their confederacy, though after a time they withdrew the common treasury from thence, and made Athens herself the pivot-state.

As time went on, the inheritance of a common literature was another bond of union amongst all Hellenes. We read in history of the wars of Sparta with Argos ; of Argos with Tiryns and Mycenae ; of Athens with Eleusis and Megara ; but are apt to forget that in the intervals of peace which after all existed the rhapsode or the minstrel passed from town to town, and delighted those who thronged around him with the same strains of epic or of lyric verse with which he had charmed his own countrymen. The Iliad was popular at Sparta while it was still comparatively unknown in Attica. Terpander of Lesbos and Alcman of Sardes were neither of them Dorians ; but their poems charmed the Dorians first and afterwards all Greece. There was more of intercourse between the various communities than we are apt to imagine. It was only in the late sixth or early fifth century B.C. that Sparta began her jealous habit of excluding foreigners ; the Greek who could afford it loved nothing better, at any time, than seeing and hearing something new. Solon left his country, not only to avoid inconvenient interviewers, but to see the world; and Plato mentions it as one of the chief miseries of the tyrant, that having the keenest thirst for seeing and hearing pleasant things, he is compelled to live like a woman in a secret chamber for fear of assassination. That is a touch extremely characteristic of the Greek mind. But the rivalry of powerful states and internal factions rendered anything like union or even federation impossible, although wise men such as Isocrates in the fourth century began to dream of combining Hellas against the Persian; until Philip of Macedon came and Macedonian tyranny put an end to the spontaneous vitality of the Hellenic states.

One of the greatest difficulties attending any general study of Greek religion arises out of this perpetual oscillation between universalism and particularism. The great Olympian deities, while they gradually came to be acknowledged as belonging to the whole Hellenic race, were at ihe same time claimed by several cities individually as belonging to them of special right. Thebes laid a special claim to Ares, Corinth to Poseidon, Argos as in Homeric times to Hera. Zeus the protector is invoked by all alike, but each nation thinks of him as protecting their own land in particular. Earth is the most universal of deities, but in speaking of her the Theban or the Argive thinks only of his own land. The travelling sun-god is perhaps the only deity who is never thus appropriated to a single state ; though he too had a special favour to the island of Rhodes. Popular imagination found it hard to separate between Artemis and Athena in general and the Artemis or Athena that was worshipped in the precincts of this or that city. Such local appropriation gave special attributes to deities as worshipped under the same name by different communities, who sometimes sought to retain them, as the Spartans did their Ares, by actually chaining them to the shrines. Artemis was one divinity in Arcadia, another at Brauron, and yet another in Aetolia, or on the Maliac gulf. The Helen who dispensed the gift of beauty to Laconian women, or whose aspect terrified the Messenian chieftain, was a divinity whose worship was independent of epic tradition.   There were Athenas who had no special care for Athens : Athena Itonia for example, whose chief seat was in Boeotia, though she was not forgotten in Thessaly her earlier home ; and the Athena Onka of the Cadmeians, whom some have identified with the armed Aphrodite. In Lacedaemon itself there were no fewer than fourteen Athenas with various attributes, all differing from the Athenian Maiden.   It fortunately matters little for our present purpose whether she were originally an Aryan lightning goddess, or a Libyan water deity (Neit), or a Babylonian Ishtar.   By her worshippers she was principally regarded as the guardian of their city.

The Athena of the Parthenon is no longer simply the divine helper, who moves beside the warrior or the coun-sellor ; she is the giver of the olive, the patroness of knight-hood, the founder of the council of Areopagus, the pro-tectress of her suppliant although a stranger, the mirror of equity and of mercy.   But when from the Acropolis of Athens we pass to the rising ground which was regarded as the Acropolis of Sparta, there stood Athena, a bronze goddess in a shrine of bronze, in the place which had been sacred to her before the Dorians came, but where she had remained as guardian of the Dorian city.   Her title Poliuchus corresponds to the Polias of the Erechtheum.   And here, as on the eastern pediment of the Parthenon, her miraculous birth was represented and she was associated with Amphitrite and Poseidon.   But instead of the metopes setting forth the triumphs of Theseus, the whole series of the labours of Herakles was embossed upon the bronze walls of the shrine : Athena doubtless standing by her favourite, as in the marble metopes at Olympia.   And ' Athena of the brazen house,' unlike her namesake of the Parthenon, shared all the sternness of Spartan discipline, and was of a rigorous unrelenting mood.   The Athenian goddess protected Orestes and shielded him from the onset of the Furies, though he was not an Athenian ; but she of the brazen house was in vain appealed to, by her own king of Hera-cleid descent, because he had been guilty of a rash act of homicide.   He found no place for repentance, though he had anxiously endeavoured to purge away the stain. Athena Alea, the Tegean goddess, whom the Spartans likewise adopted, was a deity of a different mood: in accordance with her title she gave shelter to the fugitive and even to the criminal. Her sanctuary was respected upon occasions where the violence of passion might have been expected to break through, as when she protected Leotychides and the younger Pausanias and Chrysis the Argolic priestess of Hera, through whose negligence the Heraeum had been consumed with fire.

The various attributes attaching to the same deity are illustrated by Herodotus when he describes Croesus as calling upon Zeus the purifier, Zeus of the hearth, and the Zeus of comradeship, and the historian takes the trouble to remark that in all these appellations he called upon the same deity.

The connection of religion with the life of the state often found a focus in some one sacred object, in which the prosperity of the community was supposed to be bound up. Thus the grave of Oedipus at Colonus was regarded by the hearers of Sophocles as the foundation and guarantee of victory as against the Thebans. The grave of Eurystheus in Euripides is supposed to give a similar advantage over the Peloponnesians. The recovery of the bones of Orestes made the turning point in the struggle between Sparta and Tegea, and the bringing of the bones of Theseus from Scyros to Athens was regarded as one of the most distinguished services which Cimon rendered to his country. A pathetic story is told of king Aristomenes, at the close of the second Messenian war. It was doubtless believed in by every Helot, as well as by the Messenian exiles at Naupactus, and encouraged them in those desperate hopes which led to forlorn enterprises and occasioned cruel reprisals on the side of Sparta. It occurs in Pausanias, Book iv. ch. 20 § 4, where it is told how when Messene was doomed and the Pythian oracle had proclaimed it, the heroic king, courageous to the last, buried by night in some unknown spot, far from the track of men on the heights of Ithome, a sacred thing not further characterised, on the preservation of which an ancient oracle declared that the ultimate salvation of Messene depended. He then continued the struggle, of which he foresaw the issue, to the bitter end. That is not the conclusion of the story: the deposit of Aristomenes was discovered centuries afterwards by Epaminondas, through a divine intimation when he refounded the city. His general, Epiteles, on digging in the place which had been indicated in a dream, found a roll of tin-foil on which was inscribed the ritual of the Great Goddesses, Demeter and Persephone, and this was the deposit of Aristomenes. Here, once more, there is an intricate interweaving of policy with religious feeling which it were vain to attempt to disentangle. But the fact is not the less significant.

The real presence of the Aeacidae at Aegina, of Castor and Pollux in many towns of Laconia, of Pelops at Olympia, in proportion as it was vividly believed in, helped to keep alive the public spirit and the consciousness of a common life in these several centres. The shapes which religious belief and ritual ultimately assumed depended partly on military or tribal exigencies, partly on mere chance coincidences, such as the similarity of names. Thus a whole cycle of legend grew out of the apparent identity of Perseus with Perses, and of Io with the Egyptian Isis. We cannot doubt that in many instances the conquerors came to share the beliefs of the conquered people, and hoped by showing respect to local sanctities to make their conquests perpetual. Thus many articles of popular belief, some of them extremely ancient, come to be woven into the recognised body of tradition. And hence it is that many items of folklore demonstrably more primitive than anything in Homer make their appearance first at a later stage of Greek literature. That is only another proof of the fallaciousness of the argument from silence. The ordeal by fire, so frequently dwelt on in the ' Zendavesta,' appears only once in classical Greek literature; but it is put into the mouth of the watchman in the ' Antigone,' who is a most perfect witness of its existence as a popular belief. The sacredness of certain inanimate objects, such as a tree or a stone, is seldom referred to, yet it can hardly be doubted that the Thorician stone spoken of in the 'Oedipus Coloneus' was endued with such mysterious virtue by some primitive belief, and in this connection we may refer also to the conical Aphrodite, and the aniconic pillar representing Hera in Argolis.

It is remarkable that a growth so multifarious should have retained so many broad features in common. Zeus, Poseidon, Apollo, Athena, Artemis, are everywhere adored. Apollo now adds to his other attributes that of the healer of disease. This may be accounted for, perhaps, by the law of opposites—'he who can destroy can also save'; but the belief was certainly supported by the accidental similarity between Paean, the hymn to Apollo, and Paiôn, healer. Artemis now generally assumes the attributes of Eilithyia, and presides over childbirth. This may be connected with her Homeric attribute as 'the lion of women.' She retains her characteristics as the huntress and also the protectress of wild animals. The worship of Hera is more localised—perhaps less popular ; she has her great temples in Boeotia and at Argos, and the greatest of all perhaps in Samos. Pan is a god whose reverence becomes accentuated with the rise of popular religion; his worship spreads from Arcadia to other parts of Greece and is associated with that of Dionysus and Demeter.

Lastly, in speaking of local sanctities it will not do to forget such semi-divine persons as the nymphs and rivers, and other impersonations of natural phenomena, which are imagined, not always as immortal, but as long-lived: an expression of the feeling, perhaps, that man is more short-lived than a tree. This multiplication of demi-gods of course accentuated the polytheistic tendency, giving rise not only to innumerable legends but to manifold modifications of mythology and ritual : such as for example the habit of sacrificing to the winds. The help which Boreas gave to the Greek cause at Artemisium was never forgotten by the Athenians, who prided themselves on being connected by marriage with the god who carried off Orithyia. Subordinate deities, personifying abstract qualities, such as persuasion, health, hope, love, became attached to the

L

shrines of greater gods with whom they were associated. Thus Earth is associated with Demeter (Paus. vii. 4 § 11), and we have a goddess of Calm in the temple of Poseidon at Corinth (Paus. ii. 3 § 9). The goddess of Health was similarly associated with Asclepius, who in Homer is hardly a divine personage, but whose worship existed in Thessaly probably before Homer's time, and passing from Epidaurus as a centre, spread quickly and widely over the rest of Hellas. Fortune comes to be personified side by side with Providence and Fate. We have Plato's authority for saying that Love in the earlier times had no separate shrine, though the famous Eros of Polycleitus suggests a different view. Such an image, however, might be a dedicatory offering at some temple of Aphrodite.

Many of these innovations may be accounted for by a theory which contains a large amount of truth—that legend has its root in ritual : that is, that in dwelling on some traditional ceremony no longer understood, the imagination formed to itself sometimes the object of worship, but invariably some history concerning him, which when analysed resolves itself into the elements of the ritual itself. That all Greek legends are to be so accounted for, it would of course be rash to affirm; but the theory in question has in many cases proved a valuable guide to the solution of mythological puzzles. The point to be observed is that the mythological fancy was still active, and that the personification of attributes, qualities, and powers, or even of a name, might at any time give rise to the creation of a new worship, in short of a god. The altercation between Themistocles and the people of Andros is a late example of this fancy in its lighter and more fugitive manifestation. When he sought to requisition them for supplies, he said that the Athenians came in fellowship with two great gods, Persuasion and Compulsion. They replied that Athens seemed to be fortunate in her deities, but the people of Andros were less fortunate, since they had two worthless deities that ever haunted their land, namely Poverty and Inability, wherefore they could not give. The same half-humorous invention of popular demons appears in the

potters' song which is given amongst the epigrams attributed
to Homer ; here every influence (Smash-up, Half-bake, and
the rest) which can do hurt to the potter's work and cause
its failure is turned for the nonce into a little deity whose
wrath is deprecated. See also the curious names of Spermô,
Oenô, and Elaïs quoted by Proclus from the 'Cypria' attributed to Homer. Such 'animism' is of course familiar to
the student of Roman religion.

CHAPTER VII

TRANSITION PERIOD CONTINUED—THE DORIAN STATES— MAGNA GRAECIA—BEGINNINGS OF PHILOSOPHY

THE religion of Sparta represents Dorian tradition in a pure but somewhat intensified form, modified not from without, but by the special circumstances of the community. The position of the plain of Lacedaemon, encircled by hills, the paucity of harbours, and even of roadsteads, available for the shipping of a primitive age, conspired with the pride of a military race in isolating the community. The relation of the true Spartan to the Lacedaemonian of the surrounding cities was that of an occupying army to a conquered population; while the Helots, who were mostly captives from Messenia, although kept in strict subjection, were not excluded from all warlike exercises. The peculiar constitution of Lacedaemon, in which the power of the kings was limited by the control of the Ephors and the privileges accorded to the senate, may have been partly due to the ingenuity of some great statesman, but the realisation of it must have been a gradual process. The Dorian conquest of the Peloponnese, though in some mythical accounts it is represented as a single act, was really the result of a long-continued struggle, and the same is true of the domination of Sparta over her neighbours and former allies. The conquerors, whose persistence was equal to their valour in war, seem to have used policy as well as strategy in completing their title to possession. The remodelling of the myth of Herakles, for this end, has been already touched upon. The recovery of the bones of Orestes, and the foundation of a temple in his honour on the site of his reputed tomb, which is said to have determined the last contest with

Tegea, gave the sanction of the old Pelopidan ascendency to the *de facto* rule of Sparta. In pursuance of the same wise foresight, Spartan supremacy at an early period identified itself with the Olympic games and the worship of Apollo at Delphi. The dominant note in all Laconian institutions is, that everything else is sacrificed to the unity and effectiveness of the state. Pericles speaks of Athenian public life as the education of Greece. The Spartans might be called the drill-sergeants of Hellas. The laws of marriage, of child-birth, of education, the regulations of conduct, were all laid down with a view to the perfecting of individual citizens as instruments for supporting Spartan rule, and to maintaining the number of free citizens at a constant figure. It is tolerably clear, however, that these features became intensified during the obscure contentions of the sixth century. The Dorians elsewhere, although strict in the observance of law and custom, and in the maintenance of ceremonial rites, do not present the same features of rigid militarism with the Spartans of history. Argos, at a time when she was already Dorian, was according to Herodotus conspicuous amongst Greek states for the cultivation of music. And it is impossible to believe that those who listened to the songs of Alcman, which the Lydian singer made for Laconian maidens who sported on Taygetus, can as yet have been drilled into the monotonous uniformity of life which contrasted so unfavourably with the liberal culture of the Athenians. The fragments of Alcman in fact reveal to us the complexion of a time when Laconian civilisation was full of grace and charm, and the stress of war had not yet hardened the city into a camp. And such an independent personality as that of the adventurous Dorieus, whose picturesque career is so familiar to readers of Herodotus, implies the existence of elements that were not easily subdued to the stiff framework of Spartan discipline. The celebration of the Hyacinthia which was common to all Dorian states remained to indicate the freër workings of a former time. The development of a rich civilisation, largely under Dorian laws, in Sicily and southern Italy affords further evidence upon this point. It is therefore, I think, an erroneous or at least questionable view which refers peculiarities of Spartan marriage customs to a survival from savage life, before the family had become a settled institution. The brilliant chapter on Sparta in the late Mr. Walter Pater's fascinating volume on ' Plato and Platonism ' has familiarised us with a view of the subject based on Otfried Müller's learned work on the Dorians, according to which the Spartan ideal is clothed with a severe beauty of asceticism. It is a charming paradox, and very instructive, but if we could throw our minds back into the age before the second Messenian war, when Laconia and Argolis were still good neighbours, when internecine strife between them had not yet broken Argos or stiffened Sparta, and while the Helots were still a manageable quantity, the spectacle would be more really beautiful and more truly Hellenic. Or if we could transfer our observation to the island of Cos, we should perceive a combination of order and freedom under Dorian religion that was more essentially admirable. That Greek life, of which there are so many reminiscences in the odes of Pindar, was realised in the earlier centuries more perfectly than in the later times of which more is known. Sparta had not yet recourse to alien acts, or to the exclusion of foreigners, such as were Alcman and Tyrtaeus.

The equality amongst the Spartan _élite_, which is noticed by Thucydides in his preface, and was partly due to the importance of the armed infantry, indicates a period of free development as having existed before the final consolidation of the rigid organism. Moreover, the peculiar discipline of Sparta is apt to hide from us, what would be interesting if we knew more of it, the life of the Perioeci in Laconia. When not specially levied for warlike purposes, they must have lived under conditions more natural and more like the rest of Greece than the privileged few who were subject to continual restraint. It was amongst them that certain industries, such as the manufacture of iron, for which Laconia was famous, were brought to perfection ; and some of the communities on the seaboard retained a large measure of independence, with their own peculiar modes of worship, hereditary customs, and manner of speaking. The military *cordon*, excluding fresh influences from the north, contributed to this result; and local worships in south Laconia long presented features in which Phoenician and Arcadian fancies had at an earlier time become inextricably blended.[1]

The Spartan *ephebi*, as we are told by Pausanias, each upon his coming of age performed an act of worship to the spirit of Achilles. Yet they were surely mistaken if they supposed that in their course of life they would be making him their pattern. Nothing could be less like an ideal Spartan than the Achilles of Homer. Both men are physically perfect and complete, both accomplished in spear-craft and all martial exercises. But Achilles has been led onward by his delight in action, and by his father's precept, according with his own ambition, 'ever to be the noblest, and foremost amongst all.' The Spartan has never had a thought except to do what was required of him by the laws and customs of his ancestors. Achilles plays the lyre, and sings of the glories of heroes, for his own delectation or that of his friend Patroclus. The Spartan is not without his share in music, but he has acquired it through taking part in song and dance of a severe and simple kind, in which the youth were trained to engage together at festivals such as the Hyacinthia in honour of Apollo. Beyond this his chief exercise in music consisted in listening to the martial strains of Tyrtaeus. Both men have a keen sense of honour, but the Spartan's honour lies in obeying the state, and in commanding his subordinates effectively. Achilles, and indeed all the Homeric heroes, place the point of honour in claiming and receiving their due; Achilles is nothing if not independent. Every Spartan has learnt to be subject and to rule in turn. Diomedes comes nearer than Achilles to the Spartan ideal, which, like every development of Greek life, had its germ in the Achaean period; but it is none the less significant that the main interest of the Iliad centres in one whose will is his law, and with whom

---

[1] The worship of Ammon may have come in from Libya at some very early time; how it found its way to Thebes or even to Elis, we cannot tell.

personal feeling outweighs every other consideration—the feeling in the first instance for his own honour, and then in a far deeper sense, on account of his friend. Lastly, the Spartan is a man of deeds not words, and abhors rhetoric; the speeches of Achilles in the first and ninth books of the Iliad, whether by the same author or not, are amongst the most splendid outbursts of human eloquence. When the Spartan spoke, it was sometimes to conceal his thought; Achilles acts out his hatred of the man who hides one thing in his breast and speaks another. We are warned, however, against imagining a mere dull uniformity in Spartan life by such examples as that of Brasidas or of the beautiful Callicrates, who died at Plataea, lamenting that he had not lived to do deeds worthy of him, or lift his hand against the foe.

What Thucydides says of architecture may to some extent be applied to literature. The nation which has left no striking literary remains is not therefore to be contemned as devoid of genius. The Spartans not only dominated Hellas more continuously than any other single race, but the respect in which they were held by the chief citizens elsewhere in Greece reacted on the mental life of other cities, and of Athens in particular. The Athenian who found his own institutions crumbling beneath him, and his own national life falling to decay, looked enviously at the stability and unshaken strength of Sparta. He would have found it intolerable to live under Spartan rule, but his ideal aspirations received a new direction from this cause.

The influence of the Spartan type on the later Greek imagination is almost incalculable. Even the nations that departed most widely from it from time to time reacted in its favour. The ideas of measure, of simplicity, of sobriety in word and deed, in short of discipline, in theory at least were amongst those most deeply rooted in the Greek mind ; and discipline or ἄσκησις was the first and last word of Spartan virtue. Not personal ambition ‘ to be the foremost,’ but obedience to law even to the death, is summed up in the supposed injunction of the Spartan mother to her son, referring to his shield : 'either it, or on it'; and in the epitaph on those who fell at Thermopylae :

> Go, stranger, tell the Spartans we obeyed
> Their mandate, and are here together laid.

We can hardly be mistaken in tracing Spartan influence in the institution, which appeared strange to the Persian, of the crown of wild olive for which competition was so keen at Olympia. When this is compared with the treasures, tripods and cauldrons, &c. &c., which the horses of Agamemnon had won for him at various funeral games, it seems to mark the advance in the quality of Greek ambition which had taken place in the interval. The outstanding dominance of Sparta had, as above remarked, an indirect effect in perpetuating primitive rites in various parts of Laconia, by forming a bulwark against the spirit of change which from time to time was operative in other parts of Hellas. Within the territory of Lacedaemon, for instance, Amyclae is known to have preserved traditions reaching far beyond the Spartan occupation.

So far as the objects of worship were concerned, it cannot be said that Sparta differed greatly from the rest of Hellas ; the worship of Zeus, Apollo, Artemis and Athena was not less conspicuous here than elsewhere. Even in the divine honours paid to Herakles, although they claimed a peculiar relation with him, it cannot be said that they stood by any means alone. It is a remarkable coincidence, that at Marathon as well as at Thermopylae there was a temple to Herakles in close proximity to the scene of action ; while at Tegea and elsewhere, in places under Dorian rule, as well as at Sparta itself, there stood important temples of Athena. It was only when the rivalry between Athens and Sparta had reached an acute phase that the Athenians made so much of Theseus, whose legend resembled that of Herakles ; while those who sought to foster peace between the rival cities represented Herakles and Theseus as bosom friends.

Before passing again from central Hellas to witness the expansion of Greek life in other lands, it may be observed that at the stage which we have reached three ethical conceptions which are only dimly present in the Iliad are rising into clearness : the conception of personal excellence (ἀρετή), the conception of law (νόμος), and the idea of justice as the bond of states.

The excellence for which a man is honoured is still to a great extent physical, but already contains also the essential elements of courage, forethought, fortitude, and self-control. The conception of law makes no distinction as yet between what is written and unwritten ; in both forms it is a tradition from former generations, embodying the will and wisdom of the state, to which an absolute obedience is invariably due.   Law in this sense was contrasted with the commandment of an individual ruler.   Such is the contrast drawn by Demaratus in his answer to Xerxes, who could not believe that men could be brave except under compulsion : ' they have a master over them, namely the law of their land : a master whom they fear far more effectually than your subjects are in dread of you.'   In every change of the Athenian constitution, the newly constituted authority was bound to determine according to ancestral custom.

The idea of justice is more prominent in the verses of Solon than in any previous writing, and carries a sanction with it there entirely different from anything that is associated with the word in Homer.   It is also to be observed that not only the notions of law and justice are modified but the system of jurisdiction has been placed on a new footing.   From the state of things in which the giving of judgment was a source of wealth, or in which two talents were awarded to him whose judgment met with general approval, to that in which the magistrate was bound on oath to judge honestly in accordance with the law, a long process of development must have come in.   The intervening struggles are exemplified by those described in Aristotle's ' Constitution of Athens ' respecting changes in the tenure of the Archonship, which culminated in the attempts of Damasias and of Cylon.

The effect was lasting, although the chronic disease of faction was not cured even by the heroic remedy of Pisistratus. His work, however, was a necessary stage in progress and left permanent effects for good. Ambitious as he was, he seriously loved his country, and during his lifetime, while maintaining his own ascendency, did much towards strengthening as well as adorning Athens. It is probable that some improvements often attributed to Pericles owed their first inception to Pisistratus. When the tribute of the Delian confederacy was employed in beautifying Athens and providing a brilliant existence for the people of Pallas, the tyrant city only followed in this the example of the tyrant whom they had abjured, who spent the bulk of his revenues not in building for himself a lordly palace, or in emulating the grandeur of oriental kings, but in making splendid the house of Athena, in adorning the Panathenaic festival, in providing that Homer should be worthily recited, and that the infant drama should be well appointed, all for the people's behoof. The democracy, when they obtained wealth and glory, followed up what was so worthily begun ; but it may be doubted whether even the Athenian Demos could have initiated these things.

The view of Hellenic life and culture is not completed when we have considered the mainland of Greece, the seaboard of Asia Minor, and the islands of the Aegean. Before the end of the seventh century B.C., Greek civilisation had attained to considerable development in Sicily, in southern Italy, and in the north of Africa. This came of a second flight of colonisation, proceeding partly from older colonies. Sicily had been chiefly colonised by Dorians from Rhodes and Corinth, no doubt with a certain following of Achaeans, and by Ionians from Chalcis and Euboea. Croton and Velia, the latter colonised from Phocaea, were the most important of Hellenic states in south Italy. While Dorian institutions exercised a powerful influence, and gave strength to the various cities, such influence was largely modified by circumstances, by mixture of race, and the forced amalgamation of different populations under despotic rulers. It may be said in passing that Crete and Cyprus were less affected by the changes of this period than other remote

Hellenic settlements, and retained more of the customs and modes of worship which had characterised them in the preceding age.

The object of the Sicilian colonists had been conquest and merchandise. The shores of southern Italy were occupied by emigrants from central and western Greece, mainly Achaeans, who settled as agriculturists in the rich plains near the sea. These settlements also became important as commercial centres. Greek culture in Sicily and Magna Graecia flourished greatly in the times before the Persian war, and the history of those cities, if it could be fully known, would appear even more romantic than we find it in the pages of Mr. Freeman's history. Individual character and energy had more scope than at Sparta or even at Athens in that early time. The ascendency of successive dynasties did not crush out the social and intellectual impulses, which were scarcely less active thereabouts than in the islands or in Ionia. That each city had its own peculiar worship appears from coins of Syracuse, Naxos, &c., than which none are more characteristic or more beautiful. (The importance of coinage marking a stage of culture is a topic which can only be touched on here. Beginning on the Asiatic coast, it was introduced by Pheidon into Argolis probably in the seventh century. Its significance is shown by the tale that Darius put to death an Egyptian governor who had issued silver coins rivalling the Dareicos in purity.) The literary products of this rich civilisation unhappily only remain to us in fragments; but the names of Stesichorus, Ibycus, Epicharmus, Xenophanes, Parmenides, Empedocles, represent a fresh breaking forth of originality in the higher region of the mind, which had immense influence on the subsequent growth of religion, literature, and morality throughout Hellas.

Quite another centre, and one of great interest, is the Minyan colony of Cyrene. Its early history, as narrated in Book iv. of Herodotus, is one of bold adventure, of striking vicissitude, and perseverance in spite of crushing disasters. The mixture of races is in this case specially interesting. Discovered accidentally by Samian voyagers, this rich tract of territory, of which some distant rumour had found its way into the Odyssey, was originally colonised from the island of Thera; where a settlement of pre-Dorian Greeks had blended with an earlier Phoenician population. There is therefore a dash of Semite blood in the race to begin with, which helps to explain the fact that after fresh contact with Egypt the women worshipped Isis and abstained from beef. From a quarrel in the royal house came the secession to Barca; then immigration from all parts of Greece—and apparently a blending of the Barcans with the Libyans; then a conflict between Barca and Cyrene in which thousands of the Greek settlers were destroyed. There ensued an uprising of the people against the monarchy, that was temporarily pacified by the legislator Demônax, invited from Mantinea; then the breach of the new constitution through the ambition of the queen-mother Pheretime, whose career is one of the most signal instances 'furens quid femina possit,' 'what wild work may come of a woman's rage' in the way of ambition, cruelty, and revenge. Cyrene and Barca continued Greek for many ages, and formed the last bulwark of Hellenic civilisation on the side towards Carthage. Some accidental resemblance of names and attributes between Athena and that of some Libyan deity led the Barcans into the belief that their country was the birthplace of Athena Tritogeneia. (This account of the matter is more probable than that Athena came originally from Libya.) At every crisis of their history they consulted, if they could, the oracle of Delphi, and the ambition of the royal family took the truly Hellenic line of competing in the chariot races at the great games. War chariots had long been the pride of north Africa. Arcesilaus III. and his ancestry are repeatedly celebrated by Pindar. In connection with the insurrection already mentioned, an extremely curious proof is still extant of the unpopularity of one of the kings. It is amongst the few vase-paintings that have a distinctly comic cast. The monarch appears in the act of weighing out bales of goods like a retail dealer, —the chief figure being a manifest caricature.

One more receptacle of Greek life should be specially mentioned because, although the subject is obscure, it can hardly fail to have been in some degree the channel for Egyptian influence on Greek art, and possibly on Greek religion. We know more of Greek life at Naucratis in northern Egypt in the sixth century than our fathers did, but our knowledge is still tantalisingly imperfect. To the commerce with Egypt and to the Greek colony at that emporium we may at least trace with confidence much of the mythology in which the Greeks expressed a consciousness of still earlier relations with the land of Nile. The fact mentioned by Herodotus of the existence of a class of half-breeds, part Egyptian and part Greek, is extremely important in this connection.

As commerce and navigation made progress, and the intercourse between distant parts was thus facilitated, the whole body of Greek religious culture became more complex in consequence of influences reacting on the mother-country from the remoter centres of Greek life, which are difficult to ascertain in detail, but are unquestionably real. The history of Herodotus presents a wide field, in which the result of all these influences is apparent, but except where he himself gives the information there is little ground to go upon, in assigning the various statements found in him to their several sources. He mentions by name Hecataeus of Miletus, and it is reasonable to suppose that there were other collectors of earlier tradition, on whose writings he relied. But the impression which he generally conveys is rather that of oral communication, as when he speaks of learned authorities amongst the Persians, or of the priests of Egypt. It has been suggested that the various states of Hellas had probably written archives, to which the historian may have found access ; this may possibly have been the case to a large extent, but we know too little of the literary habits of the time, and of the degree of jealousy with which such documents, if they existed, would be guarded, to be assured of more than that in his insatiable thirst for information the historian would avail himself of any and every opportunity, whether in speech or writing. In regard to Egypt it is disappointing to find that he has so little to tell us about the Greek colony, no doubt assuming the facts to be well known, and being led on by his eagerness to consult the priests of Memphis, whose information was not always either seriously intended or rightly understood.

The whole question of the mixture of other races with the pure Hellenic, especially in the countries which formed the fringe of Hellenic influence, is one which deserves to be carefully weighed in any attempt to estimate the true nature of Greek religion. When some great Phoenician colony was conquered in its turn by Dorian or Achaean adventurers, analogy points to the probability, not of an entire supplanting of the one race and religion by the other, but to a partial fusion in which the persistence of old elements would be veiled under the language of the conquering people. Herodotus speaks expressly of Phoenicians who in his day not only lived side by side with the Hellenes in amicable intercourse, but, as a consequence of this, relinquished some of their own most cherished customs, such as circumcision. Is it not likely that *en revanche* they would communicate some of their traditional notions to the receptive minds of the eager population surrounding them? The importance of Thasos as an early Phoenician settlement is exemplified by the immense remains of the mining industry of that people which Herodotus himself had seen (Herodt. ii. 44, vi. 47). In the neighbouring island of Samothrace, although by some confusion he speaks of the Pelasgians as its occupants, yet the religion of the Cabiri, which he attributes to them, is unmistakably Phoenician. This subject has been already dwelt upon, but cannot be omitted here. It is difficult not to conceive that the legendary empire of Minos, the son of Europa, who put down piracy and had the Carians for feudatories, had something to do with Phoenician influence. And if we turn again to religious phenomena it becomes manifest on comparing such fragmentary records as we possess that either the origin or at least the development of some important features of Greek religion had a Phoenician source. Granting that Herakles, Aphrodite, Poseidon, and the Dioscuri were originally Hellenic deities, they have certainly taken on to a greater or a less extent some features from Phoenician worship. I do not name Dionysus here because, although he is often traced to a Cadmeian origin, the more authentic indications point to his having come into Greece, perhaps through the islands, from a Thracian source. Yet even in this case there may have been Phoenician elements which entered into the ultimate form of the legend.

While Athens was still struggling with the difficulties of her early history, important mental changes were at work in what, for the sake of convenience, we may describe as greater Hellas. These affected religious conceptions in two chief ways : (1) Innovations in mythology and ritual ; (2) The birth of philosophy, tending to discard mythology altogether.

1. Stesichorus of Himera, in the north of Sicily, besides introducing novel forms of lyric poetry and improved modes for its production, set an example of boldness in the reconstruction of popular legends, and the invention of mythological incidents, that gave a strong stimulus to the religious imagination. Before reflection had had time to clothe itself in the language of abstraction, men had begun to be aware of discrepancies between much in the early mythology and the ethical feeling which had been cultivated in the life of civilised communities. Some of the unprecedented dramatic turns, which struck the hearers of Euripides as having the gloss of novelty, were really borrowed from Stesichorus. The best known instance of this is his reconstruction of the legend of Helen. He felt it to be impossible that the daughter of Zeus should have betrayed her husband, and been the cause of all that woe. It was a shadow for which the Achaeans fought, while fair Helen herself was kept safely in the shelter of Egypt. Another beautiful incident which Lord Tennyson borrowed from Euripides was taken by Euripides from Stesichorus. Menelaus, when about to revenge himself on Helen for her supposed perfidy, involuntarily drops his sword at the sight of all that beauty. A very similar thought had occurred independently to Ibycus of Rhegium. The latter poet's delight in flowers reminds

us of the exuberant loveliness of the land of south Italy, in which he wrote.

As mind awakened, imagination could not remain stationary. The poets who succeeded to the sacred office of the epic minstrel were more familiar with the popular religion, but in handling it could not forbear from introducing refinements required by the growth of half-conscious thought, which their vivid fancy readily supplied. And although ritual had a fixity which contrasted with the ever-shifting cloud shapes of mythology, there were not wanting innovations in ritual too. These were mostly represented as revivals of some primeval worship. And it is curious to remark that, as scepticism advanced, an elaborate formality of ritual increased along with it. The religious mind protested the more earnestly against incipient unbelief as itself began to be overshadowed with a doubt.

2. In speaking of greater Hellas and the changes which began there and subsequently influenced the mind of central Greece, it is necessary to include in one survey the east and west together. For the western colonists not only looked back to their earlier seats on the shores of the Aegean (Stesichorus dwelt for a while at Samos), but were reinforced from time to time by emigrants who left their native states and sought a newer world. Such were Pythagoras, who brought his wisdom from Samos to Croton, and Xenophanes, who withdrew from Colophon and settled at Velia. These brought with them the seeds of a revolution in opinion which worked at first sporadically, but was destined ultimately to have a wide-spread influence. This was nothing less than the sudden uprising of philosophic thought, which occurred almost simultaneously in Ionia and in Italy and Sicily. 'Athens, the eye of Greece,' was not the cradle, but rather the stepmother of philosophy. The sixth century, perhaps of all periods the most pregnant with new ideas, gave birth to this new creation in the world of Hellas. Great generative thoughts came forth unbidden, like Athena from the head of Zeus. The spirit of enquiry was already in the air. In gnomic poetry, in the attempts at a rational cosmogony, continuing the work of Hesiod in

M

the prose of Pherecydes, there were germs of speculation expressing themselves in somewhat 'mangled forms.' But the bold attempt to grasp the secret of the universe in one conception is of a wholly different order from any of these. When Aristotle says, 'all men by nature long after knowledge,' he expresses a truth which is applicable in a special sense to the Greek. The love of knowledge natural to men existed in Greek nature at a higher power. It had for some time been germinating, when it suddenly blossomed in Thales of Miletus. He was one of those men of the sixth century whom after generations counted as the seven wise men. The others were Bias of Priene, Pittacus of Lesbos, Solon of Athens, Chilon of Lacedaemon, Cleobulus of Lindus, and either Periander of Corinth or, as Plato says—for Periander is too odious a tyrant—Myson of Chêné. These represent what may be called the Gnomic movement in Greek thought, the culmination of that proverbial philosophy in which the ripening experience of mankind is provisionally summed up and recorded in pithy aphorisms. Each of these has a partial truth, which finds its proper place and worth only when the wisdom of life is harmonised by later reflection. Thales, however, while not relinquishing an interest in practical things, had a mind which soared far beyond his fellows. Doubtless there were antecedents for the great leap which he took, not into the dark, but into the region of light—'Above the smoke and stir of this dim spot, which men call earth' : just as, if men ever learn to fly, it will be possible to distinguish some links of connection between that and other modes of locomotion. Perhaps it may be said that early cosmogony following upon the theogony of Hesiod formed such a link between mythology and philosophy. It was the first outcome of that spirit of wonder and insatiable curiosity which, as Plato and Aristotle both affirm, is the mother of philosophy.

The crude attempt to imagine some affiliation of divine powers had behind it the latent need of the human spirit to discover order in nature, to attain harmony, if not unity, in the conception of the world. It has been suggested, but the suggestion is at present purely speculative, that when

Babylonian records have been explored, the beginnings of philosophy amongst Greek races on the shores of the Mediterranean may be rendered more intelligible. Certainly the jump from Pherecydes of Syros to Thales is a sudden one, and the combination of his speculative theory with his reported prediction of an eclipse does point to some antecedent origin. Whatever may have been the contact which set the spring in motion, the rise of this new spirit in several centres at once forms an extraordinary crisis, both in Greek thought, and in the history of the human mind. And the wonder is not lessened when we consider that almost simultaneously the north of Hindustan, the highlands of Persia, the shores of the Aegean, and the cities of Magna Graecia should have received independently the breathing of new spiritual influences, each destined to work for many centuries on large sections of mankind. The life of Gotama Buddha has been placed conjecturally in the seventh or sixth century B.C. Zoroaster 'flourished' about the same time; so did the great Hebrew prophets of the Captivity; while Pythagoras and Thales both appear before the middle of the sixth century.

Philosophy at its birth reacted vehemently against tradition and current opinion; and its creators were often isolated from their contemporaries. Even when, like Thales and Pythagoras, they were not without influence, they were as a matter of course misunderstood. Xenophanes and Heraclitus, above all, stood apart from the common life of their day, and it was only after many generations that their ideas, in part at least, became absorbed into the common stock of intellectual life. We shall have occasion at a later time therefore to develop the significance of these great thoughts, in connection with the philosophy of Plato. At present our chief interest is briefly to characterise each of these men, and to deal with their speculations in so far as they are symptomatic of a phase in the development of the Greek mind, and also as they reacted on the mental life surrounding them.

The religious world of polytheism did not see the danger to itself in the new strange thinking of such men, which in a generation or two would have rent the veil of mythology asunder. So long as they conformed in public, they were at first in little danger on this score. And the toleration extended to philosophy is in keeping with what was remarked above concerning the free scope allowed to individual impulse on the shores of the Aegean in the time of the earlier lyric poetry. At Athens shortly after this things were very different. Side by side with progress and speculative inquiry there was a growing spirit of reactionary fanaticism there, of which Anaxagoras, Pericles, Pheidias, and afterwards Socrates were victims. But in Ionia and Magna Graecia in the sixth century the fathers of philosophy were rather looked upon as harmlessly eccentric, though they might quarrel with their states on other grounds. Why Pythagoras and Xenophanes were exiles we do not know. Thales certainly was a good citizen and so esteemed ; and after the fall of Ionia some remembered with regret that his statesmanlike advice to have one council chamber for all the Ionic cities had not been taken. Yet his countrymen derided him for the strangeness of his pursuits. His prediction of the eclipse is simply mentioned by Herodotus, who has evidently no conception of the process by which such a result was obtained. The historian also records some of his sayings. That Thales himself observed the stars is implied in the tale repeated by Plato, that in doing so he once tumbled into a pit and was jeered at by a Thracian handmaid, who said that he saw what was far off, but not what lay before his feet. The girl spoke ' wiser than she was 'ware of,' for in gazing at the stars Greek contemplation could not rest in facts observed, but, as Bacon says of the human intellect generally, presumed and encroached on what is beyond. It was amidst such contemplations that Thales began to meditate on the question, what is the one essence of which all things consist? His answer, ' all is water,' was the first word of Ionian physiology. It had been anticipated even in the Homeric cosmogony, which spoke of Ocean and Tethys as parents of the gods ; but the new departure consists in saying not what things come from, but what things *are*, and in conceiving of the world as *all*.

That in some sense this great utterance found an echo in contemporary minds may be reasonably inferred from Pindar's saying more than once, 'water is the best thing in the world,' a phrase which otherwise would seem unmeaning. But Pindar is too much tinctured with tradition and legend to have any clear conception of the philosopher's aims. Another saying of Thales is more on a level with Greek feeling, but also carries with it a meaning above the reach of ordinary Greek thought—namely, 'all things are full of gods.' If we take the two sayings together, they may be held to anticipate the fine expression of Hippocrates of Cos, that 'all occurrences are equally natural and equally divine.'

While Thales was propounding his great thought in Ionia, or even earlier, for the date is uncertain, Pythagoras in Magna Graecia was founding something between a church and a philosophical school. Insatiable of knowledge, he had mastered all the rudiments of science that were available in the world of his age. He too reduced the universe to one idea, that which all the sciences appeared to have in common, number, i.e. measure, proportion, harmony. He is believed to have made the great discovery that the notes of the lyre were proportionate to the length of the strings, thus laying the foundation of musical science. Not content with this, he made a grand and serious attempt to reform human society upon a basis of order which was cognate to his central idea. The influence which he exercised on his immediate contemporaries must have been intense. A native of Samos—whence the interest which Herodotus takes in him, as he does in all things Samian—he left his native city, perhaps in despair, and after much travelling in quest of knowledge settled at Croton, where he succeeded in founding what may be best characterised as a religious association based on scientific thought. Perhaps such an attempt could only have been grafted upon Dorian institutions (in which the notion of a *rule* to be observed was so prominent). It is very difficult to separate the real from the legendary in what is told concerning him. But it is evident that he realised, as no Greek before him had done, the sacredness of human society; and that he succeeded in binding his followers together in a life of strict asceticism through which they sought at once for truth and virtue. He is said to have been the first to call himself φιλόσοφος, a *lover* of wisdom or of truth, rather than σοφός, wise. Herodotus distinctly asserts that he formulated the doctrine of immortality and that some Orphic practices, such as the abjuring of woollen garments, were really due to him. In his teaching immortality was associated with metempsychosis (transmigration), to which Xenophanes testifies in saying of him (not without a touch of satire) ' Once when he heard the howling of a beaten hound he said to the man, Have done! for in that piteous crying I discern the voice of a friend.' Hence came an almost Brahmanical estimate of the sacredness of animal life. The school of Pythagoras for a time obtained such power that the triumph of Croton over Sybaris was mainly due to it. But human nature rebelled against the strain of ascetic control, and the Pythagoreans were driven out and scattered. The seeds they carried with them were not lost, however; and in Sicily and southern Italy the fruits were manifest : above all, in two main products, the comedies of Epicharmus (of Syracuse, a Coan by birth), veiling in homely satire a strain of philosophic wisdom, and in the life and teaching of Empedocles, who more than any Greek combined in one the characters of prophet, enthusiastic sage, and theurgic hierophant.

Xenophanes like Thales was a native of the Asiatic seaboard, although like Pythagoras he left his native city (Colophon), and settled at Elea or Velia in Magna Graecia. It is a little difficult to reconcile the image of him presented by his few remains with the account which Aristotle gives. In his verses he appears as a genial though unconventional person, enjoying social life while gibing openly at the beliefs of his countrymen. His criticism of anthropomorphism is well known : ' if lions had hands they would make gods like lions.' He likewise anticipates Plato's strictures on the morality of Olympus : ' Homer and Hesiod,' he says, ' attribute to the gods all that is most disreputable amongst mankind.' As Alcibiades says of Socrates, this negative aspect may be taken for the Silenus mask of the man, and it is not really incompatible with the serious positive aspect of his contemplation of which Aristotle speaks : ' He looked out upon the whole heaven, and affirmed that the one was God ' ; or with his own saying : ' One God in heaven and earth is above all, not like to mortals either in form or mind. He is all sight, all thought, all hearing.' That is a summit of abstraction beyond Thales, and one which had remarkable consequences in subsequent philosophy.

Heraclitus meanwhile, at Ephesus, following after Thales, Anaximander, and Anaximenes, whose speculations do not at present interest us, rose to a corresponding height of idealism even more fruitful in results, in taking fire for his element, and energy, if he is aright interpreted, for his idea. This principle, when afterwards brought into contrast with the Eleatic unity, came to be regarded as a mere affirmation of motion against rest. But the fragments of the philosopher himself are suggestive of a more comprehensive view, not fully enucleated (a thing impossible at that stage of positive knowledge), but containing in germ many of the principles which modern science has most clearly established, and which modern philosophy most approves. This will fall to be considered afterwards, but two points cannot here be passed over : the character of Heraclitus and his attitude towards popular religion. Through all his utterances there breathes not only the loftiest pride but the bitterest contempt, especially for his fellow citizens. He is a fit prototype of the great soul which Plato describes, that is born within a narrow community, and despising public affairs turns to philosophy. Even more remarkable than Xenophanes' rejection of human gods is Heraclitus' derision of bloody sacrifice—inasmuch as ritual had a firmer hold on the Greek mind than mythological representation. Heraclitus' influence was so penetrating, although he spoke above the heads of his contemporaries, that he deserves even more attention than the rest. In resolving all things into change and motion, he summed up the ruling tendencies of contemporary thought. The first effect of reflection was some vague consciousness of flux and change. And this, as we shall find, is one of the keynotes in Herodotus, the serenity of whose narrative does not prevent a tone of sadness from pervading his whole work. It is natural to suppose that he caught this from previous tradition. We cannot credit him with having invented the whole story of Croesus and Solon, or the conversations between Xerxes and Artabanus. He wrote down what he had heard or read, and it is now impossible to say how much is original in him. It is enough to have observed the affinity of sadness which links him to the 'weeping philosopher,' and to the strain of 'Ionian pessimism.'

The early philosophical schools acted and reacted on each other. It is a mistake to follow the ancients in separating them by hard and fast lines.

The problem had arisen in Ionia: 'What is the substance whereof all are made?' Men answered in a word : 'Water,' 'Air,' 'Infinity,' &c. Pythagoras answered, 'Number' ; Xenophanes 'One supreme whole'; Heraclitus 'Fire, for which all things are exchanged, according to a universal law : the world is eternal change, a cycle of progress, energy in order.' Parmenides cried, 'No change! That is an appearance only. It is. *One is*, and *all is one*. Growth and decay are exiled to non-entity.' By and by attempts were made to reconcile these jarring notes : number, measure, proportion, were stamped upon the infinite, form upon substance, mind upon the elements, creating order out of infinite confusion. But this intellectual movement attained to completeness only in the ripest growth of the philosophy of Plato.

CHAPTER VIII

PINDAR AND HERODOTUS

HELLENIC life and culture in the broadest sense during the early years of the fifth century B.C. are mirrored for us with considerable fulness, together with much that had preceded, in the Epinikian odes of Pindar, and in the histories of Herodotus. A few of Pindar's extant songs are perhaps earlier than the struggle with Persia, but the great bulk of those that remain are subsequent to that event, and, though not referring to it explicitly except here and there, their interest is heightened by the general sense of added glory and security which now pervaded the Grecian name. Though his allusions are marked with severe reserve, ' to tie up envy evermore enlarged,' the poet had evidently some feeling of what was involved in the heroic action of Sparta, Athens, and Aegina. He comprehends in his wide-sweeping glance, from an aristocratic and conservative point of view, all that was most significant in the political movements that were at work, from Thessaly to Cyrene. He thus enables us to gauge the level to which Greek thought and feeling rose at this time, elsewhere than in Athens. In poetising men's beliefs, his genius sublimates them into a vehicle for consolation or admonition. The fluidity of Greek mythology and legend makes this possible without any consciousness of violent or abrupt modification. Pindar cannot be fully understood without taking into account the mystical and also the philosophic movements briefly touched in the preceding chapter. We note in him therefore a phase of feeling and reflection on the highest themes, in which an incipient rationalism is consistent with the heartiest faith and reverence.

Pindar was a Theban, and although when occasion calls for it he duly recognises the great achievements in which Thebes was prevented by her rulers from taking part, it is not without surprise that on a survey of his odes we find so little reference either to Athens or Sparta. The victory of Megacles celebrated in the sixth Pythian was gained in the year of the battle of Marathon, and the chief historical allusion in it is to the renewal of the temple at Delphi by the Alcmaeonidae. The second Nemean is in honour of Timodemus, whose fathers came from Salamis, and the only trace of the battle is that Athens is spoken of as 'great.' Even here Marathon seems to be known to Pindar chiefly as a place where annual games were held.

In selecting Pindar and Herodotus as representing the transition period of which the pivot was the Persian war, we are the more fortunate in that Pindar on the whole reflects the conservative, Herodotus the progressive spirit of the time. Both are pan-Hellenic, and the period to which they belong was one in which the Hellenic name came nearer than before or afterwards to harmonious unity. But broadly speaking Pindar is Achaean and Dorian, or rather simply Greek, while Herodotus is virtually an Ionian and a frank admirer of Athens. Pindar also appreciates the great deeds of Athens, but holds them in the balance with those of Pausanias and of Theron ; Herodotus too is ready to speak of the victory at Plataea as the fairest which any general ever won, but he does not conceal his hearty friendship for the Athenian people, nor the value which he sets on the liberty which they enjoyed. In reading Pindar, as has often been observed, we breathe an aristocratic atmosphere, and are in constant intercourse with the scions of great houses in whom the blood of gods still flows. The men who are celebrated in the Epinikian odes are mostly descendants either of Herakles, or of Cadmus through the Aegeidae, or of Apollo. The Aeolian and Lydian elements in his music tend to soften a little his Dorian exclusiveness and austerity, but the loftiness of his air throughout has a twofold source, the pride of genius, and the pride of race. That is his attitude towards the world at large, but the stores of legend and of earlier mythology, which it had been his cue to master, are handled by him not only with unwavering reverence but with a freedom inspired by ruling ideas, drawn partly from a wide experience and partly from the genius of Greek thought, which had now reached an advanced stage of reflection.

The singer is closely associated with great families and with the priesthood; yet his mind is not made rigid or conventional as one might expect. The expansiveness of the Greek intellect asserts itself afresh, and the spirit of the poet moves along a higher plane than that of the traditions which afford the material for his art. He shrinks from attributing to the gods any motive that in human life would involve the charge of meanness. Not Hera but Themis is, in his mythology, the first bride of Zeus and mother of the Hours, because Themis is the goddess of law and order, and supreme over the Dorian states. It is observable that while the gods, in his poetry, retain all the fulness of individual life, the generalised use of θεός for a divine being occurs in him more frequently than heretofore. The lives of heroes, including Herakles, are celebrated in such a way as to insinuate some lesson suitable to the character and circumstances of the person for whom the ode is written, and towards whom the poet bears himself with the dignity of a friendly monitor, as well as with the most penetrative and delicate sympathy. Moderation is constantly inculcated. Patience and hope, quietness and confidence, fear of the gods, the avoidance of envy even while contemning it, the changefulness of life, in which a single achievement may compensate for much labour and trial, are other thoughts repeatedly suggested. ' Excellence' (ἀρετή) is a word of constant recurrence, and in Pindar may be generally rendered ' splendid achievement.' Intrinsic worth, rather than meritorious service, is the leading thought. The aim continually set before the athlete is that of equalling or surpassing the excellence of his sires. Sometimes it is that of restoring the reputation of a house, whose fame has for a while been silent.

That the Olympic crown was a reward of bodily exercise,

which according to Christian teaching ' profiteth little,' is not the whole account of the matter. What Pindar values is the energy, the perseverance, the training in endurance and in courage, which in warlike times was really the height of virtue. He also recognises that success is not always given to the strong or swift, that fortune conquers where strength fails. This is only a fresh instance of the limitation of the human lot. Two leading thoughts of frequent recurrence are law (νόμος) and time. The famous passage quoted by Herodotus, ' νόμος the king of all,' does not stand alone. But in Pindar's view this great conception was associated with Dorian (not necessarily Spartan) institutions. The notion of time is more abstract, and even more characteristic of Pindar's thought. Time is the chief of the immortals (Fragment 4). It is he who alone realises the decrees of fate. There is a striking coincidence here between Pindar and Milton, at least in one of his moods, and the parallel of expression is so close that it seems difficult to resist the inference, very interesting if true, that our great poet read Pindar at the age of twenty-two. The words in the seventh sonnet on his twenty-third birthday—

> Yet be it less or more, or soon or slow,
> It shall be still in strictest measure even,
> To that same lot however mean or high
> Toward which time leads me, and the will of heaven—

are a close if somewhat Christian rendering of the sixty-seventh line of the fourth Nemean, ' but to me whatsoever excellence sovran destiny gave, well know I that time in moving onward shall accomplish that as decreed.'

The Epinikian odes are steeped with the spirit of the religion of Zeus and of Apollo. Athena, if less often present, is conspicuously recognised. The conquest of the Giants, the suppression of Typhon, the slaying of the serpent Python, illustrate the supremacy of the divine order over rebellious powers. The release of the Titans, on the other hand, is an example of the clemency of Zeus held up for imitation by kings. But there are significant references to other worships, which show the range of the poet's interest, and in the case of the Great Mother, perhaps, betray a personal feeling. It is observable that he combines an adhesion to orgiastic rites with his austerity, and that his worship of Apollo does not exclude an allusion to Ammonian Zeus when he is celebrating a Cyrenaic victor. He is also ready to personify attributes, such as the goddess of Tranquillity, or 'Memory with the bright frontlet,' or Mercy the divine ; the mythopoeic spirit was still active in him. The religion of the Graces, whose ancient worship at the Minyan Orchomenos under the names of Aglaia, Euphrosyne, and Thalia is the main theme of the fourteenth Olympian, is continually present to the mind of the poet. Originally nature goddesses of springtime, they had become the embodiment of all that cheers and soothes the lot of men—associated with all genial powers, above all with the power of song. Professor Bury well observes : ' The poems of Pindar " burn bright," to use an expression of his own, with the presence of the Graces. Χάρις may sometimes be translated *the spirit of art*, but the sphere of the Charites was wider and cannot be better defined than Pindar has defined it himself :

σὺν ὔμμιν
τὰ τερπνά τε καὶ γλυκέα
ἀνατέλλεται πάντα βροτοῖς,
κεἰ σοφός, εἰ καλός, εἴ τις ἀγλαὸς ἀνήρ.

("On you depends the rise of all things pleasing and delightful for mortals, if any man be wise, if any noble, if any brilliant in renown.")

It was natural that they should be sovran ladies in a world of art, which was conversant mainly with "the delightful things in Hellas," and . . . in all his epinician hymns, except three . . . of very small compass, Pindar either mentions the Graces or alludes to their influence.' Χάρις in Pindar might often be translated in Tennysonian language ' The Gleam.'

In speaking of the altar of Zeus Hellenios in Aegina the poet simply preserves the traditional title of the father of the Dorian race and of the Aeacidae. The ode in which this title of Zeus occurs was written at all events before the battle of Salamis, to commemorate the victory in the boys' Pancratium of Pytheas, a namesake of him who received so many wounds at Artemisium. The same victory of the boy Pytheas was celebrated by Bacchylides with a similar allusion to his trainer, the Athenian Menander. But the two odes in which the word 'Pan-Hellenes' occurs are probably subsequent to the Persian war.

The growth of heroic legend may of course be largely illustrated from Pindar. We may select as an example the development of the fable concerning Castor and Pollux. In the third Iliad, where Helen looks in vain for them on the field of Troy, they are both already hidden beneath boon earth. In the Odyssey, they have a partial immortality which they share on alternate days. In Pindar we have this beautiful tale, that although twins they were one of mortal and one of immortal birth, and that when Pollux was wounded to the death, Castor prayed to Zeus for him. The Father granted him either to enjoy his immortality, or to share it with his mortal brother, and he chose the latter. An earlier version of the legend appears in the eleventh Pythian, v. 63. Here they still live and die on alternate days, while in later allusions six months is the period alternately assigned to each ; and in Euripides the brothers of Helen are identified with the constellation of the Twins.

Pindar's pan-Hellenic spirit does not prevent him from showing personal preference ; his love for Thebes and pride in her appear continually. It must be remembered that he was bound to please the Hellenes generally—those also who had joined the Mede, and that his Aeginetan friends, who by the consent of Hellas had won the prize of bravery at Salamis, had not long since been openly hostile to Athens. Yet it is strange that he should so little have anticipated the full significance of the repulse of Persia or the unique position which it secured for the Athenians. Once indeed, in praising the Aeginetan Cleander, he expresses the relief to all Hellas when the impending danger had passed away ; and in celebrating another Aeginetan, Phylakidas, the brother of Pytheas, he refers briefly to the part taken by Aegina in the battle of Salamis. 'Even but now in war might

Aias' city Salamis bear witness to her deliverance by Aegina's seamen and the destroying tempest of Zeus, when death came thick as hail on the unnumbered hosts. Yet let no boast be heard. Zeus ordereth this or that.' And in the dithyramb of uncertain date, of which two fragments remain, composed for performance in the Athenian Agora, he celebrates the 'violet-crowned city' as the prop of Hellas, for which he was rewarded by the Athenians, and is said to have been fined by his own countrymen. This tradition rather confirms what has just been said, in accounting for the scant praise of Athens in his Epinikian odes. Almost the only encomium of her which occurs in them is that a good trainer of athletes, such as Menander was, may be expected to come from Athens. In the praise of the Athenian Megakles, we seem to perceive some suspicion or dislike of the forward liberal movement which threatened to place the great families at a disadvantage. 'I agree with this, that envy is the requital of fair deeds. They say, however, that prosperity is then more stable when it is not unmixed.' It can hardly be accidental that the man whose victory called forth this strain was an Alkmaeonid, and that in speaking of him the poet expressly refers to the merit of that family in having renewed Apollo's temple.

Nor can the fact be overlooked that the lover of the Dorians and their order (εὐνομία) is not known to have celebrated any Spartan victor, and that while acknowledging the achievements of Lacedaemon, and reverencing her sanctities (or rather those of Amyclae and Therapna), he hints once not obscurely that the Spartan Heracleidae forgot the rock whence they were hewn. His own family pride, as one of the Aegeidae, repeatedly shows itself, and through another line he claims affinity with Argos; thus the close relationship between Thebes and Aegina, as well as the pure Dorian stock that ruled that island, may help to account for the large proportion of Aeginetan lays. The Thessalian Aleuadae were his first employers (cp. Bacchylides, Ode xiv.), and in spite of drawbacks which are clearly felt, he heartily admires the splendour of his patron Hiero. But his friendship for Theron of Agrigentum has less of reserve, and one is bound to recognise the reality of the good side of the tyrant's character which is put forward by the poet, while the deeds of violence are suppressed in silence. He seems equally ready to praise (when paid for it) both tyrants, though they were ready to fly at one another's throats. He is at home in Rhodes, and hardly less so in Cyrene, although here again his encomium is dashed with notes of warning. His love of nobleness and of all things high and great, while held within religious limits of moderation, is commensurate with his scorn for what is base, especially of the envy which proves an empty mind.

Pindar's pride of birth appears also in his contempt for excellence that is merely acquired. Native genius, not learning, is what he values, yet in the eighth Pythian, which some think his latest ode, he expresses a well-considered recognition of the value of training, which may be set against some extravagant utterances on the other side. It must be acknowledged, however, that in some respects he does not rise above the level of his age and class. Experience had not yet taught the value of chastity as such, or the accumulated misery which the breach of it involves. The lesson which Plato only learnt in age was not taught by Pindar; it is with a strange feeling that one turns from the first Pythian to the fragments of the scolion written for Xenophon of Corinth, who had set up a house of fifty girls in fulfilment of a vow, presumably to Aphrodite. Greek euphemism could hardly go further than in the line ' In all that is pretty there is compulsion ' ; ignoring the fact that the ' necessity ' (ἀνάγκη) here is but organised brutality (ὕβρις). Well might the poet wonder what the Lords of the Isthmus would say of him. Some lines addressed to the young Theoxenus of Tenedos also prove that Pindar was not exempt from the special taint which by this time had become established in the social life of Hellas. In both these respects he has fallen far below Homer.

We turn gladly from these lapses to the passages in which, almost for the first time in Greek literature, there is expressed the hope of a blessed immortality. In the

Epinikian odes, he imagines the dead ancestors as in some way affected by the successes and the glories of their descendants. In the odes of lamentation which were written for the consolation of persons suffering from recent loss, he sang more distinctly of a happy life to be. The hope, as in Plato, is associated with a doctrine of transmigration (see Fragment 4), and is also connected with the value attached to the Eleusinian mysteries (Fragment 7). But the most significant passage on this subject is the second Olympian, in which he appears to have in mind that Theron, who was afflicted with a lingering and fatal disease, must be looking forward, like Cephalus in Plato, to the life beyond the grave :—

' The deed once done must have its issue, be it right or wrong. Not even time can uncreate it, time who fathers all things. Yet god-given success may bring with it forgetfulness of what is past. Sorrow dies hard, but yields to the prevailing power of present joy, when destiny lifts up the life and sends prosperity. . . . When one hath gained the victory for which he strove, ill thoughts relax their hold. Wealth adorned with excellent endeavour brings opportunity for divers aims, suggesting eager yearnings for high enterprise ; a conspicuous luminary, enlightening the path without fail. Only let him who hath it be aware of what ensues, that when men die their thoughts on earth shall perish, and forthwith all earthly debts are paid ; but in the underworld there is a judge, who sums the account of all the sins committed in this realm of Zeus ; and from that dire sentence there is no reprieve.[1] But for the good remains a life exempt from toil, where equally by day and equally by night for evermore the sunlight cheers them : not harassing the stubborn glebe with stalwart arms, nor ploughing the wide sea to eke out a scanty livelihood ; but companioned by deities of high renown, who delighted in their faithfulness on

---

[1] Cp. *Hamlet* iii. 3 :

> There is no shuffling, there the action lies
> In his true nature ; and we ourselves compelled,
> Even to the teeth and forehead of our faults,
> To give in evidence.

N

earth, they share in an existence free from tears. The others are yoked to torment too terrible to see.

'Now all whose constancy hath thrice in either world endured to keep the soul entirely apart from wrongdoing, ascend by the way Zeus wendeth to the high place of Cronos; where breezes from the ocean stream are ever blowing round about the islands of the blest; and flowers all-golden glow, some blossoming on stately trees that hold the ground, others nourished by the living waters : with chaplets and festoons whereof they enwreathe their arms.

'Even so determineth the righteous doom of Rhadamanthys, whom father Cronos ever keeps beside him on the judgment seat, Cronos, whom Rhea, enthroned above the world, still owneth for her husband. Peleus and Cadmus too are conspicuous thereamong, and thither too the mother of Achilles brought him, when she had prevailed upon the heart of Zeus. 'Twas he that o'erthrew Hector, Troy's resistless unsubduable stay : 'twas he gave Cycnus to his death, and Eôs' Aethiopian son.'

It remains to notice the advance in ethical reflection which is marked in Pindar, and the deficiencies which are equally marked. The solidarity of the family awakens his keenest sympathies; the inheritance of excellence in a household is prized above everything; the fathers are blessed in the sons. The poet's power of entering sympathetically into the varied circumstances of the men of noble birth who employed him, and giving them spiritual counsel suited to their truest need, is, ethically speaking, the most interesting aspect of his work. Order is the preserver of states, especially when combined with hospitality (θέμις σώτειρα Διὸς ξενίου), and faction is their destruction. Opportunity (καιρός) is another favourite idea : there is a time for speech and a time for silence ; often the word left unspoken hath the greater honour. Pindar himself has but a moderate fortune, although he tells us that he has funds deposited in the temple of a neighbouring hero Alcmaeon ; but with all his admiration of personal excellence, he is by no means insensible to the glamour of wealth and power where these are accompanied with liberality in spending and energy in use. In praising Hiero ('Olymp.' i.) he frankly says that kingship is the highest thing : so far is he from sharing the hatred of tyrants as such, which Athens felt and Sparta professed. Gold, he says, the child of Zeus, gladdens the heart of man. His praise of Theia, the goddess of the golden gleam, is not purely symbolical, nor, as some have thought, merely associated with the gilding of the Olympian crown. Yet he would not have men trust in riches, or be the slaves of fortune. ' Truth ' is often on his lips, but he acknowledges that beauty (χάρις) may sometimes obliterate truth ; what he most deprecates is the indolence that shrinks from enterprise. Time, as before observed, is a dominant idea. 'The days that follow are the truest witnesses; and time befriends the righteous.' His morality is still merged in opinion and convention, yet he has several noble maxims in accord with Aeschylus : ' It irks me not to suffer, where all are to suffer with me,' he says when overawed by the eclipse of the sun. ' The road of virtue is direct and leads to a good end.' ' War is sweet to the inexperienced ' (compare Thucydides) ; yet he disdains not to say that ' stolen waters are sweet.'

While sympathising deeply with his aristocratic friends and employers, he has none of that pure human feeling for the people which Aeschylus shows, and but little tenderness for man as man.

'Euphemia' is one of his chief notes, and is apt to conceal from inattentive readers the deep tone of melancholy which often prevails in him. Thus in praising the Pelopidae, he appears as ignorant of the horrors of that house as if he had never heard of Atreus or Thyestes. Yet the tale of Pelops' line must have been well known to him, and he knew more than he cared to tell of the fall of Polynices and the fatal son of Laius, to whom he traced his stock. His strange silences are partly due to the fear of awakening envy.

Pindar is aware of Scythian customs and of some Egyptian rites to which he refers with scorn (fr. inc. 64 ; cp. Herodt. ii. 46).

Not Sparta but Argos in Pindar is spoken of as a lover

of brevity. Pindar's Achaean pride is ultra-Dorian. The chief interest of Pindar for us lies in his comprehensive survey of the Hellenic world, from Rhodes and Tenedos to Agrigentum, Cumae, and Cyrene. We thus gain a glimpse of the condition of greater Hellas before Greek life and culture drew closely about Athens as its centre.

Herodotus like Pindar has a keen interest in all things Hellenic, but he enters with more of sympathy into the forward movement, of which Athens was the head and front. There is hardly a page of his history that does not testify to the reality and power of religion amongst the Greeks of his time. To collect into one view the more striking aspects of the subject, it will be well to treat separately (1) of his representations of contemporary belief, and (2) of the indications which he gives of his own thoughts on the subject of religion.

1. In his far-reaching survey of the world surrounding him, he takes notice of many religious customs amongst barbarians also. We may begin with these.

There is the Scythian tribe, who shoot their arrows upwards into the sky as a menace to their god when he displeases them by too much or too little rain. There are the Atarantes in Libya, who curse the mid-day sun. There are the Psylli, who made a warlike expedition against the south wind when he brought famine on them, and who perished in the desert. Then there are the Carians, who repented of having admitted some foreign worship, and marched in armed array to the border of their land, declaring that they thus expelled the foreign gods. Or to turn to more humane features of non-Hellenic rites, he describes how the Persians appeased the river Strymon by sinking white horses in his stream; how Boges the Persian rather than fall into the hands of men burned himself and his whole family on the pyre ; how the outrage done by Xerxes to the corpse of Leonidas was inconsistent with the Persian habit of admiring bravery in an enemy, of which the treatment of Pytheas, the son of Ischenoös, when taken captive off Arte-misium, is a striking proof. We read, moreover, how the

Nasamônes worshipped their ancestors only; and how the Atlantes abstained from flesh and saw no dreams. An illustration by contrast of ordinary Greek beliefs is supplied by the Getae, who claimed immortality, and the Trausi, who wept at every birth, and rejoiced at funerals; and again, by the Thracian tribe whose widows joined their husbands on the funeral pyre.

The tendency of Herodotus, and of the Greeks generally, to identify the gods of other nations with their own appears most prominently in his account of the religion of Egypt. This should make one cautious in accepting such statements, however they are to be interpreted, as that the Thracian kings considered themselves children of Hermes, or that the worship of Athena was indigenous in the neighbourhood of Barca. That the Cyrenaeans, although Greeks, revered the Egyptian goddess Isis may, on the other hand, be accepted as a fact, and this cult, as well as that of Zeus Ammon, is known to have early found its way into central Hellas. In the time of Callimachus it still flourished at Cyrene. *En revanche* it appears that the Lydians and Persians also paid respect to some of the Greek deities in whose wisdom and power they had been led to believe. We know that the Egyptian king Necho sent offerings to Apollo at Branchidae near Miletus, and that Amasis gave presents to the god of Delphi. These instances and others that might be adduced raise the whole question of the contact or contamination of religions, which will be more conveniently treated of by and by. They are mentioned here merely to illustrate the wide range of the historian's survey.

To come now to purely Hellenic worships, Herodotus supplies many illustrations of characteristic peculiarities of Greek faith and Greek superstition.

Take first, as an evidence of religious feeling allied to superstition, the power which sacred persons exercised: note, for instance, the ascendency gained by Telines at Gela in Sicily, solely through his possessing the sacred things of Demeter and Persephone, and coming amongst a people who had them not. Other examples are afforded by the prayer of the Athenians to the north wind, who had married their sister Orithyia, to come and help them, which he did effectually at Artemisium ; whereupon they raised to him the temple near the Ilissus, not far from the place where Socrates and Phaedrus afterwards conversed ; the cruelty of Periander to the women of Corinth, to which he is moved by a gloomy superstition about the dead ; the addition of the name Sôtêr, saviour, to Poseidon, after the storm before Artemisium ; the conception of the power of Zeus implied in the saying that when minded to destroy the Greeks he need not have appeared as a Persian monarch, bringing millions behind him, since his own power would have sufficed; the dread which the Greeks felt of the burning of their temples, showing the reality of their belief in the divine presences, a belief more clearly evinced by the minority of the Athenians, who sought shelter on the Acropolis behind their wooden wall; the worship of Artachaeus, the Persian, at Acanthus, because he was more than seven feet high.   The intense love of country and fatherland, which lay so near the heart of every Greek, displays itself sometimes in strange forms, as for instance in Hippias plotting for his return to Athens, where the people execrated him : an attitude which occurs repeatedly in subsequent history.   In this connection it is instructive to observe the matter of fact way in which Herodotus employs the data of poetic legend and mythology, as in his version of the stories of Medea, Io, and Europa, in the opening of his history, and numberless other statements which, without the aid of the earlier literature, it would have been impossible to translate into the imaginative form which was really essential to them.   This feature of his style may be described as a *naïve* and superficial rationalism.

2. Herodotus not only abounds with indications of contemporary religious conceptions, but in many parts of his work conveys, not obscurely, his own thought and feeling about sacred things.   Indeed the personal element in him is larger than might be inferred from the objectivity of presentment, which makes his history one of the masterpieces of Greek art.   For example, if the places in which Samos and

the Samians are referred to were collected in one view, it could not fail to be perceived that the author's own feelings had been engaged in the incidents which he records. So also a special interest is betrayed in his references to Sybaris and Croton, since these towns had been supplanted by the colony of Thurii in which he had joined. But it is not to be assumed that the ethical and religious sentiments which dominate the history were peculiar to him; they rather bear witness to the growth of a new stratum of reflection on things divine and human, which may have been due partly to the indirect influence of early philosophers, especially the Heraclitean philosophy of change, but which also has a value and interest of its own.

The chief vehicles of these newer conceptions are the maxim and the apologue. The simple genuine wisdom of the time appears in sayings obviously proverbial, which are thickly scattered throughout the work (see esp. iii. 53). Solon as a poet and a statesman had spoken earnestly of Justice as the daughter of Zeus. Herodotus makes him talk rather as a pessimistic philosopher. It is not the real Solon, but Herodotus for him, who speaks of the malignity of the divine nature. The apologue, or story with a moral, is exemplified in such passages as the elaborate account of Solon's meeting with Croesus, or of the ring of Polycrates, or again more briefly in the story of Glaucus and the Delphic oracle (vi. 86 § 12 ff.), and of Artabanus and Xerxes (vii. 46). The most remarkable change in the mode of conceiving the divine working is the generalised use of the words for god (as in Pindar) and deity. The latter expression (τὸ θεῖον) is found in Herodotus for the first time. He seems to have attached more reality to such abstract names as τὸ θεῖον or τὸ δαιμόνιον than to individual personalities, such as Apollo or Hera. Thus when Cleomenes goes within the temple of Hera at Argos, the portent which he sees there is said to indicate the meaning of the god (θεοῦ), the sex of Hera being neglected as unimportant.

The use of the word deity or divinity gives distinct evidence of a new stage having been reached in the process of abstraction, or in other words the growth of thought and the decline of polytheism. It has been said that this neuter abstract is a poor exchange for the rich variety of the Homeric Olympus. It may be so for those who cherish Wordsworth's hankering after a 'creed outworn.' Others may see in it, on the contrary, a great and significant advance towards a clearer and worthier conception of divine action. But there remains much confusion as to the attributes of the being who is thus conceived. Everything extraordinary and unaccountable is referred immediately to the divine working, and human interference with natural phenomena is regarded with superstitious dread. To make a channel through the isthmus and to bridge the Hellespont are alike impious undertakings. On the other hand some general provisions of nature which tend to the preservation of life are referred to divine forethought or providence almost in the spirit of Socratic teleology. But in regard to human life the ruling thought is that of the divine envy or malignity, which is exemplified in the countless miseries of mankind and the insecurity of all good fortune.

The conception of divine government has hardly risen beyond the notion of action and reaction. God will not suffer human beings to exalt themselves, and to provoke him by success. In this there is a continuation of the Ionian pessimism already spoken of, and a tinge perhaps of Heraclitean philosophy. But there is also a germ of ethical reflection, though only partially developed. 'A great Nemesis came upon Croesus, because he thought himself the happiest of men.' Here thought is in transition from the danger of prosperity to the sinfulness of pride. What at first seemed to be malignity is now rather viewed as just severity. Nemesis thus passes over into retribution ($\tau i\sigma\iota s$), a conception which often recurs. The fate of Oroetes, the Persian, whom Darius put to death for many misdeeds, is regarded by the historian as an act of divine retribution for the cruel death of Polycrates, the tyrant of Samos, years before. And similar to this is the story of the wrath of Talthybius, the herald, which took effect in the third generation on the Spartan family who were responsible for the death of the Persian heralds. This Herodotus speaks of as 'the most divine event' of his time (Herod. vii. 137). Some applications of this idea of retribution are quaint enough, as in the account in book ii. of the manner of the birth of snakes, where the baby snake, like another Orestes, avenges his father on his mother. But in telling the tale of Pheretime, the historian himself observes that the extreme of vengeance too provokes the gods, and in this he rises above the general level of his history, much as Iliad xxiv. (the ransoming of Hector) goes beyond the morality of the rest of the poem.

Passing from the divine into the human sphere we find in Herodotus what was conspicuously absent from the Homeric poems, the idea of Nomos,—law and custom in one. The historian gives it as his own decided opinion, that while the customs of different nations are diverse and contradictory, the sacredness of custom ought to be respected everywhere. This saying exemplifies a singular phase of thought. We can see why each people may be expected to revere the customs of their ancestors ; we can see why at a later time the difference of customs and laws led to scepticism as to the existence of any universal principles of law ; and again, why this doubt should have induced serious minds to attempt the elaboration of universal principles. But the position of Herodotus is different from all these. He lays stress upon the fact that law and custom in different countries differ irreconcileably ; but the inference which he draws is the predominance of law and custom as such, and to this he attributes a divine sanction (iii. 38).

The distinction between Nomos and Themis (the Homeric counterpart) turns partly on the more abstract nature of the conception and partly on the growing idea of the State, to which a powerful impulse had been given by Dorian and other legislative institutions (Pindar's εὐνομία). Themis in the singular is little more than established habit or the custom accepted by mankind generally ; and in the plural the same word, as Sir H. Maine has pointed out in his book on 'Ancient Law,' is used to signify the particular judgments, decrees, or commandments of the king. But before the commencement of the fifth century the idea of law as an independent authority, or dependent only on the word of the lawgiver, had acquired all the constraining force of an ideal.

The idea of destiny in Herodotus is already more fully developed than in the Homeric poems, where it is hardly distinguishable from the will or nod of Zeus, as the supreme god. Apollo answers the expostulation of Croesus by saying that even a god cannot prevent the fulfilment of destiny, though he may defer it by his influence for a time. In this and other ways the historian reflects the stage of Greek culture which is presupposed in tragedy and lies behind it. The ideas of fate and Nemesis, for example, which are so pervading in Herodotus, and the maxim that none can be called happy before he dies, are present in almost every tragic fable. But in handling them the tragic poet is inspired by other thoughts than those of Ionian culture, and especially by the consciousness of a great life which had been realised by the Athenian community. Xerxes, in Herodotus, is led onwards by a spiteful deity; in Aeschylus it is the wilfulness of Xerxes himself which precipitates before its time the doom or weird which Darius had foreknown. The ethical advance which this implies is manifest.

Some separate points may be noticed. The sacredness of the person of heralds is a genuine feeling (see vii. 133 ff.). Quite genuine also is Herodotus' belief in the essential service that the Delphians had done to Hellas in reporting to them the Pythian oracle bidding them pray to the winds; though he appears sceptical upon the subject of the Magian prayers in answer to which ('or perhaps of its own accord') the storm desisted after blowing for two days. The union in the same person of an almost mystical reverence with intellectual doubt affords a curious subject for reflection, and has perhaps been never more clearly exemplified than in Herodotus. Here and there he distinctly anticipates later philosophy, as in the discussion about forms of government, where he recognises the difficulty of finding a monarch free from envy, though if he could be found that would be best of all; or where, as already remarked (iii. 108), he discourses of the wise arrangements of the author of nature. Yet he is continually dwelling on the divinely caused fatality which prompts human folly, and appears to sympathise with the Spartans when they broke from their friendship for the Pisistratidae, in obedience to a spurious oracle, 'for they preferred divine to human obligations'; and he is deeply impressed with the warning which the Chians had had before the onslaught of their successive calamities. The earthquake at Delos also is regarded by him as a divine premonition of woes to come.

A curious indication of Herodotus' conception of religion as a human growth with some underlying divine reality is afforded by his remark that the attribution of the ravine of Tempe to the action of Poseidon was reasonable on the part of those who regarded Poseidon as the causer of earthquakes. He thinks of the Greek gods as real beings, and yet conceives of a time when either they were not or had not yet been discovered or invented. We may observe also what may be called the scientific curiosity of Herodotus (so vainly exercised about the sources of the Nile) ; as when he wonders why the lions in Thrace should have attacked the camels, a creature whom they had never seen, apparently suggesting some pre-established harmony or rather discord, and perhaps implying that the race of lions came originally from a country where there were camels.

Something should be also said of the pan-Hellenic patriotism of Herodotus. He suppresses many names, but, no doubt at the risk of odium, he deliberately names various persons who had betrayed the cause of Hellas, including the Pythian priestess Perialla, who had been bribed to give a false oracle. In other cases he mentions individuals who have deserved universal commendation, as Callias, the son of Hipponicus, whom he praises for his munificence. He also shows large consideration and indulgence for some of those who had failed in the crisis of Greek independence ; and in this he does not seem to be moved by partiality, but by equity ; for example, in speaking of the odium which the Argives had incurred by their conduct at the time of the Persian war, he dwells upon the calamities which had exhausted them and on the difficulty of their position, and says that if every Greek state would only consider its own shortcomings, Argos would not be found to have behaved the worst; to which he adds the moral, that few men would like to take upon them other men's evils in exchange for their own.

The large and comprehensive outlook of Herodotus may suggest some further observations on what I have already called the 'contamination' of worships; although in reverting to this subject some awkward repetition is unavoidable. The theory of Tiele that the growth of the higher religions has been promoted by contact and assimilation is peculiarly fruitful in its application to Hellenic religion, or rather might be expected to prove so, if our knowledge of the early history were not still so shadowy. This does not mean that the Greeks borrowed their religion from others. The effect of contact is to call forth inherent powers, and assimilation, in the only sense which makes for development, is the result of an inward vital principle acting on materials supplied from without. Each race has its special character, but this is only brought out through intercourse with other races, and the result is most apparent in those who have contributed most to the sum of human culture. The native force and vivacity of the Greek spirit, of which the lyric poetry of the islands perhaps affords the strongest proof, transmuted what it received, not only by surrounding it with the atmosphere of beauty, but through the presence of a deeper aspiration and a loftier ideal.

The Phoenicians were a Semitic people, who brought some things from their earlier home in Mesopotamia, and derived others from their intercourse with the Egyptians. The result was a crude syncretism which they cannot fail to have communicated to the races on the Mediterranean shores, whom they visited in their commercial intercourse. That they were long settled at Cyprus, on the coasts of Crete, in Thasos, at various points in Sicily, at Gades, and of course at Carthage, cannot reasonably be doubted; although their scattered empire shrank and faded, from the time when the

Assyrians threatened the independence of Tyre. Nor is there any sufficient ground for questioning the constant tradition of the Greeks, that the Cadmeians, who long held the citadel of Thebes, and checked the growing power of Orchomenos, were of Phoenician origin. If that be admitted, it points the way to a further speculation. The way from Thebes to Delphi is not far, and an early occupation by Phoenician priests and prophets of that mountain height, perhaps already the seat of an earlier religion, is, to say the least, not inconceivable. The altar of Poseidon on Onchestus appears to have been of great antiquity, and his attributes both there and at Corinth have been thought to betray indications of Phoenician influence. The Ismenian Apollo may possibly be not inferior in antiquity to the 'Far-darter' of Pytho, and the Herakles of Thebes may have been worshipped before his derivation from the line of Perseus had been imagined. The island supremacy of Minos, confirmed by recent discoveries, is associated with the myth of Europa, and Europa, in the belief of Herodotus, was a princess of Tyre. There are traces of an early association between Crete and Delphi. If Delphi was at any time a Phoenician shrine it would naturally be visited by Phoenicians from Crete. There was a tomb of Dionysus at Delphi, and a tomb of the Idaean Zeus was long an object of reverence in Cretan worship. Other legends, such as that of Dionysus and Ariadne, have an oriental colouring. The goddess whom Herodotus identifies with Aphrodite Urania had a temple at Askalon, as well as at Paphos, and in Cythera off the Laconian coast, also at Côlias on the shore of Attica. The armed Aphrodite in the Peloponnese, the Despoina of Lycosura, and the Athena Onka at Thebes had all some attributes of an Oriental divinity. The worship of 'Urania' was always liable to sink to the level of the Syrian ship-master, although the higher minds in Greece refined about her as the inspirer of a spiritual love. Castor and Polydeuces, specially worshipped in Laconia, have in one aspect a family resemblance to the Pataïci of the Phoenician mariners, and their sister Helen has some attributes of Aphrodite. Tyre was visited by the historian with the special object of examining the temple of Herakles there, which he believed to be the oldest in the world, and that of Thasos, in the neighbourhood of the Phoenician gold-diggings, appeared to him to have been founded on the same model.

When the land afterwards called Boeotia was overrun by its mountain conquerors, there followed an exodus, at once of the Minyae from Orchomenos, and of the Cadmeians from Thebes. And the Aegeidae to whom Pindar traced his descent boasted of a Cadmeian, that is to say a Phoenician origin. The island of Thera, according to Herodotus, had in yet earlier days been colonised by a kinsman of Cadmus, and from Thera went forth the expedition which colonised Cyrene, and the history of that settlement bears manifest traces of a more than Greek intensity of passionate resolve. Thales was originally a Cadmeian, that is, as Herodotus expressly says, a Phoenician. Once more, in the Eleusinian mysteries there were associated with the Eumolpidae in the performance of the most sacred rites the family of Gephyreans, immigrants from Eretria or Tanagra, but tracing their origin to a Cadmeian stock. Herodotus says that they had brought with them a peculiar worship of Demeter Achaia, not the Achaean Demeter, but that mother of sorrows of whom the sculptor of the Cnidian goddess has preserved a most impressive type. It is rather strange that the historian speaks of this as a particular or family cult, while he is fully aware of the universal sacredness to all Athenian hearts of the mystic song of Iacchus. Had the worships not yet been amalgamated, or is he drawing his information from diverse sources? In either case he seems to point to the once independent existence of rituals which were finally assimilated. He also tells us that the assassins of Hipparchus—Harmodius and Aristogiton, the patron saints of Athenian liberty—were Gephyreans. And in the intense resentment for a personal affront, to which that memorable act was due, is there not perceptible something of a Semitic strain? Herodotus tells us, in his matter of fact way, that Io was carried to Egypt by Phoenicians. The resemblance of the horned maiden to the Egyptian Hathor has often been observed (it was afterwards accentuated by Callimachus), and in the birth of Epaphus there is an obvious reminiscence of Apis, the incarnation of Ptah. The question is, whether this myth, which had approached completeness by the end of the sixth century, can have grown up in the interval which separates that epoch from the foundation of Naukratis. If that is impossible, it would seem necessary to suppose a still earlier contact, of a closer kind than could come through the Phoenicians, between Argolic and Egyptian religion. This, however, for reasons given elsewhere, I cannot but regard as improbable. That the ‘ Orphic ’ influence, which became so powerful about the opening of the fifth century, had a root in some imperfect knowledge of Egyptian rites is clearly manifest. The dismemberment of Phanes by the Titans, his re-birth as Dionysus Zagreus, and other features of that new mythology bear too close an analogy to Egypt to be accounted for by accidental coincidence. The avoidance of woollen garments, the tabooing of the bean, and other Pythagorean ceremonies, point to the same origin. Of this, however, more will have to be said hereafter.

The religion of Phrygia, so far as known to us, is of a different complexion from that which we recognise as essentially Greek, yet through the colonies of Asia Minor it exercised an early influence that is not to be ignored. The great matriarchal goddess, whose worship had already passed into Greek religion in the form of Hera, is recognisable in the Asiatic Cybele and the Ephesian Artemis. The huntress deity of central Greece, and still more the dignified Athena, are widely separated from this mode of worship, tending as it did on the one hand to an extreme asceticism, and on the other to wild orgies. The Greek spirit assimilated this only so far as to burst out occasionally into passionate reaction from the monotony of social life, and into music and dancing, accompanied with the Phrygian flute ; but the true Hellene tasted only intermittently, and in measure, of such savage delights. Yet though the foreign influence does not predominate, it is certainly there. It would be impossible to account for the varying forms of Artemis, including the Thracian Bendis and the Cretan Dictynna, without assuming some contact or contamination.

Dionysus, whom the Greeks themselves regarded as a late comer, had a stronger and more universal influence. For his worship became naturally amalgamated with the village festival of vintage time, which it is natural to suppose to have originally spread from Thracian and other centres with the cultivation of the vine. The effect of the wine of the Ciconian Maron on the Cyclops is suggestive of this. Whence came the various elements that were ultimately blended in the Greek conception of Dionysus, is an obscure question. Homer knows of him as the mad power whom Lycurgus in Thrace resisted in vain. At Delphi, and in Crete, he seems associated with the winter or midnight sun, and as a consequence of the same notion, he is the Zagreus, a form of Hades, whom the Orphics developed into the Iacchus of the mysteries. We recognise again the blending of foreign elements, Thracian, Cretan, Egyptian, that had their meeting-points at Naxos and in Thebes.

But the contact of Hellenic with foreign religions must always have been of a more or less superficial kind. It is not to be supposed that the jealousy of a priesthood like that of Memphis or the Egyptian Thebes would allow their mysteries to be penetrated by the intellectual curiosity of a Greek traveller, and the Greek spirit itself was too positive, too restlessly active in moulding all that was submitted to it, to take over alien forms unmodified. The intercommunication was, however, more frequent, and more intimate, than has often been supposed. Herodotus speaks more than once of free intercourse and even intermarriage between Phoenicians and Hellenes settled in the same locality in his own time. The Carthaginian Hamilcar, who, in the great battle with Gelon and Theron on the day of Salamis, stood all day sacrificing in vain, and lastly threw himself into the fire, had a Syracusan mother, and was called in to support the claims of Terillus, the Greek tyrant of Himera who had been exiled. Greek followers of Terillus must on that occasion have fought side by side with Phoenicians, Libyans, Iberians, Sardinians, and others. Thucydides the Athenian was the son of Olorus, or in other words had Thracian ancestry. The assimilation was not wholly on the Hellenic side. The Persians respected the sanctuary at Delos, and Croesus, Necho, and Amasis, as we have seen, made offerings to Apollo at Branchidae and at Delphi. The Persians when they conquered Miletus spared the priests of Branchidae, and transferred them to a village where their descendants were found by Alexander. Is it possible that in the interim these exiles should have broken off all communication with their former countrymen? The son of Miltiades, the victor of Marathon, was taken by the Phoenician fleet of Persia, and was married to a Persian wife, by whom he had children. Although Xerxes and Mardonius were said to have meditated violence against the Delphic sanctuary, the conduct of Datis and Artaphernes to the people of Delos shows that in some way they recognised in Apollo a congener of their own sun-god. Even Xerxes spared the precinct of Athamas out of superstitious fear. Croesus not only sent offerings to Delphi but to Abae and elsewhere in Greece, and built a temple for Athena at Sparta. Letters of his name can still be traced on one of the columns of the old temple of Artemis at Ephesus. These facts are sufficient evidence of an inter-mingling of reverence which must naturally have left an impression.

The case of Cyrene is peculiarly instructive. She retained Hellenic institutions down to the fifth century A.D., longer, in fact, than any other Grecian state. Yet her non-Grecian affinities are not less marked. The marriage of Amasis the Egyptian king to Ladike (a Cyrenaic princess), the adoption of the religion of Isis, including abstinence from cow's flesh, by the Cyrenaic women, the appeal of Pheretime to Cyprus, in preference to other allies, all give evidence of the Phoenician or Semitic blend.

Two questions remain in this connection : 1. Had the sacred places which became the rallying points of Hellenic culture been already in prehistoric ages the centres of a

o

widespread influence? Achilles, in adducing the wealthiest seats on earth, names Pytho and Orchomenos and Egyptian Thebes in the same breath. Whence came the wealth of Pytho at such an early time, if her priesthood had not long been recognised as a religious power? May not the readiness with which Necho and Amasis sent gifts to Branchidae, or founded temples for the Samian Hera and the Athena of Lindos, have been partly due to an earlier knowledge of the sacredness of those shrines; and conversely, may not a similar account be given of the acceptance of the religion of Ammonian Zeus in Hellas?

2. Granting the possibility of this, and remembering what was said above of the lines of communication between distant parts of the world in prehistoric times, is it not also possible that some mutual intelligence may have existed between the priests and seers in such favoured spots, who may have owed something of the spiritual power they exercised over their immediate neighbours to the secret wisdom which they attributed to an immediate inspiration, but really derived from a far distant human source? The legends connecting Dodona with the Ammonian oasis, and Delos with the Hyperboreans, may be interpreted as indicating something of this kind. One more conjecture is suggested by the consideration of these external influences. May not the extraordinary fascination which Argive and Theban fables had for the cultivated Athenian have been due to the strange contrast which Tantalid and Cadmeian legend presented to the spirit of moderation and of sane reflection so deeply inherent in Hellenic thought? Here, then, were two distinct channels, through which the traditions of Phrygia and of Phoenicia severally operated by the force of contraries in the moulding of Greek religion.

CHAPTER IX

EFFECTS OF THE PERSIAN WAR ON GREEK RELIGION —
TRANSITION TOWARDS THE ATHENIAN PERIOD

KEEN interest is from many causes at present concentrated on the origins of Hellenic life and culture, and the subject, however baffling, is a fascinating one. But a still more potent fascination, were it not apt to pall on us through familiarity, attends the culminating moment when a nation is, as it were, reborn, when events have roused the people to a new consciousness of growing powers yet unexhausted, when timely success has awakened in them a wholesome collective pride, and life appears more than heretofore worth living. Such a time in English history is the moment of the repulse of the Spanish Armada. That, more than any single event or series of events, gave to the English people their proud consciousness of high destinies and world-wide aims, and endued with tenfold life and force their every act of thought and imagination. The victories of Marathon and Salamis, Plataea and Mycale, (nor should Himera be left out of view,) had a similar effect in Hellas. And the parallel deserves attention in another way. We have lately heard the story of the Armada from the Spanish side, and know more fully than we did how many causes worked together with British patriotism, courage, and seamanship to bring about that overthrow. But those who felt the joy and exultation of the deliverance knew nothing of this ; they knew only that the big black cloud which threatened England had been rolled away, and they acknowledged with grateful pride the daring defence of Howard, Drake, and Frobisher, and their brave seamen, and the protecting hand of God over their land. A speaker in Thucydides, two generations after

Salamis, is made to say that the Mede failed chiefly through his own errors. But that could not have been the thought of the Athenian or Aeginetan who took part in the battle. To him it appeared that the deliverance was due to Zeus who sent the storms on Artemisium, to Boreas, son-in-law of Erechtheus, who there put forth his might, to Poseidon, who inspired the sea monsters around Mount Athos, but above all, to Hellenic bravery aided by Athena and by the sons of Aeacus, who came in their Aeginetan ship at the crisis of the battle. This is an example of the contradiction referred to above (p. 20) between the actual historic circumstances of great events and the imaginative ideals which they have awakened.

If the Persian power was a force entangling itself with strength, there were great faults also on the Hellenic side. The selfish pride and blind procrastination of the Spartan rulers, the treacherous venality of many leading men, the ignominious end of Miltiades, the double-dealing of Themistocles, the vacillation of Eurybiades, the breakdown of king Pausanias after Plataea, are familiar instances. Old sores were ready to burst forth afresh the moment pressure was removed. Yet all defects are swallowed up in the brilliance of the achievement itself, and the spirit shining through it of a free people and an indomitable race. All else is covered by the glorious rush at Marathon, the radiance of battle-martyrdom at Thermopylae, and the splendour of the victory at Salamis.

A single remark conveys much of the religious feeling of the Greek at such a time. ' Why are they combing their hair so carefully ? ' asked a Persian of a Greek in the army of Xerxes. ' It is their way of preparing themselves for death,' was the reply.

The name Hellenios as a title of Zeus from henceforth acquired a new meaning. It dated from the time when the chief god of the Achaeans was worshipped under this title by the inhabitants of the small mountain region of Hellas, whether in Thessaly or Thesprotia, and it was specially appropriated to the father of Aeacus as worshipped in Aegina. But when the name Hellenic had been extended to all Greek-speaking lands, Zeus Hellenios obtained a new significance, and the importance of the attribute, as symbolical of one race, or it may almost be said, of one nation, became indefinitely intensified after the repulse of the Persian invasion. Indeed unless Herodotus and Aeschylus are reading the present into the past, the sanction of the Hellenic gods, that is, of objects of worship held sacred alike by all Hellenes, was felt in the midst of the struggle, as a great moral support to the cause of national liberty. However this may be, the effect of those great victories was manifestly to emphasise the growing sense of unity and of common interests that found expression in common worships and beliefs. The particularism of separate communities still remained only too potent a factor, and this was no doubt strengthened by the localisation of various worships and traditions ; but the higher minds in Hellas could never forget that by a great united effort, with the help of the Hellenic gods, the temples, the tombs, and the living families throughout the mainland of Greece had been rescued from slavery. It is true that the Delphic oracle had given an uncertain sound, and that the acknowledged leaders of the Hellenes, namely the Spartans, although they behaved heroically at Thermopylae, and fought nobly at Plataea, had been behindhand in supporting the Athenians at Marathon, and, if Herodotus may be trusted, had given only a hesitating support at Salamis. But the prestige which has been won through generations is not soon cast aside ; and the Spartan leadership, by land at least, was not thus lost, nor did the Delphian Apollo lose his influence ; things had ended well, and the gods must have had a hand in the affair. But if Sparta did not lose, Athens gained enormously, and the triumphs of the Greek genius throughout the remainder of the fifth century, as these are now preserved to us, are mainly hers. She is the centre towards which the several streams converge. Could she but have continued the line of policy on which she was launched, under the guidance of Aristides and the Areopagus, while still fresh from the encounter with Persia, her subsequent history would not have so glaringly contradicted the aspirations of her noblest sons. It is in the time of rapid growth immediately succeeding the war, that the ideas of freedom, justice, equity, beneficence, acquire a meaning hitherto unfelt. And while the worship of all the greater gods is anxiously maintained, speculation becomes more active as to their true nature :—the most thoughtful minds, while scrupulously attending to religious duties, begin to form conceptions of divine action, independent of particular rituals, and tending to pantheism or even monotheism. Their vision of the world had been enlarged, and they were ready to listen to the poet or historian who spoke of the barbarians equally with the Greeks as under the dominion of Zeus ; or of Apollo as equally present at Delphi, Delos, Xanthus, Miletus or Sparta. Although Hellenic unity was sadly broken, and may indeed be said never to have been realised, yet from this time forth the pan-Hellenic idea became a powerfully recurrent motive, until under the dominion of Alexander, as it were to avenge the Persian inroad, Hellenic arms were carried beyond the Indus, and left, there also, an imperishable record.

But it was in other fields than those of military conquest that the greatest triumphs of the Hellenic genius were to be won.

In the earliest times not only had each tribe and township its own divinities, but those whom all Hellas worshipped were imagined as dwelling in different shrines under different titles and attributes, and approached with special peculiarities of ritual. We have already seen the effect of the great festivals in drawing diverse communities together. But now the rising consciousness of a common national life gave new emphasis to the worships in which all shared, and even led to their borrowing from one another. Zeus the Saviour had previously been revered in many temples and at many altars—as the special protector of Dodona, of Argos, or of Corinth ; but now he began to be regarded as the saviour not of each particular city but of all Hellenes, and the Samians appeal to Spartan aid in the name of the common divinities of Hellas. The Eleusinian worship of Demeter had in earlier days been a particular tribal cult, in which probably only certain families had cared to join; but after Marathon, initiation in the mysteries became general at Athens, and frequent amongst other Greeks. Apollo's shrine at Delphi could hardly be said to gain in authority from the invasion; but the god had miraculously vindicated his own treasure-house by rolling down rocks on the invader :—were not the boulders visible 'unto this day'?—and it was piously believed that although his warnings were neglected he had adopted the cause of Hellas for his own. Delos, his birthplace, the rallying point of the Ionian name, had been respected even by the Persian enemy. Poseidon, whom the Corinthians worshipped, had destroyed the ships at Athos and Artemisium; and did not Pan strike terror into the Persian host at Marathon, as he declared in person to the runner Pheidippides? Herakles had looked down from Oeta upon the heroic action at Thermopylae; and the descendants of Aeacus, and above all Aias the son of Telamon, had actually taken part in the Salaminian conflict, the last named hero protecting his own island, Salamis. Athena had been personally interested in the struggle; she had shouted her exhortation to those Greeks who were backing out of the fight. Her sacred olive-plant, when the Medes had burned it, was believed to have at once put forth a new shoot a cubit long, although the serpent (in sympathy with the Delphian oracle) had slunk away at the approach of Xerxes. These are symptoms of the deepening and widening religious feelings that were prompted by the repulse of the Persian invasion. For the Athenians at least, the sacredness of home and family life must have been greatly intensified. Their wives and children had been saved by the ships and by Salamis, but their homes had been devastated, their fields ravaged, and what must have been their feelings in revisiting them? With what deep gladness must they have resumed the broken thread of family life, revisited their homesteads in the various demes, and lighted again the sacred fire upon the central hearth from the embers which the priest of Erechtheus had religiously preserved! With what joy and gratitude mingled with awe must they have celebrated the first Dionysia, Thargelia, Panathenaea, Apaturia, in the following year ; and with what mystic exultation must the crowd of votaries on the Sacred Way have seen the cloud of dust rising from beneath their feet,—no vision as in the day of Salamis, but a blessed reality ! It was by reminding them of their homes that Themistocles allayed their ardour, when they were madly bent on pursuing Xerxes to the Hellespont.

Such considerations may partly help us to understand how the arts which were already blossoming now burgeoned into richer life, and dressed themselves in forms of endless beauty and significance. The temple of Athena on the Acropolis, which the Persians destroyed, had many glories both of architecture and of statuary. Some of the statues have recently been recovered, and they are most interesting, giving strange promise of the power to make marble live and breathe, which came afterwards to such inimitable perfection. Yet, had it not been for the great deliverance, for the universal or at least pan-Hellenic thoughts which it awakened,—perhaps we should add but for the pride of Athens as the head of the Delian confederacy,—that art might have been arrested in its growth, might have become the instrument of tyranny or of priestcraft, or at least have stiffened into conventionalism. A certain rigidity belonging to the earlier style is traceable even in the Aeginetan marbles, although these are probably subsequent to the Persian war. The strong emancipating influence was only beginning. When Pheidias moulded the great Pallas of the Acropolis, or the Zeus whom all Hellenic tribes should worship at Olympia, what far-reaching conceptions must have inspired him ! Or when Ageladas made the Winged Victory that surmounted the pediment of the great temple there, what power to soar was given to her, or to her proto-type, by the thought of Salamis !

Historic circumstance combined with Hellenic genius to emancipate art from literalism. An eastern or southern potentate in his hour of triumph would command the royal artist to perpetuate the monarch's features, and to represent him in his habit as he lived—perhaps in the act of con- quering with his spear and with his bow the enemy who became his captive. Thus the countenance of a Rameses or a Sennacherib is better known to after ages than those of Miltiades, Leonidas or Pausanias. The Greek feeling of Nemesis co-operated in this regard with artistic idealism. No human individual was permitted to claim the credit of the great deliverance. The name of Pausanias inscribed by himself on the tripod dedicated to Apollo at Delphi in commemoration of Plataea was immediately struck out by the Spartans, and instead of it the names of the states which had joined in the overthrow of the barbarian were substituted. When he was afterwards convicted of corruption and treason, this act of his (though the epigram was by Simonides) was regarded as his first downward step. The names of the cities are still to be seen at Constantinople on the three-headed bronze serpent that supported the tripod. It was only after the loss of Hellenic independence that the figures of Macedonian kings were embroidered on the Peplos of Athena. When the Romans took Jerusalem, the triumphal procession carrying off the seven-branched candlestick was eternalised on the arch of Titus. That was not the Greek way of celebrating a great victory. The pride of country and of race, the uplifting of gratitude, the consciousness of a noble destiny, transfused themselves in ideal shapes in which the traditional types of deity and of semi-deity were heightened and beautified. Divine forms instead of becoming petrified were more intensely humanised. The Sun and Moon, the river-god Ilissus, no less than the lords of Olympus, sympathetically surrounded the new-born Athena as she looked forth from the eastern pediment of the Parthenon in the direction of Marathon ; while on the western pediment, which looked down on Salamis, the primeval contest between the giver of the olive and the ruler of the sea reminded the Athenian of the divine protection under which he lived. The old legends, the old mythology, the old ritual, remained with clinging tenacity in the old traditional sites ; old mythological types were carefully preserved, but a new spirit from thenceforth informed them. Two great works especially bore witness to such a tendency, and both were attributed to Pheidias :—the colossal statue of Athena Promachus surmounting the Acropolis, said to be formed of bronze taken from the spoils of Persia, and the marble image of Nemesis at Rhamnus, in the neighbourhood of Marathon. This is one of those personifications of abstract ideas mentioned above (pp. 145, 146). It was anticipated indeed by the author of the ' Cypria,' who made Helen the daughter of Zeus and Nemesis. The Nemesis of Rhamnus had beheld the ruin of the Persians' pride. And according to a tale which is either true or well invented, her image was formed out of a block which Datis and Artaphernes had brought expressly from Paros in order to raise a trophy of their assured victory over the Athenians.

Of the poets who ' flourished ' during the period of the Persian wars, I have already spoken of Pindar. Of Phrynichus and Aeschylus I shall have to speak hereafter in treating of Attic Tragedy. There remain Simonides of Ceos, and his nephew Bacchylides, now better known than heretofore, since Mr. Kenyon's publication of the well-known papyrus.

Simonides, though he exists for us only in fragments, is an important figure. He is a poet who writes ' to one clear harp in divers tones.' A native of Ceos, he lived much at Athens, but like other wandering bards was also to be found at the court of Syracusan ' tyrants.' He had already reached celebrity at the time of the Persian war, 490–480 B.C., and many of the inscriptions celebrating the bravery of Greek leaders and warriors were either his or attributed already in antiquity to him. Wilamowitz-Moellendorf, in an ingenious paper, has sifted the original epigrams with their stern simplicity from the later accretions. Simonides is one of the gnomic poets, but also a lyric poet of great eminence. Of all poets of antiquity, perhaps, he presents the nearest analogy to Tennyson. The famous fragment about Danae and Perseus is unsurpassed for tenderness, while his poems in celebration of Marathon, Thermopylae, and Salamis have an heroic spirit in them, and the ring of absolute sincerity.

The following passages exemplify the strain of moral reflection characteristic of him :

' 'Tis said that virtue once dwelt on inaccessible rocks, but now she ranges the holy place of the gods, and meeteth not the eyes of mortal men, nor is seen by any, save by him who with heart-consuming toil hath poured out his sweat, and so hath mounted to a height of bravery.'

' Men have little strength and thoughts that find no issue, and labour upon labour in a scanty lifetime, and over all alike there hangs inevitable death, whereof the noble and the mean obtain an equal share.'

In connection with the personifying of abstractions just alluded to, it is noticeable that he speaks of To-morrow as a divinity (δαίμων).

The recently discovered poems of Bacchylides contain but little that contributes to our knowledge of Greek religion. The evidence they present of some early link between Ceos, Miletus, and Crete has been already noticed. The form of the Herakles legend which comes out most strongly in them is that which connects Herakles with Aetolia. The meeting of the divine hero, during his quest for Cerberus, with the ghost of Meleager is remarkably impressive, and the new light thrown on the story of Theseus is interesting in itself, and also as proving that the Athenian hero was already the centre of a living tradition. It is also most interesting to find that Croesus, as the servant of Apollo, had been already deified in poetic legend no less completely than Cadmus or Herakles. The two Cean poets reflect a period of Hellenic development in which Athens was rising in importance, while the ascendency of Sparta had not yet waned. And taken in conjunction with Pindar they mark a period in which the interest of all Hellenes, but especially of the great families, in their legendary past was at its height. The grandeur of heroic personalities and their achievements is more prominent in the productions of the Cean muse than any deepening of the conception of deity. It is a remarkable instance of independence in Bacchylides that in celebrating Alexidamas of Metapontum, who had won the boys' prize for wrestling in the Pythian games, he should hint not obscurely that his young hero had been unfairly judged at Olympia.

In previous chapters dealing with Greek religious life as reflected in Greek literature, we found great variety, yet with remarkable similarities and an approach to unity, of which the Homeric poems on the one hand, and the odes of Pindar on the other, were at once the embodiment and the support. The Greek of the sixth century, in looking backwards, whether he were a native of Sicily or of Ionia, would have a sense of community in religion with other Greeks, which had no place in the thoughts of his remote ancestry. But this common basis, if it may be so described, had been disturbed by two causes whose operation was widespread. The experience of the race was outgrowing its traditions, and the more advanced minds were having recourse either to innovations in mythology and ritual, or to philosophical speculation.

Religious innovations were connected with a natural transition, assisted by some vague foreign influence—from polytheism to pantheism. The old worships held their own, and no attempt was made either to neglect or to supplant them ; but the accompanying conceptions were losing their sharpness of outline : the attributes of the gods were generalised, and were becoming merged in mystic apprehensions of a divine nature pervading all things and encompassing human life both individual and national. In this movement, which went on side by side with the growth of hero-worship, two distinct tendencies are perceptible : (1) the attempt—anticipated to some extent in the Hesiodic poems—to introduce order into the chaos of mythology by an elaborate filiation of divine beings. In the sixth century, however, in accordance with the pantheistic drift, theogony was already passing into cosmogony. This aspect of early Greek thought or fancy is associated with the name of Pherecydes of Syros. At the same time (2) there was a deepening sense of human sinfulness, and fear of divine anger, possessing whole communities and prompting strange efforts after purification and atonement. The germs of this are of course already present in Homer, and still more in Hesiod, and are derivable from earlier sources. The plague at the beginning of the Iliad is sent by an offended deity, whose anger is averted for a time by sacrifice and by washing in the sea. But there is nothing specially piacular in the mode of sacrifice. Gifts are offered in the hope of appeasing wrath. And purification by sea water, or as in the Odyssey by the burning of sulphur, are simple and natural ideas, belonging to an age whose spiritual wounds could be healed slightly, and in which physical and moral notions easily blended. The annual washing of the Palladium at Athens was a survival of this. In Hesiod, the fear of ceremonial pollution has an almost oriental cast, but is met by a few *naïve* precepts which ' salve all.' Towards the beginning of the sixth century, however, the trouble had deepened, and we find traditions of a time when spiritual evils were met by mystical expedients : when the guilt of blood incurred during the insurrection of Cylon at Athens could only be dissipated by the coming of Epimenides, the religious sage, from Crete, and the expulsion of the attainted family, even the dead members of it being cast out of their graves ; when by the magic arts of the physician Apis, from whom according to Aeschylus the Peloponnesus was called the Apian land, the brood of monstrous serpent forms which through the anger of the gods had infested it were driven out—much as Ireland was cleared of reptiles by St. Patrick ; and when, through the timely aid of Melampus, curing like with like, epidemics of hysterical frenzy amongst women were strangely cured by the organisation of orgiastic rites. In all this movement the spread of the Apolline worship from its chief centres at Delphi, Delos, and Miletus had an important influence which is difficult to trace in detail, and the instances last mentioned are closely connected with the rise of Dionysiac religion. Without attempting to follow this connection further, I must content myself with having so far indicated a phase of religious life which undoubtedly existed, and had an important bearing on what followed.

It is true that these newer religious influences still

took the form of ceremonial observances, not of doctrines clearly enunciated. There remained much darkness as to the principles of divine government, and the nature of those actions which were supposed to provoke the anger of the gods. That sense of the divinity of justice which appears in Hesiod, and to which Solon gave such noble expression, was but dimly apprehended even by the few. The distinction, so familiar to us, between positive and moral obligation was hardly felt. Yet in the fear of an offended deity and the effort to propitiate him there lay in embryo a real principle of spiritual life.

The beginnings of philosophy were still more isolated than the outcropping of these mystical yearnings, from which, indeed, they were not altogether dissociated; for in the cosmogony of Pherecydes and his school there was already a beginning of speculation on the riddle of the universe, and the philosophy of Pythagoras and even that of Parmenides had a mystical strain. These isolated philosophic utterances had hitherto been chiefly heard in Ionia and Magna Graecia. We have already found traces of their influence in Herodotus and in Pindar.

But in treating of the fifth century, the focus of interest in spiritual matters, as well as in political life, is transferred from the outlying parts of Hellas to Athens. The achievements of the Athenian people at Marathon, at Salamis, and generally in repelling the Mede, and the defection of Sparta after the fall of king Pausanias, not only quickened all the seeds of mental growth in Attica, and greatly deepened the national consciousness there, but through the position of Athens as the head of the Delian confederacy and the new leader of Hellas against the barbarian, every stream of culture from Hellenic lands was made to flow her way. In the case of Attica the question of the sources of religious life is peculiarly interesting, for in spite of the obscurity which envelops all beginnings, especially the beginnings of mythology, there are perhaps more traces in Attica than elsewhere of primitive worships. The country, as Thucydides says, had been so long inhabited by the same race, the separate districts had so long retained their own peculiar rites, being only gradually absorbed into the main community, that that not-very-fortunate man (as Plato calls him), the investigator of early mythology and of folklore, has more material for his industry in this quarter than can easily be found in the same space elsewhere, unless in Arcadia.

Our aim, however, will be to deal as far as possible with facts obtained at first hand, and to abstain from filling up with mere guesswork, however plausibly supported, the gaps of knowledge.

The Athenian of the fifth century truly felt that the Homeric poems were the education of the race. In creating out of innumerable local worships a universal Pantheon, in which Zeus, Athena, and Apollo predominated over the lesser gods, Homer seemed to have led the way to a conception of the divine nature in which all minor phases of religion tended to become absorbed. Yet while enlarging and elevating the Greek mind, these poems failed to satisfy the religious instinct chiefly in two ways : (1) The universality of Homeric religion owed its existence partly to the fact that the Achaeans of Asia Minor, in emigrating from Thessaly, had left behind them many customs of their ancestors. To the Athenian such old customs were still in living observance, intertwined with the essential life of his family, his tribe, his city. The heroes of his race and nation, whose graves he visited, whose succour in battle or in any stress of need he relied upon, to whom from childhood he had seen his parents offering sacrifice, had a reality for him, which, if less exalted, was more immediately inspiring than that of the Olympic gods. There were also, as above remarked, deep spiritual needs which had sprung up and grown in central Hellas after the close of the Homeric canon. The sense of sin and need of atonement, vague yearnings for religious sympathy, and above all, desires and aspirations towards the world beyond, had been awakened in various degrees in different minds, and found a transient satisfaction in the development of the Eleusinian mysteries and of the Dionysiac worship, which had taken root upon Athenian soil.

Through the wisdom of the legislator, these diverse needs

had been met in the creation of the complex fabric of Athenian social life. By a law of Draco in the sixth century the worship of the local gods and heroes was to be maintained according to immemorial use and wont. The recitation of Homeric rhapsodies formed an essential part of the pan-Athenaic festival. The Eleusinia were acknowledged by the state, and obtained a firm hold on the Athenian spirit; and from the keen interest in the Dionysia, which not only Athens but her Ionian allies increasingly felt, came that unique creation of Greek Tragedy, which, while holding up the mirror alike to local legends and heroic memories, revealed so much of what lay deepest in the human soul.

The spirit of philosophic speculation which had arisen in Ionia before its overthrow, which had culminated in Magna Graecia, and had for a time been associated with political ascendency at Croton, had nothing to answer to it in the earlier life of Athens. It may be doubted whether before the time of Pericles it could have found a home there. Indirectly, it is true, great poets, such as Aeschylus and Simonides, may have reflected something of Pythagorean wisdom: a sort of glorified common sense expressed itself in the gnomic poetry of Solon; but a teacher such as Heraclitus, openly denouncing sacrifice, or Xenophanes, declaring the folly of anthropomorphism, could scarcely have been tolerated by the Athenians in the time of Cimon. When Ionia had finally come under the rule of tyrants who depended on Persia, and spirits that loved liberty were seeking a home elsewhere; when Sicily was also under despotic rulers, and Athens stood forth as the declared friend of freedom, then it was that the wise policy of Pericles brought Anaxagoras to Athens, and shortly afterwards such men as Gorgias and Protagoras came to visit her. It was a short breathing space, and precarious while it lasted, but it allowed room for that outburst of enlightenment, and for that new birth of time, to which the death of Socrates only gave fresh life,—a spiritual influence that is still active in the world.

CHAPTER X

ATHENIAN WORSHIPS

WHILE most of the worships common to all Greece had in Attica also a local habitation and a name, the spirit of the people there in combination with the facts of their history brought some forms of religion into prominence, whilst others sank into the background. Zeus, Athena, Apollo, Artemis, Hermes, Poseidon, Demeter, Dionysus, are more celebrated in Athenian literature than Hera, Aphrodite, Ares, Hephaestus, Pan, Herakles, the Dioscuri. It is true that the divinities most worshipped at Athens are also prominent elsewhere, but it is at first sight remarkable that Hera, so great a goddess in Argolis, in Samos, and at Plataea, so active in the Iliad, should be rarely mentioned amongst Athenian deities; that Ares should have so little recognition from a warlike people, and that Castor and Polydeuces the patrons of mariners should be so little thought of by a seafaring population. Some remarks on each of these points may help to clear the ground. In Laconia and the south of Peloponnesus the 'brothers of Helen' were generally acknowledged as the sailor's friends, having been probably identified in pre-Dorian times with some objects of Phoenician worship. Though they had a shrine in Attica they do not figure prominently amongst Athenian gods. They were not gods of the Ionian-Attic stock. The Athenians, when they became a naval power, continued the worship of Poseidon, who had an ancient seat on the Acropolis, and had assured to them the mastery of their own seaboard. If they looked for a more human patron, had they not Theseus, who had led the expedition to Crete commemorated in the annual mission to Delos, and who tended

P

in Athenian worship to supplant the universal Hellenic reverence for Herakles, although in Attica, especially at Marathon, the cult of Herakles also had been rooted from very early times ?

Except in connection with the jurisdiction of the Areopagus, and as included in the oath of the Ephebi, Ares was but little worshipped at Athens. Indeed, there were but few centres in Hellas, excepting Thebes and Sparta, where this deity, generally more feared than loved, was much at home. His presence on the Areopagus was associated first with the legendary invasion of the Amazons, who had sacrificed to him (with some barbarian rite), and secondly, with the avenger of blood, whose direct appeal was naturally to the god of battle, i.e. to ordeal by combat, until the law of vengeance came to be tempered with equity, through the intervention of Apollo and Athena. There is here an obvious progress of religious thought, which may partly explain the general fact that not Ares the aggressor, but Athena the defender, is the Athenian god of war. To the predominance of Athena may also be assigned, perhaps, the absence of any public worship of the great goddess Hera, who reigned over the whole land of Argolis and had such time-honoured worship there and in the island of Samos. The position of her temples in rural districts, as in the territory of Plataea, and her early association with herds of kine, suggest that she was rather a pastoral than a civic deity, whereas Athena is before all things the protectress of the city. But although Attica could boast of no great temple to Hera, yet as the goddess of married life and of motherhood she was much thought of, especially by women ; yet the oath ' by Hera,' which is put by Plato into the mouth of Socrates and others, does not occur in Aristophanes, or in any Attic writer of the fifth century.

Pan, too, (Πάων the feeder) was a deity rather of the country than of the town, and as such had been ignored by the Athenians, or rather not formally recognised amongst the deities that gathered round the Acropolis. But after the fight in the open field at Marathon and the ' panic ' fear that seized the Persian enemies on that wild coast, the people found a place for him in a grotto to the north of the Acropolis.

Hephaestus was believed in from very early times, and in one sense, in his union with Mother Earth, was regarded as the author of the Athenian race, but he was chiefly worshipped as a culture deity in combination with Prometheus and Athena.

The worship of Aphrodite Pandemos could not be absent from a system of polytheism, in which every power that ever dominates mankind must have a place, but at Athens this ritual was believed to have been imported from abroad by Phaedra, the sister of Ariadne and the unfaithful wife of Theseus. In earlier times Aphrodite Urania had been worshipped, at Colias, for example, rather as a great nature power, associated with the Graces and the Nymphs, than as the goddess of love.

The worship of Zeus at Athens had some peculiarities derived from an immemorial antiquity. We have seen how Zeus Hellenios, an epithet derived originally from Thessaly, where Hellas was a local name, and celebrated in Aegina, became after the Persian wars a type of the union of all Hellenes against the barbarian. In Attica Zeus retained much of his original nature as the god of the sky, who now smiles on men and their works propitiously, now thunders and lightens as the god of storms; who sends rain or fair bright weather as it pleases him; and he was accordingly worshipped on the height of the Acropolis, with bloodless offerings at the festival of the Diasia in the spring of the year. But he had other attributes and other functions. Zeus Teleios, the god of consummation, had a priest of the family of Buzugae at Athens; he was primarily the lord of consecrating rites, especially the marriage rite which completes the family, but to the pious mind of an Athenian, without losing this association, he became the author and disposer who determines all events and accomplishes faithful prayers according to his will. Zeus Herkeios, god of the enclosure, was, in a general sense, the protector of every home; but at Athens he had a special sanctuary in the Erechtheum, where his altar with its perpetual flame kept

the Athenians in mind of that ancient sovereignty which had
descended from their early kings and was now vested in the
sovereign people. It was the hearth of the state, the
embodiment of the goddess Hestia. There Zeus was
specially known as Zeus Polieus, the protector of the
city. So with an infinity of titles he presided over various
other functions, public and private : over the council, the
assembly, the family, the phratry, the dues of hospitality,
of friendship, and of comradeship, combining the attributes.
of a universal and particular providence ; but it is remarkable
that while he had many altars, where his worship was
associated with that of other deities, he had only one great
temple, instituted not by any popular government, but by
the Pisistratidae, and left unfinished until Athens was in
her decline. This was the temple of Zeus Olympius, to the
south-east of the Acropolis. Pisistratus may have chosen
to strengthen his own sovereignty by the worship of the
supreme god, or he may have sought to impress upon his
countrymen the dignity of the pan-Hellenic Zeus upheld by
Homer, in preference to the traditional local deity. But
after the expulsion of the tyrants, the popular imagination
clung to their ancient Zeus upon the northward cliff, who
was associated more intimately with their daily life. And
in this character, instead of building temples to him, they
preferred to worship him after their ancient wont under the
open sky and in connection with other gods who were nearer
to mankind. They thought of him now as the saviour, now
as the bringer on of fate, in a somewhat distant way, but
paid their more direct and familiar worship to those of the
kindred of Zeus who acted as his vice-gerents in human
affairs, above all to Apollo and Athena.

When Athens first rose into importance, the worship of
the Pythian Apollo had long been universal throughout
Hellas. And though we have seen reason to suspect that
the religion early established at Delphi had at one time been
reinforced by a Phoenician influence, yet like the Apollo
worship everywhere it had been thoroughly penetrated with
the Greek spirit. The ideas of citizenship, of nationality,
and patriotism entered into it with a refining and elevating

power; and the purely Aryan notion of the solidarity of the household in its successive generations was also potent therein. While Athens remained as one of a loose confederacy of Hellenic states acknowledging the primacy of Sparta, she, like the rest, looked with implicit faith for guidance to the oracular son of Zeus, whose shrine was at the centre of the world. Whatever may have been the wisdom and spiritual insight of the Delphic priesthood, there can be no doubt that the simple confiding belief in the god of Delphi had on the whole a wholesome and strengthening effect upon the Athenian mind. Not that it is to be supposed that all Athenian notions concerning this universal Hellenic deity were borrowed from the Delphic teaching, but their conception of him in some aspects was certainly coloured by it. When they claimed him as Patrôos, the author of the Ionian race, this mythological invention was due to their desire for a close relationship with the divine being to whom they looked up with a more than filial awe; and the legend sought and found its confirmation in Delphic tradition. Again, Apollo Delphinios, who purged the commonweal from the guilt of blood, was by the Athenians themselves associated with Apollo Delphicus, and the sense of blood-guiltiness as needing purgation through blood was, if not originally taught, at least greatly deepened by the influence of the Delphic priesthood. Apollo Pythius was worshipped at more than one site in Attica, and although the title may have primarily signified merely the oracular god, yet in historic times it was inevitable that by Pythius should be understood the Pythian, that is to say the Delphic Apollo.

For the rest, in Attica, as elsewhere, Apollo was, first, the averter of evil, especially from house and home; secondly, the healer (παιών) both in the literal and also in the figurative sense of the remover of annoyance or disease. His altar as Λύκειος, προστάτης, προστατήριος (protector or defender) stood before the chief doorway of all the more important houses. Thus Apollo was in a manner omnipresent at Athens. And if he ever seemed to be absent, was he not named Βοηδρόμιος, 'runner to the rescue,' on whom pious hearts might call in moments of distress? Nor had he relinquished his more primitive attributes as a nature power : presiding over flocks and fruits of the earth, perhaps no other, in his earliest conception, than the sun-god of spring.

Delphi, though the most important, was not the only centre of Apolline worship. Another was Delos, whose priests declared that their little island was the birthplace of Apollo. His festival had been a rendezvous for the islanders and the Ionian states on the Asiatic seaboard from very early times; and had been frequented even by the Euboeans of Carystos and the Dorians of Calymna and Cos. Hence, when Athens and Sparta began to stand apart, and the conservative tendencies (or the Dorian sympathies) of the Delphic priesthood inclined them to support the leadership of Sparta, the Delian rather than the Delphic Apollo came to be revered at Athens. Even the Persians under Datis and Artaphernes had respected Delos, and it seemed a capital stroke of policy for the Athenians, when they were now the leaders of the Greeks against the barbarian, to make Delos the centre of their new confederacy, which they thus brought under the protection and patronage of the Delian god of light and strength.

Before passing on to Athena, it is natural to speak here of Artemis, who in the Delian legend was the sister of Apollo. At Athens she was less a civic than a domestic deity, associated with the chief events in the lives of women— with puberty, marriage, childbirth, and the care of children. Her worship had taken firm hold in country places before it was introduced into the city. Hence in the rites performed in her honour there were traces of her earlier character as the huntress : goats were sacrificed to her, and the rite of initiation, by which young girls were consecrated to her service, was fancifully associated with her Arcadian favourite, the bear. Folklorists find in this a survival of animal-worship, supposing the ἄρκτευσις, the name for the rite of initiation, to have been a sort of bear-dance, derived from ἄρκτος a 'bear.' But may there not be something in the suggestion of Lobeck that ἄρκτος as applied to one of these young catechumens may have been originally derived from ἄρχεσθαι, to 'begin'? The word once chosen would soon come to be identified with the animal whom the goddess loved. Artemis, like her brother, has a twofold aspect as preserver and destroyer; the cruel Artemis of Brauron was much feared—and reminiscences of human sacrifice hung round her. One would be glad to think that these were not native offshoots of Greek religion, but had adhered to it from some barbaric source. That she was a 'lioness to women,' as Homer sang, was still confirmed by every death in childbed, and she was feared accordingly. Thus as associated with Hecate, originally another name for the moon goddess, and as the sister of the far-darter, she was torch-bearer to Persephone, and was often represented as holding up a flaming torch in either hand. It may not be too fanciful to find some reminiscence of this, her first nature, in the bright shafts with which in the chorus of Sophocles she darts throughout the Lycian hills. As the Delian legend gained more hold of Athens, the position of Artemis, the sister to Apollo, and daughter of Latona, became more clearly defined. But her chief function still remained, as the maiden goddess who presided over childbirth, and altogether as the patroness of women. Yet on one great occasion she was acknowledged also as the preserver and destroyer of men. A third part of the spoils at Marathon was devoted to her, because of Artemisium, and the Polemarch offered to her annually on the sixth of Boedromion (September), a season sacred to Apollo, five hundred goats.

Athena is the central figure in Athenian religion, identified in the most intimate manner with civic and national life : the protectress, guide, enlightener, instructor, of her people. She retained from early times, when Attica was inhabited village-wise, her function of presiding over the culture of the olive. The sacred olives by the Cephisus, between Colonus and the Academy, were perhaps an earlier symbol of this than the never-dying plant in the Erechtheum. Both carry us back to the dawn of history, for already in the Iliad she is established in the house of Erechtheus, and in the cata-

logue of the ships the myth determining her connection with
that god or hero is complete. Like Artemis a virgin goddess,
she is the helper not of women but of men, who regarded her
with a sort of chivalrous loyalty. As, under the influence of
Solon and of Pisistratus after him, the commonwealth grew
and strengthened, the great ideas of law and justice, of self-
devoted patriotism, of order and discipline, clustered more
and more closely about the person of Athena. She had her
warlike and her peaceful aspect; but the warlike was for the
enemies of Athens, the peaceful was for the loyal citizens.
Thus she is at once πολιάς the goddess of the Citadel, πρόμαχος
defender of the faithful, ἐργάνη the patroness of industry,
βουλαία guide in counsel, ἀρχηγέτις beginner of every work,
and is identified with Θέμις goddess of law, Ὑγίεια goddess
of health, and, at least after the defeat of Persia, with Νίκη
goddess of victory.

The worship of Athena in Attica is also modified through
her connection with other native deities. Although a
virgin herself—an attribute probably more accentuated in
later times as symbolising an unconquered land, she watched
with motherly care over the infancy of Erichthonios, the
child of earth from whom the Athenians came. His serpent
form appears on early stone reliefs discovered on the Acropolis.
In early legend he is identified with Erechtheus, an earth
deity whose worship symbolised the Athenians' belief in their
autochthonous origin. Of this son of the soil, Hephaestus
the fire god is accounted sire. Thus Athena is associated
with Hephaestus, not only as presiding over all artistic work,
but in the authorship of that prime master-work, the creation
of man. The serpent that lived on the Acropolis, and is
constantly represented on early monuments as accompanying
Athena, preserved some early association of her worship with
that of the earth, as in the case of Athena Itonia in Boeotia.

The close relationship of Athena and Poseidon has been
thought to symbolise the fusion of the primeval Attic with
the Ionian race, who are represented in the legends as
coming into Attica when driven out of Achaia by the Dorian
invasion. The mythical contest between the giver of the
olive and the giver of the horse, the war between Athens and

Eleusis, and other indications of a conflict finally reconciled by the supremacy of Athena point at least in some such direction. But in historic times (and not at Athens only) both powers are happily conjoined : Athena defending her people by land, Poseidon maintaining their sea power (although at Salamis it was Athena who reproached the Greeks for backing water) —while both together were the patrons of the Athenian knighthood, who on the hill of Colonus had an altar to Poseidon Hippios and Athena Hippia. Athena was also associated with Ares in the sanctuary of the Areopagus.

In all these combinations the worship of Athena had a civilising, humanising, and rationalising influence. The capricious cruelty of Ares was changed into deliberate severity, directed by the spirit of patriotism against the enemies who threatened Athens from without, or those professing friends within her borders who disturbed her peace. The warlike spirit of the Athenians had the love of country for its inspiring motive. It is not wonderful that the Attic type of Athena on works of art obtained a fulness of significance and an air of bounteous dignity not equally perceptible in the virgin-goddess elsewhere. Athena Nike, bareheaded, with her helmet and a pomegranate in either hand, already looked upon her citizens with an air of benignity very different from the stern maiden scarcely less repellent than Medusa's self, who in the metope of Selinus is assisting Perseus in slaying the Gorgon. And in the form of the Palladium, presiding over the court for homicide, she tempered with mercy even the severity of Apolline ritual.

Poseidon, the earth-shaker, without losing all his terrors, became in league with Athena a true and faithful benefactor, the giver of the steed, whom the knighthood worshipped side by side with her, the lord of seacraft and of the sea—giving victory to the navies of Athens, partly through their own prowess and partly by his rage against the invader. He was from early times bound up with the soil of Attica, and, in fact, identified with Erechtheus the favourite of Athena. Thus Poseidon was honoured and feared by land as well as by sea. Theseus, the peculiarly Attic hero, was his son.

There is little to be said here about Hermes, although, as the panic caused by the mutilation of the Hermae proved, he was a very popular god : chiefly in two capacities, as the guardian of boundaries, and as the conductor of the souls of the departed, and thus associated with funeral ceremonies and the continuity of family life. As guardian of the boundary he had probably gained fresh popularity under Solon, and we know from the ' Hipparchus ' attributed to Plato that the images of him which the aristocratic youth defaced had in many cases been set up by Pisistratus. As conductor of souls, and in his association with domestic worships, his presence fills a large place in tragedy.

Pericles in Thucydides, when praising Athens in his funeral speech, says with reference to feast days, ' we have not forgotten to provide for our weary spirits many relaxations from toil : we have regular games and sacrifices throughout the year . . . and the delight which we feel in all these things helps to banish melancholy.' That may seem to modern readers to be a light way of speaking of religious services and to imply that the Athenians were irreligious ; and it is possible that a priest of the Eteo-Butadae or the Buzygae would have spoken with more solemnity ; for a shade of sadness had been superinduced over the simple enjoyment which in early times accompanied all religious acts. In many of the festivals, the Diasia, in honour of Zeus Meilichios (the ancient god of piacular atonement), the Plynteria, the Thargelia, the Thesmophoria and others, there was at least one day of fasting and of gloom. The fear of the gods had to be acknowledged before men could come into their presence. But it is not the less true that joyousness was the most prominent feature of all these celebrations. I do not speak now of the Eleusinia, nor of the Dionysia, which will be considered hereafter, but of the worship of those deities who were emphatically gods of the city. On every such occasion, even if the individual citizen did not feel a joy, he would be bound to feign it, for he was assisting at the rite which showed forth the living presence of the god. The feast which followed the sacrifice was an auspicious act of communion with the divine, and the games in which the Greek delighted were the more prized by him because they were known to be well pleasing to the great power, whose heart was gladdened, not only by the steam of the burnt sacrifice, or the perfect forms of the creatures that were offered to him, but also by the human perfections of those who were chosen to do him honour. The rounded limbs of the youths moving in procession, and of the maidens bearing vessels of offering, the trained strength of wrestlers, the skill of musicians, the still higher accomplishments of the poet—all these were brought into play, and native enjoyment of them was enhanced by the glad consciousness of offering to heaven from gifts which heaven had bestowed. Hence it was that as Athenian life—especially after the war with Persia—became more and more enriched, ennobled and refined, the festivals came to be more and more adorned and beautified, until what had once been a simple ceremony lasting half a day overflowed its pristine limits so as to occupy several days. The simple foot race was not enough : there must be races of all lengths on foot and on horseback, with and without chariots, besides wrestling, boxing, and the Pancratium —this last being a combination of several athletic contests. The mere recitation of Homer was not enough : it must be extended and organised, and there must be lyric contests also. The times of festival had been appointed in connection with the seasons and the operations of agriculture, and were studiously retained so far as the chief days were concerned. But as town life increased and country life diminished in importance, the direct association with seed time, harvest, vintage, and the like, became less prominent. Features which had once been accidental grew to be essential, and partly obscured the original significance of the rite.

Of the feast-days, then, which as Pericles says succeeded one another in a bright unbroken chain throughout the year, I select for description two only, of which it happens that a tolerably full account remains : the Thargelia or spring festival of Apollo, and the great festival of Athena, in August, between harvest and vintage—the Panathenaea.

The Thargelia was celebrated on the seventh day of the month Thargelion, that is about May 25, reputed to be the birthday of Apollo. By that time in Greece the summer is fully come. It was a sacred season not only in Athens, but at Miletus, and in Delos and others of the Cyclades. It coincided with the ripening of the first ears of grain, of which an offering was made to the god. The two aspects of geniality and severity belonging to the Apolline worship are markedly apparent here. For on the eve of the festival, in order that the city might be pure from sin, it was an order of the state that two of the lowest of the people should be driven beyond the boundaries, and thrown into the sea. This act was accompanied with music of the flute. It is not certain that they were always put to death, though this probably happened in great emergencies, but the custom was clearly the survival of some expiatory rite of human sacrifice, characteristic of a time—perhaps, also, of a race—long past. Meanwhile a milder sacrifice, that of a horned sheep, was performed in honour of Demeter Euchloös, goddess of the green herb ; no doubt by way of thanksgiving, for without the green blade the full corn in the ear could never be. After these rites performed, the public conscience was ‘ as noonday clear ’ for the festival of the ensuing day, when besides the offering of the first-fruits to Apollo, and some celebration of Artemis his twin-sister, special thank-offerings were made to Helios and the Hours.

These ceremonies were not all. After the feast come ‘ the adornments of the feast,’ the lyre and song, in which Apollo was known to take especial delight. This festival was the occasion of a lyrical contest of high importance. Crowns of honour were also given to distinguished citizens, and in families the formality of adoption was performed by prefer-ence on this auspicious day. Thus domestic solemnities were associated with public thanksgiving, and with the joy of festival. For the worship of Apollo and Artemis together was one in which the grace of domestic purity held a conspi-cuous place. One would gladly know more of the details of such a celebration, but its very familiarity accounts for the scantiness of the record. One picturesque circumstance belonging both to this and to the corresponding autumn feast of the Pyanepsia was a procession of young boys carrying olive-branches wreathed with wool, the tokens of supplication, which they afterwards hung at the doorways of private houses as if to say ' Peace be to this house.' Some part of the first-fruits was attached to each. The boys sang a carol, preserved by Plutarch in his ' Life of Theseus.' The form which he gives belongs rather to the autumn celebration :

> These holy branches carry figs and cakes,
> And honey in a cup, oil for the limbs,
> And heartening wine that sends all care to sleep.

Apollo was thus worshipped as the god of healing and of pestilence, of fruitfulness and blight, the purger of the city and the home, and also as the bright cheerful patron of song.

The month that followed, Thargelion, was the time of harvest ; then came Hecatombaeon, nearly answering to August, in the interval between harvest and vintage-time. This was the high tide of festival at Athens. It was now that Cronos and Rhea, father and mother of the gods, were approached with bloodless offerings in the Cronia festival, bringing to men's minds the memories of the golden age. And it was in this month that time was found to celebrate the great event of the union of all Attica under the presidency of Athens in a festival (ξυνοίκια) that could have had no place in the primeval calendar. This was followed by the Panathenaea, the most splendid of Athenian pageants, which once in four years or, as the Greeks counted, every fifth year, was celebrated on a scale of extraordinary magnificence. Pisistratus has the credit of having given to this occasion a richness of adornment which without him it could hardly have attained.

When once this festival had become associated in men's minds with the glory of Athens, it was a point of honour with the Athenian democracy to maintain it at the height, or even to develop it further. The central point, round which all else was grouped, was the sacrifice of a hundred kine to Athena Polias, as a birthday offering. This was the

Hecatomb, which gave its name to the month Hecatom-baeon. And that she might appear in a manner worthy of the occasion, her statue, before which the altar stood, must be adorned with a new robe on which certain women appointed for the purpose had blazoned in embroidery the achievements of the goddess, especially in repelling the assaults of the giants upon Olympus. The solemn washing of the robe, the Plynteria—a day of gloom—had preceded the whole festival. The robe was doubtless originally intended for the cult statue in the Erechtheum, and it may be that this, and not the great image in the Parthenon, continued to be thus adorned. The bringing of the offering, and the carrying of the robe, to be placed in the hand of Athena's minister, were the most essential features of the great procession which was re-presented in the time of Pericles on the frieze of the Parthenon.

But in historic times these ceremonies were not all. Choice specimens of Athenian knighthood followed upon horseback, curbing their fiery steeds to the slow pace of the kine ; a dignified train of elders bore olive-branches in token of supplication ; young men brought wine for the libations in great amphorae on their shoulders ; others carried butchers' trays to receive the choice pieces of the victims which were to be distributed amongst the various demes ; maidens bore the sacred vessels, jugs and goblets, to be used in offering, while others carried on their heads baskets of meal and grain, all for sacrificial purposes. Besides the horsemen, there were chariots with armed warriors and charioteers. All these had been selected by competition. Musicians playing on the lyre and flute accompanied the sacrifice. So great and various a procession could not be kept in rank without the help of officers especially appointed to marshal them. All these may be seen to this day upon the wonderful Panathenaic frieze, where also are represented the magnates of the city, and the quiet assembly of the gods, Zeus and Athena in the midst, looking graciously upon the offerings of the people. There also remain elaborate inscriptions, some of the fifth, but mostly of the fourth century, which help to illustrate the ceremony as it existed then.

Special magistrates were appointed to assist the priests in ordering the sacred rites. One part of their duty was to superintend the distribution of the portions of beef to the heads of the different tribes for the banquet which followed; in accordance with the primeval custom that all worshippers should eat of the sacrifice. This banquet took place in several centres, the members of each tribe feasting together. There were also special functionaries for the buying of kine. One heifer of distinguished beauty was to be selected for Athena Nike, goddess of victory. It appears from the frieze that there were also sheep amongst the victims. To whom these were offered is uncertain, possibly to Erechtheus, but more probably to Pandrosos, the genius of fruitfulness, whose worship was subordinate to that of Athena. The marshalling of the procession was entrusted to the Demarchs or parish magistrates, who each arrayed his deme in the Cerameicus among the tombs of distinguished citizens, and conducted them through the city and round the Acropolis to the Propylaea, from whence they ascended and passed along the northern side of the Parthenon in due order to the east end, where they took their stand until the sacrifices were accomplished, thence returnng to the place of the banquet. According to some accounts, the procession made a detour to Eleusis along the Sacred Way.

So much for the ceremonial part of the festival which occupied the 28th day of the month, and was preceded by a vigil or night festival, and a preliminary offering to Athena Hygieia as the goddess of health. But at the greater Panathenaea there had been already several days of organised gaiety, all consciously associated with the worship of the goddess, and calculated to do her honour. There was first the musical contest in the Odeum, commencing with the recitations of epic poetry, which had been introduced and set in order by Pisistratus (or according to others by Solon). Next came a competition in lyric song for which a golden or gilded olive-crown was the prize; then a flute competition, then one for playing the lyre, in both of which there were separate prizes for men and boys. All this must have occupied more than one day. The gymnastic contest followed, with separate prizes for grown men, youths, and boys, in footraces, wrestling, boxing, and in all combined. The prizes for these feats and also for the fluteplayer were amphorae filled with oil from the sacred olive trees, the Panathenaic vases, of which so many specimens have been happily preserved, and whose decoration forms an epoch in Athenian art. And it is not a little remarkable that foreigners from Argos and even from Cos were admitted to the competition. For these contests also more than one day seems to be required. Then came the equestrian contest, chariot racing and horse racing of various kinds. Some of these events were for all comers, and they occupied the greater part of a day. One purpose in all these competitions was to decide the choice of persons who should take part in the final procession—those whom Heaven had thus favoured would naturally be pleasing to the goddess—but there was furthermore a special choice of individuals from each tribe by magistrates appointed for the purpose. The choice was called Euandria. These preliminaries were concluded with a dance in armour called the Pyrrhic dance, which again was separately performed by boys and youths and men ; the armour consisting of a shield and helmet. The night festival began on the evening of the twenty-seventh, with a torch race followed by auspicious cries on the part of the priestesses of Athena, expressing the joy of harvest and thanksgiving for Athena's birth. There were also chants by choruses of men. Hence, other officers besides those hitherto mentioned were required, such as the arrangers of the games, one from each tribe, the superintendents of the torch race called gymnasiarchs, and others.

The Panathenaea taken as a whole may be said to place the religious characteristics of the Athenian in the clearest light. One cannot but observe the atmosphere of purity, of genial serenity, and of ordered grace and harmony which surrounded it. The joy of festival was a religious gladness in realising the immediate presence of the gods, who had done such great things for Athens, and on whose continued favour depended the well-being of the state. Nothing mean or imperfect must be brought into their presence. Not only must the kine for the hecatomb be without blemish, but the persons young and old accompanying the sacrifice or carrying the vessels for ministration must be of the highest type of Hellenic manhood or womanhood. The boys and maidens, for example, must be children of parents who are in full life. Such festivals could not but accentuate the conscious unity of the Athenian people. No doubt, in the earliest times, there had been sacrifices to Athena in the several villages, probably at the same season, but each under the separate management of the local demarch. Now all the demes were organised into one procession, accompanying one great sacrifice on the commanding height of the Acropolis, the ancient seat of Erechtheus and Athena. The Athenian spirit had beautified, ennobled and enlarged what might otherwise have been a mere scene of butchery.

The preparation of the garment and the bringing of it to the temple already indicated that Pallas delighted in something else besides the blood of heifers. The altar was decorated in such a way as to hide any part of the performance that was necessarily unseemly, such as the breaking up of the victims, from the public view. Then the prayers and chants which from of old accompanied the sacrifice were now developed into the occasion of a lyric contest, occupying many hours and giving the poets and musicians a subject for their labours during the preceding years. Not only was the procession glorified by the presence of the knights on horseback, the chariots, the armed warriors, and the rest, but in order that only the best might appear before the goddess, these also were selected through competitions, which gave a noble opportunity for the exercise of manly accomplishments of strength and skill. Thus art of every kind was vivified by having its root in religion, and yet was allowed a free development into which all that was essentially human became absorbed. From the rhapsode who recited Homer to listening crowds, to the young boys dancing the Pyrrhic with shield and helmet, or the torchrunners in the night festival, all were stimulated to do their very best, and the crown which they received in recompense was rendered more delightful by being the gift of Athena, whose honour they upheld. Beneath this perfect blossom of Athenian life, ideas were germinating which were destined to have their course in after ages, but they were latent in the form of feeling, until they were drawn out by the poets and thinkers of a succeeding time. The duty of defending one's country, of struggling for the right, of maintaining power by equity, and liberty by well-ordered discipline, could not but occur to the reflective mind, that in the earlier part of the fifth century either witnessed or took part in the Panathenaic ritual.

We have seen that at some public festivals, as at the Dipolia, there were bloodless offerings (like the Hebrew meat-offering), as of cakes and honey, or of the first fruits, or frankincense, or of a mere libation. Such innocent oblations were frequent in the religion of the home, which continued side by side with that of the city. The harmonious co-existence of state ceremonials, local worships, and the religion of the hearth, not rivalling each other but blending in one complex and harmonious system, was the peculiar happiness of the Athenian. His loyalty to the state did not diminish his affection for his ancient neighbourhood, nor his sense of obligation to those of his own house. Although at the chief festivals the various districts of Attica might seem to have become absorbed in the whole community, every deme or district also retained its own peculiar worship, which circumstances brought into prominence from time to time. Thus Athena and Poseidon were worshipped specially at Colonus, as well as on the Acropolis, and although the Eleusinian Demeter had a sacred place under the central rock, close to the Areopagus, she retained her full honours at Eleusis in the time of festival. The Eumenides, or Dread Powers, were alike revered at Colonus and on the Areopagus. The great Dionysia did not supplant the ancient observances in honour of Dionysus at Icaria and Salamis.

Still more inseparable from the district was the local hero, whose reputed tomb was not forsaken. The worship of ancestors, from which hero-worship was derived, had never been discontinued on the Hellenic mainland. In the time following the migrations, the increasing religiousness before spoken of, the causes of which are but vaguely known, fastened on these local worships and developed them. The rifted rocks so common in Boeotia were supposed to be inhabited by powers once human, which had passed from the upper air but still lived on beneath the ground, and in some cases, as in that of Trophonius or Amphiaraos, might be consulted by men in their extremity who descended thither, and saw them in a dream. Something like this appears in Attica also, where the resting place of Oedipus, whither he has passed mysteriously, was the security of Athenian victory over Thebes. But that fear of ghosts which oppressed other parts of Hellas, where wicked ' heroes ' or disembodied spirits were known to rise out of their graves at night and devastate a region till they were propitiated or exorcised, pressed but lightly on the Athenian mind. The Attic heroes were of the nobler order, going forth to battle in great emergencies to defend their people, and extending protection to the men of their tribe so long as they were fed with sacrifice at stated times.

There are many indications of the great number of such buried lives which dominated Athenian soil. Some of these have been already mentioned ; the most striking evidence of their importance, perhaps, is that in the time of Cleisthenes ten heroes were selected from a hundred names submitted to the Delphic oracle to be acknowledged as the protectors of the ten tribes. That such worship was fully alive in the fifth century appears from the fact that it was thought worth while, on the morning of Salamis, to send to Aegina for the Aeacidae. The sense of close neighbourhood and of blood-relationship between the members of the same phratry was maintained by the annual feast of the Apaturia, celebrated in October towards the beginning of winter time, by every phratry in common, and also by every household apart. The chief ceremony was that of placing fresh faggots upon the hearth, so renewing the sacredness of home, and honouring Hephaestus, the fellow workman of Athena, and author of the Attic race, and also Prometheus the giver of fire. The word Apaturia signifies a festival of common parentage, and if we speculate on the transition from patriarchal to village life, we may suppose that this general feast day took the place of that on which each family had severally worshipped its own ancestors. The celebration was not peculiar to Athens, but was shared by other members of the Ionian race.

The prominence naturally given to public life in all Hellenic records tends to throw into the shade the life of the family, which was not less real ; each household was bound together by ties of affection, which sometimes proved stronger than death. Great families doubtless still retained their private altars, on which offerings were made on special days. A welcome light has been thrown upon this subject by the discovery of the graves in the Cerameicus, the chief public burial place. These tombs were adorned with sculptured reliefs of pathetic interest, which, although the groups from their very simplicity are often enigmatical, attest the depth and tenderness of feeling with which the survivors sought to perpetuate the forms of the departed. Here the moderation and simplicity of the Attic spirit is strikingly exemplified. The unmeasured pomp of ancient funeral ceremonies, having something of an oriental cast, with formal lamentations, of which reminiscences appear in the plays of Aeschylus, had been restrained by the legislation of Solon ; the superstitious rites which had survived from an earlier time, in which the chief anxiety of the living was to prevent the spirits of the dead from coming back again 'as ghosts to trouble joy,' had been forbidden, and only the weaker sort of women were inclined to them. No such anxiety appears amongst these sculptured stones.

The representations of the dead on monuments in all ages are principally of four kinds. The departed friend is represented (1) either as a divine being of more than mortal stature, receiving tribute from his puny descendants, who walk beneath ; or (2) in form and habit as he lived, perpetuating the impression that is cherished by surviving memory ; or (3) as at the moment of death, with some indication of the circumstances of that never-to-be-forgotten hour ; or once more (4) symbolically, as if asleep.

All these modes of representation may be found amongst Hellenic monuments, but the second is that which characterises the early fifth century in Attica. The most valuable example of the first-named motive, indicating a time when the worship of ancestors was in the fullest life, has been preserved in a monument found at Sparta, and now in the Sabouroff collection. The departed parents are enthroned like gods, with the smile familiar to early statuary, and redundant locks falling on their shoulders. Before their knees appear their offspring, of Lilliputian stature, approaching them with reverence, and carrying one a cock for sacrifice, and one a lotus flower. Behind the seated figures is a great writhing snake, symbolising the good demon or spirit of the world below, who has them in his keeping. Primitive customs, especially in regard to sepulture, were retained longer in Laconia than elsewhere. (See the account, in Herodotus vi. 58, of what happened on the death of every Spartan king.)

In passing from this monument to the stelae of the Cerameicus, we find a remarkable change. There is no exaggeration in them, no fear of ghosts, hardly even the oppressive sense of awe, much rather the desire that ' the dead should still be near us at our side,' with ' every lovely organ of their life ' in undecaying freshness,—their lightest fancies gratified, the warmth of welcome never cooling. The figures stand before us as in the fulness of life, with their names and nothing more inscribed above them. In a few instances, in the space above or beneath the group, some symbol of their occupation appears, and the name of the father or of the deme is sometimes added. The variety as well as the simplicity of the grouping is very striking, and even at the risk of rash conjecture one is tempted to read between the lines. One recurring type is that of an aged patriarch gazing wistfully upon a youthful figure unclothed and in the prime of manhood. It is natural to suppose that the father has died of sorrow for the untimely death of his son. A still more frequent motive is the grasping of hands. This has been variously interpreted. Is it welcome, or farewell, or simply the record of a true attachment ? In some groups at least there is a name above either figure, indicating that both are buried there. Else if the standing figure only were going upon the long journey, why has the one who remains seated her name written above her in the place of tombs ? Is it that the youthful person so full of a kind of tranquil awe is being received there by a mother or father or another relative who has gone before ? Another frequently recurring type is that of the lady who is looking out her jewels, while a maiden holds the casket. Yet another grouping represents the mother who has died in childbirth ; she sits listlessly playing with some ornament while she gazes at the child that is held in the arms of a nurse who stands before her. In these latter instances no names appear for the subsidiary figures. Or a youth is represented with some favourite animal, as a dog or rabbit in his hand, or at his side ; a child at his mother's knee often reaches his hand to take a bird that is held out to him. In one family group a little dog is much in evidence : he jumps up and fawns upon a young boy whose father places a hand upon his head. Some modifications appear towards the end of the fifth century, the time of the restoration of the democracy. There is no longer the absolute simplicity of remembrance ; short inscriptions are added, indicating the status of the deceased, or additional symbols, as the figure of a siren or a lyre. One of the most beautiful of all the monuments is that of Dexilaos, a young knight who died in the Corinthian war, 394 B.C. It is an equestrian group in high relief, and in a very noble style, in which the youth appears in the act of spearing his adversary and riding over him. ' He died at Corinth in the archonship of Teisander : he was one of the five horsemen.' What incident of the battle is thus alluded to, we can no longer guess, but it was no doubt at the time not less famous than the charge of the six hundred at Balaklava. In others the dead person is represented as fainting, with head reclined, perhaps indicating the suddenness of the death. Here comes in the third of the motives enumerated above. In another strange group of an uncertain period, Charon in his boat is represented as intruding on several persons at a feast, and laying his bony hand upon the shoulder of one of them (cp. the fresco of Orcagna at Pisa). The nearest approach to the fourth category above mentioned is the very interesting stele on which in low relief is the prow of a trireme, with the mark of the water-line, and on the deck of the vessel a man's figure seated in profound slumber, with his shield and helmet laid behind him. He is voyaging no doubt to the islands of the blest, in that deep repose, 'most like to death,' which overcame Odysseus as the Phaeacian ship was wafting him to his home. He may have been a trierarch or general, killed in some naval battle. Last, and belonging mostly to a later time, are the very frequent representations of the funeral feast in which the dead person appears at his own banquet amongst his friends.

This evidence of monuments helps to realise for us the unity of the household, and in considering Athenian life one should bear in mind the influence which domestic piety must have had on the young, who saw the heads of their families worshipping their special gods and heroes. These were by no means always the same, for Athens from early times had been hospitable to gods as well as to men : witness the Gephyraei who had their own peculiar worship of the sorrowing Demeter, and the family of Isagoras who sacrificed to the Carian Zeus.

Asclepius is one of those forms in Greek mythology that fluctuate between the divine and human. In Homer he appears as the father of Machaon and Podaleirios, the leeches of the camp, and is inferred to be a man of noble strain, like the other god-descended chieftains. He is said to have been taught by Chiron, the godlike centaur, who was also the teacher of Achilles, and his sons are leaders of the Thessalians from Trikka. But this need not prevent our supposing that in yet earlier times he had divine honours on the Greek mainland.

The original seat of the worship of Asclepius seems to have been this same Trikka in Thessaly, where, like Amphiaraos and Trophonios, he was believed to have his habitation underground, and was consulted as an oracular power who gave intimations in dreams. The god of Thessaly was carried by the emigrants whom the Dorians displaced to their new seats in Epidaurus, Cos, and elsewhere. He had hitherto been more allied to Zeus than to Apollo, and his function had not been limited to that of healing. But the Ionian Apolline worship grew and spread and absorbed the elder worships into itself, drawing them into the light of day; thus Asclepius became a son of Apollo; but his divine honours were not universally recognised until in the Hesiodic poetry, much influenced by the Delphic priesthood, his legend was humanised and took the shape which remained more or less fixed in literature. In historic times at least his power was associated, even at Trikka his original seat, with that of Phoebus, who, according to the legend which became established at a comparatively early time, was his father by the nymph Corônis. The epithet of Apollo in this connection is Maleates, a word of doubtful origin. In Messenia and Arcadia there were other legends which connected the family with Poseidon.

It was probably from Epidaurus that the Asclepian worship found its way to Attica. There are other indications, for example in the legend of Theseus, of religious intercourse between Attica and the opposite shore, where Calauria, the modern Poros, had been the centre of an important amphictiony. The worship of Asclepius, the authentic son of Apollo, supplanted that of many local gods of healing to whom the people had been accustomed to bring their sick, amongst others Alkon, the god of succour, of whom Sophocles was priest.[1] Such ancient divinities now took the rank of subordinate ministers.

Athena herself, as we have seen, was worshipped on great occasions as the goddess of health, but this was in a large sense, less intimately affecting individual and family life. The Asclepian cult was established in Attica from the middle of the fifth century and was the most popular of all minor Hellenic worships; its vogue went on increasing with the centuries until, in the schools of Cos and Epidaurus, it became systematised into a genuine art of healing.

[1] Sophocles is believed to have written a hieratic ode or hymn in honour of Asclepius.

The physicians there, and seemingly at Athens too, were formed into a guild or brotherhood, professing to be the descendants of the god, and in their practice combined in various degrees a mystical enthusiasm with scientific observation, relying more on diet than on drugs and charms. Of the innumerable cures attributed to the influence of Asclepius many may have been fanciful, and many what in modern times would have been called examples of faith-healing; but in the school of Cos, at any rate, which late in the fifth century produced Hippocrates (while the literary glories of that splendid island race were reserved for Alexandrian times) there was a most genuine and sincere endeavour to ascertain through science, in a religious spirit, the best and surest means of probing and alleviating human ills. The feeling at first prompted by the belief that disease was a divine visitation was modified but not extinguished by the discovery that all bodily affections were equally natural and equally divine. (See above, p. 165.) There was also amongst the Coan communities much disinterested devotion to the service of humanity, comparable to that which has created the modern hospitals; this appears from the inscriptions which record noble examples of individual public spirit. The scene at Epidaurus, where the precincts of the temple enclosing the sacred snake, which represented the good genius of the earth, were continually surrounded with anxious groups of those who brought their sick for healing, must have resembled nothing so much as the modern festival at Tenos, where the Virgin works miraculous cures, or the sacred place at Lourdes.

From the form of medical oath which was in use in the fourth century, and perhaps much earlier, it appears that the descendants of Asclepius adopted others into their brotherhood. The Asclepiadae had the exclusive right to practise medicine amongst the Athenians as well as at Epidaurus and in Cos.

The school of Croton, which flourished at a still earlier time, and of which Democedes was a brilliant example, may have owed their skill in part to a separate tradition, derived perhaps from Cyrene, or ultimately from Egypt.

The Asclepius-cult at Athens betrays the signs of a recent worship : first, in the fluctuation of certain details in the legend of the god ; e.g. his relationship to Epione, Aegle, and Hygieia, whether as husband or father, and secondly in his being surrounded with such clearly allegorical beings as Akeso and Iaso, spirits of healing, and Telesphorus, the perfecter of cures. On the other hand the doubtful derivation of the name is indicative of an early origin. The snake is his constant symbol as the good genius of earth, indicating the Chthonian nature of the god. The victim sacrificed to him was a cock, the bird of dawn, an immigrant from the east, probably because of his association with the sun-god. The words of Socrates to Crito just before his death : ' We owe a cock to Asclepius, be sure to pay it,' have given rise to various comments. Some think he would not leave his comrades without showing them that he still observed the religion of his countrymen ; others treat the saying as symbolic of thanksgiving for recovery from the long disease of life in a mystical Pythagorean sense ; or again, as symbolising the hope of an awakening. May not the message have meant more simply that the god of health is regarded as the author of Euthanasia, or painless death, the safe transition from this world to another ? May not Socrates have prayed for this as Cassandra did, or rather, had he not prayed for it in 'Phaedo' 117 B C ; and would not Crito receive comfort from the assurance that the prayer was heard ? Neither of the other two suggestions seems in accordance with perfect art ; compare Soph. ' Oed. Col.' and the dirge in ' Cymbeline ' (' Quiet consummation have ').

Asclepius was one of those deities who obtained a site for his temple not within the circle of the Acropolis, but just beneath it, outside the containing wall. Not far from this, and similarly situated, was the temple of Aphrodite Pandemos, said to have been founded by Phaedra during her passion for Hippolytus. Aphrodite in both her characters, as Urania and Pandemos, had probably a source in Phoenician religion, as it spread from Cyprus to Cythera and elsewhere. But in the earliest times the Athenians had retained a severe and stern conception of the great nature-goddess, who shaped the tree and flower, gave produce to the herd, and in her dealings with mankind conferred or withheld the charms of which she was the sole mistress. Her worship was not yet associated with the mere indulgence of sexual licence. But after the Persian war, through increasing intercourse with maritime populations, such as that of Troezen, where a distinctly Tyrian influence had long prevailed, a different and lower spirit appears to have sprung up, of which the establishment of the temple by the Propylaea gives visible proof. The string-course of marble pigeons still visible upon that site attests the relationship of this Troezenian goddess to her of Paphos, whose symbol was always the dove. But at Paphos itself, where, as Mr. Hogarth tells us, the worship of the Virgin to this day retains some features of the Aphrodisiac cult, it is hard to say what aboriginal or Achaean superstition may have survived under the Phoenician rite. The retention of the ' Cypriote ' syllabary and the rarity of Semitic inscriptions in the island are facts hard to reconcile with the sole prevalence of a Phoenician influence. The way in which the more refined Athenians regarded the votaries of this religion which had appeared in their midst may be inferred not only from the conduct of Hippolytus in Euripides, who, as Mr. Grote remarks, refused to worship her ' because she was a very bad goddess,' but from the words of the Platonic Socrates in the ' Phaedrus ' (he is refer- ring to his former speech describing the harm which may accrue from an intemperate love)—' would not any one who was of a generous and noble nature and who loved or ever had loved a nature like his own, when he heard us speaking of the petty causes of lovers' jealousies and of their exceeding animosities, and the injuries which they do to their beloved, have imagined that our ideas of love were taken from some haunt of sailors in which good manners were unknown? ' See also the speech of Pausanias in the ' Symposium,' assert- ing that there are two loves as there are two Aphrodites— ' the love who is the offspring of the common Aphrodite (Pandemos) is essentially common, being such as the meaner sort of men feel . . . and is of the body rather than of the soul.'

Polytheism could not but acknowledge all powers that sway humanity, nor omit one whose potency is so evident as that of sexual desire, but it by no means acknowledged all powers as of equal worth. Nor, while allowing some practices which long experience and a series of high examples have led the modern world to discountenance and to forbid, did it therefore view them with respect, or include them in its ideal of human virtue.

The question whether there existed an organised tolerance of vice at Athens is not quite a simple one. In the time of the Orators and of Plato it is evident that public morals were considerably relaxed, and a poet of the new comedy, Philemon, who wrote after the loss of Athenian freedom, had the hardihood to assert that Solon, because of the difficulty of restraining youth, had instituted regular provision for licentiousness. I refuse to accept this on the authority of a comic poet, although a comparatively serious writer in the following age (Nikander of Colophon) seems to have taken him literally. Such literalism has been a fruitful cause of mistakes in history. It is certain, however, that at Corinth, early in the fifth century, an institution of the kind was founded by a certain Xenophon, and that Pindar was not too fastidious to write a hymn on the occasion. In this he showed a very different spirit from that of Aeschylus, who described with deep and true feeling the misery of the poor captive women in the sack of a city. I see no reason to doubt the assertion of Isocrates (' Areopagitica,' § 48) that in the later fifth century there had crept in a corruption of manners in private life unknown to previous generations. The example of the said Xenophon only shows that Corinthian laxity began early under Phoenician influences, and that the ' silver sound ' of Pindaric verse was responsive to the chink of coin. It is observable that in Athens, as in modern Europe, those who pandered to men's vices were mostly aliens or outcasts from the state.

During the same period, as the number of foreign residents increased, many strange worships were introduced at Athens, and in some instances at least sites were accorded

to them by the state, not, indeed, within the charmed circle
of the Acropolis, nor in its immediate neighbourhood, as in
the case of Aphrodite Pandemos and Asclepius, but in the
outer precincts of the city, and more particularly in the
Piraeus, where men of foreign nationalities, even when
partly naturalised, chiefly made their abode. Thus it was
at the Piraeus that Socrates, having witnessed the inaugura-
ting festival of the Thracian goddess Bendis, went home to
the house of Polemarchus, the resident foreigner, which the
Thirty Tyrants afterwards despoiled. And it appears from
inscriptions that land was granted in the same district for
the specially Tyrian worship of Aphrodite, that is of Astarte
—hence, perhaps, Plato's allusion to the haunts of sailors.
That amongst the sworn votaries of some of these foreign
cults native Athenians of eccentric tendencies were counted
is no doubt true, but the number of such persons was probably insignificant compared to the mass of Athenian citizens.

The admission of these foreign worships not only shows
the pliability of polytheism, except where fanaticism had
been aroused through panic, but their influence also indicates
the fact that the formalities of the national religion had
failed to satisfy the religious cravings of the people. The
innovations in mythology, which began with Stesichorus, and
the growth of the orgiastic worships presently to be described
belong to the same tendency, characteristic of a stage in the
evolution of religion which has been well described by
Professor Menzies in a recent work. He points out two
causes which tend to counteract the completeness and permanence of national religions : the one that tribal and
family traditions persist side by side with the national
worship which might be thought to have absorbed them ;
the other, that in the mental evolution of the race individual
minds outgrow the forms which were an adequate expression of religious feeling at an earlier stage and have become
fixed through the increasing influence of the priesthood.
At Athens both these causes were at work and helped each
other, while the fixity of public ritual was less rigid than
elsewhere, because of the plastic nature of Attic genius and
the indefiniteness of local traditions.

CHAPTER XI

THE MYSTERIES

THE Greek had religious yearnings that were not satisfied either by the public or the private worships which have been described. (1) He had reminiscences of an earlier world in which the state was not yet organised, and in the life of the country he had lived in more immediate and continual dependence upon Mother Earth, and the powers which give increase to the flocks and to the fruit of the ground. Survivals of tree worship and of animal worship had lingered on as elements of village life, and could not be relinquished without leaving a void, which imagination laboured to supply. (2) As humanity became more conscious of itself, the great recurring fact of death awakened more and more anxiety and wonder about what lay beyond. And (3) the sense of sin or of an offended god, of which the germs are found in Hesiod, although in the Homeric poems there are only distant echoes of such thoughts, had suggested rites of purification and atonement which wrought upon men's hopes and fears.

The religious movements which brought temporary aid to these human needs may be considered in two stages : the first earlier and more primitive, the second more advanced. In both we cannot but trace the working of influences from abroad, although in every instance the Hellenic, and more particularly the Attic spirit, is accountable for what is essentially characteristic. Simple mysteries, such as belong to most religions, were not absent from the earliest known phase of Hellenic worship. The ceremony of the sacred marriage of Hera, performed with cognate rites at

Samos, in Argolis, and in Boeotia, was essentially of this nature; and although the Samian Hera had Asiatic associations, and the Argolic Hera, in historic times at least, bore traces of Egyptian contact, the mysterious rite referred to had a deep root in Hellenic soil. The procession of the ἀρρηφόροι carrying secret things in honour of Athena was analogous to the Thesmophoria, and belonged to the most primitive of Athenian worships. The worship of the mother of the gods, already known as Rhea in Homer, stood undoubtedly in some relation to the Phrygian worship of Cybele. When Sophocles describes her as seated on a chariot drawn by lions, he seems to recognise this connection. It will be remembered that the scene of the 'Philoctetes' where this occurs is laid in the island of Lemnos, and that this play was not produced until the last decade of the fifth century. But it is uncertain how far such recognition was really present at Thebes in the time of Pindar, or at Athens in the early years of the Peloponnesian war, when the Great Mother is mentioned in the inscriptions as one of the gods whose treasures were drawn upon for supplies. Her temple (the μητρῷον) was one of the earliest of those at Olympia. Whether there were mysteries connected with her in these earlier days or not, or whether, as in Homer, she was simply regarded as the parent of the Olympian gods, must be left uncertain.

All such worships in historic times are composite, and have been developed both from within and from without. The difficulties attending the attempts to analyse them have not yet been solved by archaeology. The Egyptologist is inclined to attribute all mystic worships to an Egyptian source. The student of Semitic origins is apt to look everywhere for traces of tribal religion. Both sometimes ignore the Aryan element to which language unmistakably points as prior to either of these. What came in through Phoenician commerce and colonisation, what through contact with Asiatic peoples, and what was due to the supposed suzerainty of Egypt over the shores of the Levant in the second millennium B.C., can hardly be distinguished with accuracy. The tendency of the Hellenes, after their settlement in lower Egypt in the seventh century, to refer many features of their own religion to an Egyptian source should make us hesitate in accepting without reserve the statements of Herodotus and other writers on this subject, whatever proofs may exist of subsequent contamination of Hellenic with Egyptian rites. This caution is especially necessary in considering the worship of Demeter. Even if Minos were, as is sometimes affirmed, not a Phoenician potentate, but an Egyptian viceroy, it does not follow that Hellenic village populations would be inclined to accept a religion imposed on them in consequence of the suzerainty of the Pharaohs.

In Homer the underground Zeus and Persephone are the god and goddess of the world below, while Demeter is simply the goddess of the grain, and in a late passage one of the many consorts of Zeus; while in a myth apparently of Cretan origin she is the wife of Iasion. This hardly justifies the supposition that the Eleusinian ritual and mythology had been developed to any extent in the heroic age.

Besides the Eleusinian mysteries, Demeter and her daughter Persephone had another important festival, the Thesmophoria, which Athens shared with many other localities. It belonged essentially to the country, as appears from the fact that when the Chians passed through the Ephesian territory, the women were all in the fields, on account of this festival. Its universality, especially amongst Ionian peoples, is a strong evidence of antiquity. Herodotus even refers it to Pelasgian times. In Attica it never underwent the modifications to which the kindred festival at Eleusis was continually liable. It was first a festival of seed-time, being celebrated in the month Pyanepsion, our October, and it occupied four days. Only the married women of the state took part in it; and, as the name implies, it was observed with strictness according to ancestral precepts (θεσμοί) which the goddess herself had instituted. The reason of its continued importance was that not only the produce of the ground but the fruitfulness of married life depended on it. The elder women gave precepts to the younger, which they had themselves received from those before them; thus it was a sort of initiation into the duties of the wife and mother. On one day they went in procession to the point of Colias, where was a shrine of Aphrodite Urania: on the next they returned. The third day was a day of fasting in sympathy with the sorrowing Demeter, in honour of whom young pigs were thrown into a chasm and destroyed; this was a day of gloom, when no religious-minded person would show a cheerful countenance. The fourth day was a day of rejoicing, again in sympathy with the goddess, who had her child restored to her; certain objects not to be beheld by men were carried solemnly in closed caskets, and the day ended with a feast, the means for which were supplied by the richer matrons of the community. It appears that at some uncertain time a procession of the Athenian women to the temple at Eleusis formed part of the ceremony. M. Foucart, accepting the testimony of Herodotus that this ritual was brought by an Egyptian colony to Argolis, and assigning its arrival to the period of the eighteenth dynasty, further assumes that another colony brought it also to Eleusis at the same time, the sorrowing Demeter being thus supposed to have been already identified with Isis. But the sorrows of the earth goddess have given rise to similar observances in many centres not associated with Egypt, and the Gephyreans, who were said to have brought the rites of the Demeter of sorrows into Attica, were not Egyptians, but Phoenicians from Thebes. Without affirming or denying M. Foucart's hypothesis, I hold that it is at least conceivable that some Asiatic influence working upon an Aryan village rite may sufficiently account for all that is known of the religion of Demeter before the seventh century. Her worship seems to have sprung up independently of Eleusis. Demeter was by no means the only earth deity in Hellas. The worship of Erechtheus and of Aglauros on the Acropolis, of Athena Itonia in Boeotia, that of Asclepius, and other worships in which the serpent as the son of Earth appears, bear traces of primitive religious feeling. Poseidon as god

R

of earthquake had similar associations, and even the
Omphalos at Delphi seems to have been a primeval symbol
of the earth.   Nor is it clearly proved that such forms as
Damia and Auxesia in Aegina and Epidaurus, or the name-
less goddesses of Triteia in Achaia, were derivative, and not
rather an indigenous growth arising out of feelings connected with the cultivation of the soil.   Earth has, in fact,
two aspects : she is the mother of all things, the nurse of
all things, the producer of ' our sustaining corn ' ; but she is
also in close relation to the darkness beneath, into which
all that live upon the ground must pass away.   Vague
emotions thus suggested lay at the root of religious forms
that sprang up, no one can tell how.   It is hardly conceivable
that rites, which appear at so many different centres, and
remain longest in places most remote from the outer world
(see, for example, the Demeter Erinnys and the ' black
Demeter ' in Arcadia), should be entirely of foreign origin.
Even the rape of Persephone was identified with many
separate localities : for instance, with Lerna, where in the
time of Pausanias there was a stone enclosure surrounding
the place where the daughter of Demeter descended with
Pluto to their under realm.   This festival of the Thesmophoria was, in any case, the native Attic worship of
Demeter, as distinguished from that in which Athens had
joined hands with Eleusis.   Aristophanes made fun of it in
his ' Thesmophoriazusae,' where he takes occasion to satirise
Euripides and the Athenian women.

The wisdom of early Athenian statesmanship was in
nothing more remarkable than in its frank acceptance of
the Eleusinian and Dionysiac rituals under the patronage of
the state.   The Eleusinian rite became interwoven with
Athenian patriotism hardly less intimately than the worship
of Athena herself, and this helped to perpetuate it in its
main features.   That of Dionysus came in time to be equally
inseparable from the national spirit, to which it gave expression in its most universal pan-Hellenic aspect.   Dionysiac
rites in prehistoric times had already had a vigorous growth
in Attica, especially on the east coast and on the northern

border. In Dionysus there are traces of primeval tree worship, and also of the midnight or winter sun, distinct elements which must have blended in very early times. His winter festival at Delphi, with the midnight torch processions on Parnassus, belong to the latter phase of him, which reached Athens through Thebes by way of Eleutherae. Which of his many seats in Hellas was the earliest it would be hard to say, but his oracle in the Thracian highlands seems to have been of great antiquity. His ritual probably spread together with the planting of the vine, but not the vine alone was sacred to him. All fruit-trees, the mountain pine, and the lush growth of ivy were evidences of his universal power. He was associated with the mythical mountain Nysa, which was variously located in Euboea, in Naxos, and far away in Ethiopia. In Sicily also there was a Nysean plain. The Greek habit of identifying foreign deities with their own makes an already obscure subject still more confused. It may be incidentally illustrated by the curious interlacing of flute music with that of the lyre in the worship of Athena and Apollo, which gave rise to fables such as that about the flutes of Marsyas, found by a shepherd in the river Asopus near Sicyon, and dedicated by him to Apollo. Compare the Sicilian story of Arethusa and the Alpheus.

That in the Hellenic Dionysus worship, Phoenician, Thracian, and Phrygian elements have been engrafted on a primitive stock is extremely probable. This religion seems to have entered Attica through two principal channels —by way of Icaria, perhaps from Naxos, and through Eleutherae on the way from Thebes. Thespis, the inventor of tragedy, was a native of Icaria, while, on the other hand, the place of honour in the Dionysiac theatre was assigned to the priest of Dionysus of Eleutherae. The reception of the god by the mythical Icarius is the subject of a strange and elaborate legend, which was still represented on the ὑποσκήνιον of the Attic stage in the latest time. In accordance with the spirit of the festival, the cries of joy and grief alternately had less of native Greek moderation than in other rites. This worship embodied the 'violent delights that have a violent end,' the exuberance of nature, whose transience awakens profound sadness, the infinity of natural desire in which, as Plato felt, there is involved the spiritual longing after immortality. It should be remembered that the Greeks were descendants of a race who had first been huntsmen, then nomad herdsmen, leading a wandering life under the covert of the sky. Coming down to arable land and settling in villages, they had felt the periodic exhilaration and depression of agricultural life : the springing of the corn, seed-time and harvest, and the hardships of the winter season had impressed their minds. Their feelings had been deeply engaged in the precarious growth of their fruit-trees, above all of the vine. That in some ways, even before the Orphic symbolism entered in, the sufferings of the god were celebrated in the Bacchic dance, appears from what Herodotus tells of tragic choruses at Corinth in the earlier part of the sixth century. Hence, amid the wild licence and unbridled mirth of the spring festival, in which Sileni and Satyrs danced, there were notes of poignant melancholy, which had a sobering effect, and opened deeper fountains of emotion. It was out of these, as will be presently seen, that Attic tragedy sprang.

Another worship, partaking still more obviously of the underground or Chthonian strain, is that of the Erinnyes, who, whatever may have been the origin of the name, came to be in fact an impersonation of the 'dead man's curse' surviving him. These Dread Goddesses, whom the Athenian feared to name, had a habitation assigned them in a cave under the hill of Ares, and also in the precinct of Poseidon at Colonus. Their worshipper, fearing to offend them, addressed them as the 'gentle ones,' a euphemistic and propitiatory epithet, describing them as he would have them to be. This special attribute did not diminish the awe with which they were approached, but was an index of the aspect which they assumed for the Attic spirit. They were no longer merely blind and passionate avengers, but the executors of divine justice, the guardians of domestic sanctity, bringing to those who worshipped them in spirit and in truth a blessing and not a curse. We shall have to say more of them in speaking particularly of the Aeschylean religion, for it was Aeschylus who gave expression to the peculiar form of this belief and ritual which afterwards prevailed in Attica. The imagined struggle between powers of light and darkness, appearing in the conceptions of Typhoeus and of the Titans already known to Homer, is a common feature of early religious thought, and may be recognised on the Babylonian monuments as well as in the mythology of Egypt. But there are plausible grounds for recognising in some Greek forms of it an early influence from without. Typhon, in Homer, has his lair amongst the Arimi in Cilicia, and in Aeschylus he is said to have dwelt formerly in Cilician caves.

We have now to consider a most important movement which had an extraordinary influence on all the after development, but whose early history, like that of all beginnings, is extremely obscure. The existence of Orphism throughout the fifth century is an indisputable fact, but of its precise scope and nature during that period little trustworthy evidence remains. A religion which from the first was imparted to a clique of votaries in a mystery, which in the course of centuries attained extensive influence, and was continually modified through the absorption of fresh elements, affords a subject of enquiry which is almost impossible to disentangle. Quotations from the Orphic poems or from 'Orpheus' abound in writers of the early Christian centuries, both sacred and profane. And that such poems existed in much earlier times is clear ; but it is known that they were continually recast, augmented or interpolated, as the doctrines of the sect were altered or improved ; and the only evidence that can be really trusted is that which was either derived from Aristotle, Plato, and writers preceding them, or which is confirmed by direct allusions in such writers. We may now add the golden plates or tablets inscribed with a sort of ritual for the dead which have been lately found in Greek tombs anterior to the Christian era. Lobeck did an immense service by collecting the fragments, whether genuine or spurious, and discussing them ; and the labours of Hermann, and more recently of Lenormant, of Abel, of Ermin Rohde, of Foucart, and E. Maass, have supplied us with grounds on which we can proceed with some confidence, though much remains vague and indeterminate. Partly with their help I will try to give such an account of the matter as may be in keeping with the general tenor of this volume.

Before the middle of the sixth century individuals at Athens and elsewhere had begun to form new conceptions of the divine nature and of the religious life. They dimly but strongly felt the contradictions and confusions of the traditional mythology, and strove to formulate the notion of a universal Deity pervading all things and essentially One. At the same time they were painfully conscious of the limitations of mortality. In giving form to their conception, and still more in recommending it to others, it did not occur to them, and it would have been futile if it had, to give their thoughts an abstract and clearly defined or an openly controversial expression. For abstractions were a language not yet understood, and negation would also have been premature. In promulgating a new form of religion, a new mythology and a new ritual having some felt relation to the old were indispensable. But in this case, unlike that of more primitive religion, the mythology was not subsequent to the ritual, but suggested it, and was itself subject to conditions of precedent thought. These men were impelled to impart to others their own aspirations and emotional impulses, but to teach novelties as novelties, and to do so openly, was impossible in that state of the world. They found a basis for their doctrine in the Thracian worship of Dionysus, which with important changes had long been naturalised in Hellas. Thrace was the cradle not only of Dionysiac worship but of the religion of the Muse, and under the traditional names of Orpheus the Thracian singer, and his son Musaeus, as well as of Olen, Thamyras, and other legendary figures, they indited long poems in hexameter verse embodying their mystic theosophy. The Hesiodic poems supplied them with some hints, for, as we have seen, there are already in Hesiod germs of an almost oriental mysticism, and there is a strong probability, which modern research has made more substantial, that through the recent settlement of Greeks in Egypt in the seventh century, this rising sect derived important suggestions from Egyptian theology. The result was a creation of great originality and fulness of symbolic meaning. The exact steps of the Theogony in its early form are uncertain. The primeval egg, the birth of Phanes, his disappearance and rebirth, cannot be traced to the fifth century, though it is possible that they may have already been present then. Rohde's reason to the contrary, however, has considerable force, viz. that the similarity between the swallowing of Phanes and the disappearance of Zagreus (as presently described) looks like an after development or reduplication. But the central feature of the mythology is tolerably clear. The son of Zeus and Persephone (the goddess of the under-world) is Zagreus, an old epithet of Hades, whom the Orphic pantheism identifies with Dionysus, and also in a manner with Zeus. The holy child, like the infant Zeus in Crete, is entrusted to the Titans, powers of evil, who cajole his infancy with toys, and while he looks into a mirror which they have given him, surprise him, and attempt to seize him. He assumes various forms in endeavouring to escape from them, and last assumes the shape of a bull; in that disguise he is torn to pieces by them. They devour the members all but the heart, which Persephone rescues, and it is swallowed by Zeus, who thus becomes Zeus and Dionysus in one, the supreme being, the beginning, middle, and end of everything. Zeus smites the Titans with his thunderbolts, and reduces them to ashes, which are collected and become the material from which mankind are formed. Man thus partakes of a nature both evil and good, infected with the Titanic element, but having a portion of the divine. To subdue the Titanic to the divine, and to reunite what has been violently sundered, is therefore the highest task of humanity. Many writers have dwelt upon the obvious parallel between the discerption of Zagreus and what follows it, and the Egyptian legend of Osiris. If the primeval egg and the birth of Phanes were proved ancient, the analogy would be strengthened; but this would not disprove the supposition that the pulling to pieces of the bull and devouring the portions is founded on the ancient Thracian ritual, of which there are many other reminiscences, a ritual having many analogies in savage rites. The doctrine lends support, however, to the suggestion of Herodotus that Osiris and Dionysus are the same. To the Orphic mystic the whole legend symbolised the high doctrine that birth is an evil, and that the manifold is a hindrance to the good. And with this accords their ethical doctrine, that the soul of man is imprisoned in the body as a punishment for previous sin. This involves the teaching of metempsychosis and continuance after death. Whether this last doctrine had an independent existence in Thrace, it is difficult to say. That for the Orphic theosophist it was confirmed by stories of Zamolxis and other mysterious beings in the northern region (such as Aristeas of Proconnesus), as well as by the return of Orpheus from Hades, is probable enough.

Another question arises which is not yet solved : the relation of Orphism to Pythagoreanism. They have many points of resemblance, which cannot be accidental. There are three ways of explaining these : either (1) both systems had an Egyptian (or other earlier) source, or (2) Pythagoras borrowed from the Orphics, or (3) the Orphics from Pythagoras. The first supposition is countenanced by many ancient writers who support the Egyptian origin, and has perhaps been too rashly thrown aside by modern critics. Rohde declares for the second view, that Pythagoras borrowed certain details of his scheme from the Orphic teachers. But it seems more consonant with analogy to suppose that the authors of a vague theosophy, groping their way by feeling more than by thought, and desiderating some intellectual substratum, should lean on a half-understood philosophy, than that a great original philosopher should have condescended to follow such a doubtful lead. But here again we are met by the chronological difficulty. Onomacritus, the only person who can be credited with the authorship of Orphic writings in early times, flourished about the middle of the sixth century, and Pythagoras is said to have left Samos in 532. We are thus thrown back upon the first hypothesis, viz. : that what is common to both schemes of doctrine was due to some influence to which both were subject; and this is supported by the theory of Diels, that mystic doctrines of similar complexion arose simultaneously at various centres. The doctrine of transmigration, however, is not Egyptian at all, and is common to many forms of religious speculation. It was adopted by Brahmanism and Buddhism, no less than by Pythagoras. Thus we may be justified in supposing that besides Egyptian influence, or even apart from it, some phase of pantheistic or at least of ascetic and pessimistic teaching, of which no clear trace remains, existed antecedently both to Pythagoras and Onomacritus. But to return. The hope of the mystic who carried the reed in the train of the Orphic priest was, that by performing the ritual prescribed, not only outwardly, but in spirit and in truth, he might ultimately escape from the circle of successive births and deaths, and fly away into some unknown heaven, perhaps becoming an inhabitant of one of the stars. To this end, not only were religious forms prescribed, but a mode of life, unlike that of the world, was instituted.

Greek asceticism never reached the extravagance of the Indian self-tormentor. It chiefly consisted in abstinence from fleshly indulgence and especially from the use of animal food. This latter practice was denounced by the Orphic teacher as a sort of cannibalism. The doctrine of transmigration implies that all living beings are akin, so that to eat animal food is to devour one's relations. Abstinence was also prescribed from eggs, and (emphatically) from the bean. The former prohibition was in later times attributed to the legend of the birth of Phanes, but may have simply expressed the reverence of the sect for the beginnings of life. The latter was also a Pythagorean observance and coincided with some Egyptian rites. It has been accounted for by the fact that beans were amongst the usual offerings to the dead. The Orphic, in this also agreeing with the Egyptian, would not be buried in wool. Even his dead body must not benefit at the expense of an animal.

The hope of a future state of ultimate blessedness was balanced by fears of judgment to come. The uninitiated, and the adherent of Orphism who had broken the rule, were threatened with torments or with degradation in a future state, from which they could only be released through repentance and suffering. Eternal punishment in Tartarus, such as was dimly foreshadowed even in Homer, and is distinctly provided by Plato for incurable offenders, does not seem to have been preached by these mild mystics.

Some general remarks may be more profitable than any further discussion of uncertain details.

1. Any one of the resemblances between Orphism and the religion of Egypt taken singly may be accidental, and it is uncertain at what period each was introduced. But taken all together they do afford *prima facie* evidence of some real connection. To recapitulate them briefly there is : (1) the primeval egg ; (2) the tearing to pieces of Zagreus by the Titans, the saving of the heart, and collection of the remains, compared with the destruction of Osiris by Set, the saving of the head, and the finding of the body by Isis ; (3) the prohibition of the use of wool in burial ; (4) the belief in a future judgment. Compare the ' Book of the Dead,' of which we are also reminded by the inscriptions on gold plates above referred to, in which the hope of the dead person relies upon his strict observance of the Orphic rule. The resemblance is after all superficial, for the chief doctrine of the Orphics, the immortality of the soul, combined with metempsychosis, and with the hope of ultimate deliverance from the body, is essentially different from the Egyptian belief in the Ka or double of the dead man, which enjoys an intermittent life so long as the body is preserved, and the ritual of the dead is maintained.

A deeper affinity is implied in what is called the Theocrasy or blending together of distinct divinities ; as when Zeus becomes Dionysus or Dionysus Zeus. But this again may be accounted for by the pantheistic spirit, which is inherent in either religion.

2. The coincidences between Orphism and Pythagoreanism are more striking, extending as they do, not only to

detailed points of doctrine, but to minute requirements of ritual. The data which are available seem to point, as said above, to some common antecedent influence out of which both came. Orphism may then be related to Pythagoreanism, much as the Asclepian school of Epidaurus was to that of Cos. The one was far more influential for a time, but lost itself in vague aspirations in which true feeling was alloyed with credulity ; the other contained within it a germ of philosophic truth, which is of endless value, and is in fact still operative amongst mankind.

3. The indirect influence of Orphism, even in the fifth century, must have been considerable. The curiosity of enlightened Greeks would be a sufficient motive for initiation, and it is obvious, for example, that Herodotus, though not a consistent adherent, had been initiated. It is, therefore, not surprising to find pantheistic tendencies and innovations in mythology existing side by side with orthodox polytheism in the plays of Aeschylus and even of Sophocles, as well as manifestly in Euripides. From the way in which Plato speaks of Eumolpus, side by side with Orpheus and Musaeus, it is evident that there had been a secret alliance as well as no doubt occasional rivalry between the Eleusinian and the Orphic priesthood. But this fusion must have been comparatively recent, else why should Aeschylus, who is learned in all the wisdom of Eleusis, betray so little consciousness of future blessedness for the righteous dead ? Probably also they had something in common with the priests of Cybele, the Great Mother, of whom Plato speaks in similar terms. It was in the nature of these orgiastic worships to become interlaced with one another. The reader of the ' Bacchanals ' of Euripides might suppose that Dionysus had as much to do with Phrygia as with Thrace or Naxos.

Pausanias, the antiquarian writer in the times of the early Roman empire, surprises us with the observation that the Orphic poetry appeared to him as great as, or greater than, the poems of Homer. We should not attach too much weight to such a criticism, from one to whom a vein of religiosity probably appealed more powerfully than the perfection of art. But still we are led to think that he must have had access to these works in an earlier and less interpolated form than that from which most of the fragments which have descended to us were taken. It may be worth while to quote here some of those passages which have the strongest claim to be considered authentic.

' One power, one Deity, was born, great gleaming Heaven ; all things were framed as one, wherein all these are rolled, fire, water, earth.

' Zeus was the first, Zeus of the bright thunderbolt shall be the last of things ; Zeus is the head ; Zeus fills the midst ; all things are framed of Zeus. Zeus is the foundation both of earth and starry heaven ; Zeus is male, Zeus the divine feminine ; Zeus the breath of all things ; Zeus the rushing of irresistible fire ; Zeus the great fountain of the deep ; Zeus the sun and moon ; Zeus is the king ; Zeus the leader of all ; for he of the bright thunderbolt, after hiding all within him, brought them forth again from his sacred bosom to the gladsome day, doing ever wondrously. None saw the firstborn except holy night alone ; the other powers admired as they beheld an unlooked for light in the sky ; such radiance shone from the immortal form of Phanes.'

The following is probably a somewhat later development of the description of Zeus just quoted :—' For all these things lie within the mighty frame of Zeus. His head and fair countenance is to be beheld in the gleaming sky, adorned with the golden rays of glittering stars, as with beautiful hair ; and on either hand are two golden horns as of a bull, the east and the west, paths of the heavenly gods ; and his eyes are the sun and shining moon ; his royal ear that tells him all things truly is the imperishable ether, wherethrough he hears and hath intelligence of all things. Nor is there any voice or cry or noise or rumour, which escapes the ear of all-prevailing Zeus, the son of Kronos. Thus immortal is his head and faculty of thought, and his body, all radiant, immeasurable, impenetrable, unshakeable, of mighty limbs and all-subduing, is thus framed. The shoulders and the chest and broad back of the god is the wide circumambient air, and he hath wings, moreover, whereon he is wafted every way. And his holy abdomen is the earth, mother of all things, and the lofty mountain tops; and the girdle of his middle is the swelling and sounding sea. And the ground he treads are the inward parts of earth firmly rooted beneath in gloomy Tartarus. Hiding all these things within him, he brings them forth again into the gladsome light, doing ever wondrously.'

One more short piece, though not from the poem itself, is worth quoting because it refers to the Orphic tradition at an earlier stage. It is the place in Apollonius Rhodius' 'Argonautica,' where he describes the singing of Orpheus, and has been imitated by Virgil in a well-known passage. 'And Orpheus, lifting with the left hand his lyre, essayed to sing.—He sang how earth and sky and sea beforetime fitted in one perfect frame were sundered by dread strife, and stood apart. And how the stars and moon and pathways of the sun hold evermore their limit in the ether without fail; and how the mountains rose, and how the roaring rivers came into being with their attendant nymphs, and all the creatures were born. And he sang how first of all Ophion, and the ocean nymph Eurynome, held the sway over snowy Olympus. And how, by force and violence, Ophion yielded his honours to Kronos, and Eurynome to Rhea. And they fell into the ocean waves, and Kronos and Rhea for a while ruled over the Titanic brood of happy gods, whilst Zeus was yet a child and still with infant thoughts was dwelling in the covert of the Diktaean cave, and the earthborn Cyclopes had not yet provided him with the might of thunder, lightning, and the thunderbolt. For these things give to Zeus his renown.—He spake, and hushed his lyre, together with his immortal voice.'

4. The Orphic ritual may be credited with two great contributions to religion—the belief in immortality, and the idea of personal holiness. Each contribution was made more valuable by the fact that both were combined, so that without holiness blessedness could not be secured hereafter. A third contribution had in it the seeds at once of good and evil. The idea of redemption or of atonement entered largely into this religion. So long as this was received in a

spiritual sense, and the great Orphic saying ' Many bear the reed but few are pure ' was understood in its full significance, it could not but have a profoundly salutary effect. But when the ritual degenerated into formalism, and it was imagined that by rites and ceremonies duly performed not only might a man's self be acquitted for past sins but he might redeem the souls of his ancestors from future punishment, what should have been a law of life became a law of death. It is this degenerate Orphism that is denounced and satirised by Plato, whose disgust at the hypocrisy of the sectaries whom he had known, and who made a gain of godliness, led him into a possibly exaggerated abhorrence of the whole doctrine of forgiveness and absolution. He, too, holds forth the hope of release for the wrongdoer, but it is through the conversion of the whole soul from error to truth, by living in the light of truth, and holding firmly to the right way. Many a weak brother whom Orphism had comforted and really edified was beyond the reach of Plato's teaching, and could not have benefited by meat that was too strong for him. More will have to be said of this when we come to Plato.

5. It is a paradoxical circumstance, and one that illustrates the contrariety that may exist between the germ and the completed form of a spiritual fact, that the Orphic sect, the central point of whose mythology had been suggested by a savage ritual of bloody sacrifice, not only themselves abstained from animal food, and therefore cannot have tasted for instance of the hecatomb to Athena, but lived amongst a nation of sacrificers without partaking in the act. This consideration also brings into a clear light the tolerance of polytheism when not directly challenged or provoked. The Orphic teaching may have led to acts which were severely punished for impiety, but the sect does not seem to have been the object of anything like an organised persecution.

To return from these generalities to the special worship of Demeter at Athens, which in historic times had two chief forms—the Thesmophoria above described, and the Eleusinia. The former, as we have seen, was common to the Attic population with other members of the Ionian race, and apparently also to the early Achaeans. So much at least may be gathered from what Herodotus tells, that this rite at the conquest of the Peloponnesus retired from Argolis into Arcadia, where it remained in green observance. But there is a question behind. There is no doubt that some elements derived from Egypt were infused at an uncertain period into the Eleusinian ritual. The historian believed that the earlier and immemorial rite was brought by the daughters of Danaus into Argolis, and that they had also visited Lindus in Rhodes. The students of Greek history have long discarded that belief ; but it has recently been revived by Foucart, who suggests that as the victories of Thoth-mes III extended to the shores of the Aegean, and as Achaeans seem to be mentioned amongst the enemies of Egypt during the twentieth dynasty, there is every proba-bility that the whole religion of Demeter, together with the cultivation of wheat and barley, may have been introduced into Greece by way of Egypt. The proof, however, seems incomplete, and if Hellas was early occupied by an Aryan stock who brought with them the words for ploughing, sowing, and reaping, it is probable that, notwithstanding the poverty of the soil, agricultural habits may have been accompanied with a native village festival. Still it deserves to be remarked that if the hypothesis of Foucart should be substantiated, it would appear all the more natural that the worship of Demeter should in later times have assimi-lated the exotic features which I have just referred to.

When the Homeric ' Hymn to Demeter ' was composed, a time that can hardly be placed later than the beginning of the sixth century, Eleusis was already the home of an elaborate myth which gave the reason of a ritual already considerably developed. This seems to have prevailed not at Eleusis only, but also at Paros, no doubt in the temple which Miltiades violated to his cost. And it included various features which were permanently imbedded in the Eleusinian celebration. These are :

1. The interval of three months between the lesser and the greater Eleusinia (the latter at Eleusis, the former at

the village of Agrae near Athens)—i.e. from the disappearance of the seed in the ground to the springing of the corn. 'Persephone remains with her dark lord for one third of the year.'

2. The nine days of preparation for the greater Eleusinia in spring—' Demeter wandered for nine days with torches in her hands.'

3. The association of Hecate and of Rhea the mother of the gods with this worship. Hecate is a light-bearing deity who dwells in a cave.

4. The position of the temple below the citadel of Eleusis on the rising ground above the spring of Callichoron. This locality, as well as the rock of sorrow on which the image of the Mater Dolorosa sat, has been verified by recent excavations.

5. The fertility of the sacred Rharian plain—from which barley was taken for the sacrifices.

6. The joyousness of the procession along the Sacred Way, perhaps also some sportive features in the celebration, contrasting with the solemn silence of the main ceremony. 'Iambe with her pleasantry succeeded in diverting the mind of Demeter from her sorrow.'

7. Certain abstinences forming part of the preparation— as from wine and from pomegranates, or, at least, pomegranate seed. Also downright fasting for some time. 'Demeter remained without tasting food or drink.'

8. The drinking of the potion made of barley water flavoured with an aromatic herb.

9. Demeter has the power of conferring immortality, and this is associated with the sacred fire of the Hearth.

10. The happiness of the mystae in the world below. They are not yet removed to Islands of the Blest.

11. A sort of sham fight which followed all the other ceremonies on the concluding day, which was a day of festival.

No trace appears in the hymn of several things which are described by later writers as belonging to the Eleusinia, some of which have been referred with probability to the fifth century. The sacred marriage of Zeus and Demeter, and the birth of the child, whether Triptolemus, Eubulus, or Iacchus, are the most important of these. The Egyptologists who suppose the whole rite to have been introduced from Egypt at a very early date attribute this silence to some mystic reserve; but the supposition is hazardous, and no confirmation of it has yet been cited from any source that is shown to be earlier than the hymn. If we compare the manner in which the Panathenaic festival was developed out of a crude sacrificial rite, another hypothesis seems at least tenable, namely, that the Eleusinian ceremony, under the guidance of the Eumolpidae, may have assimilated foreign elements by gradual stages, of which the adoption of the Gephyreans with their Cadmeian sanctities may have been the earliest.

M. Foucart, in supporting the Egyptian origin, makes much of the name Eumolpus and the requirement of great vocal power in the hierophant and intelligible utterance in the initiate. This he accounts for after the manner of Egypt, by supposing that the mystic formula to be dictated and repeated was of the nature of a charm, which lost its effect if any tone or modulation were imperfect. He rejects the usual tradition that by intelligible utterance was meant that of a true Hellene. This hypothesis he states with becoming modesty, but the other views which he puts forth on this subject are hardly more substantial. It is true that amongst the sanctities of Eleusis, to which the hymn makes no allusion, there are a god and goddess, simply mentioned as such, while the god is sometimes identified with Pluto. This fact has, indeed, a primitive air, but not more of an Egyptian look than the worship of Zeus and Dione at Dodona. That the Thesmophoria was the more ancient rite seems clear. The rite of Eleusis may not have been originally distinct from it, but gradually modified through special influences. Two statements of Herodotus, however, must be considered before we finally lay aside the theory in question : (1) that the Thesmophoria were brought by the daughters of Danaus into Argolis, and carried by them, under the stress of invasion, into Arcadia; and (2) that the Eleusinion at Miletus was founded by the Ionians, who brought the rite from Athens in the time of Codrus. That the simpler rite of the Thesmophoria has

s

some primeval connection with Egypt, I would neither affirm nor deny ; in any case it does not pass beyond the limits of an ordinary village festival, securing by traditional custom the blessing of fruitfulness and the ordering of married life. What rite may have been brought over from Eleusis to Asia, in the time of Codrus, it would be difficult to say, but the continuous intercourse between Athens and Miletus in historical times would be a sufficient reason for assimilating the ritual of Demeter in the neighbourhood of Miletus to that of Eleusis, and assigning to the worship so developed a date coeval with the foundation of the city.

It is clear at any rate that the Eleusinia already differed from the Thesmophoria in promising to the initiated a peculiar blessedness in the world of the dead, and in attributing to the goddess the power of conferring immortality on her nursling and favourite. The latter attribute, however, does not go beyond the privilege assigned to several of the gods in Homer, and it is remarkable that in the promise of blessedness there is no allusion to the Islands of the Blest, but only to some special immunity, such perhaps as Teiresias already enjoys in the eleventh Odyssey, while dwelling in the darkness underground (ὑπὸ ζόφῳ εὑρώεντι, cp. Od. xi. 155 ὑπὸ ζόφον ἠερόεντα). The grave question whether these features were added to the original rite through a process of internal development, or, if they came from without, whether they were brought directly from Egypt, or through a Phoenician channel, must unfortunately be left undecided. But it is important to note that the probable date of the hymn excludes the supposition that such development was due in the first instance to the influence of Orphism. The Eleusinian priesthood may claim the right of precedence as to the honour of holding forth the hope to the initiated, that if faithful they will be happy after death ; but it may be cited as making against the hypothesis that they derived this doctrine immediately from Egypt, that the power of Demeter to confer immortality on her favourite is directly associated with the sacred fire of the hearth, which, as we saw at first, is a conception of Aryan origin.

We may now pass to the consideration of the ritual as

it existed in historic times. The details of the nine days'
preparation—the rush to the salt water, the sacrifice of
young swine, the tumult at the bridge, the purification for
uncleanness and bloodguiltiness, and so forth, have been fully
described by Lenormant and Foucart. The following are the
essential points :

1. Although there could be no strict test of probation so far
as pure Hellenes were concerned, when once the celebrants
were multiplied by the admission of foreigners, yet the warning
of the Archon Basileus and of the Eumolpidae, that none
should take part who had not ' the hands and the heart pure,'
implied something more than a ceremonial test, which those
elect spirits that were ' finely touched unto fine issues ' could
not fail to apply to themselves. Even in Aristophanes, the
initiated declare ' we only have bright sun and cheerful light
who have been initiated and *lived piously in regard to
strangers and to private citizens.*'

2. Another incident of great importance and solemnity
was the proclamation of the sacred truce—which was
religiously observed until the intense embitterment of
relations which came after the disaster at Syracuse, and the
establishment of a Spartan garrison at Deceleia.

3. The carrying of the image of young Iacchus from
Athens to Eleusis—occupying the whole of a day : ' the procession which set out at sunrise did not arrive at Eleusis till a late
hour of the night, by the light of the thousands of torches
carried by the mystae.'

4. The order of the ceremonies at Eleusis itself. We
may note in passing, as indicating the high development of
the later rite, that there were no less than twenty distinct
titles for the various ministers, and it was a fact which gave
added solemnity that the hierophant and high priestess
when once appointed were never known again by their birth-
names.

The day preceding the mystic celebration was occupied
with many sacrifices. The greatest of them is described in
an inscription said to be earlier than the age of Pericles, i.e.
early in the fifth century. ' A goat to Earth the nourisher
of Youth, to Hermes of the public place, and to the Graces ;

a goat to Artemis ; a goat to Triptolemus and Telesidromus' (Telesidromus is not mentioned in the 'Hymn to Demeter ') ; 'a bull, a ram, and a boar ' (cf. the Roman Suovetaurilia) 'to Iacchus and the Great Goddesses.'

That night the mystae went to visit the places which bore witness to Demeter's grief, carrying torches as she had done—the well by which she was found, and the rock of mourning on which she had sat awaiting her reception by Metaneira. Then, if not before, they fasted, and on returning from the wandering all drank together of the temperate potion, whereof the goddess had tasted when Metaneira had prepared it. This was part of the ' communication of the sacred things ' preceding initiation, which is implied in the mystic formula : 'I have fasted : I have drunk of the potion : I have taken out of the casket, and after having tasted I have deposited in the basket : I have taken out of the basket again, and have put back into the casket.' Before all this the mystagogus put the question to each initiated person, whether he or she had tasted any of the forbidden aliments—as fish, fowl, or pomegranate seed.

Once more the herald proclaimed silence, and warned off the profane ; and a new phase of the ceremonial began. It was continued through two nights of vigil. Those permitted to take part in it were crowned with myrtle and carried a short staff with mystic emblems on it. They assembled at the gates of the temple some time before the ceremonies began, not now with torches, but in darkness, with the mystagogues no doubt keeping order amongst the novices. Presently a light was seen to gleam through the aperture in the roof reflected on high. A torchbearer threw the gates open, and the farther end of the hall was seen under a strong illumination which revealed the forms of the statues of mystae of former days. In the middle was the seated image of Demeter with new and gorgeous apparel, and probably also figures of the other divinities of the place. On either side stood the hierophant and the torchbearer. Then, while the audience remained in breathless silence, moving and breathing pictures were presented—a series of tableaux representing the carrying down of Persephone, the sorrow of

Demeter, the return of Persephone with her child in her arms, and lastly the triumph of Triptolemus, Demeter's foster son, in his chariot drawn by serpents, in which he goes forth to spread the blessings of husbandry amongst mankind. These successive scenes were probably accompanied with sacred words delivered by the hierophant in exalted tones adapted to produce a profound impression on minds so carefully prepared.

In the legend as known in the fourth century Iacchus, the child of Persephone, or according to another view of Zeus and Demeter, was identified with Zagreus, the suffering Dionysus of the Orphic theogony. M. Foucart supposes this to have been the case as early as the sixth century, but perhaps Lenormant is right in thinking that the change coincided with the building of the larger temple begun in the time of Pericles. Iacchus in Herodotus means only ' the song of the mystae.' Iacchus in Aristophanes is the god whom they invoke ; but there is no proof that he is there regarded as Dionysus, though this identification seems to be already implied in a choral ode of the ' Antigone.'

The name Zagreus occurs in a fragment of Aeschylus, apparently as an appellation of the god of the underworld, but not as in any way associated with the Eleusinia. We can only say that probably before the time of Plato both Dionysiac and Orphic elements had been engrafted on the Eleusinia, and in the mysteries of *the second night* of vigil, in the tableaux reserved for the select number of those who had been initiated at least a year before, and who were only admitted on presenting tokens,[1] scenes were enacted recalling the mystic marriage of Zeus and Demeter, the birth of Zagreus, his dismemberment by the Titans, and the pursuit of the Titans by Zeus—points of Orphic doctrine closely resembling the Egyptian legend of Osiris. If these incidents recall Egyptian theology, so also does the culminating act of these advanced mysteries. The horror of that scene of apparent annihilation is said by a somewhat late authority to have been followed by the blissful apparition of a perfect ear of corn, which was contemplated with adoration amidst absolute

---

[1] Some of these have been recently discovered.

silence—the symbol at once of life and death and of life after death. As I have said, this second night is not proved to have existed before the fourth century. With the exception of this solemn hour of silence which concluded all, not only were the eyes of the mute throng on either night engaged with visions, but their sense of hearing, too, was filled with impressive sounds. The hierophant who managed the display accompanied each successive scene (in which there were both live impersonations and plastic moving figures) with solemn words, spoken or chanted in awe-inspiring tones. And at the critical moment of the descent of Persephone, he struck a bronze bowl, a sort of bell or gong which resounded through the hall. What the words then uttered were, we never shall know, but it is unlikely that they contained any elaborate statement of doctrine. The effect was not that of listening to a sermon, but much more that of assisting at the Easter ceremonies at Rome, when the Pope still gave his blessing *Urbi et Orbi*. This is said to have been Aristotle's view. 'The initiated learned nothing precisely, but received impressions and were put into a certain frame of mind, for which they had been prepared.'

M. Foucart in a memorable brochure, published at Paris in 1895, has argued with great probability in favour of the following hypothesis :—That the words heard by the mystae, which might not be repeated to profane ears, were simply directions for the passage of the soul from this life to happiness in the next, analogous to the elaborate guide-book with which the Egyptians provided their dead. If we suppose with him that the Eleusinian rite in its full development was derived from Egypt with due adaptation to Hellenic religion, his view seems plausible, and it is strikingly supported by the mystic inscriptions on gold plates which have been mentioned before in connection with Orphism, discovered in Greek tombs, not only in Magna Graecia, but in Crete, and dating at all events from pre-Christian times, in which the departed spirit is advised to keep to the right, leaving the pool of oblivion by the cypress tree on the left hand, and to beg for a draught from the springs of memory ;—then to declare itself as an offspring of heaven and earth, and as having partaken of the rites of Persephone.

The same author reasons with much force in favour of another view, viz. that the drama of the second night presented not only the legend of Demeter but also the contrasted pictures of future misery and blessedness ; the dangers which the soul must pass before arriving at its Elysium, the slough of despond in which the uninitiate were plunged, the monsters threatening the disembodied spirit, and finally, the state of blessedness which would be reached by those who bore in memory the mystic pass-words.

The remark above quoted as attributed to Aristotle brings us back to the point which is of main importance in connection with our subject : What was the frame of mind of the initiated ?   What impressions did they receive and carry away ?   The effect must have varied greatly with the degree of impressibility, of depth, of aspiration, and of preparedness in the nature of the recipient.   What frivolous or sentimental fancies may have been awakened in the mind of the average sensual man is really not our concern.   That to many the promise of future blessedness meant only an earthly paradise may be quite true.   Antinomianism dogs the steps of every spiritual revival, as the shadow the substance.   Hence the mocking question of the Cynic—' Shall the thief who has been initiated fare better after death than Epaminondas ? ' But there is a phase of religious growth in which persons gifted with a deeper religious impulse than is satisfied by the established worships infallibly draw together. To such, the requirement that those who approached the goddess of sorrow and of consolation must have clean hands and a pure heart had much more than a merely ceremonial meaning.

To some also, as to the Antigone of Sophocles, the hope of blessedness in another life was inseparable from the thought of reunion with loved ones who had gone before.

In the sixth century B.C. or early in the fifth, even if no Dionysiac or Orphic rite had been engrafted on the native ceremony, there must already have been an inner

circle ever growing amongst the initiated and amongst the
Eumolpidae themselves, not marked off from others by any
outward sign, yet consciously distinct, who were acquainted
with Orphism,—with that new mythology, embodied in
strangely sounding poems, in which Hesiodic traditions,
cosmogonic speculations, and a daring theosophy were
blended in a haze of pantheism. What ineffable thoughts the
mysteries may have suggested to minds so prepared, who
can say ? Many mystagogues on each occasion were instruct-
ing the novices how to conduct themselves. Each was an
Athenian, active in mind and fluent in speech. Can we
doubt that the results would be rich and various ? We cannot suppose, for example, that Themistocles and Aeschylus,
or Herodotus and Sophocles, would be alike impressed, or
that their meditations would be of the same order. All this
must have gradually reacted on the body of legend that was
sure to form itself around such a religious centre, and which
as thus gradually modified supplied rich material for
tragedy.

One thing may be certainly affirmed—that high authorities whose gravity and depth of mind cannot be disputed
bear witness with one voice to the elevating influence of the
Eleusinian mysteries. Sophocles dwells emphatically on the
incomparable happiness of the initiated both in life and after
death ; and Plato, who had a far clearer vision both of God
and immortality than any child of Eumolpus, can find
no more fitting vehicle for his most transcendent thoughts
than the imagery which he borrows from the contemplation
of the mysteries.

And long afterwards, when the philosophy inspired by
Plato had become the acknowledged guide of life for those
who could receive it, and the Eleusinian ceremonies had lost
much of their early freshness and simplicity, Plutarch, in
speaking of death and a future state, could find no language
more impressive than what belonged to the same line of
allusion :—' To die is to be initiated into the great mysteries. . . . It is there that man, having become perfect
through his new initiation, restored to liberty, really master
of himself, celebrates, crowned with myrtle, the most august

mysteries, holds converse with just and pure souls, and sees with contempt the impure multitude of the profane or uninitiated, ever plunged or sinking of itself into the mire and in profound darkness.'

Lastly, it is a significant fact that Marcus Aurelius, in his anxiety to keep touch with the religion of his contemporaries, when he visited Athens took care to be initiated at Eleusis.

How many of the higher thoughts about another life, and about the divine nature, which we find in Pindar, Aeschylus, Sophocles, or Euripides, how much of the tradition concerning immortality to which Plato refers in the ' Meno,' may have been originated in some such way as I have indicated, it were vain to inquire.

Demeter and Persephone were closely associated both in ritual and mythology with the Erinnyes of the household, i.e. with the religious sanctions for domestic purity and for righteous dealings amongst kinsmen. Here also existed a true germ of moral and spiritual religion.

Tiele and others have observed that the great historical religions have all grown out of voluntary associations (θιασοί) which stood apart from national or tribal worships. And in this connection it deserves to be noted with respect to the mystical side of Greek religion generally that its votaries differed from those of the national or patriotic gods, in being possessed with the missionary spirit. No Athenian priestess of Athena, no Corinthian devotee of Poseidon would think of carrying the sacred things of either into other realms, unless in connection with the foundation of an Athenian or Corinthian colony. The case is different with the rites of the Great Goddesses. Take, for example, what Pausanias tells us of the bringing of the Eleusinian rites into Messenia (Book iv. ch. 1 § 5) : how Caucon, the son of Celaenus, the son of Phlyus, came bringing the orgies of the Great Goddesses, Demeter and Persephone, from Eleusis to the court of Polycaon, in Messene. This is one of many similar traditions, and the universal spread of these worships may have arisen partly from this cause, but partly from the fact that they were congenial to the native mind, and that the germ of them already existed in the universal village festival. A still more unquestionable instance occurs in Herodotus (vii. 153), where he tells how Telines of Gela owed the ascendency which he obtained over his countrymen to nothing else than his possession of the sacred things of the subterranean goddesses. He led back a body of exiles and made terms with his fellow citizens on condition that his descendants should succeed him as hierophants of the same holy rites. This achievement, Herodotus says, would seem to have evinced high qualities of mind and manlike energy, whereas the Sicilians repute Telines to have been of a soft and effeminate character.

There is something akin to these phenomena in the persistence with which certain ancient families, especially in Elis, successfully maintained the power of divination (μαντική). See for example the elaborate account which Herodotus gives of the soothsayers on either side before Plataea : Tisamenos, the son of Antiochus of Elis, a Clytiad of the Iamidae, whom the Spartans had secured upon the Greek side by the rare gift of Lacedaemonian citizenship ; and Hegesistratos, also of Elis, a distinguished Telliad, who served upon the Persian side through resentment against the Spartans for their maltreatment of him. Thus it appears that the religious authority accorded to the race of prophets was independent of national prepossessions.

There has been no room in this chapter for the mention of mysteries of a more vulgar kind, which became rife at Athens in the fourth century, and were increasingly influential in the decline of Hellas—such as those practised by the votaries of Sabazius (a spurious Dionysus) or by the mendicant priests of Cybele. We must be content with following the more important lines, merely glancing aside at such as these : ' Let us not discourse about them, but look and pass them by.'

CHAPTER XII

The Dionysiac Worship—Origin and Growth of Tragedy.

IN that early state of Hellas of which we can only entertain conjecture, there must have been many gods with comparatively few attributes. The gods many and lords many, belonging severally to each locality or to each tribe, would have had for an enlightened observer, had such been there, a strong family resemblance, differing only as the small communities of the same race, at the same stage of culture, may be imagined to have differed. If, as some have thought, the Greeks gave to many local gods the common name of Zeus, this was only an appellative, denoting the fact that each so-named god was supreme over that particular land ; much as the various tribes of Canaan had each their Baal, whom they worshipped under special titles, all much in the same way. When from various causes, amongst which Homer, the Delphic oracle, and the Olympian games were not the least, the Greek tribes had been partly drawn together under one universal name, a select number of divinities under the headship of Zeus were organised, again only in part, into a generally accepted Pantheon. Many deities, once reverenced at particular shrines, were eclipsed by the more modern sanctities, while others were retained as satellites of the chief divinity, or figured as local heroes, worshipped at their tombs :—as if in a firmament sown with innumerable stars of the seventh magnitude great constellations of the first and second magnitudes were to shine forth, either dimming or eclipsing their elder rivals. Polytheism does not stop here.   Attributes of the great gods are again personified, and at each centre of worship there is a cluster of divinities, grouped together in some order.   Each of the more brilliant stars in the newly adorned firmament gets a planetary system round it, and each planet has its accompanying moons.   In some places, at Argos for instance, the custom had obtained of combining several of the great divinities round one high altar (κοινοβωμία), probably in groups of eight or twelve, as in Egypt and Babylon.[1]

Now under cover of this long-continued process there has been a growth of thought.   The greater gods have had their characters modified by the changing circumstances and experience of the communities who support their worship ; by the imagination of great poets educating the race ; and, in the later stage of which we now speak, also by the influence of the priesthood.   The 'Olympians' are frequently addressed under this common title.   And amongst the subordinate deities who now claim the reverence of mankind are some which in modern language would be called abstractions, but to the personifying imagination of the early fifth century were beings as full of life and power as the deities of the older tradition.   Such, for instance, was the goddess Nemesis, whose temple at Rhamnus, on the Marathonian shore, was adorned by her statue attributed to Pheidias, commemorating the defeat of Xerxes as the most signal of all examples of the fall of pride.   Such was Peace, whom the Athenian with all his quarrelsomeness loved as the protector of his fields, his olive and his vine and fig-tree, that Peace (Εἰρήνη) whom the sculptors were wont to represent with the infant Wealth in her arms.   Such was Fortune, who was often imaged forth in the same way ; and such was Adrasteia, the goddess of the inevitable, whose worship the daughters of Oceanus commend to Prometheus. So far the growth of ritual and mythology in this direction was natural and spontaneous.   Then came the Orphic teacher with his pantheistic blending of divinities, and his vague suggestions of great thoughts on the divine nature, which he was unable clearly to express, and the Eleusinian

The foundation of such an altar in Attica was attributed to Solon.

mystagogue, not uninfluenced by Orphism, but also having spiritual aspirations of his own.

Such in general outline was the condition of Athenian religion when Aeschylus, who had fought at Marathon and been present at Salamis, entered on his vocation as a votary of the Dionysiac worship, and the new creator of Tragedy.

Before going further it is necessary to speak more fully of Dionysus, of whom in the preceding chapter comparatively little has been said. His worship like that of Demeter was in historical times an extremely complex phenomenon. I will not attempt to determine here exactly the sources of the stream that gained such fulness on Athenian soil. Some aboriginal strain had been developed through Phoenician, Thracian, and possibly Egyptian influences. As it existed within the bounds of Attica this religion again resembled that of Demeter in retaining a more primitive celebration side by side with that which ultimately proved most important. The spring festival of the Lenaea was more ancient and remained more simple than the greater Dionysia, originally a winter festival, which took place earlier in the year. Instead of giving a detailed account of either of these, which have been described in many popular works, it must suffice to speak generally of the spirit which informed the worship and the probable motive of its adoption as part of the state religion. The Dionysus whom the tragedians celebrate is the god of Thebes, the son of Semele, the nursling of the Nysaean nymphs, whose worship had been adopted not without a struggle at Thebes and previously in Thrace. The legends of Pentheus and of Lycurgus are extremely significant in this regard.

This Dionysus is not only the god of wine, but also primarily the embodiment of all great powers of vegetable and animal nature, and his festival is one in which the feelings awakened in primitive humanity by the succession of the seasons, the joy of vintage, the gloom of winter, the rejuvenescence of the spring-time, had found a natural expression. In a dithyramb composed by Pindar for performance at Athens, of which a fragment has been preserved, the chorus, after invoking the Olympian gods, Zeus above all, pass on to celebrate Bacchus and his mother Semele whose power is seen in the opening of the year, ' when the chamber of the Hours is disclosed and sweet flowers spread their fragrance, when the prophet of Zeus at Nemea perceives the first shoot of the palm-tree, when rosy chaplets are worn, and songs resound to the accompaniment of the flute.'

As the tribe came before the family, and the village before the city, so the annual festival either of the tribe or of the village preceded that organisation of the state and of national religion which in Hellas found a general rallying point at Delphi. The Delphic legend of the conquest of Dionysus by Apollo was a symbolic embodiment of this truth. But the tribe or the village community which had submitted to the restraints of civic life was liable to a periodic recrudescence of the old Pagan impulse. We may imagine them as seized with an epidemic of orgiastic frenzy, returning to some wild rite of their ancestors, going forth into the pine-woods, tearing in pieces the victim who was identified with the tribal god, partaking of his blood, and giving vent to the exuberance of their animal nature, not unaccompanied by a diviner stimulus, with shouts and cries. Such an outburst would threaten a manifest disturbance of the more settled organisation. Now the wise tolerance of some Greek ruler, at once priest and king, is to be imagined as obviating this danger to the order of the state by the institution of an annual festival associated with the joy of vintage time, or of broaching last year's wine cask, in which these aboriginal feelings might find utterance with a minimum of mischief. The story of Melampus is instructive from this point of view. The women of Argolis (including the daughters of Proetus) had all at once gone mad, and Melampus, a sort of medicine man, cured them by the introduction of Bacchic rites (which the historian thinks that he had learnt in Egypt) and so obtained a third share of the kingly power. Thus in its first institution the Bacchic festival was a means of healing or purgation, at once indulging and regulating emotions that could not be suppressed; so rendering them harmless and preventing the turbulence that might arise from continual restraint. Now in such a festival, especially amongst the Dorians, the regularly ordered dance accompanied with singing was a prominent feature ; and the poetical genius of the people, or of a succession of poets, developed this into complex and beautiful forms. And at Athens, where things beautiful were not rejected because they were of foreign growth, the Dorian tragic chorus became an adjunct of the Dionysiac celebration.

In the course of centuries Athenian life and culture had passed through many phases, in which primitive rites were not abandoned, but expanded and modified. The recitation of epic poetry, which in the time of Pisistratus or earlier had come over from the Asiatic seaboard, now formed an accompaniment of the great national festival of Athena. In this body of recited verse many legends of the heroic age of Greece, to which every Greek looked back with pride, had found a splendid record. Why should not the festival of Dionysus also be adorned with some of these time-honoured tales ? The leader of the chorus had long since in the intervals of song and dance recited in vernacular Ionic Greek some appropriate narrative with gestures approaching to impersonation. The legend of Theseus or of Herakles, by an agreeable licence, now sometimes took the place of the myth of Dionysus ; and other deities, as in Pindar's dithyramb, were invoked to favour the celebration which had found acceptance with the state. The old Bacchic impulse thus dressed itself in novel forms. When by a further change, in addition to the chorus leader, a second speaker or answerer was introduced, a more finished impersonation was at once made possible : tragic dialogue began, and the drama in the proper sense was born. The spirit of these changes is well expressed by Nietsche, in his essay on the birth of tragedy, when he says that through the influence of music the more artistic Apolline element was grafted on the Dionysiac wildness. What had once been a mere village festival had now become a public institution, and this process was consummated just at the time when Athenian national life was rising to its height. The grosser elements were reserved for the satyric drama as a separate mode, but the Bacchic enthusiasm was not therefore withdrawn from the more serious performance which now took definite shape. The orgiastic impulse was refined and clarified, but not extinguished. The fire still glowed, although the decoration of the altar was different and the tone of the worshippers more solemn.

Aeschylus is distinctly said by Aristophanes to have owed his inspiration to Demeter and her mysteries. But his genius is too great to have ever taken the mould of any priest-made form. If, as Aristotle tells us, he was accused of having divulged in his dramas some part of the Eleusinian secret, this may probably count as one of the groundless accusations of plagiarism to which great poets have always been liable.

Familiar with every aspect of Greek religion, he had meditated profoundly on the great questions which it raised, concerning life and death, good and evil, crime and retribution, the state of the departed, the relation of man to higher powers, and that of the new world in which he found himself, and in which he exulted, to an earlier and less harmonious dispensation which he imagined as having preceded it and given it birth. He is in entire sympathy with polytheism while he is representing the thoughts of ordinary men and women ; yet he feels also for the patriot, who despises those who cry to heaven when they should be acting for the common good, and allows Eteocles to remind the frightened maidens, with something of ironical scorn, that the gods are said to desert a falling city.

But throughout his tragedies, wearing as they do the many-coloured garb of popular religion, there is a dominant tone,—a strain of higher mood. Religion means for him something more than sacrifice or ceremonious prayers. The dark traditions of the past, which it is his cue to dramatise, are transfigured with a light from heaven, calculated to lead mankind into a more excellent way. The deliverance of Hellas through the agency of Athens has penetrated her poet with the conviction that in the higher mind of the Athenian people while they remained faithful to it, or in other words while they followed the guidance of Athena and Apollo, lies the salvation of the world.

This conviction meets in his mind with far-reaching contemplations concerning the nature and attributes of the divine, the first principles of human conduct, and the sources of good and evil. In all he recognises growth from discord towards harmony, from Chaos to Cosmos, from tyranny and rebellion, action and reaction, to the triumphs of liberty and order.

In himself, also, there is a growth observable.

1. In his early plays, as compared with the 'Agamemnon' and the 'Prometheus,' his religious as well as his artistic attitude is comparatively crude. Nothing can better illustrate the workings of a great religious genius still struggling with the swathings of mythology than to compare the passages in the 'Suppliants,' in which Zeus is spoken of as the lover of Io when transformed into a heifer, and those other lines not far remote from these, in which the power of Zeus as the supreme god is expressed in language almost worthy of the book of Job :—

> Divine Protector, now beyond the sea,
>   Son of the Highest, the wandering heifer's child,—
> For while she roamed and cropped the flowery lea,
>   Zeus breathed on her, and, ever undefiled,
> She felt the touch that filled her veins with thee,
> And made her to be mother of us all ;
> Epaphus, named of Fate, on thee we call !

> .   .   .   .   .   .

> Let highest in mind be most in might.
>   The choice of Zeus what charm may bind ?
> His thought, mid Fate's mysterious night
>   A growing blaze against the wind,
> Prevails :—whate'er the nations say,
> His purpose holds its darkling way.

> What thing his nod hath ratified
>   Stands fast, and moves with firm sure tread,
> Nor sways, nor swerves, nor starts aside :
>   A mazy thicket, hard to thread,
> A labyrinth undiscovered still,
> The far-drawn windings of his will.

T

> Down from proud towers of hope
> He throws infatuate men,
> Nor needs, to reach his boundless scope,
> The undistressful pain
> Of Godlike effort; on his holy seat
> He thinks, and all is done, even as him seems most meet.

Yet even this last expression appears vague and incomplete when compared with the conception of Zeus—or should we rather say of God Himself?—in the first chorus of the 'Agamemnon.'

> Zeus,—by what name soe'er
> He glories being addressed,
> Even by that holiest name
> I name the Highest and Best.
> On him I cast my troublous care,
> My only refuge from despair :
> Weighing all else, in Him alone I find
> Relief from this vain burden of the mind.

> One erst appeared supreme,
> Bold with abounding might,
> But like a darkling dream
> Vanished in long past night
> Powerless to save ; and he is gone
> Who flourished since, in turn to own
> His conqueror, to whom with soul on fire
> Man crying aloud shall gain his heart's desire,—

> Zeus, who prepared for men
> The path of wisdom, binding fast
> Learning to suffering.   In their sleep
> The mind is visited again
> With memory of affliction past.
> Without the will, reflection deep
> Reads lessons that perforce shall last,
> Thanks to the power that plies the sovran oar,
> Resistless, toward the eternal shore.

And not less wonderful is the teaching of the Promethean trilogy, in which it is shown that even the supreme God, if exercising power apart from wisdom and beneficence, would be less than divine.

2. In dealing with the principles of human conduct there

is a corresponding advance. The virtues of mercy to the suppliant, and of self-devoted bravery in defence of one's fatherland, were not unknown to those of old time. Yet in the ' Suppliants ' and the ' Seven against Thebes ' the poet has so enforced these duties as to invest them with a nobler sanction. The hesitation of king Pelasgus, whether or not to protect the fifty maidens who appealed to him for succour, at the risk of ruin to the state, is borne down by the unanimous voice of the people, who declare for the higher law. Here already Aeschylus shows that confidence in the people under rational guidance, as the supporters of all things good, which has its greatest expression in the description of the fight at Salamis. Observe also his manly tenderness towards women, of which the description of captivity in the chorus of the ' Seven against Thebes ' is a signal example. But his thought has not yet the comprehensiveness which it attains in the Orestean trilogy. His moral and political conceptions have not risen to their full height.

3. The figure of Eteocles, who goes forth to battle for his country, well knowing his impending doom, and of Amphiaraus, the righteous man enlisted in a wrongful cause, will never cease to fire the human breast with a sympathetic glow. But there are yet deeper tones in the ' Eumenides,' where the love of country is transfused with a love of goodness and of equity, of gentleness and purity of life.

4. In his ' Persians ' Aeschylus appeals not merely to Athenian pride but to the frank and generous spirit of his countrymen, which could sympathise with the vanquished, and reflect upon the causes of success. ' Not unto us, but to thy name, O Athena, be the praise.' It is the paean of rational freedom. Here also appears the Aeschylean aspect of Nemesis, a conception which in the ages following Homer had obtained a powerful hold on the Hellenic mind. It will be remembered that Herodotus was in sympathy with that forward current of Hellenic feeling, of which Athenian life, after the Persian wars, was the main channel. But his notion of the divine nature was still overclouded with early pessimism. In recommending that law of moderation,

which was the chief note of incipient reflection in Hellas, he based his argument on the supposed malignity of the gods. The Solon of Herodotus, most unlike the real Solon, speaks of God as the author of confusion and as full of envy. The envy of the gods was, in fact, the crude form under which the moralists of Ionia seem to have couched the all-important lesson of wise self-control. The impetuosity of passion and desire thus found a check. This traditional doctrine had, of course, a prominent place amongst the motives of tragedy, but Aeschylus takes occasion to correct such perverted theology, and to teach a higher morality at the same time. It is not the successful, the eminent, or the wealthy, whom the gods cast down, but the proud, the impious, and the unjust. Human calamities are not accounted for by divine jealousy, nor even by a blind inexorable fate, but by the misdirection of the human will. Xerxes is overthrown, not because it had been prophesied that disaster should attend the Persian arms, but because he did violence to the sacred Hellespont, destroyed the temples of Hellenic gods, and trusted in his own might. The Greeks are delivered, not only because heaven favoured them, but because freedom had inspired them with the love of country. Thus, not all at once with perfect clearness, but with irresistible fervour, the religious spirit is moralised. Man is represented as in part the master of his own fate, and the fear of the gods becomes a rational motive. No breath of doubt is thrown upon religious customs or traditions, but they are transfigured into the expression of thoughts transcending them.

God is no longer merely envious of prosperity, but rather jealous of the right, determining that all shall have their due ; and for this not Phthonos, envy, but Nemesis, the spirit of distribution, is the more correct expression. The religious spirit of this age anticipates what a century afterwards Plato well summed up in the fourth and fifth books of the ' Laws,' in following up his retrospect of the course of Hellenic history. Although it is coloured with a somewhat later strain of reflection, the passage may be quoted here :— (' Legg.' iv. 716 c—718 b) ' God ought to be to us the

measure of all things, and not man . . . . and he who would
be dear to God must as far as possible be like Him and such
as He is. Wherefore the temperate man is the friend of
God, for 'he is like Him, and the intemperate man is unlike
Him, and different from Him, and unjust. And the same
applies to other things ; and this is the conclusion, which is
also the noblest and truest of all sayings—that for the good
man to offer sacrifice to the gods, and hold converse with
them by means of prayers and offerings and every kind of
service, is the noblest and best of all things, and also the
most conducive to a happy life, and very fit and meet. But
with the bad man the opposite of all this is true : . . . from
one who is polluted neither a good man nor God can without
impropriety receive gifts. . . . Next to the gods, a wise
man will do service to the demons or spirits, and then to the
heroes, and after them will follow the private and ancestral
gods who are worshipped as the law prescribes in the places
which are sacred to them. Next comes the honour of
living parents, to whom, as is meet, we have to pay the
greatest and oldest of all debts, considering that all which a
man has belongs to those who gave him birth, and brought
him up, and that he must do all that he can to minister to
them, first in his property, secondly in his person, and thirdly in
his soul, in return for the endless care and travail which they
bestowed upon him of old, in the days of his infancy, and
which he is now to pay back to them when they are old and
in the extremity of their need. And all his life long he ought
never to utter or to have uttered an unbecoming word to
them ; for of light and fleeting words the penalty is most
severe ; Nemesis the messenger of justice is appointed to
watch over all such matters. . . . And let a man not forget
to pay the yearly tribute of respect to the dead, honouring
them chiefly by omitting nothing that conduces to a perpetual remembrance of them . . . . Living after this manner
we shall receive our reward from the gods and those who
are above us ; and we shall spend our days for the most part
in good hope.'

5. In speaking of Hesiod and of Solon, I had occasion to
remark that justice or righteousness, as a personified abstrac-

tion, was revered by the Greek poet and legislator, with
something of the zeal of Hebrew prophecy. But for the first
clear conception of the divine righteousness, we must turn to
Aeschylus. The law of retribution was inherent in the very
subject of tragedy, but in his treatment of the Orestean
legend the thought of the poet pierces beneath the superficial
view of human suffering, ' an eye for an eye, a tooth for a
tooth,' and while he is profoundly aware that the consequences
of human conduct spread far beyond any single life, his sense
of individual responsibility is clear and strong, and divine
justice, in his view of it, is tempered with equity. The weary
course of action and reaction, and of wild justice in the shape
of personal revenge, is ended by the application of the higher
law which changes the Erinnyes into the Eumenides, the
Furies into gentle powers, the curse into a blessing.

6. Lastly, in the Promethean trilogy the daring genius
of the poet imagines a corresponding progress in the superhuman sphere. Time was when power and wisdom were at
war, but now they have been reconciled, and the reign of
Zeus is one of unchanging beneficence, since power works
together with wisdom, uniting liberty with order. Power
and truth have met together, sovereignty and peace have
kissed each other.

Aeschylus is credited with certain innovations in mythology. Herodotus tells us that in some play that is lost to us
he represented Artemis as the child of Demeter ; [1] and that
he was led to this through having identified Artemis with
the Egyptian Isis. However this may be, it is a striking
fact that in his ' Prometheus Bound ' the mother of Prometheus is named indifferently Themis and Earth,—'One
nature, having many names,'—while at the opening of the
'Eumenides' Themis is the daughter of Earth ; and that
at an earlier time, in the ' Supplices,' he speaks of the god of
the world below as another Zeus, who keeps a strict account
of the wrong that is done upon this earth.

Such blending of divinities, whether original or borrowed,
has an evident affinity with the Orphic movement. And in
characterising the Eumenides as the guardians of public and

---

[1] Cp. the Arcadian Despoina.

domestic order, the poet combines in a new way the blessings of peace, fertility, and plenty with the law of retribution of which the Erinnys was the traditional expression. The evil of faction and of civil strife, which no man ever felt more profoundly, is regarded by him as a curse resulting from hereditary crime. The Marathonian warrior had also a deep sense of the horrors of war, for which he found the surest remedy in civic justice and equity. The old blood-feud has been transformed into a pervading consciousness of the widespread pollution derived from acts of violence. Ceremonial purgation with the blood of swine (obviously associated with the religion of Demeter) is not held sufficient, without the intervention of Apollo, testifying to the integrity of a good conscience and a pure intention. The wilful wrongdoer is not freed by death. If not overtaken by divine judgment in his lifetime, he awaits it with trembling in his passage to the other world, and it will find him even in the darkness below the ground. His children and his children's children bear the consequences of his act, but he himself shall reap the main penalty.

Such are a few of the conceptions which reading between the lines we may attribute to the poet himself. Other notions, of which he makes dramatic use, survivals from the past, had evidently still a hold upon the popular imagination. Darius rising from his tomb is worshipped by the Persian elders, whose reverence makes them dumb in the midst of sorrow. He has tasted of the libation which Atossa brought to him, not as in the eleventh Odyssey the blood of a black sheep, but the bloodless offering of honey, wine and milk ; bloodless also are the ingredients of the libation poured out by Electra at her father's tomb, over which his children utter their constraining cries for help against his foes. He does not appear visibly to them, but by this religious service the spirit of Orestes is bent up to the terrible deed. Orestes himself, in promising to the Athenians a firm alliance with Argos, threatens the Argives that, if they fail in supporting Athens, he will send them afflictions from his tomb. The curse of Oedipus survives him, and with dry hard gaze impels Eteocles to the fatal conflict with his brother. Such passages show clearly the effect of hero-worship as a living force. I have spoken above of the crude simplicity of the mythological fancy so tenderly portrayed in the 'Supplices.' Not less crude is the notion of sacrifice implied in the warning of Orestes to Zeus, that if he suffers the race of Atreus to perish, he will lose the rich savour of many a victim which that royal house will offer to him ; and to Agamemnon that if he fails to help his children he will remain portionless among the dead. In mutilating the body of her murdered lord, Clytemnestra betrays a survival of that fear of ghosts which had so largely disappeared from Greek religion. In attempting to gather the purport of Aeschylean theology, we are confronted with the anomalous position of a sublimely gifted mind expressing itself through forms in which the popular imagination was steeped, and by which it was itself affected, yet darkly conveying truths of universal and even eternal significance.

On the other hand it is important to observe that in Aeschylean tragedy the dead even when deified are never spoken of as blessed. There is no reference to Elysium or to the islands of the blest. Agamemnon though a king among the dead still appears unconscious or even non-existent as in Homer. The blessedness to which the poet looks forward is to be realised by present and future generations upon the earth.

Where Aeschylus seems most original he may be quoting from lost writings or from oral tradition, as when the chorus in the 'Supplices' say that honour to forefathers comes third amongst the laws of the supreme, or when the Pythian prophetess describes the successive holders of the oracular seat, from Earth, the first prophetess (of whom the Omphalos was perhaps a primitive symbol), through Themis and Phoebe (a name rarely heard) to Apollo, Dionysus not being left out. The counsel of the ghost of Darius to his elders to be cheerful under sorrow, because wealth does no good in the grave, has with much plausibility been thought to indicate an acquaintance with Persian learning.

No such sudden advance in religious thought as appears in Aeschylus is to be found in either of his successors. He set the tone of tragedy. But the originality of Sophocles, not merely as a poet but as a religious thinker, is notwithstanding great. His attitude towards the divine is individual and distinct. Aeschylus dwelt on the imagined contrast between the order of the present and the confusions of the past. Painting the struggle between good and evil with unique vividness, he had a sublime faith in the ultimate triumph of the good. The path of justice is with him a process from savagery to humanity, from discord to law and order, from war to peace, in which the human will bears an essential part, by conforming itself to the divine. In his later years, when he saw the emergence of a spirit in the Athenian people at once more rash and more exclusive than that embodied in the policy of Aristides, he turned to yet wider contemplations, and found comfort in the speculative realisation of the divine attributes in their ultimate harmony. Sophocles, with less of sanguine expectation either for the immediate or the distant future, rather dwells on the unchangeableness of the divine order, and the futility of human efforts to contravene it. The immemorial unwritten laws of piety are stronger than human edicts, and will outlive them. ' Not now or yesterday they have their being, But everlastingly ; and none can tell The hour that saw their birth ' ('Ant.'). The lives of individuals are in the grasp not of a blind fate, but of an inexorable and mysterious will, that works according to eternal law. Amongst the extant plays of Sophocles also there is perceptible an advance beyond his earlier conceptions, chiefly as regards the law of retribution. Every act brings inevitable consequences, but in the divine judgment it is not the act but the motive of the act that ultimately weighs. Oedipus is ruined in this world, but having suffered here for his unconscious crimes, he is accepted of the gods, and after his death becomes a spiritual power. There is even an approach to the doctrine which the Hebrews learned in their captivity, of the blessedness of sorrow. God seeth not as man seeth. Philoctetes is rejected by the army, who condemn him to untold sufferings, until it is revealed by Herakles that the despised solitary of Lemnos is their destined saviour. In the ' Ajax,' however, which is perhaps the earliest of the extant plays, there is an anticipation of the general conception which underlies the action of the two latest, the ' Oedipus Coloneus ' and the ' Philoctetes.' In all three there is a similar contrast between appearance and reality, between the human and the divine point of view. The essentially noble spirit may be harshly used by men in consequence of some error, and for a time may be afflicted by the gods, but ultimately obtains redemption. And it is especially significant that the vindication of Ajax is assigned not to the ruling powers but to Teucer, the bastard son of Telamon, and Tecmessa, the captive concubine.

In studying Greek tragedy, it is important to distinguish between the poet's own point of view, which is to be gathered from his work considered as a whole, and his representation of persons and events adapted to the beliefs of his audience. Athena in the ' Ajax,' for example, appears in various aspects, in some of which her divine wisdom may seem to be overshadowed with caprice and cruelty, but the real motive of her introduction into the play is to inspire Odysseus with that moderation and clemency towards his enemies which is the keynote of the concluding scene. (Compare the colloquy between king Pausanias and Lampon of Aegina in Herodotus ix. 78.) It is evident that while retaining their reality for the imagination, the gods of polytheism were becoming virtually, for the higher minds, either the exponents of popular religion or the symbols of some dominant idea. In the language of the fifth century the notion of Theos, god, has become generalised so as to receive many applications outside the sphere of customary worship. When Sophocles says that Time is an ease-giving god (χρόνος γὰρ εὐμαρὴς θεός), the deified abstraction becomes transparent, and when Euripides goes further and says of Shamefastness (αἰδώς) that it is an ineffectual goddess (ἀργὸς ἡ θεός), we see that the traditional notion of deity itself is wearing thin. The prominence given to individual deities in the several plays is found to vary according to the data of the legend, the scene of the action, and other external circumstances. In the ' Trachiniae,' for example, not Apollo but the Dodonean Zeus is the giver of the oracle. This would not be the case unless the poet himself sat somewhat loose to the actual religion of his countrymen.

A wide interval separates the Homeric conception of the world of shadows, whose powerlessness only serves at once to accentuate the brightness of our brief existence and to give it a deep undercurrent of sadness, from the belief in an existence after death, which is prominent in the earlier tragedies. This belief had its roots in primitive observances which in central Greece had never lost their force, although the Ionians of Asia Minor had forgotten them, but which had received a new impulse from the growth of hero-worship, and a new meaning from the teachings of Orphism. Aeschylus, as his manner is, points us back to a past stage of culture, or, as in the ' Persians,' to what he imagines to be the stage of culture attained in barbarous lands. Greek imagination thus works by contrast, whether of time or place. But his supernatural scenes, such as the apparition of Clytemnestra or of Darius, have a convincing force and true sublimity which implies the actual survival of beliefs akin to them. The long Kommos or lament in the ' Choephoroe ' at the grave of Agamemnon would not have been permitted in actual life by the Solonian law ; yet the poet's contemporaries must have still really imagined that the spirit of the dead could be revived by libations and incantations at his tomb. The state of mind which prompted the summoning of the Aeacidae to Salamis was still a living power. This close association between Hades and the grave is less clearly present in Sophocles, although of course the tomb of Ajax in the Troad, like that of Oedipus at Colonus, is still imagined as containing the hero himself. Such imaginative belief is inseparable from the fable of either play ; but the underworld is thought of by the poet himself in a manner not less vivid, but less concrete. The land of souls, as well as Olympus, the habitation of the gods, is to his mind all the more venerable because it is unseen. Neither to Olympus nor to Hades is a distinct place assigned, except above and beneath. The blessed are not exempted from Hades or sent to ' islands of the blest,' but their condition in the unseen

world is different from that of others : such at least is the
belief implied in the well-known lines about the happiness of
those who have seen the mysteries :—

How blest are they,
Who ere they travel to the viewless land
Have seen these mysteries. They alone in Hades
Have life. The rest have nought but misery.

But the characteristic difference is, that whereas in
Homer the body is the man, while the shade flits underground, in Sophocles it is the person himself who passes
beneath, taking with him all that was essential to him here,
retaining his affections and relationships, and finding a true
welcome from his kindred who have gone before. (See
above p. 230, sepulchral monuments.) He retains also (this is
part of the popular belief) the power of being a source of
bane to his enemies. The change which is thus implied in
the manner of conceiving the state of the dead must have had
various phases, some of which have left no trace. A curious
light is thrown upon the subject by the epitaph over those
Athenians who fell at Potidaea in 432 B.C. on a tablet now
in the British Museum, in which the souls of the brave are
spoken of as having gone into the sky : a belief which increasingly prevailed in the later centuries. (See esp.
Soph. 'Aj.' 1192, Eur. 'Suppl.' 533.)

In some points of view Sophocles, as compared with
Aeschylus, may be regarded as reactionary. He relies more
on Homer and the epic cycle, and less on the innovations of
lyric poetry which looked back to Hesiod. He is less pan-
Hellenic and more purely Attic, and his aristocratic feeling is
more severe, although if Aeschylus had lived another twenty
years, one cannot tell how he might have regarded the party of
Cleon. Sophocles' notion of eternal law is coloured by the
immemorial tradition of the family or the clan as opposed to
those enactments which had a political motive and set expediency before traditional right. If there is any truth in
the story that he was appointed general because of the
success of the 'Antigone,' this may have been due rather to
the sympathy and support of the great families than to the

acclamation of the people. Antigone defies Creon, not merely as an arbitrary ruler, but as a *parvenu*. And together with the all-searching humanity which is his chief note as an artist and a poet, there is traceable here and there an esteem for princely qualities and a contempt for the vulgar which make it credible that he may really have been one of the Probuli in his eighty-second year. Even should the hypothesis which I formerly advanced as to the date of the ' Oedipus Coloneus ' prove unfounded, it is certain that the poet's deep and tender piety towards the sanctities of his native deme betrays his sympathy for the knightly dwellers at Colonus, whose assertion of their ancient privileges made the precinct of Poseidon there a suitable place for the inauguration of the aristocratic constitution of the Four Hundred. Poseidon Hippius, Athena Hippia, and the Dread Goddesses who haunt the favoured spot, are set against the deities of the same name whose seats in the Acropolis formed the centre of the popular religion. The hope of the Eupatridae lay in reviving the ancient local rites which had been supplanted through the constitution of Cleisthenes. Yet his poetry reflects the changes of the time : the harsh vindictiveness of Electra and the dark end of the ' Trachiniae ' seem to have coincided with the embitterment that preceded the close of the first part of the Peloponnesian war, while in the last-mentioned play his human sympathy extends (if I am right in my conjecture) to the captive Heraclidae. And the solitary of Lemnos is allowed to exclaim, when he hears that Thersites has survived Ajax, ' What is one to make of these things when, in praising what is divine, I find the gods doing evil ? ' That is the nearest approach in Sophocles to the occasional cynicism of Euripides. But in other ways the 'Philoctetes,' certainly a drama of his latest years, exhibits a stage of ethical reflection passing beyond the limits which the Greek consciousness had hitherto attained. Taking a hint from the Homeric picture of Achilles as one who scorned to conceal his thoughts, he represents the son of Achilles as an ingenuous youth who in the last resort finds it impossible to persist in falsehood. Veracity had nowhere until then been so distinctly recognised by any Greek as an element of ideal nobleness.

Before passing for the time from tragedy, it is worth while to take account of one circumstance that gave exceptional scope to its creations, in addition to the freedom which belonged to Dionysiac worship. The greater Dionysia, at which most, if not all, of the extant tragedies were produced, occurred in early spring, at the time when foreigners were most wont to visit Athens. The members of the Delian league, or at a later time the subject allies, were present in great numbers, and formed not the least important part of the audience. The plays were composed, not for Athens only, but equally for all Ionia. This may even help to account for some of the peculiarities of tragic diction, which have given rise to several rival theories. The word translated ' tyrant ' had long since become odious at Athens, where the memory of the tyrannicides Harmodius and Aristogiton was fondly cherished, and yet in representing the heroic age, the term is continually employed with no disparaging association. This is more easily accounted for when it is remembered that the Hellenic cities of Asia Minor had long been familiar with despotic government, and in many cases had learned to tolerate it. Even under democratic institutions, the 'monarch' (μόναρχos) continued to be the title of the chief magistrate of Cos.

A question of some interest remains. It is a curious circumstance, though hitherto it has hardly received the attention which it deserves, that Attic tragedy from the first revolved continually about the legends of Thebes and Argos. Dionysus was a Theban god, and in passing from his legend to other fables the tragic poets may have been first attracted by his congeners of the Cadmeian stock. Also the horrors of the house of Labdacus supplied subjects eminently suited for tragic handling. This last reason also applies to ' the tale of Pelops' line.' Both these traditions had figured largely in epic poetry, especially the poems of the cycle. Yet there may have been an additional reason. The birth of tragedy coincided with the reign of Pisistratus, who strengthened himself by close alliance with Argos and probably with Thebes. ' The friendship with Argos,' says Aristotle, ' began when Pisistratus married the Argive woman.' May not this circumstance have influenced the early development of tragic art ? If that may be conceded, the conservatism always attending an art when once established, in regard to the choice of subject, will account for the rest.

The other fine arts, as we call them, followed in the wake of poetry, but had their own independent growth and development, of which we are beginning to know more than formerly. As they were mainly applied to the building and adornment of the temples, they were still more thoroughly penetrated than poetry was with the religious spirit. But they also fully shared the humanising poetic impulse, becoming more and more emancipated from the stiffness of convention. As the Greek gods delighted in nothing so much as a perfected humanity, the Greek sculptor applied all his powers to the representation of the divinely human. The Argive and the early Attic schools vied with each other, and in comparing the Aeginetan marbles with even pre-Pheidian art at Athens, we see how rapidly the artists of this period had advanced towards the unimpeded expression of their ideal.

Of the art of Pheidias and his disciples enough still remains to give us a glimpse of the spiritual atmosphere which it shed around it, and which made the Athens of Pericles so glorious an embodiment of those perfections which Athena loved. His master-work, the great Zeus at Olympia, was said by the consent of all antiquity to lift the mind of the beholder above mortal things. The strongest testimony to this effect is Livy xiv. 28, where Aem. Paullus (B.C. 167) is making his progress through Greece. He came to Olympia : ' ubi et alia quaedam spectanda visa, et Iovem velut praesentem intuens motus animo est.' Perhaps with the exception of some modern strains of music, art was never more effectually employed in the service of religion. The genius of Pheidias and the accomplishments of his scholars have tended to eclipse the labours of his predecessors and immediate contemporaries, such as Myron of Athens and Ageladas and Polycleitus of Argos. This, however, is partly due to the fact that so much of Pheidian work, comparatively speaking, remains in the original. Recent dis-coveries have shown that the art of this period had reached a height of conception and execution, before the work of Pheidias culminated, which has hardly been equalled since, and also that it was far more varied and more rich in character than was conceived by the generation of whom Winckelmann in Germany and Flaxman in England are the types.

Those softening influences which we have seen working in the later plays of Sophocles produced a modification of Pheidian art in the work of Praxiteles, in which perhaps there is some loss of strength, but an even more penetrating humanity and a more absolute freedom. There remained another aim for sculpture of a more doubtful kind, but of unquestionable value, while it was held within the limits of Greek moderation : this was the attempt to give to human groups the perfection not only of form but of action and expression. According to Sir Charles Newton, the great master in this kind was Scopas, who in other ways introduced a degree of minuteness and naturalism hitherto unattained. The art in all these stages was applied to religious uses, and even the portrait statues of the earlier time were doubtless intended to be dedicated and set up in the precincts of some god (Paus. vi. 4 § 5). Together with the humanising tendency of Praxiteles came the increasing love of representing beard-less youth, in which at once the skill of the sculptor was put to its last test, and an idiosyncrasy of the Greek mind was gratified.

The earlier statues of Hermes were bearded, more in accordance with Homer's description than the Hermes of Praxiteles. Another beardless form was that of the boy Zeus of Ageladas, worshipped by the people of Aegae (' behold divine-ness no elder than a boy '). Very noticeable in the religious aspect is the persistence of the type under all these changes of treatment. Compare for example the metopes representing the labours of Herakles in the earlier and later temples at Selinus and again at Olympia. In all there is the simple figure of the hero and of that which he is vanquishing, with the person of Athena standing by. The later representation conveys a sense of purity and strength combined, and of a perfection of form after which the primeval artist strove in vain. Yet how strictly, down to the fifth century at least, the conventional limits are maintained. The same is true of such groups as Theseus and the Amazon, Lapith and Centaur, and many others. But I leave it to the archaeological enquirer to illustrate this observation more in detail.

The charm of the old ritual and mythology is still unbroken, but within that charmed circle a work of experience and reflection has already begun, which is destined to pass beyond the magic boundary and to assert claims which the old religion could not satisfy. In an age of striking vicissitudes it was impossible that gifted minds roused into extreme activity should acquiesce in the mere repetition of outworn formularies. The higher minds had already separated from the majority more widely than was imagined even by themselves. New thoughts were being cast into the ancient moulds without bursting them, for they were elastic and capable of expansion. So long as the forms of ritual were maintained, and these also were continually expanded and adorned, the descendant of Eumolpus, or of Buzyges, or of Butades, might have misgivings, but he had no power to stem the advancing tide. There is no separation as yet between religion and enlightenment. The most religious minds are the most advanced. All this was presently to undergo a change ; but for the time being, until after the outbreak of the Peloponnesian war, such may be taken as a general description. No doubt there was already some opposition between the elements of progress and of conservatism, between the party of Cimon and that of Pericles, when the latter was not yet the leader of the state ; but there was no such rift in the religious harmony of the commonwealth as soon afterwards became manifest. Before the supporters of immobility and of obstruction had rallied their forces, the liberalising tendency had taken head. The characteristic note of the age of Pericles may be expressed in a word as the ' human ideal.' Without breaking in any way from the past, the central energy of the most active minds

U

was expended on the contemplation of human nature in all its aspects. The phrase 'human nature,' so familiar to ourselves, hardly occurs in Greek before Thucydides, but he employs it again and again. He belongs in some ways to a later stage of thought than that which I have tried to delineate in this chapter, but in this expression he sums up explicitly the general aim more or less consciously pursued by the Athenian poets and thinkers who had preceded him— viz. to penetrate the secret of human life and to infuse it with a divine spirit.

CHAPTER XIII

PHILOSOPHY AND SCEPTICISM

Early philosophers—Age of Pericles—Religious reaction—
Euripides—The Sophists.

THE beginnings of philosophy in Asia Minor and in Magna
Graecia had exercised no direct influence at Athens, except so
far as we may suppose that minds such as that of Aeschylus
or of Sophocles or even Simonides may have gathered something indirectly from Ionia and Sicily, or that the Orphic
theosophy contained an element which it had borrowed from
some half-understood phase of incipient philosophy. The
flower of the old mythology could not but fade, for it was a
child of the twilight, and too fragile to endure the full light
of awakening reflection. But beneath that many-coloured
exuberance were the germs which I have tried to indicate of
substantial thought—ideas which gradually came to ripeness
in bold and reverent minds, eagerly persevering in the search
for truth. It does not belong to the present work to
examine into the purely philosophical aspect of those early
thinkers, or to criticise the views that have been held concerning them ; but it is a truth which cannot be too often
insisted upon, though it is constantly lost sight of, that, as
imagination comes before thought, so thought comes before
logic, in the order of human development. If mistakes have
been made by those who from Bacon to Hegel have felt their
affinity with the great spirits of the past, and have coloured
with their own reflections these anticipations of truth, there
is also a danger lest, in rejecting their unverified appreciations,
we should leave the first notions of that 'stammering' philosophy, as Aristotle happily described it, too bare and colourless,
because they cannot be expressed in the terms of later

systems. This would be an error like that of some theorists who, because Homer has only a few words for the infinite shades and hues of coloured objects, concluded that the ancients as compared with the moderns were colour-blind. If it be wrong to say that Thales or Anaximenes spoke the language of symbolism, because the symbol and the thing signified were to them inseparable, and they could not conceive the universe apart from some imaginary object of perception, it is equally wrong to take that sensuous image to have been all in all to them, or to deny that it was the vehicle of a deeper meaning. Even Aristotle could not conceive of divine thought or energy except as moving in a circle, or of the divine nature apart from the form of a sphere. It may be impossible to draw out in modern language the significance of the few great words, spoken with intense vehemence, in which the first philosophers put forth their conceptions, and yet they are alive and palpitating with significance even for us at the present day. We have here to deal, however, not with philosophical tendencies as such, but with the *religious aspect* of the pregnant thoughts through which they were conveyed. For to speak of the early philosophers as irreligious would be an abuse of language. Some of them thought slightingly enough of the form of religion which existed amongst their countrymen. Nothing can be more sweeping than Xenophanes' remarks on anthropomorphism, or the saying of Heraclitus about expiatory sacrifice ; but they did not set themselves openly to denounce traditional customs, and amidst the social and individual freedom which existed on the Asiatic seaboard (p. 115), they were tolerated as perhaps they would not have been tolerated at Athens in the days of Cimon. Meanwhile they were themselves impelled by what was essentially a religious spirit, different indeed from that of priest or soothsayer, but also deeper and more enduring. It was not a dead universe of which they sought to give an account. Thales, who spoke the first word that implied a universal principle, and so laid the corner stone of science, was also the author of the saying ' that all things are full of gods.' Xenophanes had said or sung ' one god is highest both in heaven and earth ; unlike to mortals both in form and mind ; all sight, all thought, all hearing.' He does not deny the plurality of gods, but asserts the supremacy of one, whose transcendent being cannot be represented in a human form. Heraclitus, who in making fire the primordial element resolved the universe into a process of energy in harmony with law, said also 'that which ever wills to be expressed and yet will never be expressed, is the name of Zeus, the supreme god.' Religious thoughts which are at least latent in Heraclitus, if not explicit, are the relativity of evil, and its necessity as the condition of good ; the universality of truth, in which opposing elements co-exist in ultimate harmony ; and in a vague pantheistic sense, the unreality of death. 'There await men after death,' he says, 'things other than what they look for or expect.' 'It is not good for men to get what they desire ; sickness brings health after it, hunger satisfaction, weariness repose.' He sought to awaken his disciples to the conception of a moving world encompassing them, and full of vitality, in contemplating which the mind awakes from stagnation and from the sleep of sense, and ranges the pure dry element above the mists of earth, the waters of forgetfulness, the cold obstruction of the nether ground. The ' dry soul ' is exempt from narrow personal views, and bounded only by universal law. 'We can speak with confidence,' he says, ' only while we follow that thought which comprehends all things, even as the law of the state controls the citizens, only much more firmly. All human laws are fed by the one divine law, which prevails as far as it chooseth, and is adequate and more than adequate to every need.' 'The universal soul is infinite, you may travel every way and never find the end.' (Compare the words of Zophar in the Book of Job : 'It is as high as heaven : what canst thou do ? deeper than hell : what canst thou know ? ') The phrase ' dry light of intellect,' which Bacon has made proverbial, was borrowed from Heraclitus.

Parmenides, the founder of that opposition between being and not-being which made logic possible and indirectly also physical science, asserted with the energy of a Hebrew prophet the eternal fulness of that supreme substance or existence which is one with thought. I will not here discuss his philosophy, but rather dwell on the fervid enthusiasm with which he proclaimed it. For if wonder, as Plato and Aristotle both say, is the beginning of philosophy, the combination of awe with eager boldness, which characterises these utterances, contains in it an essential element of religion. To illustrate this I will first quote the prelude of his great poem :

> Ye steeds that bear me, ye that bore me then,
> When I assayed the path of wisdom's way,
> Straining the yoke ;—the daughters of the sun,
> Rending the veils from off their temples fair,
> Were leading us from darkness into light,
> To where the gates which sever night from day,
> Stand o'er the threshold ; held by Righteousness.
> Whom then the maidens, with caressing speech,
> Persuaded to draw back the massive bolt ;
> Then through that yawning gateway flew my car
> Led by those maids on the direct forth-right.
> The goddess took my hand and spake to me,
> ' Hail, youth ! no evil destiny hath brought
> Thy car this way—far from the track of man.
> For 'tis thy blessed fate to learn all Truth,
> Truth sound of heart, convincing, unreproved ;
> And also to discern the thoughts of men,
> Deceiving and unprovable, that so
> With understanding thou mayest guide thy way.

This contempt for ordinary thinking is a note which is common to all the early philosophers, especially to Parmenides and Heraclitus :—

> All speech and thought must hold that Being is,
> Not-Being is Nought. Mark that, and turn thy mind
> Away from following that path : and then
> Avoid this also, on which ignorant men
> Are wandering ever with divided brain,
> Helpless, distraught, deaf, blind, amazed and dumb.
> To be and not to be to them are one
> And diverse, so perverse are all their ways.

I will quote one more passage in which Parmenides, with prophetic fervour, declares the attributes of his supreme being :

> 'Tis all alike and undivided still,
> Continuous all throughout ; in equal strength ;

All full of being; indiscerptible;
For Being touches Being everywhere.
Unmoved, in limits of eternal bonds,
It is—without beginning, without end.
Growth and decay are banished far away,
Driven off by proofs irrefragable and sure.
Ever the same, abiding in the same,
In its own place it rests immovable.
Sovereign necessity holds it in strict bonds,
And keeps it in all round. Being cannot be
Unlimited : for nothing can it lack.
Were it not-being, it had lacked of all.

That which characterised the religious consciousness of all these early thinkers was pantheism, not theosophic or mystical, as in the Orphic teacher, but philosophic and speculative. Anaxagoras of Clazomenae approached even more nearly to what we understand by monotheism ; for in setting mind over against the elements which it informed and regulated, he asserted the supremacy of a spiritual principle, uncreated, invisible, and eternal. To ordinary Greek intelligence this assertion seemed blank atheism, because denying the divinity of what was visible and material, such as the orb of the sun.

When Pericles was at the height of his power, in what Thucydides describes as a democracy in form, but in reality a rule of the chief citizen, distinguished foreigners were glad to be invited to form part of the inner circle surrounding him. Aspasia, the *illuminata,* had probably some influence in promoting this. Amongst these visitants was Anaxagoras, who had uttered the last word of the Ionian school. His visit was like the letting in of waters. The full stream of Ionian culture, imperfectly realised, was poured upon sensitive minds in a condition of abnormal activity. The result was an access of enlightenment resembling the *Aufklärung* which preceded the French Revolution, and equally with that to be followed shortly by a religious reaction or fanatic outburst. While these elements were fermenting there began the great interhellenic conflict, in which the two chief powers of Hellas were to exhaust each other. The invasion of Athenian territory and the desolating effects of the plague at once reinforced the scepticism of strong minds, and drove the weak into wilder superstition. What is most hard to realise is that intermediate mental condition, perhaps the commonest of all, in which sceptical doubts and questionings grew side by side with religious anxieties and an increasing scrupulosity of observance. Such mingled states of faith and unbelief are frequent amongst ourselves, and yet thought sometimes refuses to admit their possibility. For there is a curious fallacy to which many persons in an intellectual age are liable : that of supposing that a mental attitude which is inconsistent or self-contradictory is inconceivable and therefore impossible. Whereas the possibility of the phenomenon is proved by its actual frequency. That such mingled states of mind existed actually at Athens at the time I speak of, is manifest in every page of Euripides. Even in the last plays of Sophocles there are not wanting touches in which such *fin de siècle* moods are reflected.

Let us first look at the contradiction between the facts of experience and traditional feeling, which is implied in that opposition of the just to the expedient so familiar to the readers of Thucydides. The colonist felt it right to support the mother state ; to this he was bound by religious sanctions of the most stringent kind ; but under the stress of circumstances these bonds were repeatedly loosened or broken through, when it appeared that prudence dictated the alliance of the daughter community with some stronger power. Thus simple piety was overborne by enlightened policy, and the prudence of such a course was proved by its success.

This is one of several rhetorical antinomies, of which the advocates of this or that course of action availed themselves, and it was now that the art of speaking came to be recognised as a source of power and instrument of ambition, and as such reacted on contemporary thought. The ascendency of Pericles was largely due to his highly cultivated gifts as a rhetorician. If any of the speeches ascribed to him by Thucydides truly report him, he had learned much in this respect from the rhetors of Sicily. So brilliant an example could not but be followed by others, whose ability was not always guided, as his had been, by a single aim for the good of the state. The advocates in the law courts and speakers in the assembly soon became aware that, as Protagoras of Abdera taught, every question admits of two lines of argument opposed to one another. The position of Athens as a tyrant state began to warp the sincerity of her goodwill towards those allies who had at first joined with her to defend Hellas from the barbarian. Thus old beliefs and rules of conduct were undermined, while no commanding spirit had as yet arisen to point the way towards a more comprehensive ideal. Action was determined at one time by the impetuosity of passion, at another by acute reasonings about the necessities of the hour. Pericles had advised the war, but he was no longer there to direct the conduct of it ; had his life been prolonged he might have repented of having launched his countrymen on a course that could not but develop into one of ruinous ambition. The extraordinary fund of energy and resource which lay at the disposal of the state concealed even from her wisest citizens the hollowness of the motives which had prompted it. The Athens of that day was profoundly conscious of the obligation of the allies to her, but thought less of her obligation to the allies, or of the promises and professions under which the confederacy had at first been formed.

Meanwhile, the popular religion seems to have had only the effect of intensifying the passions of the people. The priesthood saw their opportunity in the anxiety and alarm which the plague, the repeated invasions, and the loss of valuable lives had awakened in many minds, and they used their power to counteract the tendencies which they regarded as hostile to religion. The embitterment of the last days of Pericles by the prosecution of his friends, Aspasia and Pheidias, the expulsion of Anaxagoras, and the like, although only known to us from comparatively late authorities, may be taken as a clear indication of the violence of this reaction. The laws against impiety were maintained in their full strength, and men suspected of irreligious acts were virtually excommunicated. They could not assist at any sacred function, such as the Eleusinian mysteries, except at the peril of their lives. This bore hardly upon those who in their early youth had been led by the champions of enlightenment to mock at sacred things, but who, as they advanced in years, felt the need of religious sympathy and the support of those common acts of worship which their fathers had shared, and in which those most near and dear to them profoundly believed. The danger of impiety was, of course, greatly aggravated by the fact that in the popular belief the very existence and safety of the state, the growth of the harvest and of the vintage, the fertility and soundness of the race depended upon the right performance of certain acts of worship. Thus the spirit of fanaticism when once awakened was ruinous to all who defied it, and the danger was greatest in moments of popular excitement; for example at that great moment, the turning point of the Athenian fortunes, when the ill-fated expedition, so brilliant at the outset, was on the point of sailing for Sicily. Then came the mutilation of the Hermae and the panic that followed. Although some features of that strange incident must ever remain obscure, the attentive study of what is known of it is essential to a right understanding of the general condition of thought and feeling with reference to religion in the later years of the fifth century—the last decade but one before the death of Socrates.

The views of the ordinary Athenian of this time as to the supposed motives of divine powers may be illustrated by some quotations from the prose literature of the day.

1. Andocides had been accused of acts of impiety in regard to the mysteries several years before. He had been in exile since the time referred to, and was allowed to return, but his enemies refused to let the matter sleep. Here is the argument by which he tried to persuade his hearers that Demeter and Persephone were not angry with him. ' My accusers would have you believe that the gods have brought me safely hither over seas that I might be condemned by you.' (We are reminded of the belief that one who is saved from drowning is reserved for the gallows.) ' But I, Athenians, do not think thus of the gods; if they felt that I had wronged them, when they had caught me in the midst of dangers they would then have taken their

revenge. What danger is greater than a sea voyage in winter-time? Then they had power over my person, my life, and property, and they preserved me. Could they not have even prevented me from obtaining decent burial? Moreover, it was a time of war, and there were warships and pirates then at sea, by whom many have been caught and lost their all, and dragged out their life in slavery; there were also barbarous shores, where many ere now, having been cast away, have been involved in torture and indignities even to the mutilation of their persons before death. Out of so many and great dangers the gods preserved me in order, as my accusers say, that Cephisios, the vilest of Athenians, should be their vindicator, an Athenian citizen in profession, not in reality, whom not one of you would entrust with anything of his own, because you know his character. For my part, sirs, I think such dangers as I now am in are human dangers, but those upon the sea are divine. If, then, it is right to speculate about the motives of the gods, I think they would be very angry and indignant if they saw those whom they had preserved destroyed by men.'

2. The following are the words in which Nicias, the most pious of the Athenians, tries to revive the hopes of the remainder of his army in their extremity after the disaster before Syracuse. He has a fatal disease upon him, but still leads his army.

'Even now, Athenians and allies, you ought to hope. Others have been saved out of greater perils than surround us now. Do not think too slightingly of your remaining strength, either by reason of our disaster or of our present miseries, which you feel to be undeserved. Look at me, who am weaker than any of you, for you see how I am distressed by my disease. I have been counted fortunate exceedingly, both in my own career and in my public acts, and now I am in the same suspense of danger with the meanest of you. Yet the course of my daily life was full of religious observances, and I have been just and unoffending towards men. Wherefore I have still a confident hope of what is to be, although our disasters so far beyond our deserts are indeed terrifying. But maybe they will grow lighter, for the fortune of our enemies has reached the full, and if our expedition, so brilliant at the outset, provoked the envy of some one of the gods, surely we have already paid sufficiently for our pride ; we are not the first who have been aggressors against a neighbouring power : it was a human error for which other men have not suffered beyond endurance, and we may reasonably hope that the hand of God upon us will be gentler than it has been. They cannot envy us now, but must rather pity us.'

In both these passages, which are couched in the language of contemporary piety, the gods are spoken of, not individually, but generally, and Nicias speaks once of God in the singular. This shows that the generalising movement, which tended to obliterate sharp distinctions between different deities, had influenced common language ; but it is equally clear that such grand conceptions of the divine action as those to which Aeschylus and Sophocles had given shape were far from having effectually permeated the public mind.

On the other hand, the arguments of Andocides reflect a condition of popular belief which has been unconsciously modified by the reasonings of enlightened persons.

An important solvent, both of religious and moral continuity, was the violence of faction, and the activity of political societies within the state. The effects of this are described by Thucydides in speaking of the Corcyrean sedition, in language so admirably chosen that it would be a pity to paraphrase it. I give it here in Professor Jowett's translation :

'Revolution brought upon the cities of Hellas many terrible calamities, such as have been and always will be while human nature remains the same, but which are more or less aggravated and differ in character with every new combination of circumstances. . . . The meaning of words had no longer the same relation to things, but was changed by them as they thought proper. Reckless daring was held to be loyal courage ; prudent delay was the excuse of a coward ; moderation was the disguise of unmanly weakness ;

to know everything was to do nothing. . . . The tie of party was stronger than the tie of blood, because a partisan was more ready to dare without asking why (for party associations are not based upon any established law, nor do they seek the public good ; they are formed in defiance of the laws and from self-interest). The seal of good faith was not divine law, but fellowship in crime. . . . Neither faction cared for religion ; but any fair pretence which succeeded in effecting some odious purpose was greatly lauded. And the citizens who were of neither party fell a prey to both ; either they were disliked because they held aloof or men were jealous of their surviving. . . . When men are retaliating upon others, they are reckless of the future, and do not hesitate to annul those common laws of humanity to which every individual trusts for his own hope of deliverance should he ever be overtaken by calamity ; they forget that in their own hour of need they will look for them in vain.' Thucydides iii. chap. 82–84.

The tendency of religion to become the tool of politicians, which is visible in Hellenic life from the first page of the Iliad, was naturally much aggravated in the Athens of this period. The party of enlightenment and progress was perpetually hampered and tripped up by reactionary conspiracies. It will be remembered that at Athens more than elsewhere certain priesthoods were hereditary in great families, such as that of the Eumolpidae, who were naturally prepossessed against religious change. Their influence worked on the superstition of the people, while the democratic leaders were equally unscrupulous in branding their opponents with impiety. Religion in the time of Socrates was altogether in a bad way. And yet a singlehearted devotion to the state upheld many a noble career.

To follow private interests, apart from the state, was a course which inevitably led to moral disaster. How completely morality for the average human being was bound up with the state is shown by a signal example in the case of Phrynichus, the Athenian general. In the earlier part of his career he was a noble servant to the Athenians, but when once exiled, and without a country, he broke down into utter unscrupulosity. In him, as in Hippias and Alcibiades, the love of the country which he had lost took the form of an endeavour to regain her by foul means. Nothing can more evince the need of a moral sanction transcending the narrow limits of the Greek community and linking the individual to the whole race of men. The great work of Thucydides, on the other hand, shows how a mind of exceptionally strong temper and essential dignity could retain its integrity, even when deprived of native country, while contemplating human affairs with an interest not less profound because detached from partial views, and subordinating present interests to a forecast of futurity. Whether his failure to save Eïon, which led to his banishment, was in any degree influenced by some natural care for his possessions further eastward in Thrace, we cannot know. But in his twenty years of exile his noble employment of that enforced leisure has earned him the gratitude of mankind. An adherent of Pericles when at the height of his power, he had shared to the full those intellectual novelties then so rife in Athens ; but they had cleared his mind without enfeebling it, and unlike Themistocles, whose practical philosophy enabled him to adapt his way of life to any environment in which he found himself, he held firmly by the resolution to make use of his singular opportunities for the lasting benefit of Hellas, and of mankind at large. The most penetrating human sympathy was combined in him with a dry light of unembarrassed observation, or to use the phrase of Matthew Arnold, with ' disinterested objectivity.'

A slave to no illusions, he sought for truth in the direct and simple record of facts laboriously ascertained, and through their help he obtained a grasp of the universal springs of human action which no preconceived theory or traditional doctrine could have given him. The contemporary of Socrates, he shows no trace of Socratic influence, and, indeed, he was absent from Athens during the greater part of the time when that strange personality was most prominent there. He has shown us many things, but amongst the lessons of his history, perhaps none is more valuable or convincing than the proof which it contains of what may be achieved by sheer strength of character and force of intellect in an age of confusion, while other men are the victims of passion and prejudice, and amidst the decay of old beliefs are distracted by the want of higher guidance :

> The rudder of their course is gone, or only points in vain
> The shore to which their shattered sail shall never make again.

For the condition of ordinary minds during this period of transition we must look to the early orators and to Euripides. The inscriptions also afford some guidance, but they only prove the scrupulosity with which, amidst all changes, ancient forms were maintained. Religious anxiety went hand in hand with doubt as to the substance of religion. In reading the orators one is struck by the frequency with which religious topics are brought in, the appeal to the sanction of the oath, to the authority of the legislator, to the sacredness of use and wont, to the fear of what the gods may do. Yet one feels that the speakers protest too much, that whichever side is the gainer in some disputed cause there must have been a good deal of perjury in the case and a good deal of secret contempt of things divine. In regard to religion the orators are chiefly valuable as showing what institutions were still in green observance, what notions had still a hold on the popular belief.

Euripides is an excellent witness if well employed, but the interpretation of his evidence requires unusual care. He is an artist and a poet, and in applying his words to any purpose one must know beforehand the conditions of his art. Now this is a subject on which there is still a good deal of dispute. Euripides is not only a poet but, like Edmund Spenser, a poet's poet, the favourite of Milton, of Goethe, and of Robert Browning, or perhaps one should rather say of Mrs. Barrett Browning, whose taste inspired the author of ' Balaustion.' And yet to the critic who approaches him in the expectation of finding the perfection of tragedy his work appears full of flaws, answering rather to the conception of our modern melodrama. Some ingenious theories have lately been propounded to account for this. It is argued that so accomplished an artist in producing works so anomalous must have done so with profound design. The tragic poet was still, it is assumed, the teacher of his age; but the age could not bear the lesson which he desired to impart. He was therefore driven to insinuate this, under the ancient forms, so moulding the legends as to make it manifest to the more intelligent amongst his countrymen that these forms were morally untenable and inconsistent with the highest notion of the divine, while they were yet so handled as to entertain the common herd and to excite their emotions. Something like this had occurred to Mr. Robert Browning, whose Balaustion sums up the lesson to be derived from the poet she admires by saying, ' There are no gods, no gods; Glory to God, who saves Euripides! ' I venture to think that in all this the poet is taken too seriously. It appears to me that in the latter part of the fifth century, no longer the tragic poets, but the rhetorician and the sophist, were the acknowledged teachers of the age. Sophocles, while with rare adaptability conforming himself to the requirements of the time, still upheld a noble standard of true piety, conveying moral lessons while retaining ancient forms in their integrity; but he belonged to the previous generation. The task of Euripides was rather to interest than to instruct. What Plato calls the Theatrocracy or tyranny of the audience had already begun. The poet had not only to aim at producing an effect, as all dramatic poetry must, but he must produce the effect which the audience desired—like our *fin de siècle* politicians, watching how the cat would jump, and obtaining suffrages by catching at the passing breeze. Dramatic art was already sinking to the position described by Dryden, in which ' those who lived to please must please to live.' It is true that the tragic poet was still a sacred functionary, but we are approaching the time when priesthoods were bought and sold, and the price fixed by public edict, as we learn from inscriptions. Euripides stands, in fact, half way, or more than half, between the latest work of Aeschylus and the ' Poetics ' of Aristotle, in which tragedy is regarded simply as a branch of ποιητική, with little reference to its religious origin.

We are told by the historians of Greek art that the vase-painter of this period is less serious than formerly in his rendering of legendary scenes, treating them rather as the vehicle for producing through some human group a beautiful or striking effect. Thus similar changes are observable in different regions of art. An apt illustration may be drawn from the Renaissance period of Italian painting, as compared with the deeper and simpler religious feeling of the preceding generation. Compare, for example, Paul Veronese with Giovanni Bellini or Cima da Conegliano ; Guido or Correggio with Giotto or Fra Angelico. Artistic convention, no less than religious prescription, confines the later artists within the same cycle of subjects ; but in the handling of these, they assert their new-found liberty, and have descended from the type of superhuman holiness to the more familiar aspects of contemporary humanity. In Euripides the change is still greater, because of the more plastic nature of language, and the more intimate relation of the dramatic poet to a popular audience, which required him to adapt his work to the incongruous tastes of many sorts of persons at once.

But we are not to leap to the conclusion that the old traditions which are losing something of their reality are therefore consciously discarded and laughed to scorn. Men do not so easily divest themselves of the garments of the past ; for a time at least they content themselves with shaping them anew, and patching them with vivid colours taken from present things. They do not at once realise that the new piece will rend the old ; that the new wine will burst the outworn bottles. To ask whether Euripides believed in his version of the story of Orestes is like asking whether Milton believed in the fall of the rebellious angels, or Wagner in the Venusberg and the swan-chariot of Lohengrin. In popular belief the fables had still enough of substance and of actual hold to be accepted when embroidered afresh by the fancy of the poet, who, with his eye on present things, could give even ' to airy nothing a local habitation and a name.' This is not the place for a detailed discussion of the art of Euripides, which, as I have said, is more akin to melodrama, or at most to the romantic drama, than

x

to tragedy, in the Aeschylean or Shakespearian sense ; but the point of view I have indicated may enable us to glean from him something of the attitude of his contemporaries towards divine powers, and even of his own thoughts concerning them.

1. Men had begun to claim that the gods, if they existed, must make for righteousness, and in moments of despair they were prone to cry out, ' This tyranny of iniquity proves that there is no God.' They felt, also, at many points, the inconsistency of the old mythology with this requirement, and sought anxiously to find a reconcilement. The simple mind of Ion, a sort of Delphian Timothy or Samuel, is shocked by the discovery of Phoebus' apparent unfaithfulness. Yet the Delphic oracle maintains its authority, when merely human modes of divination are discredited. Thus the moralising of religious thought has begun, and men are half awakened to it, but they are at the same time eager to find a temporary resting-place in some superficial explanation.

2. The Orphic teaching is now less of a secret than at first, and has become a familiar fact of contemporary experience. Even the thought of a future life in the mystic sense is occasionally present. One who dies is said to have entered on a new phase of existence. Alcestis after death will be a *blessed* divinity (μάκαιρα δαίμων) to whom at her tomb the passers-by will pray. ' The mind of the dead lives not but hath intelligence, being launched into the deathless aether ' (' Hel.' 1014).

3. How far the fusion of worships originally distinct had proceeded in the time of Euripides it is difficult to say. But there is hardly any limit to the freedom he assumes in combining kindred rites and weaving them into a single picture. There is a choral ode in the ' Helena ' where the Greek captive maidens describe ' the mountain mother of the gods ' as wandering in search of her lost mystic child (who has been rapt away from the cyclic dance). She is drawn by wild animals, surrounded with rattling castanets and Bacchic cries, and in her following is Artemis and Gorgo armed with the spear (Athena Gorgôpis). She passes the heights of

Idaean nymphs (a Cretan touch), and the land is desolate because of her sorrow. Then Zeus sends the Graces and the Muses to allay her grief with the noise of cymbals and of timbrels; at the sound whereof Cyprian Aphrodite takes up the flute. After this description the Chorus proceed: 'Sacrifice to the great mother, put on the fawn skin, take in hand the sacred reeds wound with green ivy, and let the booming of the rhombus fill the sky. Loose your hair wildly to Bacchus, keep nightlong vigil for the goddess' (Cybele?). What ritual answered to all this?

4. It is not to be supposed that the poet himself sets out with any consistent philosophical point of view. He is reported, indeed, by late writers to have been a friend of Socrates. But if he was one of the poets referred to in the 'Apology,' the friendship is not likely to have gone very deep, and we have the far better evidence of Plato for the existence of familiar intercourse between Aristophanes and Socrates, yet the comic poet was certainly not a Socratic philosopher. In adorning situations with reflections and observations suitable to them, or striking to the audience, Euripides often images forth to us contemporary modes of thought, just as Shakespeare has made use of the wit and wisdom of Montaigne. But that he does so more sympathetically when he asserts the just government of the supreme power, than when he complains of the blindness and cruelty of fortune, can hardly be maintained.

5. For his scepticism appears to me to be more profound than is commonly assumed. Aeschylus firmly believed in a divine order, fraught with blessings for those who sided with justice and maintained their integrity under trial. Sophocles, with equal firmness, upheld the supremacy of eternal laws of holiness and purity, the breach of which involved inevitable calamity; while for the innocent who suffered he foresaw divine compensation in another world. The bitter experience of the internecine warfare between Athens and Sparta had shaken the foundations of these beliefs. One fate appeared for the righteous and the wicked, for him that sacrificed and for him that sacrificed not. The cloud of pessimism, which the earlier tragedy in a somewhat strug-

gling fashion had broken through, came down again with a more chilling power, because it seemed to be confirmed by the facts of life. The interference of the gods to bring disaster to a happy end, so often represented in Euripidean drama, had less reality, both for the poet and his audience, than the sorrowful complications which had preceded. It was a requirement of the contemporary stage, but had more to do with the framework than with the substance of the art. It was adapted to the weakness of those who could not bear a story to end badly, and may have led simple minds to 'faintly trust the larger hope,' but could leave no impression on the thoughtful spectator, compared to that of the troubles which had moved his sympathy.

6. These troubles came home to the audience all the more because they were such as occurred in daily experience. Under the transparent mask of Electra or Andromache, Peleus or Orestes, men saw themselves and their neighbours, in strange circumstances no doubt, but with the feelings, passions, reasonings and disputings of ordinary Athenian humanity. This effect was produced with an intimacy of realistic portraiture, which, more than anything in Euripides, is an evidence of commanding genius. The life of the Athenians during the whole time of the Peloponnesian war is as clearly visible in his pages as in those of Lysias and Andocides.

7. The life so represented is a strange mixture of nobleness and meanness, of tenderness and cruelty, of national prejudice with occasional gleams of an all-embracing humanity. We have only to compare Aeschylus's treatment of vanquished Persia with the invectives againt Sparta in the 'Andromache'; the pity for Xerxes with the hewing in pieces of Eurystheus by Alcmena, to appreciate the change which a few years of inter-Hellenic contention had produced in the Athenian mind. The pictures of domestic life are especially interesting. The troubles produced through any deflection from the strict law of monogamy, the rare but admirable virtues of continence and self-control, are exhibited in a manner which convinces us that the spread of licence in these respects, which marked this period of transition, had not corrupted the ideal of home

affection and of personal purity. But revenge for individual wrongs is still regarded as a note of virtue and a ground for pride. In the emotions, characters and reasonings thus realistically depicted, while there is much that is specially Athenian, there is often something strangely modern. Persons who are impelled by passion and circumstance into some fatal action on insufficient motives hesitate long beforehand and repent immediately afterwards. This is utterly unlike the solidity of Aeschylean and Sophoclean *dramatis personae*. Both sides of some case of casuistry are carefully hammered out before a course is taken or a judgment pronounced. Local colour is minutely observed, and the phenomena of sickness, both of mind and body, are elaborately studied. These are the 'touches of things common,' of which Mrs. Browning spoke, but they do not altogether ' touch the spheres.'

8. I have left myself but short space in which to speak of the most singular of the productions of Euripides, in a religious sense, and in some ways the most brilliant of his works, the play of the ' Bacchantes.' This goes beyond those ' touches of things common ' which characterise what I have ventured to call the melodramatic manner of Euripides. The culminating motive, Agave returning in triumph from the unconscious murder of her son, is in all conscience tragic enough. But is the poet serious or ironical here? The meaning of the old legend must have been the power of Dionysus upon his enemies. The death of Pentheus had already been the subject of an Aeschylean drama ; but in Aeschylus the play was one of a trilogy, and it was open to him, as in the Oresteia, to compensate the horror of this first advent of the new god with some gentler dénoûment in the concluding play. This does not seem to have been the case with Euripides. If he were serious, he must have simply intended to terrorise his audience into a revival of the worship which they were tempted to neglect. Such a motive would not be in accordance with the tenor of his other extant dramas. If, as has been supposed, the play was written for performance at the court of Archelaus, he may indeed have employed his genius in recommending to the Macedonians the revival of a worship once predominant in that northern region, or, as some have

imagined, he may have repented of former impieties and thought it safer to propitiate Dionysus before leaving the world.

But let us suppose that his motive is ironical. Then the cruelty of Dionysus might be as effective in discrediting his worship for the enlightened auditor as his cowardice in the ‘ Frogs ’ of Aristophanes. But what then becomes of tragic effect ? And one cannot but admit that there is a strain of seriousness in parts of the play, as in the passages which recommend a self-controlled enthusiasm which only vulgar minds confound with insobriety. ‘ These are not drunken, as ye suppose.’ We are reminded of the curious juxtaposition of a gory mythology and ascetic practice in the Orphic religion. The puzzle remains, but belongs to what I venture to think the inherent inconsistency of Euripides, reflecting as he does the distracting influences of a time of transition. That the divine power of Dionysus should be asserted and at the same time his personal existence rationalised away is only too closely in keeping with what we find in the ‘ Ion ’ and other plays.

A partial clue to the difficulty may perhaps be found in the following considerations :

1. According to a tradition repeated by Herodotus, Bacchic rites were originally introduced by Melampus as a cure for some epidemic of mania or hysterics among women. This is one of many similar legends. The remedy was homoeopathic, to borrow a much abused word, curing like with like : an outlet for superabundant emotion, calming and purifying undue excitement, as in Aristotle’s famous definition of tragedy.

2. The Orphic religion, which in the time of Euripides had become widely prevalent, was based in theory, as we have seen, on the most violent form of the Dionysiac myth, the tearing in pieces of Zagreus or of Phanes by the Titans. Yet the whole tendency of Orphism was to an ascetic life in which abstinence from animal food and from the slaughter of animals held a prominent place. The contradiction is a striking one, but is analogous to many other incidents in the gradual spiritualising of religion. I may instance the

Epistle to the Hebrews, from which it appears that after the daily sacrifice had been discontinued the idea of sacrifice and of atonement through blood was dominant amongst the Jews of the dispersion.

3. In reviving the myth of Pentheus and thus emphasising the terrible power of a god whose worship was neglected, the tragic poet and sworn votary of Dionysus, by what may be described as a religious oxymoron or unresolved antinomy, encourages the belief in what Plato afterwards spoke of as divine madness, a temperate enthusiasm resulting not in vicious excesses but raising ordinary virtues to a higher power. (Compare ' Is any among you merry, let him sing psalms.')

4. This, however, I suppose him rather to have shadowed forth than consistently to have embodied in his drama. In dramatising the fable, he has been led onwards by the tragic motive to the development of the given situation apart from any moral, mystical or otherwise. The moralising as in his other plays is incidental and rather insinuated than expressed.

The old world was dying, the new world was not yet born. It was an age of intellectual growth, but of religious and in some degree also of moral decay. Yet humanising influences were at work, which were destined to have a far-reaching effect. The relation of the slave to his master was one, for example, on which a volume might be written : he is a chattel, and yet a human being, perhaps a captive prince, yet compelled to do another's bidding. The law requires that in the interest of justice he may be demanded for torture, yet bright examples of faithfulness and tenderness on both sides are not infrequent, although it is elsewhere taken for granted that slave nature is necessarily base and will always take the part of the latest master. The contrast of Hellene and barbarian is often emphasised with patriotic scorn,—' the Greeks are freemen, in barbarous countries only one is free.' Yet the conduct of Thoas and his obedience to Athena must be admitted to do him credit, and the spectator cannot but be sorry for Theoclymenus, the mild and ingenuous

Egyptian, when he is over-reached by Hellenic cunning. Again the examples of self-devotion in Euripides, recurring as they do with almost monotonous frequency, belong to an ideal which had many counterparts in the actual life of the time. Altogether it was an age in which contradictory elements were fermenting together, which were afterwards separated,—the dregs of old tradition and convention still occupying the lower sphere, while exceptional minds were gradually shaping an ideal world of thought, which should have more lasting consequences than the round of commonplace observances which were continued even by those for whom they had lost their life and meaning.

No doubt it is possible, and would be more so if more of him had been preserved, to gather out of Euripides much of serious thought on religious subjects, as Bishop Westcott has done, in the very able chapter on Euripides which he has published in his volume on 'Religious Thought in the West.' And it is only fair to the poet to credit him with sincerity, where the strain of reflection in him appears deepest, as when Theonoë says, 'I have within me, in my nature, a great temple of Justice.' But in order to appreciate his spirit aright, it is necessary to break through the rule of criticism which bids us consider each great literary production as a whole. His best thoughts come in sudden flashes that surprise us out of dark places, amidst some thorny tangle of sophistry or verbal disceptation. One frequently recurring notion is that of the Aether, or Empyrean, which with Euripides, as with the Aristophanic Socrates, often appears as the native home and nutriment of the human soul. ' O mother earth, the wise of mortals call thee Hestia whose seat is in the sky.'

The influence of philosophy is perceptible, but in the secondary phase which is sometimes described as 'theosophy.' 'The happiest man is he who contemplates the ageless order of immortal nature, and beholds how it is framed. The ruler of all things shall be worshipped, whether he chooseth to be named Zeus or Hades.' Such vague beliefs have something of an Orphic colouring, and are not associated with philosophic speculation, which is scouted as a dangerous extravagance, not only by the chorus in the ' Bacchae,' but in many other places, for example in Fragment 969 :—

'Wretched and ill-starred is he, who, beholding these things, doth not perceive a god in them, and cast away from him the crooked deceits of theorisers, whose disastrous tongue throws out conjecture without sense about things unseen.'

Like other great poets Euripides reflects not always consistently the many-coloured atmosphere surrounding him, in which doubt and superstition were crossed with aspiration after better things, and imagination still played around the traditions of the past, remoulding them, and in the same act, melting them away or transfusing them with a light that was really alien to them. It has been sometimes said that religious music is the euthanasia of dogma ; Euripidean poetry may be similarly described as the euthanasia of mythology. But the great influence which he exercised over later ages in Greece, evinced by the very frequent quotations from him, is enough to secure for him a lasting place amongst great poets. If his vision is often disturbed, it has gleams of a light beyond his age. And even his honest doubt claims respectful sympathy. For it carries with it the promise and the potency of a higher faith. He is oppressed with 'the burden of the mystery,' 'the heavy and the weary weight of all this unintelligible world,' yet at times he seems on the point of solving the great problem. It is a passing moment and associated with an unworthy desire of revenge, and yet a moment of true exaltation, in which Hecuba cries

> O Earth's upholder that on earth dost dwell,
> Whate'er thy name, hard to be understood,
> Zeus, or necessity of nature's course,
> Or mind of mortals,—before thee I bow ;
> For on thy noiseless pathway thou dost guide,
> As righteousness commands, all human things.

After the departure of Anaxagoras, whom they had not understood, the Athenians received the great doctrines of Heraclitus and Parmenides in a secondary phase from teachers whose aim was practical or even mercenary. In the first instance the interest they awakened came from the pleasure of keen discourse, and the practice thus obtained in public speaking, which was the way to power. The most intelligent of the Athenian youth, however, found a disinterested enjoyment in the novelty of abstract ideas, their oppositions and relations, which was an end in itself : while at the same time, the incessant activity of political and social life at Athens made it impossible that abstract thought should be long dissociated from actual reality. Protagoras of Abdera was the most prominent of the new teachers. In theology he professed himself what we should call an agnostic :—' Concerning the gods, whether they are or are not, I refuse to say ; there are so many things to hinder that knowledge ; the matter is uncertain, and human life is short.' He came from Abdera in Thrace, but if Plato is to be believed, he was in part a disciple of Heraclitus of Ephesus. This, however, may be only one of those combinations by which Plato indicates the manner in which he thinks philosophers ought to be grouped together. Yet, if an arbitrary combination, it is also a suggestive one. For the Heraclitean doctrine—that all is motion and transience, that nothing is but what immediately is not—has its human application in the Protagorean doctrine of the relativity of truth. No statement can be held to absolutely ; truth and goodness are alike matters of degree ; human life, like animal and vegetable life, may be improved by circumstance and training, but there is no fixed standard ; no irremovable good at which to aim. The man is the measure of truth, and custom is the only standard of virtue. This had its logical counterpart in the saying that about every matter there are two lines of argument, opposed to one another and equally tenable.

It is tolerably obvious how such theories might work upon minds prepared by those lessons of experience which are described above. Meanwhile Zeno, the younger friend of Parmenides, was amusing the finer intellects and sharpening the wits of youth, by his paradox supported with elaborate arguments, that Change and Motion were impossible ; and Gorgias, from Leontini in Sicily, even at an earlier time, had impressed the Athenians with the stateliness of his antithetical style, imparting to them the graces of rhetoric, while professing a philosophy which was the negative counterpart of the great assertion of Parmenides. While Protagoras asserted the relative, Gorgias denied the absolute. Starting from a different point he came to a result hardly distinguishable from that of Protagoras, the incomprehensibility and the inexpressibleness of absolute being. The truth is that pure scepticism and pure transcendentalism continually pass over into each other ; and something like this is really what Plato meant by his paradoxes in the ' Parmenides.' Thus what was most alive in the mental condition of the more enlightened Athenians in the time of Socrates was not the ritual, which the old priestly families sedulously maintained ; nor the mythology, which, from being the expression of spiritual thought, was becoming merely the food of fancy and imagination ; but a spirit of enquiry, keen and bold at the outset, and having as yet no clearly speculative aim ; suspected by the older generation, but stimulated at once by sheer intellectual activity and by practical ambition. This last was for long the ruling motive, and philosophy, still immature, was in danger of being corrupted by it. John Selden has described the sacramentarian doctrine of the Middle Ages—the belief in Transubstantiation—as ' Rhetoric turned into Logic ' ; the intellectual danger of the pre-Socratic age in Greece was that pure thought might be prematurely turned into rhetoric, and that logic might become a mere barren exercise in logomachy and verbal disputation. Sceptical doubts in matters of religion were threatening, as we should say in modern language, the very foundations of morality ; for the ancestral laws and customs, whose sanction was religious, shared the suspicion which had begun to spread over religious convictions as hitherto received. Men had become aware of the variety and even contradictoriness of customs in different lands, and were not slow in drawing inferences. Yet amidst all these confusions, there was a spiritual force awakening that could not cease to work until it found a resting place. And while speaking of the great Sophists as forming a solvent of traditional morality, it is not implied that they were themselves conscious of an immoral tendency. The impression left upon the mind by the great figures of Hippias and Prodicus, imperfectly as we are able to distinguish them, and of Protagoras himself, is that of men who were seriously inclined to use their gifts for the improvement of their fellows. In recalling his hearers from convention to nature, Hippias, like Rousseau, believed himself to be inculcating a higher morality. The famous apologue of the Choice of Herakles, with which Prodicus is credited, was a permanent contribution to the literature of ethical exhortation. And Protagoras, even as Plato represents him, and probably more so in reality, presents the appearance of a moral teacher of no mean order. Meanwhile, the common morality was maintained, not without religious fervour, by the persistent teaching of Plato's dignified contemporary, Isocrates, ' the old man eloquent,' whom there is not room to consider at all worthily here.

In the intervals of the Peloponnesian war, as well as after its conclusion, when the democracy was restored and the aristocratic leaders retired to Eleusis, the lessening of interest in home politics turned the minds of cultivated persons towards foreign travel. They would thus be brought into contact with the original philosophies, which they had hitherto only known at second-hand. At Ephesus, Miletus, Elea, Thurii, Agrigentum, Syracuse, Tarentum they would find the actual disciples of the various schools. We may therefore now divert our thoughts from Athens for a while and look once more at other centres, where this love of truth for its own sake had sprung up and flourished in the preceding century. The Pythagorean league had been broken up long since, but the school scattered over the towns of Italy and Sicily had rather gained in influence when the political association was no more. Pythagoreanism had two sides, which seem hard to reconcile, and which perhaps at the time now spoken of were represented by different sections of the professing followers of the sage. 1. There was the mystical and ascetic doctrine, closely allied, as before said, to Orphism, and depending on the belief in immortality and transmigration. 2. There was the mathematical and scientific learning pursued in reliance on the first principle of the master, that 'number is the world.' Philolaus combined both these aspects by teaching that the soul is a harmony, which, as Plato shows in the 'Phaedo,' is an insecure foundation for the belief in an existence after death. The two sides are also linked together in the use of music as a means of religious purification. This notion still retained much of the formalism of a magical rite, and had little as yet of a really exalted morality ; but it prepared a mould into which Plato's moral teaching could afterwards be poured. It is not to be forgotten that the Pythagoreans are credited with the scheme, already traceable in Pindar and afterwards adopted by Plato, of the four cardinal virtues. Nor was their ethical doctrine, negative as it may seem to us, by any means barren of great exemplars of true nobleness. Virtue, as we may remember, was described by the Pythagoreans, not only as the harmonising of life, but as the 'following of God.' In the scientific theory also, and its applications to cosmogony and psychology, much was crude and imperfect ; but just as alchemy prepared the way for scientific chemistry, while it gave occasion to much quackery and self-deception for a time ; and as the worship of Asclepius gave rise both to the science of medicine and to many forms of mere empiricism and imposture : so the Pythagorean school, while on the one hand degenerating into wild fancies about the occult virtue of numerical ratios and the like, was also the ground on which the true science of Archytas, Euclides, Hipparchus, and Archimedes built their enduring monuments. Meanwhile, the ideas of harmony, rhythm, proportion, symmetry, and of orderly evolution, in all their various applications, had become an inalienable heritage for mankind. This notion of the applicability of number and measure to all things is one of those anticipations of truth, which, as afterwards enforced by Plato and formulated by Aristotle, have obtained a fixed place in the development of thought, and are apt to seem to us mere truisms or original elements in the constitution of the human mind. If they have since been abundantly verified, that is not a ground for detracting from the merit of those who first clearly conceived them.

The strange and wonderful career of Empedocles of Agrigentum is a most striking example of the influence which could be exerted in Sicily and Magna Graecia, in the fifth century, by one who to a fervent belief in himself and his own destiny, and an irresistible impulse to excite and elevate mankind, drew from Pythagoreanism its magical power of forming men's lives anew, and from the Ionian philosophers, theoretic conceptions concerning the nature of things. The two elements are doubtless inconsistent, but when fused by his genius into a whole, they assured for him an ascendency over his compatriots, of a kind that is unique in Greek history. His bold assertion of his own immortal destiny raised not only wonder but a desire to follow him. And though he passed like a comet across the stage of Sicilian life, he could not fail to leave traces of spiritual influence behind him. His resolution of the universe into four elements,—earth, water, air, and fire, although in a manner borrowed from the Ionians, is memorable as having stamped itself on common language ; and his employment of the principles of love and hate, or in colder words, of attraction and repulsion, as the efficient causes of natural phenomena, is also the anticipation of much that has been fruitful in subsequent philosophy. One of Matthew Arnold's early poems represents him in the hour before his tragical end ; but as usual with this poet and thinker, the thread of the discourse ascribed to the Sicilian sage is strongly tinged with stoicism. Instead of quoting Matthew Arnold, therefore, I will make a few extracts from the genuine fragments of this strangely inspired being. Although they are meant to be an expression of universal truths, the form of them is full of what may be described as a noble Ego-mania.

1. ' Human birth is one of a series of transmigrations which are the punishment of some original sin.

' When one of the blessed has incurred bloodguiltiness, he must wander thirty thousand years away from blessedness, passing through all forms of mortal life : so now I am a wanderer and banished from heaven, a victim of the principle of strife. . . .' ' Oh, from what a place of pride and high renown I fell to move amongst mankind ! . . .

I wept and wailed when I beheld the region in which
I was a stranger . . . this joyless place, where hate and
murder and many forms of death and dire diseases and
corruption flow. Here wander we up and down the dark
valley of disaster.'
2. 'Friends who inhabit lofty Akragas, industrious in
good works, receiving strangers, all hail! I come amongst
you all, a god, immortal, not a mortal any more, but
honoured as is meet with crowns and garlands; and when I
come to any thriving town, both men and women reverence
me, and follow in countless numbers, asking me the way to
happiness and wealth ; some for true oracles, some to heal
disease when racked with tedious torments and with agonies.
They learn from me the beauteousness of Truth.'
3. 'It cannot be that one and the same thing is lawful
in one city, and forbidden to others ; but universal law
stretches throughout the widely ruling sky and the immeasurable beam of light.'

The travelled Athenian would therefore find in his converse with the men of Italy and Sicily much to stimulate
that intellectual wonder which is the parent of true philosophy. He would be led back from the ingenious paradoxes
of Zeno to the words of Parmenides, conveying deep thoughts
in poetic language, which would be a revelation to him,
though he could not fathom their full significance. On the
Asiatic shore, again, he might mingle with the little band of
the adherents of Cratylus, who was expounding the dark
sayings of Heraclitus to an enthusiastic audience. Their
extravagances would at once amuse and interest him.

To puzzle him still further, he might come across adherents of the early atomistic school, whose scepticism as to
sensible phenomena was as profound as that of any philosopher, but who believed themselves to have reached reality,
to have got down to the granite as it were, by asserting that
the world was made of irreducible, solid particles, moving in
a void. The penetrating mind of Leucippus in dwelling
upon the Eleatic philosophy, as represented by Melissus and
Zeno, conceived the germinal idea of accounting for difference and relation through a primordial reality of two elements,

the atom and the void. This thought was developed by his followers, including Democritus, into a consistent theory of perception and the object of perception. Mechanics thus became for them the basis of universal science. Their first motive, however, was controversial. Heraclitus had said 'the non-existent is : all is and is not at once.' Parmenides had asserted the absolute fulness of one Being, which is all in all. The atomists declared reality to consist of Being and not-Being in combination, of fulness and emptiness together. That conception, in a scientific sense, was the most fruitful of all, although it was lightly passed over or contemptuously ignored by Plato. Democritus was almost his contemporary ; hence perhaps the impersonal manner of his rare allusions to him.

Once more our Athenian traveller might find himself in the Dorian island of Cos, amongst the worshippers of Asclepius, and might chance to come across the great Asclepiad who was destined to become famous as Hippocrates and had actually visited Athens. Here was an entirely independent origin of scientific thought, immediately based upon religion, and associated with practical life. It was a science relying on tradition, but on tradition concurrently with experience, and perpetually revised and corrected by fresh observation and investigation. 'Life is short, art is long, opportunity flies, and judgment is hard': so runs the foremost aphorism of Hippocrates. In the body of writings which pass under his name, there is much that is of later growth, and in his genuine work there are no doubt many theories, traditional illusions and rash anticipations which have been since exploded ; but the spirit of the whole is that of observation, patiently conducted, cautiously generalised, and conscientiously recorded. There is no reason to suppose that the central conception of Nature was derived by Hippocrates from the Ionian physiologers. The connotation of the word was probably different for him and for them. As Professor Burnet has shown, the early Ionians in speaking of the 'nature of things' meant rather the substance whereof they are made than a process of growth or manner of becoming : although in Heraclitus the two notions seem to coincide. Nature in Hippocrates is rather the *modus operandi*, the process to be investigated, which goes on independently of human thought and action, but, when closely followed and understood, becomes the secret of right treatment and successful cure. This is not a borrowed notion, but rather what we may venture to call, in modern language, an original induction. And with all his untrammelled zeal of investigation, he never departs from an essentially religious standing-ground. He is the author of the great saying, as true for our generation as his own, ' I believe these affections to be divine, as I do all other ; no one affection is more divine or more human than any other, but all alike are both human and divine ; each having its own nature, and none arising but in the way of nature.' Any one who compares this saying with the passage from Andocides above quoted (p. 298) will see at once how far Hippocrates was in advance of the average Athenian mind. Plato himself was for a while impressed with the genius of Hippocrates, and sought to transfer his method from physical to mental philosophy.

If we now suppose our travelled Athenian to return to Athens, he will find Socrates there, towards the close of his career, in the city which he has never left, and to which he has devoted his life, still busied in awakening his compatriots to a line of enquiry at first sight very different from those hitherto described, and standing in no relation to them ; but destined by and by, through the genius of Plato, to be interwoven with almost all of them, and to interpenetrate them with a new spiritual force.

CHAPTER XIV

SOCRATES AND THE SOCRATICS

The historical and the Platonic Socrates—Religion in Xenophon—
Aristippus—Antisthenes.

THE attitude of Socrates towards the ideas which prevailed amongst his contemporaries was at first a negative one. That his curiosity was awakened by the discussions which he heard around him may be taken for granted, and what Plato tells us in the 'Phaedo' may possibly be true—that he at one time busied himself with speculating about the nature of thought on a physiological basis, until the book of Anaxagoras carried him off into a higher region, in which, not the blood or the brain could be accepted as a cause of mental action, but only mind or reason. Dissatisfied with Anaxagoras too, who failed to show the connection between his cause and the effects which we experience, Socrates as he is there represented was thrown back upon discourse, in which, as in a mirror, the operations of universal mind could be dimly perceived. This is one of several ways in which the Platonic Socrates seeks to account for the strangeness of his career.

The main facts of his life-history, so far as known to us, are, as in this instance, suffused with afterthoughts, and decorated with fancy. Not the man himself, but his reflected image, is all that we can discern. The son of a sculptor, he had for a time practised his father's trade, but, as we cannot but believe, had spent his leisure time in eager talking, up and down the market-place, only interrupted by unaccountable fits of abstraction, in which he remained silent for hours together. His conversation already impressed some listeners as having an inexhaustible interest, unlike that

of the ordinary Athenian, however acute or discursive.
Amongst these constant listeners, if we credit Plato's
'Apology,' was his friend Chaerephon, one of the most im-
pulsive of human beings, who boldly went and asked the
Delphic oracle whether Socrates were not the wisest of men.
The oracle was understood to give an affirmative answer ;
at which, when Chaerephon reported it, no one was more
astonished than Socrates himself. He had thought deeply,
and had talked much with many who had seemed wise, and
the result had been only to convince him of the depth of his
own ignorance. But he shared the religion of his countrymen, and would not gainsay the response of Phoebus without further proof. So he gave up all other employments,
and went about interrogating all who had a reputation for
wisdom, continually expecting to find some one wiser than
himself. But he found no man, for each interlocutor, after
asserting what he thought he knew, could give no reason
of it that was not found to be self-contradictory when put to
the test of persistent enquiry.

From this strange tale we may gather so much with confidence—that he regarded himself as the devoted servant of
Apollo, the enlightener of men, the lord of music, but of a
higher and grander music than Terpander or Stesichorus had
conceived—the harmony of human life, the melodious concord
of thought and action. That harmony had been disturbed
and broken in the Greek world by causes which have been
roughly indicated in the preceding chapter ; and the penetrative glance of Socrates, piercing through all the plausible
appearances and brilliant colouring of the life surrounding
him, was deeply conscious of a universal need. Mankind
seemed to be perishing for lack of knowledge and wisdom.
Yet where was wisdom to be found ? The old philosophers,
great souls springing up in petty communities, had risen
far above their neighbours, and, despising practical affairs,
had gone each his own way, not caring to take mankind
along with them, while they speculated about the substance
of the universe, and proclaimed the principle which each
maintained concerning it in symbolic language, too high for
ordinary comprehension. To Socrates, as to the average

Athenian, all this seemed 'meteorology,'—a meddling with things remote from earth, which men could never know, and were not meant to know. Remaining, as he did, superficially in touch with his neighbours, and holding silent communion with himself, it was not the universe but man that interested him. To outward observers he appeared at first sight like any other Athenian, except that he consistently abjured all the softnesses and refinements which had become habitual amongst men of leisure,—seldom changed his garment, wore no shoes, and never seemed to feel the inclemency of the sky. But he kept all religious observances with scrupulous fidelity, attended social gatherings with unaffected enjoyment, and in his address preserved a perfect urbanity, which irresistibly recommended him to other men, though he was far from possessing that beauty of feature which was so attractive to all Athenians. His snub nose, wide nostrils, and great eyes set far apart were a standing joke amongst his friends. His straddling gait, indicative of strength, was often ridiculed. But when you got beneath the surface, there was something unaccountable and even mysterious about him: courage, endurance, physical strength, sociability, and many-sided humanity were combined with spiritual yearnings never satisfied; a mind that was ever probing the deepest questions; soaring contemplations, which yet seemed to put no strain upon the firmly anchored cords which held him to his country and his countrymen, amongst whom and for whom he lived. To the busy politician, the poet, the artizan, he appeared idle and useless; spending his time in endless talk about matters in which no man was immediately concerned. And yet the whole bent of his activity was to find a firmer standing ground for public and private life than the Greek world had hitherto attained. Until this were reached, it seemed to him that no idleness could be more futile than the sweating labour of the contemporary politician.

Such were the contradictions that met in the life of Socrates—eager sociability, intense self-concentration, a passionate nature held in absolute self-control, strength, endurance, courage at the height; mystical anticipations of worlds unrealised, suspense of judgment about present things : a practical aim, leading to abstinence from active life ; a sceptical attitude, rooted in an absolutely firm conviction of the reality of truth and justice—of goodness, human and divine. This attitude of enquiry is what distinguishes Socrates on the one hand from the dogmatism of the philosophic schools preceding him, and on the other from those sceptical doctrines of the mere relativity of truth and the incomprehensibility of being, with which the age had been amused by the great sophists, Protagoras and Gorgias.

A great English poet was called by one of his friends ' a little crooked thing that asks questions.' In the same spirit of banter, some of his associates might have called Socrates a snub-nosed Silenus who had never done with catechising. The form of his discourse was stamped by later philosophy into the formula, ' *What is it ?* ' (τί ἐστι;). The subject-matter is described by Xenophon, when he says that ' Socrates went about asking his fellow-citizens *What is a state, what is a statesman, what is government, what is it to be a ruler of men ?* ' The scope of his labours was characterised more closely by himself as a continual endeavour to fulfil the precept ' Know thyself,' by interrogating other men. This was the first step in the great sciences of ethics, of logic, and of psychology.

But our immediate concern is rather with the religion of Socrates. He was accused of abandoning the gods of his city, and of introducing other new divinities, but he disclaimed this accusation, and no impeachment was ever more unjust. Although we cannot take quite literally the view of the simple-minded Xenophon, who may have strained a point in representing him as orthodox, there does not seem any ground for supposing that he had ever any thought of separating himself from the majority of his countrymen with regard to formal religion. But his piety, which was, perhaps, the deepest thing in him, had more in it than was conceivable to the average Athenian. Thinking of the gods generally, more often than of any particular god, he was convinced, as none before him had been, of the moral and spiritual nature of the service which they required. He was quite sincere in speaking of himself as the servant of Apollo, in worshipping the sun at dawn, in joining his countrymen at public festivals, in paying his vow to Asclepius in token of thanksgiving for peaceful death. But in and beyond all these formalities, he had the sense of a divine presence in the world, and especially in the soul of man, which was inseparable from the inmost springs of his being.

It was this which inspired his persistent faith in an ultimate discovery of truth, which should be a light to guide humanity, since he was profoundly assured that men would not wilfully persist in error. The light he sought for was an intellectual light, no doubt, as it appears to us ; but are we sure that *knowledge*, in the mind of Socrates, did not comprehend some anticipation of what we most value as religious enlightenment ? Thus the philosophy of Socrates was in one sense a sceptical philosophy, yet it was by no means a philosophy without prepossessions or without assumptions. The two great postulates which underlay it were the existence of truth for the inquiring mind, and the identity of truth and goodness. But on the other hand, it was assumed at the outset that truth was not yet found ; that goodness was something more than custom and tradition, and that the confession of ignorance was the preliminary condition of all sound enquiry.

Knowledge is the central word in the philosophy of Socrates, but a knowledge to which he laid no claim, and which he believed to be hitherto unattainable, yet one which could be gradually approached by reasoning : the knowledge not of this or that phenomenon or matter of fact, but of universal principles, which, once known, can never be gainsaid, but will prove ' the light of all our seeing.' The search for this knowledge is a religious duty, the highest fulfilment of the will of God, the highest service to mankind. In the pursuit of this, Socrates was never stopped by the familiar voice that checked him unaccountably when on the point of doing this or that. Only when men came to him for guidance, if he instinctively felt that their motives were idle, or that they themselves were for the time incurably conceited, his instinct sometimes took the shape of this warning intimation which was so mysterious to himself.

The life of Socrates was devoted not only to the pursuit of truth, but in the same act to the education of his countrymen. Whether we take the evidence of Plato or of Xenophon, we cannot doubt that his influence in this respect, even in his own generation, must have been incalculable. Like other great teachers, he formed sanguine hopes that were not always realised. Socrates did not succeed in making of Critias or of Alcibiades patterns of justice and morality, yet the hold which he obtained on them must have raised them above themselves for a time, and even in that he may have done a service to the Athenians. But when Critias, as one of the Thirty, would have given Socrates the commission of fetching in Leon to be executed unjustly, the tyrant met with a firm refusal, just as the Athenian populace had done, when they wanted him to put to the vote the question of the execution of the generals after the disaster at Arginusae. He had a power of acting upon others without being reacted on or influenced by them; moving straight along his chosen path imperturbably, and turning neither to the right nor to the left. Such common human features as his lifelong friendship with the faithful Crito, who had no philosophy but only simple worth, are probably as real as anything which has been handed down concerning him. The impression he made on his contemporaries was that of an extraordinary person, but very few appreciated him at his full value, and his greatness was only known through the manner of his death.

In what, then, did that greatness consist ? 1. He had steadily upheld an ideal standard of truth and right, at once intellectual and moral, scientific and practical, which he set before himself and others as the goal—unattained, perhaps unattainable, yet indefinitely approachable—of all thought, all effort, all care to live. 2. For the pursuit of this new aim he had invented a novel method of proceeding, in the re-examination of those cardinal conceptions to which all men constantly appealed, while a brief cross-examination was enough to show that the terms so confidently used were imperfectly understood. In other words, it was by the application of negative instances to current notions that he sought to obtain definitions of moral ideas, which would hold without exception, and might thus be relied on as rules of conduct and tests of sound thinking. 3. He imposed this task upon himself and all who came within his influence, as a religious vocation. Thus the paths of religion and philosophy, which had diverged, or seemed to diverge, in the preceding generation, were united in him.

1. It may seem paradoxical to say that the confession of ignorance and the bringing of others to the same confession was equivalent to the setting up of an ideal standard ; but it is the simple truth. In saying ' I know nothing,' Socrates implied that knowledge was a higher thing than his contemporaries had dreamed of : that the only knowledge worth having was the knowledge of something universal and unchangeable ; that it was clear and definite ; above all, that it had a real ground, which no man ought to despair of finding : —something very different, for example, from the notion of justice that was bandied to and fro in law courts ; or from that of expediency, on which men dwelt so complacently in the popular assembly ; or of holiness as preached in the Orphic or Dionysiac mysteries : notions to which those who employed them so freely attached no distinct content. And the Socratic ideal of knowledge involved not merely a speculative but an intensely practical aim. It is the knowledge which begins with knowledge of oneself, and ends with true beneficence towards other men, while it is enlightened throughout with ever enlarging conceptions of the relation of man to the divine.

In this first great effort of earnest ethical enquiry, much is blended which by later reflection was analysed into several parts. In the white light of Socrates the several rays which coloured later ethics are combined. To know the right is with him to follow it. Perhaps his own instinctive moral strength prevented him from adequately estimating the possibilities of human weakness. He did not stop to dissect the sophistry of vice, on which Aristotle dwells so ingeniously. Vice with him is folly, ignorance, stupidity. Real knowledge of the good could not but issue, he thought, in good action. The good is what all men desire, and if once clearly seen, must draw the whole man to grasp it.

A word may be added on what have been called the utilitarian ethics of Socrates. It is hardly fair to credit him with particular opinions on the doubtful report of conversations by which he tentatively approached conceptions admittedly partial and imperfect. In pointing out that virtuous action was based on the calculation of pleasures, he was really opposing an intellectual to a merely conventional standard, a principle of some kind to the uncertain dictates of custom and tradition.

2. The method of Socrates belongs rather to the history of logic than of religion, but cannot be passed over in giving any account of him at all. His power of conversing easily with all and sundry enabled him always to start from a common ground. That once obtained, he asked the question which pierced to the root of the matter, and by examples of the most obvious kind brought out some contradiction which led to a further tentative definition. Some of the reasoning may appear puerile to our modern experience, but it should be remembered how little as yet the Greeks were accustomed to the abstract expression of general ideas. In his method, no less than in his aim, the work of Socrates is to be distinguished from that of Protagoras on the one hand and the Eleatic Zeno on the other. These were necessary moments in the evolution of incipient thought ; the work of Socrates was the beginning of an evolution which bore in it the seed of endless progress, and can never lose its applicability to human experience.

3. The religious aspect of the work of Socrates is deeply rooted in his individual nature. What seemed his self-chosen mission, in which he continued labouring for forty years, was, as he conceived it, a long course of obedience to a divine call. If the truth which he sought was not only speculative but practical, it had beyond both these factors a spiritual element, in which the practical and speculative

were combined. In defending his country and his friends, in obeying the laws, throughout his lifetime and more conspicuously on the approach of death meeting injustice and cruelty with the firmness of a law-abiding will : he acted throughout with a profoundly religious motive. But for this it may be doubted whether he would have made on other minds that deep impression which has secured for after ages the continuation of his lifework, and has provided philosophy no less than faith with the image of a proto-martyr, never to be effaced. In this sense he is indeed the founder of a religion. The lives of many saints reflect to us the graces of faith, hope, and charity ; the love of truth, that other grace of the religious life, without which all else is incomplete, is represented, as has well been said, by none so fully as by ' Saint Socrates.'

Did Socrates believe in immortality ? He who professed to have attained no adequate knowledge of human things could not consistently profess to have unravelled the secrets of the grave. On the one hand lay the Orphic belief or imagination, which had by this time become traditional amongst a few ; on the other, what tended to be the prevailing notion of a sceptical age, that with death there came the extinction of all conscious life. Socrates in Plato's ' Apology ' is represented, probably with truth, as holding his judgment in suspense between these different views, and saying that to assert either would be to seem to know what one does not know. In reliance on the goodness of the divine power, he is ready to accept either alternative not only with resignation but with an untroubled mind. If death be a dreamless sleep, are there many days of life to be preferred to that ? If it be a continuation of existence, as represented in poetic legend, what joy must it be to converse with the great and wise of former ages, some of whom were unjustly used by their contemporaries, and like himself were wrongfully condemned !

Consistently with his general aim, Socrates speculated less about the divine nature than about the attitude of men towards superior powers. There is no reason to doubt that he discoursed upon the right use of prayer, pointing out that men should exert themselves to obtain what the gods had placed within their reach, and only have recourse to prayer and divination in cases of perplexity and doubt. Also that, considering human blindness, every prayer should be accompanied with the reservation, that such and such a wish should be accomplished only if God saw that it was for good.

Once more, the simple anticipation of the famous doctrine of final causes, i.e. of the evidence of a divine providence in the adaptation of organ to function, attributed to him by Xenophon in the 'Memorabilia,' may have been really suggested by him in some discourse or other, at least as a pious opinion. But in this connection it is necessary to repeat that his discourse upon particular themes, no doubt imperfectly reported, should not be interpreted too rigidly. More unequivocal, and fortunately more important, are those general lines of thought and action, the direction of which I have been trying to indicate.

In what precedes I have attempted to describe the religious aspect of the work of Socrates, as far as seemed possible, in itself, and independently of the impressions or representations of his younger contemporaries. In dealing with the Platonic Socrates. as such, one can use a freer hand. The only caution to be observed is to prefer the evidence of those dialogues which were written while the influence of the Master was still vividly present, and Platonism had not yet received its final development in the mind of its author. We are thus confronted with the difficult question of the order of the Platonic Dialogues, a problem which may never be completely solved, but of which a partial solution has received pretty general assent, according to which six dialogues at least—the 'Sophist,' 'Politicus,' 'Philebus,' 'Timaeus,' 'Critias,' and 'Laws'—belong to the writer's latest manner, and present comparatively few features of that strange and potent personality which dominates the greater number of Plato's writings. It is also admitted that in the work of his maturity, to which the 'Phaedrus,' 'Republic' and 'Theaetetus' belong, many things are put into the mouth of Socrates which he could never have spoken. But the person of Socrates is there throughout, and the living philosopher sincerely believes that his philosophy is the genuine outcome of a faithful application of the Socratic method. This method has its destructive but also its constructive side. The Platonic Socrates begins by examining some of the simplest and most universally recognised moral ideas, such as courage, temperance, holiness, and friendship. Conversing with Laches the great general, who is a type of soldierly qualities, and with the ill-starred Nicias, he brings his hearers to the admission that neither physical nor moral courage, as commonly conceived, is an adequate notion of this virtue, and the only courage worth having would be one derived from a general principle of conduct, inseparable from true knowledge, on which both courage and all other virtues ultimately depend. Again, in his fascinating talk with Charmides, the most temperate of young men, he brings him to utter confusion in the confession that he does not know what temperance is, thus exhibiting the need of a scientific principle without which the conduct of life must be a haphazard affair. In the ' Lysis,' Socrates is introduced to two young boys, whose inseparable friendship is described as exemplary ; and in a strain of banter, in which many theories of friendship are lightly touched, he concludes that neither he nor they can tell what friendship is, except that to be worth anything it must bear some relation to the highest good. In the ' Euthyphro,' another simple dialogue, a deeper question is involved, and the contrast between the piety of Socrates and what passes with the religious world for piety, although not explicitly stated, is powerfully suggested. Socrates is about to stand his trial for impiety, and he meets with Euthyphro, who is bringing an indictment against his own father, for having accidentally caused the death of a slave. Socrates is naturally interested to know what one whose religious principles are so deeply rooted as to support him in such an exceptional act has to say about the nature of piety or holiness. This may stand him (Socrates) in good stead, when called on to defend himself before his judges. He leads poor Euthyphro an uneasy dance amongst various trite definitions of holiness,. and states the central problem, which has had an interest for other ages than his own : ' Is an action holy because the gods command it? or does God command it because it is holy ? ' At the end of the dialogue he declares himself to be no wiser than he was, but the reader feels that Euthyphro must have gone away a wiser and a sadder man.

The ' Protagoras ' contains the first great outbreak of Plato's dramatic power, and it is here that the Platonic Socrates appears with most of vividness and freshness of detail. It is the only one of the longer dialogues about which it is open to question whether it may not have been written before the death of Socrates. Mr. Grote's view, who is inclined to regard it as the most finished and therefore, perhaps, the latest of the dialogues, is a curious instance of the effect of preconception on criticism.

It is still grey dawn, and Socrates, a man of mature age, is fast asleep upon his truckle-bed, when the young and noble Hippocrates brusquely awakens him, with the thrilling intelligence that Protagoras is in town. Socrates takes the news quite coolly, having heard it the night before, when Hippocrates had gone into the country on a personal errand. He rises, however, and rallies the youth on his enthusiastic eagerness, asking him, amongst other questions, whether he wants to be made a sophist ; whereupon he detects the rising blush on the cheek of Hippocrates, for it was now near sunrise ; then he proceeds with his cross-questioning, while preparing to yield to the young man's importunity. They go together to the house of the rich Callias, which is thronged with the greatest sophists ; the porter, who has suffered many things from his master's guests, is unwilling to admit them, but being assured that they are only plain citizens (not sophists from abroad), gives way. The scene within the house is then vividly described. Protagoras, Hippias, Prodicus, and the rest come before us in lifelike procession ; then Protagoras is cross-questioned as to the nature of his art, which is the teaching of virtue. Socrates doubts if virtue can be taught. Protagoras, in a brilliant argument, in which some think that the sophist has the best of it, shows that the relative civic virtues, which alone have worth or substance, can be imparted through intercourse with relatively wiser or better men. But this does not satisfy the doubt of Socrates; for he is straining after a virtue whose substance is not relative but absolute, and which could only be taught through the attainment of a perfect science or art of measurement, a power of gauging pleasures, present and future, which he does not find that any man has yet attained. The conversation breaks off without a positive result, but in the course of it Socrates has not only provisionally expounded his 'utilitarian' theory (the greater amount of pleasure being the criterion of action), but has announced his central postulate, 'that virtue is one, and is the subject-matter of an ideal science.'

Socrates in the 'Protagoras' is in the prime of life. In the 'Meno' he is advanced in years, and the shadow of his prosecution is already approaching. Meeting with Meno, the light-minded Thessalian youth, who has been a disciple of Gorgias, he suddenly asks him to define virtue. Meno betrays his ignorance of the nature of Socratic definition by enumerating the several virtues, and on being made conscious of the futility of his attempt, compares Socrates to the torpedo, whose touch benumbs at the first shock. The difficulties of the 'Protagoras,' about the unity and nature of virtue, here recur, but there is a slight change or progress in the point of view. The relative conventional virtue of civic life is not now denied, although Socrates has not yet found his teacher of virtue. It is admitted that a certain measure of goodness is undoubtedly imparted through human intercourse. And this is accounted for by some unconscious inspiration or divine *afflatus*. But the virtue so imparted does not carry with it the power of infixing a principle of conduct that will hold. That can only come through science (the reason of the cause), which in other words is the reminiscence of truths apprehended in a former state of existence. Here Platonism is already growing out of Socratism. Socrates ironically refers Meno to the sophists for further information, whereupon Anytus, who is present, bursts forth with an indignant protest. Socrates darkly hints that, if this anger of Anytus can be appeased, the Athenians will reap a certain benefit; so foreshadowing the fact that Anytus, confusing Socrates with the sophists, was to be one of his accusers.

The reader of the 'Meno' is thus prepared to find Socrates in conflict with the Athenian world; armed for the battle *à outrance* between the principles (so called) of the prevailing doctrine and practice, and his own. The occasion for this is provided by a supposed visit of Gorgias to Athens. The magnificence of the sophist's pose, worthy of the follower of Empedocles, and the grandeur of his condescension, implying a strain of real nobility, are dramatically portrayed. It is Chaerephon, the same who had so impetuously consulted the oracle about the wisdom of Socrates, whose impatient eagerness brings on this debate. When Socrates is condescending on particulars that seem beneath the notice of the reverend sage, Polus, the ardent disciple of Gorgias, interposes for a while. The use of rhetoric, says Polus, that art which Socrates denies to be an art at all, is to increase men's *power* by enabling them to persuade their fellows, and so to effect what they desire. Here Socrates joins issue by maintaining that to effect what one *wishes* is not to effect what one really *wills*; for the wish of the moment may be based on ignorance of true principles of life, and may lead to disaster, which is not according to the will of any man. ' *Vis consili expers mole ruit suâ.*' He thus carries the discussion into a region into which Gorgias and Polus cannot follow him, but Callicles, who has had a smattering of philosophy in his youth, rudely breaks in by asking Chaerephon whether Socrates is not in jest? Chaerephon answers that he is profoundly in earnest. Thus Callicles, the man of the world, with enough of sophistry to state his principle clearly, and Socrates, the prophet of truth and righteousness, are confronted. The noble paradox is now further developed, 'to do wrong is worse and weaker than to suffer wrong'; and 'for the wrongdoer it is better to be punished than to escape from punishment.' This is maintained by arguments which Callicles is unable to refute, and is finally reinforced by a description of the judgment of the dead, where the soul standing naked before her disembodied judge, cannot hide the self-inflicted wounds of her own evildoing.   It is obvious that Plato, having his Master's fate before his eyes, sees revealed therein the sublimity of the truth for which he suffered : that 'because Right is Right, to follow Right were wisdom in the scorn of consequence.'   The subject is resumed in the opening scene of the ' Republic,' which is perhaps the last appearance of the genuine person of Socrates.   We have before us the real man, but idealised and transfigured by the imagination of Plato, and teaching not precisely what he had taught in life, but the doctrine which Plato has evolved from the contemplation of that life and teaching.   This last remark is still more clearly true of those great dialogues in which Plato has embodied the most ambitious of his speculations, the ' Phaedo,' ' Symposium,' and ' Phaedrus.'   Nowhere is the unique personality of Socrates more livingly displayed, and yet the substance or philosophic content is still more remote from the merely Socratic point of view.   The wild playfulness, the humour, the spiritual insight of the two latter dialogues ; the imperturbable calmness of the ' Phaedo,' are the essential attributes of the living Socrates, only heightened through reverential contemplation.   But the doctrine of immortality, in each of the three forms, which are diverse in themselves, as will appear by and by, is essentially different from what Plato himself reports in the ' Apology,' as the belief of Socrates, when condemned to death.   And the ideal theory, here formulated in three different ways, though not unrelated to the Master's lifelong search for truths unrealised, certainly goes beyond anything which Socrates in his lifetime would have asserted.   We are not, for that reason, to reject the evidence of these dialogues as to personal traits : such as that of going barefoot except when called to a feast ; of never leaving Athens, even for a walk in the country, unless led onward by the interest of conversation with a friend ; of standing stock-still for long spaces of time, while he thought out something with himself ; or gently caressing some younger friend, as when he playfully strokes Phaedo's hair and says : ' I suppose to-morrow you will cut off these fine locks in token of mourning for me ' ; of his conduct in the field of Delium, or in the winter quarters before Potidaea ; least of all, perhaps, the beautiful relation between the philosopher and the simple friend of his own standing, honest Crito, who has no tincture of philosophy.   Hardly any of the dialogues have more of pathetic interest than that in which this aged friend, who has provided a way of escape, vainly urges Socrates to take advantage of it.   The ' Crito ' may have been written with a motive, viz. to prove that Socrates, though he took no part in active politics, was a good citizen ; but the im-pression which it· produces of perfect faithfulness to life must surely reflect, in common with the mention of Crito in the ' Phaedo,' an aspect of Socrates not less precious than his speculative energy—his affectionateness towards a true and lifelong companion.   That the substance of the ' Phaedo ' is largely an invention, Plato as good as confesses by stating that he was not present, being prevented by illness from attending Socrates in those last hours.

The Socrates of the ' Theaetetus ' and ' Parmenides,' al-though still a lifelike image, has more of the deliberateness of Platonic art, and less of the spontaneity of an immediate transcript from memory.   The description of Socrates by himself as a man-midwife of the mind, although wrought up with admirable skill, seems rather to embody Plato's conception of Socrates as the greatest of educators than to repeat what Socrates is likely to have said about himself. And when the youthful Socrates, in answer to Parmenides, sets forth his inchoate theory of ideas, that is Plato's way of confessing that his own doctrine of ideas, in its earlier form, as developed from Socratic teaching, was liable to objections which, in the interest of truth, he now saw must be encountered and grappled with.   In the dialogues which follow these (including the ' Philebus ') the person of Socrates is retained, more in form than in reality, as a conventional element of the Platonic dialogue, until in the ' Laws ' he dis-appears altogether, and the leader of the conversation is an Athenian, presumably Plato himself.

z

Amongst the many *dramatis personae* that enliven Plato's writings, standing in various relations to the central figure of Socrates, it is somewhat remarkable that Xenophon nowhere appears. He was a true disciple, although, like Crito, he was incapable of realising the speculative aims and wider philosophic bearing of his master's teaching, still less of adorning them after the manner of Plato. If Plato's representation of his master must not be taken too literally, it would be still more dangerous to regard that of Xenophon as adequate or complete. What we learn from him, so far as Socrates is concerned, is, that besides the intellectual ardour and mystic enthusiasm which prompted his own lifework, there was in Socrates a fund of practical wisdom, of serviceable commonplace morality and good sense, which, in numberless cases, proved of infinite benefit to his friends and disciples. When he compels some youthful aspirant to refrain from public speaking until he has studied more, or when he brings the weapon of ridicule to bear on vicious propensities, or when he reasons with one who makes religious services an excuse for the neglect of plain duties, we catch a glimpse of the man in everyday life and conversation, as we find him little if at all in Plato. Xenophon has been described as the military brother of the Socratic family; and he is interesting, apart from anything which he has learned from Socrates, because he reveals in a fine literary form the religious mind of an ordinary well-educated Athenian and an accomplished soldier. He is strict in all religious observances, and in his retirement at Scillus builds a temple to Artemis, which he surrounds with a sort of park or hunting-ground, perhaps in imitation of what he had seen in Asia. His ideal of virtue, or true manhood, is that of a practised soldier; an essential part of it is to have the body always in serviceable condition, to bear heat and cold and hunger, and keep the muscles hard and dry, and at the same time to have the mind ready, in the Spartan sense, to rule and to be ruled in turn, to observe discipline and to maintain it. But he has also thoughts which pass beyond this world: the wise and good who die are to be held in honour and to be counted blessed, without too nicely determining whether they are conscious of their blessedness or not. The most perfect of Xenophon's writings, apart from the 'Anabasis,' which is mere narrative, is his embodiment in the 'Cyropaedeia' of his ideal of a ruler of men. The last exhortation of Cyrus to his sons and to his friends and comrades illustrates, as well as anything could, the religious feeling of a cultivated Athenian of the fourth century about a good man's death. The genuine piety of such a highborn Athenian is also clearly apparent in the 'Economist' of Xenophon, especially in the delightful picture of the manner in which Ischomachus is supposed to educate his child-wife, and to fit her for the position to which she is called. The constant reference to the gods (not to any particular god), the exhortation to begin every important course of action with prayer, is balanced by a mild appeal to the practical reason, in which the method of Socrates is watered down to suit a childish apprehension. This glimpse of an Attic interior, idealised though it may be, teaches us more about Attic religion than the information that the person thus instructed had danced the bear-dance at ten years old, or had carried the sacred basket in honour of Athena at fourteen.

Three others of the disciples of Socrates require special mention, since each became the founder of a separate school : Euclides of Megara, Aristippus of Cyrene, and Antisthenes the Athenian. Socrates had not taught any positive doctrine ; he rather sought to awaken the minds of his disciples to independent thought. But the minds so awakened were apt to hark back on one or other of the earlier dogmatic systems, which were still in full life, although the Master himself had turned away from them.

Euclides combined the Socratic moral idealism with a modification of the Eleatic logic. His dialectic differed from Plato's in making more formal use of negative argument, the *reductio ad absurdum* ; but he held firmly by the belief inspired by Socrates in the reality of human good, which he identified with conscious thought or wisdom. A late tradition represents him as having given shelter to his brother disciples after their master's death. The school of Euclides degenerated into barren subtleties, but for a time had a distinct influence in the development of the science of logic, especially of that chapter of it which treats of fallacies.

The doctrine of Aristippus had a more lasting effect, appealing as it did to a constant factor in human experience. Plato, in expressly mentioning him as absent from the scene of the 'Phaedo,' would seem to indicate that he had broken off from discipleship before the end, perhaps crediting himself with independent discovery. I have spoken of the utilitarianism sometimes imputed to Socrates, and in the 'Protagoras' he is certainly represented as making the amount of pleasure, if calculated over a whole lifetime, the test of good. That is only a moment in the process of Socratic thought ; but pleasure more simply conceived became the centre of the teaching of Aristippus in the form of Hedonism. Resuming the sceptical theory of Protagoras respecting the relativity of truth and good, and applying it to life, he found in the impression of the moment the sole attainable reality, and in the pleasure of the moment the sum of attainable good. This is the Cyrenaic doctrine, which afterwards, in combination with the atomism of Democritus, formed the substance of the teaching of Epicurus and his followers. The couplet of Horace well expresses the ethical spirit of the school :

Nunc in Aristippi furtim precepta relabor ;
Et mihi res non me rebus subiungere conor.

Antisthenes was a faithful disciple, but wanting in imagination. He had a Thracian mother, and Th. Gomperz argues with some probability that his mental peculiarities were partly due to the fact that he was not of pure Greek blood. He is said to have lost or to have spent a handsome fortune, and to have taken to philosophy in old age when he was disgusted with the world. He was less influenced by Socratic reasoning, which did not convince him, than by the strong and independent personality of Socrates ; and his predilection for Heraclitus amongst the earlier philosophers was less due to the Ephesian's speculative sublimity than to his proud scorn for the generality of mankind. He shared the tendency of some earlier sophists to shake off all social conventions and return to an imagined primitive simplicity of 'nature'—Glaucon's 'city of pigs.' Accordingly he followed Socrates in the simplicity of his mode of life, and made individual self-sufficingness his ethical ideal. Like the Megarians, he seems intellectually to have been influenced by the paradoxes of Zeno, which he carried into sophistical extravagances, destructive of thought and even language. Some of the logical difficulties which he raised have perhaps the merit of having stimulated Plato to important metaphysical determinations. Great doubt still hung over the nature of predication; and until such doubts were removed, all thought was liable to fallacies which hindered its true development. The importance of Antisthenes, however, turns rather on his having founded the Cynic school, whose doctrine, again in combination with another great philosophy, that of Heraclitus, formed the chief factor in the ethical teaching of the Stoics. Individualism was his strong point, and the tendency to excessive distinctions between logical terms was his intellectual weakness. Diogenes exaggerated the individualist tendency, while Crates accentuated the logical, which his pupil Zeno of the Porch combined with the Megarian tradition.

Thus it appears that all the ethical theories which prevailed amongst the ancient world had their root in Socrates, whose teaching they more or less perverted or only partially understood. The Stoic, the Epicurean, the Academic, the Peripatetic, and the Neoplatonist all derived from this abundant source their separate and narrower streams.

CHAPTER XV

PLATO AND PLATONISM

IT was through Plato that the spirit and wisdom of Socrates came forth to Hellas and to the world. The minor currents of Cynicism, Cyrenaicism, Megarianism and the cultured religiosity of Xenophon, though all had important consequences, are comparatively of little account. Platonism is the main stream deriving from the Socratic fountain, but the channel has given shape and colour to the moving waters. In the Platonic philosophy, the whole spirit of the master's life and teaching is embodied, but there is something more. When Plato first attached himself to Socrates as a younger companion and disciple, he was already accomplished in all bodily and mental graces which the highest circle of Athenian society could bestow. He was a poet of no mean aspirations, though when he came under the influence of Socrates he destroyed his verses so effectually that only a single couplet can with any probability be assigned to him :

ἀστέρας εἰσαθρεῖς, ἀστὴρ ἐμός· εἴθε γενοίμην
οὐρανός, ὡς πολλοῖς ὄμμασιν εἰς σὲ βλέπω.

'Thou gazest at the stars, my star ; would I were Heaven,
With countless eyes to give thee back that gaze ! '

He had also a considerable tincture of the earlier philosophy, and as we are told by Aristotle, a sound authority, had studied under Cratylus, the contemporary Heraclitean. But in the talk of Socrates he found a depth of wise suggestiveness which eclipsed for him all other culture, speculation, dogma. And when that strange and fascinating life came to its tragic end, the poet-scholar could not rest in the suspense which had been so often the last word of the Socratic teaching; the aim and scope of that teaching, negative as it had seemed, was revealed to him as having a positive substance of which other doctrines were but the shadows. These discourses alone had mind within them, they lived and breathed, and were instinct with a life-giving power. Socrates had not died for a negation, but for an ideal of justice, which Athenian wits had pared away to nothing; a standard of goodness to which the world was still a stranger; an absolute truth which, if discovered, would afford the only sure basis for human life and conduct. To develop these conceptions, to give them literary form, to recommend them to the select spirits of his own generation, and if possible to posterity, was thenceforward to be his lifework. In this he was not unmindful that Socrates had been throughout impelled by a profoundly religious aim; that he believed himself to be acting in obedience to a divine call; and that the ideas of justice, goodness, truth, by which he measured contemporary standards and found them wanting, were inseparable from a right conception of the nature of God.

1. There had grown up in the Athenian mind, as we see from Thucydides, a radical opposition between justice and expediency. Ordinary men were in the habit of praising justice, while they did what they found expedient. But here and there, one bolder than the rest would discard justice altogether, as a word only 'devised at first to keep the strong in awe.' Such a person is the Callicles of the 'Gorgias.' Plato sees that in their highest realisation the just and the truly expedient are at one, that it can be for no man's genuine interest to do wrong, and so to lose that integrity which is beyond all price. But he sees also that the narrow conceptions of justice which have hitherto obtained must be revised, if human society is to continue or to be improved; that man cannot live by sentiment alone, but human life, both individual and social, must have a ground of reason. Hence, not content with exhibiting Socrates against the world in the person of Callicles, as alone determined 'to live by law, acting the law he lives by without fear,' he further represents him as engaged in a search for ideal

justice, in conversation with Plato's younger brothers Adimantus and Glaucon. This is the theme of the 'Republic,' in which Plato has also inwrought many of his own highest thoughts on cognate subjects.

2. There is another aspect of life, rather individual than social, in which the questions that occur have less to do with conduct in relation to other men than with the art of living. The secret of this art, according to Plato, is a reasoned enthusiasm, such as Socrates inspired in his best disciples, and of which they realised the depth and permanence only after his death. This mystic impulse is symbolised as Ἔρως, Love. The passion so described is not, however, mere personal attachment, though that may sometimes kindle it ; but the love of that ideal which, to the mind so inspired, is alone the real,—an absolute universal goodness, a beauty of holiness, which becomes the standard to which all actions, lives, thoughts, doctrines, are referred. This is the leading conception of the two great dialogues, the 'Symposium' and 'Phaedrus,' in which Socrates treats of philosophic love under a form which is often misunderstood—and not unnaturally, since he starts from a phase of manners, belonging to that time and race, to which nothing in modern life bears strict analogy. But the meaning is independent of the starting-point, and it is this : that the only life which is worth living is one in which the contemplation of truth and goodness in their highest realisations is prized beyond all other objects, and has a practical effect in subordinating all other motives to the endeavour to attain moral and spiritual perfection.

3. It is evident that a mind so inspired cannot rest short of the highest intellectual satisfaction which is attainable for man ; for that ideal which is alone the real is not the object of a mere vague yearning, like an earthly love, but of the most strenuous mental effort, in accordance with the laws of reason. The conversations of Socrates had aimed at defining, with a precision that should be invulnerable by counter-argument, those moral truths which all men everywhere acknowledge, but of which, when questioned, they are found to have such hazy and confused notions. Plato's way of representing this is to say that Socrates was in search of the

form, εἶδος or ἰδέα, of temperance, of courage, of justice, of the state, &c. This perfect form, which was only to be grasped by reasoning, he opposed to the changing impressions or first-thoughts which the dialectic of Socrates was engaged in setting aside,—so approaching ever nearer to the certainty of truth. Thus philosophic truth became for Plato a constellation, as it were, of abstract forms or ideas, which alone had reality, and could be reached only by discarding, through a process of reasoning, the fleeting appearances or impressions which were their shadows. This was the first crude sketch or outline of the doctrine of ideas ; but to take this as a distinct and separate dogma, and call it Platonism, would be untrue to Plato. He had been, as we have seen, a pupil in the Heraclitean school ; and in the method of Socrates, dislodging men's apparently fixed opinions, and making them move away, as Euthyphro puts it, like the tripods of Daedalus, of themselves, he saw a living illustration of the Heraclitean doctrine of flux and perpetual change. But beneath this he saw also the permanence of the ideal, a fixity not like that of the Eleatic ' Being,' that stood out of relation to human things, but an unchangeable reality which imparted to human life, as nothing else could do, a true element of stability. All round him were raging the contentions of philosophic disputants, overthrowing one another in argument, and caring little for truth or human good in comparison with a polemical victory. How was the ground which Socrates had gained, and which Plato had enclosed with his ideal theory, to be secured against polemical attacks ? How was he himself to hold it, or his disciples to cultivate it, in the face of all this controversy ? What had been intellectually gained could only be held intellectually, and the Socratic teacher, above all, could not maintain positions that lay open to disproof. Hence Plato was brought face to face with the great intellectual difficulty of his time, the fruit of a philosophy in which a grand anticipation of truth had degenerated into a tyrannous form of thought. Euclides and the Megarians, and in a different way Antisthenes and the Cynics, had fallen under the dominion of the Zenonian logic. Plato, in his first enthusiasm, had carried his theory of abstract indefeasible ideas beyond the ethical region, which had been the province of Socrates, into all other subjects of human inquiry ; but he was arrested by the logical difficulty how to conceive the relation between the idea and the phenomenon, the real and the apparent—or, what comes to the same thing in Platonic theory, the universal and the particular—which Eleatic reasoning tended to regard as incommunicable. This difficulty is developed with consummate skill in the 'Parmenides'; and in the 'Theaetetus' the cognate difficulty of the relation of knowledge to sensation and opinion is similarly evolved. In a series of dialogues probably composed a good while after these, a determined attempt is made to solve this problem of the age, by disposing of the prime fallacy of reasoning through contraries, in which it is assumed that things different are mutually exclusive. This fallacy had been carried to its extreme by those who denied predication because the subject was not identical with the predicate, and it is the same illusion which, under infinitely varying disguises, has haunted controversialists and polemical disputants of every subsequent age. The dialogues in which this phase of Plato's philosophy is embodied and expressed are the ' Sophist,' ' Politicus,' and ' Philebus.' These represent a long period of intellectual conflict, at the end of which the conviction remains, as firmly as at the first, that goodness and truth are in their highest forms inseparable and can be made the objects, in part at least, of scientific determination. But the ground for rational discussion has been cleared by the discovery that, as Renan saw, ' the truth of a thing does not necessarily establish the falsehood of its apparent opposite ' ; or as John Selden put it : ' When a doubt is propounded, you must learn to distinguish and know wherein a thing holds and wherein it doth not hold. " Ay or no " never answered any question. The not distinguishing where things should be distinguished, and the not confounding where things should be confounded, is the cause of all the mistakes in the world.'

What concerns us more (as students of Greek religion) is to observe that in these later dialogues Plato's ethical conviction assumes more and more the nature of a religious confidence. According to this, mind and the object of mind are the supreme realities, the measure of all else in the universe, at once the end and the cause of all that is, or comes to be.

4. Plato nowhere sets himself directly in opposition to the religion of his countrymen in such a way as to provoke an accusation of atheism or impiety. Like Socrates he conformed to the traditional worship, but he is all the while absorbed in theological speculations, which really stand apart from tradition, but which he probably felt to comprehend it, as the less is comprehended in the greater. His quarrel is not with the religious teachers, whether Apolline, Eleusinian, or Orphic, whose symbolism he sometimes adopted, seeking to infuse into it a higher spirit, but rather with the poets and the mythologists, and their anthropomorphic and immoral representations of things divine. His Socrates confesses in the 'Euthyphro' that he had been accused of impiety because he could not accept current fables which implied immorality amongst the gods ; and it is on this ground that Plato in the ' Republic ' does violence to the cherished feeling of his adolescence by excluding Homer from his ideal state. God must be represented, even in fiction, as He is : that is to say, as perfectly good and true. God cannot be the author of evil : if He afflicts mankind, it is because they need such chastisement to purify them from their own unrighteousness ; nor can God be ever tainted with falsehood or deceit, nor is He liable to change, for He is absolutely perfect and all-powerful, and no being that could avoid it would alter from a state of perfection. Such views of the divine nature are far in advance of any earlier theology; indeed, it may be questioned if much of what has been called theology in later times might not bear to be revised by Plato's rules.

In no respect is the height of Plato's moral idealism more striking than in the contrast which it presents to the common Greek tradition, which even Herodotus maintained, concerning the divine *envy*. ' Envy stands apart from the concourse of the gods,' it is said in the ' Phaedrus ' ; and the God of the ' Timaeus ' in creating the world, because He is exempt from envy, is determined that His work shall be very good. The idea of Good is, in fact, hardly separable in Plato's mind from God Himself. The reason of the best is all but identical with the great First Cause. In Plato's religious philosophy, as perhaps in all natural theology, there is a lingering doubt as to what in modern language may be called the personality of God. Of the reality, beneficence and wisdom of the Supreme Being, there is no doubt at all ; and how these attributes should exist without personality is inconceivable : (' Soph.' 249 A)   ' Can we ever be made to believe that movement and life and soul and mind are not present with Absolute Being ?   Can we imagine Being to be devoid of life and mind, and to remain in awful unmeaningness an everlasting fixture ? '   Yet on the other hand, even where the language is so full of personal emotion as to incur the suspicion of anthropomorphism, we are conscious of a certain impersonality and remoteness in the mode of thought.   At the same time it is made abundantly clear that the way for man to rise above himself is by imitation of the divine.   ' God is in no way by any means unrighteous, but as righteous as can possibly be ; and nothing more resembles Him than whosoever of mankind becomes as righteous as he can ; in that consists man's real ability, and in the want of that his nothingness and inability.'   From these speculative heights, in which moral aspiration and spiritual emotion are blended with the most intense and indefatigable efforts of the mind, Plato surveys ' all time, and all existence '—that is to say, all human experience, so far as realised hitherto by the Hellenic race.   He does not go to work with a ready-made system, into which particular facts are forced ; but he brings to the test of his highest conceptions whatever the Greek mind had felt, imagined, or conceived.   He does not stand aloof from traditions, which he regards as good servants although bad masters ; nothing is left unexamined or uncriticised, and yet all are in some way woven in,—the old mythology, where it admits of being moralised ; the Orphic mysticism, except where it ministers to immoral delusions ; the old philosophies, as witnesses to high truths which they had partially disclosed.

Plato is quite aware that, as Professor Jowett has expressed it, ' the religious truth of one age may become the religious poetry of another.'

Pythagoreanism is an important element, not in Plato's thought so much as in assisting him to body it forth. The ideas of measure and symmetry, of harmony and rhythm, of limitation and the infinite, afford a meeting-point for that antinomy of the one and many, of similarity and diversity, of the fluxile and the stable, which, while remaining in sheer abstraction, seemed so hard to grasp. More especially he sought the aid of Pythagoreanism in dealing with those astronomical and cosmological theories which had fascinated him, although he still so far agreed with Socrates as to regard them as only capable of probable conjecture. Morality in Plato is the subject of exact science ; physics only of doubtful speculation—the contrary of our modern point of view.

It is possible that he may have borrowed some of his imagery from Zoroastrianism, as for example the subterranean pilgrimage of Er, the son of Armenius, who, according to Clement of Alexandria, is Zoroaster himself. But this must remain in doubt until M. Darmesteter's view (rejected by Tiele) that Zoroastrianism, as we know it, has received a tinge of Platonism, is either confirmed or set aside. The substance of Plato's thought is independent of all such modes of expression, and to revert once more to his ethical doctrine, it is far more important than the resolution of any such questionable details, to observe how he differs from his own countrymen of old time (who made it a point of honour to revenge an injury) in maintaining that a good man cannot harm any human being, no, not even an enemy. This paradox Socrates maintains against Thrasymachus, and in the conversation with his old friend Crito, he refers to the same principle as having been long since agreed upon between them. The good man therefore only needs to be understood to be accepted of mankind. But he is misunderstood, and therefore rejected, tormented, crucified. Yet he wins the race at last, when the unrighteous who made a splendid start comes lagging in with shoulders up to his ears, breathless and faint.

The wars of Greeks with Greeks appear to Plato unnatural, and to hang up in the temples of the gods (as had been done at Delphi) the trophies of such internecine strife, he accounts nothing short of impious. On the subject of marriage and of sexual relations Plato's philosophy was only gradually matured. In the ' Symposium ' the picture of Socrates as absolutely exempt from the weaknesses of his countrymen in this respect is somewhat marred by the tolerance apparently extended to the errors of the average Greek. In the ' Republic,' the famous institution of communism is intended, not to encourage licence, but to minimise the indulgence of sexual desire. In the ' Laws,' his latest writing, while professing still to hold the theory of the ' Republic ' as a pious opinion, he lays down for the citizens of the imaginary Cretan colony a series of precepts upon this subject which fully satisfy the requirements of a pure morality. As before remarked, he regains in theory the freedom from the special failing of the Greeks in this respect which is hardly to be found elsewhere except in Homer.

For once in the history of Greek thought religion, philosophy, and ethics are interfused. They all meet together in the Platonic doctrine of the Immortality of the Soul. The distinction of soul and body is sometimes regarded as a comparatively late development of human thought ; but in one sense the separate existence of the soul is the most primitive of religious conceptions, and is implied in the earliest forms of sepulture. It had faded indeed into something very thin and shadowy for the age of Homer, but retained its vitality in central Greece, and had gained in warmth and intensity long before the time of Pindar and of Aeschylus. The Orphic teaching and the Eleusinian mysteries had given a more distinct shape to yearnings never long absent from humanity, when becoming conscious of itself. What is peculiar to Plato is not the assertion of a life of the soul after death, but rather the identification of soul with mind. This places the idea of immortality on a new footing. For on the condition of the soul in its relation to truth and righteousness depends her state of blessedness now and hereafter. Hence Plato, while often treading, as his commentators affirm, in the footsteps of Orphic mysticism, regards with unmitigated abhorrence those ceremonial rites by which it was pretended that the soul could be purged from sin and satisfy offended gods. Such doctrines of redemption are to him abominable, for they imply an utterly unworthy notion of the moral nature of God.

In the ' Republic ' he describes with bitterness, successfully veiled with ironical scorn, what may be termed the purchase of indulgences, by which rich sinners hope to escape from punishment in Hades. And in the 'Laws' there are three classes of heretics whom he proposes to visit with the utmost rigour : (1) the atheist, whose offence is the least ; (2) the believer in gods who are indifferent to human things ; and (3) worst of all, the believer in gods who can be bribed by prayers and incense to the remission of sins. That is his way of expressing the truth that the only assurance of salvation for the human spirit lies in ceasing to do evil and learning to do well. Yet perhaps these utterances may also serve to indicate wherein the highest philosophy may fall short, when seeking to provide a religion for humanity. The Eleusinian mystic, the Orphic preacher, and even the juggling priest of Sabazius had an inkling of human needs and requirements, which the intellectual scorn of Plato overlooked : disorders which they contented themselves with healing slightly, in their ignorance of a more prevailing remedy. And it is certain that in emphasising the sacredness of domestic life, Greek tragedy had given currency to an aspect of religious truth which Plato when he composed his ' Republic ' failed to estimate aright.

The great thought of immortality, like other great thoughts in Plato, is variously expressed. The reasonings of the ' Phaedo,' in which Socrates holds converse with the pupils of Philolaus, the disciple of Pythagoras, have naturally some tinge of Pythagoreanism, but were doubtless felt at the time by Plato himself to be entirely convincing. The substance of them is that since truth is eternal, and truth only exists as apprehended by the mind, the mind must also be eternal. Modern critics, perceiving that the inference is not distinctly drawn from the universal to the individual mind, assume that Plato has only thrown into a mythical form his doctrine of the eternity of knowledge. His argument as judged by logical standards may be defective, but no one who reads the dialogue with simplicity and without metaphysical prepossessions can fail to see that when he wrote it Plato was profoundly convinced of the continuance of life for the individual after death. Especially convincing in this regard is Socrates' remark on Crito's question, ' How shall we bury you?' and the same view is emphatically repeated in support of the rules about sepulture which are given towards the end of the ' Laws.'

In the ' Phaedrus ' we have a partly mythical exposition of the nature of mind or soul. It begins as follows :—

' The soul is immortal, for that is immortal which is ever in motion ; but that which moves another and is moved by another in ceasing to move ceases also to live. Therefore only that which is self-moving, never leaving self, never ceases to move, and is the fountain and beginning of motion to all that moves besides. Now the beginning is unbegotten, for that which is begotten has a beginning ; but the beginning itself has no beginning, for if a beginning were begotten of something, that something would not be a beginning. But that which is unbegotten must also be indestructible ; for if beginning were destroyed, there could be no beginning out of anything, nor anything out of a beginning ; and all things must have a beginning. And therefore the self-moving is the beginning of motion ; and this can neither be destroyed nor begotten, else the whole heavens and all creation would collapse and stand still, and never again have motion or birth. But if the self-moving is immortal, he who affirms that self-motion is the very idea and essence of the soul will not be put to confusion. For the body which is moved from without is soulless, but that which is moved from within has a soul, for such is the nature of the soul. But if the soul be truly affirmed to be self-moving, then must she also be without beginning, and immortal. Enough of the soul's immortality. Her form is a theme of divine and large discourse ; the tongue of man may, however, speak of this briefly and in a figure. Let our figure be a composite nature—a pair of winged horses and a charioteer. Now the winged horses and the charioteer of the gods are all of them noble and of noble breed, but our horses are mixed; moreover our charioteer drives them in a pair, and one of them is noble and of noble origin, and the other is ignoble and of ignoble origin; and the driving, as might be expected, is no easy matter with us.'

In this great passage the soul is mythically regarded as composite, having higher and lower elements, over which pure reason ought to preside. This notion of the composite nature of the human soul appears at variance with the argument in the ' Phaedo,' according to which the soul is one and indiscerptible. In the ' Republic ' reason, anger, and desire are again assumed as distinct elements or aspects of the soul for the purposes of the dialogue; but in Book x. it is said that if we could see her as she really is, the soul might appear to have no parts at all, but to be one and indivisible. In the ' Timaeus,' which represents a later phase of speculation, anger and desire are not allowed to share in immortality but are inseparable from their seats in the bodily frame.

There is yet another aspect of immortality, hardly reconcilable with the preceding, and belonging to another mood, in which the divinity that shapes our ends is regarded, not as a stranger to the world of sense, but as permeating and commanding it, immanent rather than transcendent. This is suggested by the contemplation of the ideal Socrates, not as in the immediate prospect of death, but in fulness of life, amongst his friends and comrades, entering heartily into their enjoyments and rejoicing in their success. Here man is represented as partaking of immortality in so far as he partakes of higher life at all. In love, in action, in the productions of poetry and art, and in the contemplation of ideal truth, not only do his works live after him, but during his brief life on earth he lives in the light of eternity.

The ' Symposium,' that strain of glorious music, was probably the outcome of Plato's heyday of success, as a leader of Athenian thought, in the early days of the Academy. But in looking rather on this world than another, it bears some analogy to Plato's latest writing, the twelve books of the

A A

'Laws.' This is not the most attractive outwardly, but in some ways the deepest and, taken in connection with the time of writing it, the most pathetic of his works. I know nothing in this way to be compared with it, except Shakespeare's 'Tempest,' and the last scene of the second part of Goethe's 'Faust'; perhaps I might add the 'Oedipus Coloneus' of Sophocles. Only in none of these is the fading light of the parting luminary transfused with the same wistful glance at mankind whom he has yearned to save. At the end of the ninth book of the 'Republic' Plato had comforted himself with the reflection that if unrealised in any community his ideal might still awaken aspirations in individual minds. In his extreme old age, having lost nothing of his belief in the reality of ideal truth, or in the eternity of mind, and some good thing in reserve for the philosopher after death, himself on the verge of that other state, finding that his pattern Republic was not to be realised in his lifetime, he turns aside from his own fondly cherished ideal, and casts a last lingering glance on the Hellenic world, in which Athens, by her own fault, was no longer the chief factor. He sees that there is only one hope for the communities of a single race, loosely held together : namely, that each of them should be governed honestly and sincerely in accordance with laws framed after Greek models but purged from errors which experience no less than philosophy condemned.

Plato's most persistent aspiration was to reform mankind, both communities and individuals; and while perhaps his greatest effort had been to clear the sources of knowledge, and so to make intellectual progress possible, this intense endeavour was throughout associated with a practical aim. In the 'Gorgias' an absolute principle of moral rectitude was asserted, while current modes of ethical and political thought were utterly renounced. In the 'Symposium' a parallel but not identical doctrine was conveyed through the idealised image of Socrates, as reflected in the confessions of Alcibiades— an image of purity and spiritual elevation, that is in the world though not of it, and has the power of leavening the world. The 'Phaedo' breathes a still loftier tone, in which the ideal is that of a mild asceticism and withdrawal from the world, and from the experience of sense. In the 'Republic,' without lowering the ideal standard, a certain balance between the higher and lower views is obtained. While the state as a whole is to be possessed of all the virtues, and the rulers are to rise to the summit both of contemplation and of action, the remaining guardians and the industrious populace are to partake, through willing obedience, of a wisdom beyond their own. Even the nature-philosophy of the 'Timaeus' was only the prelude of a more comprehensive strain that should have hymned the triumph of the perfect human commonwealth in actual achievement. But some cloud had risen to obscure the vision of a reformed humanity which in the 'Republic' had appeared so bright. The reception of that great dialogue, and possibly the failure of some attempt to realise it in Sicily or elsewhere, the continued decline of political life at Athens, and other causes, of which we know nothing, must have intervened to account for the profound strain of disillusionment and misprision of mankind, which we meet with for the first time in the 'Politicus.' Another change of a different order goes along with this. From a patriotic Athenian (the author of the 'Crito') Plato is becoming cosmopolitan. Such hope for mankind as he still retains does not centre in Athens but ranges about the Hellenic world. Even the distinction between Hellene and Barbarian is fading away, and is attributed to the partiality of local pride. Linguistic indications, such as the admission of Ionic vocables and the like, confirm our impressions of this tendency.

In the 'Laws' we have the philosopher's final attitude towards Hellenic religion. There is no trace of irony in the passages, and there are many of them, in which he prescribes conformity to traditional worships. The great rule, that the beneficial is the holy, is carefully observed ; but Plato's selection of the deities who are to preside over various public functions, while in each choice we find a Platonic motive, is in true accordance with Hellenic feeling. The introduction of Dionysus in the earlier books, in order to counteract a bare asceticism, is perhaps not to be taken too seriously.

But the consultation of the Delphic oracle on matters not determined by the law, the punishment of sacrilege, the special honours given to Hestia, to Pluto and Eileithyia, the dedication of the artisan class to Hephaestus and Athena, the description of Nemesis as the messenger of Justice, the distribution and ordering of festival days, the consecration of the lot as the judgment of Zeus, the institution of priest-hoods, the solemn appointment of the law-guardians in the temple of Apollo and the Sun, who are closely identified, the similar consecration of the appeal tribunals (945 E)—these and the like provisions are seriously intended to maintain genuine religious sentiment in connection with a strict obser-vance of the laws. The inculcation of a spirit of reverence pervades the whole work.

On the other hand, Plato is as firmly convinced as ever of the necessity of purifying mythology and diffusing worthy conceptions of the divine nature.

The gods of the national worship (οἱ κατὰ νόμον ὄντες θεοί, 904 A), above all Zeus, Apollo, and Athena, are still to be revered ; but a higher and more substantial divinity is attri-buted to the heavenly bodies, or rather to the souls that animate them and regulate their motions—it is blasphemy to speak of any of them as ' wandering stars '—and higher yet is the silent worship given to the supreme invisible mind that moves and guides the world (ὁ βασιλεύς). In this con-ception Plato rises out of the pantheism which had already permeated and transformed polytheism, but in legislating for the men of his time this higher thought appears to him rather as the harmonising medium which is to dominate and reform the old traditions, than as a mere abstract or trans-cendent notion which is to annihilate them.

I will conclude this chapter by quoting some of the more striking passages illustrative of the ' Spirit of the Laws ' according to Plato.

1. The lawgiver's prelude to his citizens :—' Friends,' we say to them, ' God, as the old tradition declares, holding in His hand the beginning, middle, and end of all that is, moves according to His nature in a straight line towards the accomplishment of His end. Justice always follows Him,

and is the punisher of those who fall short of the divine law. To that law, he who would be happy holds fast and follows it in all humility and order; but he who is lifted up with pride, or money, or honour, or beauty, who has a soul hot with folly, and youth, and insolence, and thinks that he has no need of a guide or ruler, but is able himself to be the guide of others, he, I say, is left deserted of God; and being thus deserted, he takes to him others who are like himself, and dances about, throwing all things into confusion; and many think that he is a great man, but in a short time he pays a penalty which justice cannot but approve, and is utterly destroyed, and his family and city with him. Wherefore, seeing that human things are thus ordered, what should a wise man do or think?'

2. The soul is to be honoured next to God:—'When anyone prefers beauty to virtue, what is this but the real and utter dishonour of the soul? For such a preference implies that the body is more honourable than the soul; and this is false, for there is nothing of earthly birth which is more honourable than the heavenly, and he who thinks otherwise of the soul has no idea how greatly he undervalues this wonderful possession; nor, again, when a person is willing to acquire dishonest gains, does he then honour his soul with gifts: far otherwise; he sells her glory and honour for a small piece of gold; but all the gold which is under or upon the earth is not enough to give in exchange for virtue. In a word, I may say that he who does not estimate the base and evil, the good and noble, according to the standard of the legislator . . . does not know that he is most foully and disgracefully abusing his soul, which is the divinest part of man.'

3. The Athenian stranger is apostrophising the imaginary atheist:—'O my son,' we say to him, 'you are young, and the advance of time will make you reverse many of the opinions which you now hold. Wait, therefore, until the time comes, and do not attempt to judge of high matters at present; and that is the highest of which you think nothing —to know the gods rightly and to live accordingly. And in the first place let me indicate to you one point which is of

great importance, and of the truth of which I am quite certain:—you and your friends are not the first who have held this opinion about the gods. There have always been persons more or less numerous who have had the same disorder. I have known many of them, and can tell you that no one who had taken up in youth this opinion, that the gods do not exist, ever continued in the same until he was old; the two other notions certainly do continue in some cases, but not in many: the notion I mean, that the gods exist, but take no heed of human things; and also the notion that they do take heed of them, but are easily propitiated with sacrifices and prayers.'

4. The next passage is addressed to disbelievers in divine providence:—Let us say to the youth, 'The ruler of the universe has ordered all things with a view to the preservation and perfection of the whole, and each part has an appointed state of action and passion; and the smallest action or passion of any part affecting the minutest fraction has a presiding minister. And one of these portions of the universe is thine own, stubborn man, which, however little, has the whole in view; and you do not seem to be aware that this and every other creation is for the sake of the whole, and in order that the life of the whole may be blessed; and that you are created for the sake of the whole, and not the whole for the sake of you. For every physician and every skilled artist does all things for the sake of the whole, directing his effort towards the common good, executing the part for the sake of the whole, and not the whole for the sake of the part. And you are annoyed because you do not see how that which is best for you is, as far as the laws of creation admit, best also for the universe. . . . Whenever the soul receives more of good or evil from her own energy and the strong influence of others—when she has communion with divine virtue and becomes divine, she is carried into another and better place, which is also divine and perfect in holiness; and when she has communion with evil, then she also changes the place of her life.

" For that is the justice of the gods who inhabit heaven."
O youth or young man, who fancy that you are neglected by

the gods, know that if you become worse you shall go to the worse souls, or if better to the better, and in every succession of life and death you will do and suffer what like may fitly suffer at the hands of like. This is a divine justice, which neither you nor any other unfortunate will ever glory in escaping, and which the ordaining powers have specially ordained ; take good heed of them, for a day will come when they will take heed of you. If you say :—I am small and will creep into the depths of the earth, or I am high and will fly up to heaven, you are not so small or so high but that you shall pay the fitting penalty either in the world below or in some more savage place still, whither you shall be conveyed. This is also the explanation of the fate of those whom you saw, who had done unholy and evil deeds, and from small beginnings had become great, and you fancied that from being miserable they had become happy ; and in their actions, as in a mirror, you seemed to see the universal neglect of the gods, not knowing how they make all things work together and contribute to the great whole.'

5. Lastly the following are Plato's reasons for moderation in funerals :

' We must believe the legislator when he tells us that the soul is in all respects superior to the body, and that even in life what makes each one of us to be what we are is only the soul ; and that the body follows us about in the likeness of each of us, and therefore, when we are dead, the bodies of the dead are rightly said to be our shades or images ; for that the true and immortal being of each one of us which is called the soul goes on her way to other gods, that before them she may give an account—an inspiring hope to the good, but very terrible to the bad, as the laws of our fathers tell us, which also say that not much can be done in the way of helping a man after he is dead. But the living—he should be helped by all his kindred, that while in life he may be the holiest and justest of men, and after death may have no great sins to be punished in the world below. If this be true, a man ought not to waste his substance under the idea that all this lifeless mass of flesh which is in process of burial is connected with him ; he should consider that the son, or brother,

or the beloved one, whoever he may be, whom he thinks he is
laying in the earth, has gone away to complete and fulfil his
own destiny, and that his duty is rightly to order the present
and to spend moderately on the lifeless altar of the gods
below.' [1]

[1] ' The wheel has come full circle ' from the Homeric notion that the slain
heroes were themselves a prey to dogs and birds.

CHAPTER XVI

RELIGION IN ARISTOTLE—SUBSEQUENT DEVELOPMENTS
CONCLUSION

RELIGION in Greek literature finds its culminating point in Plato : he absorbs the previous elements of religious feeling and reflection, recasts them, and forecasts the future. In what came after him of Hellenic culture there is nothing higher, if so high. But before leaving the subject of the present volume it is desirable to note very briefly the most important changes which within the limits of the Hellenic world preceded the great change brought in by Christianity.

Much that in Plato's mind remained in fusion became crystallised in Aristotle. But besides this external difference, and underlying it, there is an essential difference of spirit between the two philosophers. The reigning motive in Plato was the moral ideal. His cherished object is the reformation of human society and the education of the individual man, following out his interpretation of the meaning of Socrates. Metaphysical speculation and the dialectic on which he laid such stress were, if not subordinated to, at least inseparable from, this essentially human aim. Aristotle in earlier years had drunk deeply of the spirit of Plato, but as his own philosophy took shape, the science of ethics became for him a branch of the study of man as a social being, and the study of man altogether came to be a branch of universal knowledge. Knowledge as such, for its own sake, as contemplated by pure reason, is, for Aristotle, the consummation of all intellectual endeavour. The forms of nature—and of these human life is one—have each an end, at which they aim unconsciously or consciously ; their own complete and perfect realisation in subordination to one great final cause, ' towards

which the whole creation moves.' Philosophy is the contemplation of these ends, and of the means which lead to
them. Man is not 'the roof and crown of things,' but an
item in the universe; it may be, not the most important
item. Thus a sharp line of distinction is introduced between
intellectual and moral virtue, the latter being subordinate
and relative. This view is quite alien from the whole tendency
of Plato, whose one excursion into the region of cosmogony
was intended to be the porch and vestibule of a great structure of ideal human history, the prelude to a magnificent
prose poem on human destinies—celebrating the triumph
of good over evil, and of moral over material forces : good
absolute, and good for man are with him inseparable. The
chief attribute of the God of Aristotle is not justice in the
human sense, but the energy of pure contemplation, thought
in excelsis—Knowledge not in possession merely, but in
constant exercise.

Aristotle also was ready to guide mankind into the right
way, to shape desire into accordance with practical wisdom,
and to bring both into the light of philosophic contemplation. He carried further than Plato had done the psychological analysis of ethical conditions. But the speculative
philosopher, contemplating human life and all else that
he could bring within his intellectual ken, was in Aristotle's conception nearer to God than the just ruler or
the wise teacher of mankind. In the decay of Hellenic
nationalities, politics were becoming an abstract science, of
which ethics only formed a part. Science, in fact, tended to
be all in all, and Aristotle, 'the chief of those that know,'
stood at the head of an age in which the prosecution of
particular sciences or departments of human knowledge
became the absorbing occupation of the best minds. This
gives to his productions an air of coldness, but at the same
time one of calm impersonality, which renders them, if not
so attractive at first sight, extraordinarily impressive on a
more persistent study. Though he is often only stamping
Plato's ideas with logic, yet the precision of statement, the
crisp categorical tone, the very bareness of the literary style,
give to his writings an incisiveness which to many minds is

more satisfactory than the *chiaroscuro* of Plato ; although we are always haunted by the suspicion that what we know of Aristotle is really some disciple's version of him.

Aristotle's idealism is that of abstract thought, but a thought which is ever seeking, through logical determinations, to clasp with more and more of closeness the concrete actuality of things. He had at one time studied medicine in the school of the Asclepiadae, and he combines the Hippocratean method of observation with his own special form of speculative idealism. It is strange to find him at so advanced a period of thought still clinging to the notion that the Supreme Being has the form and motion of a rotatory sphere. Like the early philosophers, and like Plato himself in his mythological mood, or like the Hebrew prophet who saw God sitting on the circle of the earth (while the inhabitants thereof were as grasshoppers), he cannot wholly get away from sensuous symbolism. His real conception is that of pure reason at its highest realisation of energy : thought evolving thought from itself, and consciously reflecting on the thought so evolved. It is thought, however, engaged in contemplating reality, and reality for Aristotle is composed of substances, in which form and matter are combined. In this metaphysical effort to unite the individual with the universal, he anticipated some modern philosophers, but it can hardly be said that such an endeavour, although fruitful as a logical method, has in either case been crowned with absolute success. In his doctrine of the soul there is a similar contradiction or obscurity, leaving it doubtful whether he to any extent agreed with Plato in believing in the continuance of the individual after death. In the early dialogues, of which the fragments have been restored by Bernays, he appears to have done so. In the ' De Anima,' however, the human soul has indeed an immortal ever-active element, that mingles with the vital principle and controls it, but at death this portion of the divine, the active reason, is absorbed again into the divinity from which it came. That seems to imply a breach of continuity, although Plato in the ' Timaeus,' in speaking of the lower parts of the soul as mortal, had failed to draw this inference. The passage of the

' Nicomachean Ethics,' in which Aristotle leaves it doubtful whether dead ancestors are affected by the calamities of their race, refers not to Plato, but to traditional beliefs, such as we find in Pindar, Aeschylus, and Sophocles.

Religion is not the word that first occurs to one in thinking of Aristotle. Yet in steadily regarding him, one is aware of an elevation and a colossal greatness which is not dissociated from religion in the truest sense. The very keystone of his philosophy consists in a conception of the divine life, and of the divine nature, which is really sublime. The description of the philosophic life in the tenth book of the ' Ethics,' if more calm, is hardly less impressive than the speech of Diotima in the ' Symposium '; and the account of God in the ' Metaphysics,' Book xii., is in a similar strain :—

' There must be some eternal substance that is exempt from change. For substance is the primary existence, and if all substance were perishable the world would perish. But motion can have no beginning and no end—it is from everlasting,—nor can time; and the only motion that is continuous is that from place to place, and especially the revolution of a sphere. And this prime motion must be ever in act, and not potential merely ; so that it is useless to suppose eternal essences, such as the [Platonic] *ideas*, unless there is admitted some principle of change. And this must ever be in act, whereas the ideas may be potential merely, which allows the possibility of a non-existent universe and of a potentiality that is prior to actuality. But we cannot admit that theologians were right in creating all things out of night, or the natural philosophers who supposed a primeval chaos. For how can there be beginning of motion without some cause that is ever in act? It is not the timber that makes a fabric, but the principle of carpentry : nor is it the passive element in procreation that generates, but the active seed : wherefore some do introduce an ever-active energy, as Leucippus in one way, and Plato in another ('Phaedrus,' p. 246), for they say that motion is from everlasting. But they do not tell us wherefore or what motion, nor the manner of it, nor the cause : for nothing has its motion by chance, as in the philosophy of Leucippus, but there must always be some precedent cause, and then what is the primary motion ? That makes an enormous difference. Nor can Plato be allowed to say, as he does sometimes, that the self-moving is the first principle of motion ; for he makes the soul a secondary birth created together with the heaven (' Timaeus '). Now to think of potentiality as prior to actuality is not unmeaning, but that actuality is really prior, Anaxagoras witnesses, for his ' reason ' is ever in act. And so does Empedocles with his love and strife, and so do those who like Leucippus say that motion is from ever-lasting. Therefore chaos or night cannot have lasted for an infinite time, but there must always be the same universe, either in recurring cycles, or in some other way. And for this there must be a first cause. For there is something ever moving with a ceaseless motion, and the only ceaseless motion is the revolution of a sphere. It follows that the first heaven must be eternal ; but there must also be a first cause of motion ; the heaven both moves and causes motion ; but there must be some central thing which causes motion while itself unmoved, an eternal substance ever in act. Now this is the ultimate object both of thought and of desire, whose first principles are identical. For true perfection, as conceived by absolute thought, is the object at once of reason and of will. But reason is the first mover, set in motion by the object of reason, which is substance and attribute, absolute, and ever in act. The Final Cause, there-fore, and the First Cause are one : and on this depends the heaven and the whole of nature. And its life is such as ours may be for a little while,—such is that life eternally. Wherefore waking, perception, thought are pleasant in themselves, and hope and memory because of them. But absolute thought belongs to that which is absolutely good, and which in contemplating the object of thought con-templates itself, for thought is inseparable from its object. Now if God is everlastingly as we are for a little while, that is a marvellous thing ; still more so, if his life is more in-tense than ours : and so it is. Now the Being of whom we speak has neither magnitude nor parts, but is indivisible ; for it causes motion during infinite time, and nothing finite has an infinite power; nor has it passions or possibility of change, for no change is prior to locomotion, and the cause is prior to the effect. All this is manifestly so.'

The great task of Aristotle was to sum up the knowledge of his own and previous generations, to formulate it, and to reduce it to a system. His works are a repertory of the opinions of former Greek thinkers; but the statement of these is always modified by reference to his own first principles. Yet if there is much truth in Bacon's saying that Aristotle, like an Eastern potentate, cut off the heads of his elder brothers that he might reign supreme, the comprehensiveness of his view of nature and of the world regarded from the standpoint of his own first philosophy is so stupendous an achievement as to have left its impress on all succeeding ages, often dominating minds that were incapable of apprehending his full meaning. As Plato has been repeatedly overlaid with Platonism, so has Aristotle, especially in the middle age of Christianity, with Aristotelianism; but the greatness of his influence is all the more apparent. Bacon tries in vain to eliminate the Aristotelian forms of thought which had tyrannised over the Schoolmen from Averroes downward, and three centuries of modern science have not enabled men to dispense with methods first formulated by him of Stagira.

The philosophic life, which Aristotle upheld as a religious ideal, is more obviously restricted to a select few than that life to which Plato invited all in whom there was any awakening germ of higher consciousness. Yet the teaching of Aristotle has had by far the wider prevalence. Plato more profoundly influences those who love him; but the world at large finds it easier to elude his meaning. For *system*, though it often arrests intellectual progress, is far more comprehensible to common minds than the spirit of a living method of thought. It is partly, indeed, the result of accident that the younger philosopher has with most ages had the greater name : Aristotle lived again in Averroes, Aquinas, and the Schoolmen; it was not Plato but rather Proclus or Plotinus who was revived in the great lights of the

Florentine Academy.   Milton himself puts Hermes Tris-
megistus and the spirit of Plato in successive lines, so
betraying an unworthy association.

The time is still to come when the respective merits of
the two leaders of Greek thought shall be justly weighed ; I
will leave them with a single remark.   Aristotle himself has
said that thought by itself is ineffectual apart from practical
ends.   It is the enthusiasm for the highest ends combined
with ever-active thought that makes the secret of Plato.
Philosophic thought, metaphysical, logical, psychological, or
physiological, might after this revert to one or other of the
great precedent thinkers for its inspiration ; but ethical
reflection was henceforth bound to take account of Socrates
and his immediate successors.   And religion amongst
thoughtful men could no longer be divorced from an elevated
morality.   Civic life in the Macedonian period no longer
supplied an adequate standard ; individuals who sought for
a rule of life were thrown back upon themselves and on the
contemplation of universal humanity.   In idealising politics,
Plato had upheld the pattern of a perfect life for the individual also.   And Aristotle in formulating an end for man
had furnished a general scheme which no subsequent thinker
could dispense with.   The ground was laid for the great
conception of a City of God, whose citizens owed allegiance
not to this or that race or country, but to mankind.   And
this conception, passing though the crucible of Roman life,
attained its fullest realisation both in thought and conduct
when the world-wide Roman Empire also was hastening
to decay.   From thence it passed over into Christianity.
Epicurean and Stoic alike sought in allegorising mythology
to secure a *modus vivendi* through which to live in harmony
with traditional religion ; but the religious Stoic, while
' fulfilling all righteousness ' in obedience to the laws of the
state, found a deeper support for his exalted morality, not in
any assured continuance of conscious life, but in dwelling on
the supreme cosmic order which amidst endless change
moved in unison with his truest self, with the law of reason,
and with ' the god within.'

While philosophy was thus laying the foundation of a new and higher life of religious devotion, which in that age and country could never have free course, but has mingled subsequently with all religion that deserves the name, the old worships were continued in their several localities with extraordinary tenacity. The foreign rituals, some of which had already been introduced from Thrace and Phrygia, were reinforced by magical and mystic rites from Egypt and the far east, and for the world at large religion meant either an unmeaning formalism or an orgiastic craze. The Graeco-Egyptian mysteries of Isis and Serapis, confirming tendencies already awakened by Pythagoreanism and Orphism, supplied the void which, in the decay of national spirit, became more and more intolerable to individual souls. Faith-healing, like that associated with the Asclepian worship of Epidaurus, and dream oracles, like those of Trophonius and Amphiaraus, were more and more in vogue, and the darker side of the same tendency is still apparent in the *devotiones*, or curses against private enemies, inscribed on brazen tablets, and registered by individuals at certain shrines,—a lasting record of the ever-recurring bond which unites malignity to superstition. Philosophy had little power to counteract such influences, but it continued its efforts both in the Greek and in the Roman world.

Philosophy itself, however, was no longer whole and sound as it once had been : it broke up into sects. In all of these the ethical impulse given by Socrates is still to be traced, but, unlike Socrates, each Scholarch thought it necessary to have a theory not only of man but of the universe, and none of them possessed the wide glance of speculative originality which appears both in Plato and in Aristotle.

Zeno the founder of the Stoic school was like Antisthenes not of pure Hellenic blood. And considering the deep personal note that was persistent in Stoicism, it is perhaps not superfluous to remark that he was partly of Phoenician ancestry. There is a fresh influx of a Semitic strain, and we may observe that about the same time a Tyrian, Theron, the son of Budastratos, was commended by the people of Cos and made their Proxenus, with high privileges for himself and his descendants. Zeno was the disciple of Crates, the Cynic follower of Antisthenes and Diogenes, and also of Stilpo the Megarian, whose dialectical subtlety seems to have enabled him to combine the crude individualism of Antisthenes with a theory of the universe in which the Heraclitean flux of opposites was reconciled in a higher unity. A materialistic cosmogony was fused with an ethical theory resting on the precept to live according to nature. The universal reason, moving in a predetermined cycle and periodically consuming all things into the primal element of fire, was hard to reconcile with the nominalism of the Cynic. Yet the moral influence of Stoicism was incalculable. The wise man, respecting the God within and living in communion with the universal, was an ideal which satisfied aspiring minds in a distracted age. It is needless to go further into the metaphysics of Stoicism, which found its true development less in the Hellenic than in the Roman world. The subject has been lately touched with equal skill and insight by Dr. Rendall, in the introduction to his masterly translation of the Private Thoughts of the emperor Marcus Aurelius. I will only say that in reading those thoughts, although the cosmic theory of Zeno is always present in them, one is continually reminded of expressions in Plato and Aristotle, whose speculative point of view was different, while the essential substance of their moral and religious doctrine was nearly the same. It is the note of personal experience which gives to the great Roman's communings their unique and distinctive value.

The effect of Stoic precepts on modern ethical tradition can hardly be over-estimated. The reader of Epictetus is continually reminded of our moral commonplaces of the seventeenth and eighteenth centuries. From his 'Manual' to Sir H. Wotton's 'Character of a Happy Life,'[1] or from the Hymn of Cleanthes to Pope's 'Universal Prayer,' there is but a step.

Epicurus supported the art of life which he took from

---

[1] This man is free from servile bands
   Of hope to rise, or fear to fall;
   Lord of himself, though not of lands;
   And having nothing, yet hath all.

Aristippus by the mechanical atomic system of Leucippus and Democritus. The Epicurean possessed his soul in peace, consoling himself for the inevitable cares and troubles of life by the thought that consciousness would have an end when the round particles conglobated in a particular soul were dissipated into the universe at death. For the rest he sought to minimise the pain of existence by rational enjoyment and the avoidance of unreal anxieties, especially those fanciful cares which had been imposed on mankind by the teachers of the old religion. For this end he also dwelt on a psychological analysis of the passions, especially of Anger. Of this philosophy Roman literature contains a glowing poetical exposition in the work of Lucretius ; world-weariness had never a more persuasive voice.

The New Academy followed their master Plato in his negative dialectic, but had no comprehension of his constructive aims. The Peripatetic school contented themselves with repeating their master's formulae and annotating them, or in following out his encyclopaedic system through the development of particular sciences. Pythagoreanism in combination with some of Plato's later views, while stimulating mathematical enquiry, degenerated on the purely philosophical side into an unmeaning symbolism.

Apart from literary criticism the intellectual endeavours which had most success in the last period of Greek culture were in the Mathematical and Medical sciences, in which we have such great names as Hipparchus the astronomer, Archimedes the mechanician, and Galen the physician. The Asclepian tradition, in which the name of Hippocrates stood eminently forth, had been sustained by the practical devotion of many useful lives, which, in accordance with the oath taken on apprenticeship, were spent for the relief of human misery, the improvement of therapeutic methods, and the close experimental study of pathology. But this contribution to the religious life of Hellas was mainly external to the literary sphere.

Lastly, there came a time when the best minds, finding no scope in active life, sought a response to their vague aspirations in the mystical side of Plato, which they developed to the neglect of his practical and scientific aims. Philosophy lost all distinctness in a haze of speculation. Yet in the contemplation of the ocean of infinite being, in which the Neoplatonic thinkers were absorbed, there was a sublime elevation which exercised a genuinely religious influence on the votaries of the school, and in some instances, as in that of Origen, directly prepared the way for Christianity.

Between the philosopher and the peasant came an intermediate class of cultivated persons who stood in various relations to tradition on the one hand and philosophy on the other. ' Thought turned into rhetoric ' was the staple of all higher education. Latin literature affords examples that will occur to every mind, Cicero, Horace, Tacitus, Quintilian. As I do not mean to travel beyond Hellenic ground, I will confine myself to three examples, Pausanias, Plutarch, and Lucian. I will only remark in passing that it was from Cicero that Hume derived his acquaintance with the sceptical reasonings of the New Academy. If instead of learning from so late a disciple he had sought inspiration from the master of the first philosophical school, the course of metaphysical speculation in modern Europe might have been other than it has been.

Pausanias, the antiquarian, shows the keenest interest in the dying forms of paganism, which retained an obstinate vitality at many local shrines. He thus becomes the mouthpiece of contradictory beliefs. But from time to time he betrays his own opinion, and both in his credulity and scepticism he shows himself the child of a decadent age. The superficial theory by which mythology was partly rationalised was that which, from Euhemerus, the man who first gave it currency, is called Euhemerism. The gods of popular worship and belief are simply deified men, who for their never-forgotten services to mankind have been raised to some higher sphere. This sphere is not distinctly localised, except that it is above and in the light of day. The deification of the Ptolemies was a natural outcome of this conception. One popular belief Pausanias distinctly denies. His disbelief may have been borrowed from the Stoics. That there is a place underground where Hades or

Pluto rules over the spirits of men departed is a tradition or invention of the poets which he will by no means accept. But he is ready to receive any number of wonderful tales about the magical virtues of sacred wells and the like, and if a story relates to ancient times or to a former dispensation, it cannot be too marvellous for his belief.

No writer of the silver age in Hellas has deserved so well of posterity as Plutarch. His 'Parallel Lives,' translated into French and English in the sixteenth century, have given to the educated classes in modern Europe a conception of the serious aspect of Paganism which is a good antidote for more flimsy notions which have occasionally prevailed. Plutarch is not a philosopher, but he is a moralist, and in that capacity often shows himself a true disciple of Plato. In the infancy of science he is, of course, the victim of many more or less innocent delusions which are gravely stated in his 'Convivial Discourses.' In his 'Isis and Osiris' he has described the contemporary phase of Egyptian religion, as understood by the Greeks. In his 'Essay on Superstition,' in his reasonings on the 'Failure of Oracles,' and in his discussion of the brief inscription at Delphi, he shows how difficult it was for a commonsense man of the world to form distinct and reasonable opinions on matters of religion in that strangely complicated time. One convenient distinction, which he and others probably owed to their reading of Plato, is worth dwelling on, because it was taken up for apologetic purposes by the early Christian Fathers. This is the distinction between gods and demons. In Plato's 'Symposium' Diotima tells Socrates that love is neither divine nor human : —not a god, but a great demon or spirit. Plutarch has recourse to this conception in seeking to obviate the difficulty arising from the immoralities of mythology. The gods, as Plato says, are good, and the authors of good ; demons, or spirits, are both good and evil, and to them is to be attributed whatever in the old religion is inconsistent with moral excellence. A kindred notion had been expressed by Plato himself in 'Laws' x. 897.

Lucian, as everybody knows, is a licensed jester, but behind the jest there is often a touch of earnest meaning.

He openly professes that scorn of irrational beliefs which with less of certainty has sometimes been attributed to Euripides. Nor has he anything to put in its place, except a commonsense view of human life, which, as the world then was, a wise man could not value very highly. A tone of sadness and world-weariness may often be detected underneath the laugh. A striking example is afforded by the little essay on ' Mourning ' in which not only the absurdities and hollow conventionalities of funeral rites, which had long since lost all meaning, are freely ridiculed, but a bitter laugh is raised against the irrationality of grieving on behalf of one who has escaped from the cares and sorrows of life into the silent land. The dead man in Aristophanes, when asked to do a service for something less than a living wage, instead of saying ' I'd sooner die first,' exclaims ' I'd rather come to life again.' In Lucian the young man who has died is imagined as looking on at his own funeral and scornfully addressing his parents and other survivors, who are weeping and wailing for his untimely death : ' I should burst out laughing at you,' he ends with saying, ' but for the horrid thing which you have tied about my chin '! —Lucian's account of the Syrian goddess—if it is by him— is a wonderfully faithful transcript of a part-eastern part-Hellenic worship in that age of syncretism.

Against such sceptical impieties as that just quoted from Lucian, it is right to set on the other hand those hopes concerning a future state which were cherished by many persons who had been initiated into the Orphic or other kindred mysteries. These hopes are recorded in the inscriptions of uncertain date which I have before mentioned as having been found in south Italy, Sicily, and Crete. They are engraved on gold tablets which had been solemnly deposited in Greek tombs. They contain directions which are to guide the soul of the dead man to his destined dwelling-place where he is to enjoy the blessedness obtained through initiation. He is to declare himself the son of earth and heaven. He is to take the path to the left of the well and the cypress tree, and ask to drink of the water flowing from the spring of memory. Then he shall take hisplace amongst the other heroes and become divine. It is a question of some importance whether any of these inscriptions can with confidence be traced to the age preceding Plato. In some of them which bear distinct reference to the worship of Osiris there are obvious indications of a considerably later time. One thing is certain, that Aeschylus, who was learned in all the wisdom of Eleusis, was unacquainted with any such beliefs.

Although that reformation of Hellas for which Plato longed so earnestly was never to take effect, his efforts in following up the work of Socrates had not been altogether in vain. Not only an intellectual, but an ethical standard had been set up, whose influence extended far and wide wherever Greek culture spread, not moulding states indeed, but guiding and controlling many individual lives. Looking back from the vantage-ground of the modern world, we are apt to think of the higher thought of the fourth century in Greece as a light that failed; but that is not the impression we receive in reading the fragmentary remains of the succeeding centuries. There is a want, indeed, of fresh inspiration, but what there is of noble aspiration or of generous emotion is mainly a reflection from the life of Socrates and from the mind of Plato. The emancipation of faithful slaves by formally devoting them to the service of deities such as Apollo and Asclepius is a pleasing illustration of a growing sentiment of humanity; and of this practice abundant evidence remains in inscriptions of the Alexandrian and Roman periods found at Naupactus and Delphi.

We have brought down our account of Greek religion (though the later stages have been only hastily sketched in) very nearly to the time when Hellenic teaching centred in ' the school of one Tyrannus,' or of Posidonius, or Crantor, or Epictetus, while the parallel stream of Hebrew prophecy had shrunk into the synagogue, where the successors of Hillel or Gamaliel expounded the Law and the prophets; and the syncretism of both influences appeared in such writings as those of Philo Judaeus.

These were the forms in which the confluent currents of

Heathenism and Judaism passed over into the life and thought of Christendom, which they may be said to have enriched, but also in some measure to have darkened and disturbed. Readers of the 'Praeparatio Evangelii' by Eusebius of Caesarea or of the works of Origen will have no difficulty in apprehending what this means. Our endeavour has been to understand what the religion of the Hellenes was to that people themselves in its earlier stages, while they were still a people, and rather to hint than to explain the manner in which the religious experiences of that unforgettable past, the higher mind of Hellas, may still be profitable amidst the complex and conflicting circumstances of a radically altered world, 'for doctrine, for reproof, for correction, for instruction in righteousness.'

It remains that we should endeavour to estimate what has been so described, in relation to some of the larger issues of contemporary thought. In order to do so it is necessary to clear our minds of some lurking prepossessions. The attitude that was right and natural for the first Christians, who sought to keep alive the glowing spark of the new religion amidst the corruptions of the degenerating heathen world, is no longer required of those who have been brought up in Christendom. Yet more or less unconsciously all thought upon this subject, whether orthodox or not, is apt to be coloured by what is now a conventional attitude. When we look steadily at Greek civilisation regarded as a whole, we find that it has been unfairly dealt with both by the apologists and the assailants of Christianity. The words of Scripture, which are quite intelligible when viewed in their original connection, exert a traditional influence, which carries with it a degree of unreality when they are employed by ourselves. 'No idol is anything in the world' is an incontrovertible saying, as uttered by St. Paul ; and yet, when we think of Athena Promachos, or Athena Polias, as she was worshipped by the Athenians of the fifth century, our thought inevitably follows a different line. On the other hand, when he says, 'the things which the Gentiles sacrifice, they sacrifice to demons and not to God,' he uses language which Plutarch would have understood, attributing a real existence to those inferior spirits, which were as much the creation of mythological fancy as the Beings whom the Greek reverenced as supreme. These last are they whom St. Paul thus seeks to degrade in the eyes of his followers. ' We have not followed cunningly devised fables,' says another Apostle, contrasting a supposed artificial system invented by priests with the facts of the Gospel. The phrase has a possible significance, if referred to the inventions of Onomacritus and the other teachers of Orphism. But we have been led by the study of history and of comparative religion to look upon Greek mythology as a natural and inevitable growth, not wholly unmeaning, nor due to any man's invention, although largely modified by the creative imagination not of priests so much as of poets and theosophists ; and under its many-coloured veil half concealing, half revealing many germs of spiritual truth.

Over against the traditional view of the opposition of Christianity to heathenism, there stand some neopagan doctrines which have recently come into vogue. These new teachers seem frankly to accept the orthodox apologist's estimate of Hellenic life, and to regard it, not as derogatory, but as essentially favourable. With the gloom of Christian asceticism they would contrast the genial naturalism of the imaginary heathen. Thus on both sides Paganism is apt to be identified with Hedonism, if not with licentiousness. Such views are a ridiculous travesty of Hellenic life. The life of an average Greek citizen was pestered with many a dark scruple from which Christianity has set men free. To hear some people talk, one would suppose that frivolity was a characteristic of the Greek. Whereas, in point of fact, it is the *seriousness* of this people that is so remarkable : not that false seriousness which is the negation of humour, but the seriousness of unimpeded energy. Whatever they undertook, they took seriously, nay, more, in a religious spirit, and therefore they performed it better than any others have done before or since. It is due to them that the moral problem was at last set forth as one for all men.

In the study of comparative religion the mistake is often made of comparing the perfection of one religion with the corruption of another : the ideal of one age with the practice of another. If the conduct of an ordinary Athenian of the time of Aristides were compared with that of an average Hebrew of the time of Ezekiel, or of a Portuguese of the upper classes in the present day, I have a strong conviction that the comparison would not be to the advantage either of the Hebrew or of the Christian. Even the code of morals prevalent from time to time in Christian countries has been demonstrably unchristian. Look, for example, at the last century in England. Could any one who read some faithful transcript of English manners by Fielding or Goldsmith suppose that it embodied the morality of Johnson or the religion of John Wesley or of Bishop Butler ? Consider again the savage vindictiveness with which the noblest efforts of our own Protestant ancestors were alloyed. The Athenians at Melos were hardly worse than the Puritans at Wexford. To argue from hence that the leaven of Christianity was powerless or without value for that age, would be far wide of the mark ; but it is not less irrelevant to suppose, because of the inhumanity or the abnormal sensuality that prevailed in Greek communities, that the pieties of the Iliad and Odyssey, the passionate idealism of Aeschylus, the home affections manifested on the sepulchral stelae, and the aspirations embodied in many funeral inscriptions were unmeaning, or that the religion which they represent is even now dead or ineffectual. It is an often repeated saying of the great Lessing that Christianity has been tried for eighteen centuries while the religion of Christ remains to be tried. So also, not as hostile to Christianity nor as a rival to it, but as conspiring with it, in a lower grade, if you will, it may be said that those things noble and of good report which lie enshrined in the records of centuries before Christ still remain to prove their healing and elevating effect on human life ; and the noblest among these are Hebrew prophecy and Hellenic culture, of which the *religion* of the ancient Greeks is the highest and not the least important aspect.

Two contemporary sayings may be quoted in support of what is here advanced : one, the lines of ' In Memoriam, ' paradoxical as they seemed to many when they first appeared

> What keeps a spirit wholly true
> To that ideal which he bears ?
> What record ?—*not the sinless years*
> *That breathed beneath the Syrian blue.*

The other is an expression of Professor Jowett's in concluding that portion of his essay on Natural Religion which is devoted to the Graeco-Roman world. The whole passage may be quoted here.

' Such was the later phase of the religion of nature with which Christianity came into conflict. It had supplied some of the needs of men by assisting to build up the fabric of society and law. It had left room for others to find expression in philosophy or art. But it was a world divided against itself. It contained two nations or opinions "struggling in its womb " : the nation or opinion of the many, and the nation or opinion of the few. It was bound together in the framework of law or custom, yet its morality fell below the natural feelings of mankind, and its religious spirit was confused and weakened by the admixture of foreign superstitions. It was a world of which it is not difficult to find traces that it was self-condemned. It might be compared to a fruit, the rind of which was hard and firm, while within it was soft and decaying. Within this outer rind or circle, for two centuries and a half, Christianity was working ; at last it appeared without, itself the seed or kernel of a new organisation. That when the conflict was over, and the world found itself Christian, many elements of the old religion still remained, and reasserted themselves in Christian forms; that the " ghost of the dead Roman empire " lingered "about the grave thereof "; *that Christianity accomplished only imperfectly what heathenism failed to do at all,* is a result unlike pictures that are sometimes drawn, but sadly in accordance with what history teaches of mankind and of human nature.' [1]

' Christianity is not a doctrine, but a life,' was a saying

---

[1] *Epistles of St. Paul*, third edition, vol. ii. pp. 224–5. The italics are mine.

of John Newton's in his later years ; and it is a life that is fed by kindred elements from without, which it has the power of discriminating from things alien or hostile, of assimilating and of directing and controlling. Consciously or unconsciously this has been the case with Christian teaching since the first age : such men as Clement of Alexandria, Origen, and Augustine owed much of their influence to their education in Greek learning ; and the study of Hellenic life, not as it seemed to the Fathers, but as it was in itself, is of real assistance towards the growth and spread of an enlightened Christianity amongst ourselves.

The fresh outburst of intellectual and social life known as the Renaissance was greatly stimulated and encouraged by the rediscovery of Greek literature and art. But the humanism which then prevailed rested largely on an uncritical appreciation of those long-hidden treasures which acted like new wine upon undisciplined natures. It has accordingly been ridiculed by Goethe under the image of the *Homunculus* in the second part of ' Faust.' But may we not, in a more critical age, anticipate the more wholesome working of a higher humanism, in which a spirit, not of revolt, but of obedience to the essential principles of Christianity, will hail with gladness the inestimable worth of those records of the nobler things in man, coming down to us from a remoter past, in which some Fathers saw the working of the divine Logos, and Christian philosophy recognises more that is akin to the mind of Christ than in much that has been thought and written in His name ?

1. The contemplation of the Hellenic record, as a whole, supplies us with facts which, when rightly considered, tend rather to confirm than to weaken our conviction of ' the truth of Christian inspiration.' That in two races so entirely separate from each other (I don't speak now of prehistoric times) as the Hebrew and the Greek, the development of spiritual and moral conceptions and aspirations should have so much in common, is a welcome evidence of our belief that mankind are not deserted by their Creator, but are drawn continually upwards, in the course of a divine education. ' There is a spirit in man,

and the inspiration of the Almighty giveth them understanding.'

Let us glance once more at some of the points in which
the education of the two races, the Hebrew and the Greek,
led to the expression of similar feelings or beliefs. In
Homer, although religious *thought* is for the most part
implicit, there is yet a deep *feeling*, founded on experience,
that sin breeds sorrow, that there is a God who supports
the wronged and punishes the wrongdoer. In Hesiod
this breaks forth more explicitly in the cry of the oppressed,
and Justice is herself personified as the daughter of Zeus.
In Solon the same thought comes out with striking clearness
in its application to social and civic life ; and in Aeschylus
we find an ideal of divine righteousness which is strikingly
parallel to that of Hebrew prophecy. The eternal law in
Sophocles is far exalted above the caprice and wilfulness
of man. A time of doubtful disputation and of religious
discouragement follows, until Socrates raises again the
standard of an absolute morality, which he endeavours to
base upon an ideal of knowledge,—the love of goodness,
for once, conspiring with the love of truth.

Meanwhile the idea of justice or righteousness has been
insensibly modified by the notion of equity taking the
place of mere retaliation or retribution ; and by the conception of a moral government extending beyond the limits of a
single community, and of human rights participated even
by barbarians and slaves. The just man, says the Platonic
Socrates, cannot do harm even to an enemy.

Another development which in our modern age is
closely identified with religion can be traced more distinctly in Hellenic than in Hebrew culture : I mean, the
hope of immortality. The absence of this from all but
the latest books of the Old Testament has been often
noted. It sprang up during the depth of national distress
after the Captivity, ' growing,' as Jowett finely says, ' like a
green plant within the hollow rind of Pharisaism.' The
question need not here be pressed, whether this belief was
not already implicit in the doctrine of a living Jehovah. In
Hellas, as we have seen, the primitive belief which found

expression in funeral rites and in the worship of ancestors had faded in the age that is reflected through the Homeric poems, but rose into new life with the growth of hero-worship, and became prominent in the Orphic and Pytha-gorean teaching ; though it is still a strange language to Herodotus, and seems to have had no place in the first period of Attic enlightenment. The Eleusinian mystic, indeed, cherished a bright hope, but this was too apt to rest on merely ceremonial conditions. Socrates, possessing his soul in peace, was content to leave the matter to God ; but Plato, giving substance to Pythagorean fancy through the strength of moral conviction, and identifying soul with mind, attributed to the human spirit a participation in that eternity which he held to belong to truth. Hellenic faith could go no further.

The remaining stages have been too recently discussed to need recapitulation, else we might trace in a similar manner the gradual moralising of the ideas of temperance and purity, which reached their acme in the precepts given by Plato to young men in pp. 836–842 of the 'Laws.' What I desire to emphasise is, that in all this, for one who believes in a supreme wisdom and goodness, in other words, in a God of righteousness and truth, there is much which he cannot fail to recognise as of divine origin. The corre-spondence between the living pattern set before the Chris-tian and the ideal of a perfect life as conceived by Plato is an argument that both are real. One appeals more to the heart, the other to the intellect. The higher nature of man, taken as a whole, can only find satisfaction in contemplating both in one. The spirit of the Christian life gives motive and direction towards the realisation of per-fection, but that spirit is reanimated and invigorated by breathing in whatever in the world at large has an affinity to it and bears the stamp of kindred authorship.

2. If the story of Hellenic culture gives support and encouragement to what is best and highest in our modern life, it also supplies us with a warning which is not less valuable. It began with ceremonialism, and rose gra-dually towards a pure and elevated morality. The idea

of God was purged from the beggarly elements of primitive superstition and the accretions of fanciful mythology until the most sacred names corresponded to the highest aspirations of the noblest men. But as the race declined, or became contaminated with other races, the Greek came again under the power of local superstitions which had never lost their hold, or of irrational mysticisms brought in from abroad which soothed but could not satisfy; while in comparison of these, an elaborately reasoned philosophy exercised only a limited power. Shall we not take the warning, and place our reliance, neither on mere reasoning, nor on traditional rites and ceremonies which are now unmeaning, but on those truths whose evidence is moral and spiritual, which are consecrated for us by great examples, and which speak convincingly at once to the emotions and to the mind and will?

Thus the sympathetic study of antiquity on critical lines may help not only to invigorate but, what is not less important, also to purify traditional Christianity. It is no blind imitation, even of perfect models, that I am advocating, but the rational use of that liberty which is our inheritance as Christians and as protestants, in comparing spiritual things with spiritual, casting off old garments, whether ancient or modern, but interweaving the brightest and best of their colours into the new.

The question of questions remains behind. We have sought to delineate successive phases of religious life and thought which did not annihilate but supplanted one another, and were finally supplanted by Christianity. Are we to infer that all these phases were alike devoid of objective reality, a mere phantasmagoria, collapsing into nothingness with the men who conceived them? That is a consideration which, from time to time, must haunt the minds of all honest theologians. For it may be applied, not to one series of beliefs or worships only, but to all alike, even to those which are most sacred to ourselves. We are beginning to learn that the Jahve of the Hebrews was not quite the same as the God of Wesley or of John Henry

Newman ; we do not therefore think that the religion of Isaiah was unreal. It cannot be said that the God in whom John Knox so intensely believed was precisely the same Being whom Archbishop Leighton worshipped in spirit and in truth. Yet the religion of both men was unquestionable, and we cannot doubt that, notwithstanding subjective imperfections, it had a real object.

The true point of view was anticipated by St. Paul, when he spoke of the old Hellenic worship as a feeling after God : a groping in the darkness, as Plato said, yet like other instinctive motions, having a real aim. The right consideration of the facts which have been here set forth may help at once to confirm belief and to modify unbelief. Those who believe that the one God whom Christians worship made the world and all things therein : that He has made of one blood all nations of men that dwell on the face of the whole earth : that He has ordained the times before appointed, and the bounds of their habitation ; will recognise in the noble feelings and great thoughts of the religious Greeks the working of the same spirit whose fulness is in Christ. Those, on the other hand, who in reacting from Christian tradition have been led to suspect that the idea of a God who reigns supreme over man and nature is an empty dream, a relic of the metaphysical stage of human culture, may at least admit that the parallel and independent growth of that idea amongst the Greeks and Hebrews, and the correspondence between the ideal just man of Plato and the living pattern in Christ, is a remarkable and not insignificant fact. I need not add that similar analogies may be found in other regions that lie beyond the scope of the present volume, and that the cumulative argument for the moral and spiritual nature of true religion is thus strengthened. I leave it to others to dwell, for example, on the Egyptian ' Book of the Dead,' or the contemplative lives of Indian sages, or the religious enthusiasm of some great Eastern conqueror ; but nowhere, I think, can the growth of those higher thoughts which are the sustaining nutriment of the most blessed life be traced more vividly, or to more edifying purpose, than in the Hellenic world.

It is not too much to say that these thoughts correct and supplement some extravagances and defects to which Christianity, in the historical sense, has been often prone. (1) Self-denial is amongst the Christian graces ; self-culture, not less a Christian duty, is sometimes forgotten. Greek life, on the whole, is a standing protest against a merely negative and cloistered virtue. (2) Not only Christian teachers, but preachers of another sort, wisely exhort us to live for others. The French word 'altruism,' which has somehow come lately into vogue, is not, I believe, of Christian origin, yet it expresses what by many is regarded as the sum of Christian duty. 'The enthusiasm of humanity' is another phrase which has a more Christian sound, and has inspired much noble conduct ; yet there is a certain vagueness in both of these when compared with that ideal of duty which was set before the citizen of an Hellenic state. To serve other men by doing the duty that lies nearest ; to live for mankind by self-devotion to the interests of a community, however small or obscure ; to realise one's higher self in ministering to others, are Christian conceptions, which find an added support in the life of heathenism.

To dwell once more in conclusion on the central difficulty, it may be said with truth, although the saying is paradoxical, that the great historical religions of the world stand or fall together. If Christianity is true, then there is a relative truth also, though with obvious limitations, in Judaism, in Hellenism, in Buddhism, and even in Mahomedanism. The criterion of that truth involves the reality of the ideal. If we have lost faith in that, because humanity everywhere falls short of it, that is equivalent to losing faith in the existence and beneficence of God. So long as we maintain the struggle to lessen the distance between what men acknowledge ought to be, and that which through their will and deed actually is, so long we are upholding the belief in a Supreme Being, who, in mysterious ways, is drawing His creatures nearer to Himself. That is a truth which can never be seen perfectly under the limitations of our mortal state, and yet, though seen in part, is the most inspiring of all truths.

The nearest approach to a solution of the speculative difficulties which surround it lies perhaps in the words of Bishop Butler when he speaks of the moral government of God as 'a scheme imperfectly comprehended.' The naturalist hypothesis, which has made an epoch in modern science, and has won its way to all but universal acceptance, rests on the postulate of an illimitable period of past time. The religious hypothesis, of which the words of Butler are an expression, demands for its support an illimitable future duration for the individual and for the world. Neither the naturalistic nor the religious postulate admits of demonstration. If the one provides us with an account of things which harmonises with experience, and with that other postulate of the uniformity of nature, on which modern science rests, the other is in accordance with that belief in a divine union of omnipotence with beneficence which has grown with the growth of the human spirit, and cannot without violence be eradicated from the religious mind.

We are still far away from the 'new definition of God,' of which I spoke in the beginning of this volume, and the 'vision' is still shadowy and evanescent ; yet if in the future thought should keep pace with knowledge, and the crowding of new facts should not weaken judgment, it may be that both the vision and the definition may be simpler, more comprehensive, more far-reaching than anything which mankind have hitherto conceived.

INDEX

D D